DRINK

ALSO BY ANDREW BARR

Wine Snobbery: an insider's guide to the booze business

Pinot Noir

DRINK

ANDREW BARR

BANTAM PRESS

LONDON · NEW YORK · TORONTO · SYDNEY · AUCKLAND

TRANSWORLD PUBLISHERS LTD
61–63 Uxbridge Road, London W5 5SA

TRANSWORLD PUBLISHERS (AUSTRALIA) PTY LTD
15–25 Helles Avenue, Moorebank, NSW 2170

TRANSWORLD PUBLISHERS (NZ) LTD
3 William Pickering Drive, Albany, Auckland

Published 1995 by Bantam Press
a division of Transworld Publishers Ltd

A catalogue record for this book is available from the British Library

0593 035100

Typeset in 11/13pt Linotype Sabon by
Kestrel Data, Exeter, Devon

Printed in Great Britain by
Mackays of Chatham plc, Chatham, Kent

For Johanna

ACKNOWLEDGEMENTS

I should like to thank Ruth Barr, Isobel Bowler, Jane Clarke, Jim Cochrane, Peter Duff, Luciano Guernieri, Nigel Higgins, Johnny Holbech, Alastair Hook, Andrew Lownie, Charles McMaster, Mary J. Ryan, Erik Skovenborg, Richard Smith, Don Steele, Will Sulkin, Neil Ward, Susan Wilkie and Fiona Wood for assisting me beyond the call of duty.

CONTENTS

PREFACE

THIS BOOK AROSE OUT OF MY DESPAIR AT THE NARROW-MINDED approach of virtually all other books on drink. In the first place, they restrict themselves to dealing with a single drink, usually wine, when for most consumers the choice is not between one type of wine and another but between wine and spirits and beer and tea and coffee and a soft drink and water and nothing at all. Moreover, they devote their efforts to describing how particular types of wine are made, and to describing their taste by reference to other forms of flora and fauna. Thus they separate wine from its context: they divorce it not only from other drinks, but also from the food with which it is usually consumed and from the cultural influences that are generally the most important factors in determining what someone chooses to drink. Books on drink, and especially books on wine, demonstrate the popular notion that the British are embarrassed by the idea of sensuality: they do not deal with alcoholic drink as the pleasure that it undoubtedly is, but as an object of intellectual analysis.

This book is about pleasure; it is about sensuality; it is about the cultural, social and political influences that determine what we choose to drink, where we choose to drink it, and with whom. Its purpose is to try to understand why we drink what we do.

If it is the aim of history to try to assist in our understanding of the present by examining the past, then this book is a social history of drink. But it does not adopt the principles of dispassionate analysis that modern historians are taught to follow. It is not only history; it is also polemic. It uses history to make judgements on issues of current political controversy, such as the liberalization of the licensing laws, the opening of borders within the European Community, and the possible healthy or unhealthy effects of moderate alcohol consumption. While some of the opinions that are expressed may give pleasure, it is quite possible that others may cause offence. In this respect, *Drink* follows the pattern established by my first book *Wine Snobbery*, which was described by one reviewer as 'a book to hurl against the floor but which bounces back, demanding your attention'.

ANDREW BARR
London, June 1994

INTRODUCTION: DRINK AND DRUGS

FOR TEN THOUSAND YEARS, EVER SINCE HUMAN BEINGS SETTLED down to the cultivation of cereals and vines, alcohol has played a fundamental role in society. It has served as an object of religious ritual, a focus of secular ceremonies and a lubricant of social intercourse; it has been employed as an aid to the digestion of food, a means of slaking thirst without risk of contracting disease and a source of nutrition in its own right; it has been used in the treatment of wounds and disease and as both a stimulant and a sedative – as well as being valued for its taste.

In the Western world, for many centuries, societies have not generally felt the need for other forms of drink or drugs, because beer, wine and other fermented alcoholic drinks have been available to them. This has not, however, been true of the Near East, where followers of the Prophet Mohammed are forbidden to drink alcohol. According to legend, the prohibition was imposed following an incident that occurred while the Prophet's disciples were drinking together after a dinner in Medina. One of his Meccan followers began to recite an uncomplimentary poem about the tribe of Medina, whereupon one of his Medinite followers

1

picked up a bone from the table and hit the Meccan on the head. Although the wound was not serious, the incident caused Mohammed such concern that he asked Allah how he could prevent it from happening again. Allah replied, 'Believers, wine and games of chance, idols and divining arrows, are abominations devised by Satan. Avoid them, so that you may prosper. Satan seeks to stir up enmity and hatred among you by means of wine and gambling, and to keep you from the remembrance of Allah and from your prayers.'

It was not, however, until several hundred years after this incident that the followers of the Prophet found an appropriate alternative to alcoholic drinks, in the form of coffee, and an alternative institution to the tavern, in the form of the coffee house. It was only when coffee houses began to appear at the turn of the fifteenth and sixteenth centuries that respectable Muslim men were able to indulge in the practice of going out of the house for a drink. Not everyone approved of this new development. In 1511 the city of Mecca was under the control of the Mamluk Sultan in Cairo. The *muhtasib* (the civil official charged with overseeing the morality of the marketplace) was one Kha'ir Beg al-Mi'mar. The story goes that, while on his way one day to perform his evening prayers, Kha'ir Beg saw a group of men with lanterns in one of the precincts of the mosque. When he approached them, they hurried to extinguish their lanterns, which made him suspicious. On investigating their actions, he learned that they were consuming some drink 'in the fashion of drinkers swallowing an intoxicant'; and was told that this drink, which was called *qahwa* (coffee), had become popular throughout Mecca, and was drunk in places 'like taverns', where a variety of forbidden things went on. He sent the men on their way and next day called a meeting of the *ulema* (leading religious scholars) of the city. At this meeting two doctors stood up and declared that coffee was unhealthy; others then supported them by saying that they had drunk coffee and that they had suffered mental and personality changes as a result. The *ulema* believed them and decided that coffee-drinking was contrary to Islamic law. Kha'ir Beg had it proclaimed throughout the city that the sale and consumption of coffee was prohibited. Coffee was burned in the streets, and many of those who trafficked in or consumed it were beaten. The *ulema* then wrote to the central authorities in Cairo asking for them to confirm the prohibition. However, when the official decree arrived some time later, while expressing disapproval of the social gatherings at which coffee was drunk, it did not ban coffee itself. So coffee-drinking in Mecca was once again permitted.

It is unlikely that Kha'ir Beg can have been ignorant of the existence of coffee and coffee houses, as this story suggests. It is more probable that his action reflected the doubts that were already entertained by both religious and secular officials about the spread of coffee. Having two doctors stand up at the meeting of the *ulema* and say that coffee was unhealthy was simply a pretext for introducing a ban. Religious zealots were opposed to coffee-drinking because it was an innovation that was not explicitly permitted by the Koran or by the traditions of the Prophet. Religious officials were concerned that people were spending time in coffee houses that they would previously have spent praying in mosques. The connection between coffee- and wine-drinking was also a cause for concern. It had become the practice to drink coffee from a common cup that was circulated in a manner similar to that in which wine was shared among its drinkers; many devout Muslims were opposed to coffee, wrote the Turkish scholar and encyclopedist Katib Çelebi, because 'the fact that it is drunk in gatherings, passed hand to hand, is suggestive of loose living'.

Secular officials were also concerned, not so much about coffee itself as about the coffee houses – especially in Istanbul, the capital of the Ottoman Empire. In 1622 the young, idealistic, reform-minded sultan Osman II was deposed and murdered by mutinous Janissaries (members of the imperial guard), the first clear-cut instance of regicide in Ottoman times. He was succeeded by his uncle Mustafa; but then Mustafa was in his turn deposed and replaced by Osman's brother Murad IV. Since it was in coffee houses that mutinous soldiers were inclined to meet, Murad, not wishing to suffer the fate of his brother, ordered them to be pulled down – using as his pretext the disastrous fires that sometimes started in them. This was in 1633. A decade later the coffee houses were re-established under Murad IV's successor,* another of his

---

*On coming to the throne, Murad had also protected himself from Osman's fate by executing three of his four surviving brothers, but (being childless himself) had spared the fourth of them, Ibrahim.

brothers, Ibrahim I. Ibrahim in his turn was forced by mutinous Janissaries to abdicate in favour of his son Mehmed IV, who at the time of his accession was seven years old.

For much of Mehmed's reign, the Ottoman Empire was effectively ruled by a dynasty of Grand Viziers from the Köprülü family. It was the first of these, Mehmed Köprülü, who, in 1656, during war with Venice, once again ordered the coffee houses to be closed down. Adopting a favourite practice of Ottoman rulers, he had gone around the city *incognito*, and visited a number of coffee houses. Here (according to the account of one of his family's physicians) 'he found men gravely discussing the affairs of the Empire, disapproving of most of the measures that were being taken by the administration, and deciding themselves what ought to be done, as though they were themselves members of the imperial council. In order to deprive these dangerous critics of the opportunity of involving themselves in matters that did not concern them, he did not hesitate to close the coffee houses.' Indeed, Köprülü imposed extremely stringent punishments upon those who disobeyed his order: for a first violation, the offender was to be cudgelled; for a second, he was to be sewn into a leather bag and thrown into the Bosporus; there would consequently be no likelihood of a third violation.

Köprülü closed the coffee houses, but he left the taverns alone. This may have appeared surprising, given that wine was forbidden both by imperial law and by the Islamic religion. While wandering in disguise round the city, however, Köprülü found that taverns, far from being places where men discussed politics and might have plotted against the government, were frequented by people who 'enjoyed themselves, who sang, and who talked of their loves or of their exploits in battle'; many of the customers of taverns, moreover, were soldiers, to whom 'he preferred to leave this liberty rather than give them the opportunity to gather into a mob and to mutiny'.

By the time that Köprülü introduced his prohibition, the use of coffee had spread from Eastern to Western Europe, and the first coffee houses had been opened in England. This was the period of the Commonwealth, when Puritan values prevailed. The first coffee houses that opened in London during the 1650s offered no intoxicants of any kind but only temperance drinks: as well as coffee, they generally served tea, chocolate, sherbet and betony. Just as the coffee houses of the East fulfilled the needs of observant Muslims who wanted to go out for a drink, so the coffee houses of the West satisfied those sober and hard-working members of the new middle classes who had neither the time nor the inclination to get drunk. ''Tis found already,' wrote the professional author James Howell, 'that this coffee drink hath caused a greater sobriety among the nations: for whereas formerly apprentices and clerks with others used to take their morning's draught in ale, beer or wine, which by the dizziness they cause in the brain make many unfit for business, they use now to play the good-fellows in this wakeful and civil drink.' Another pamphleteer of the time offered a more political explanation for the rapid acceptance of the new drink. 'Coffee and Common-wealth', wrote the anonymous author of *The Character of a Coffee House*, 'both came in/Together for a Reformation/To make's [sic] a free and sober nation.'

Coffee houses continued to grow in popularity after the restoration of the monarchy in 1660. They served as a place for men to sit and talk, as a focus for the exchange of information; it was the coffee houses that enabled the first newspapers to be produced. This was not necessarily pleasing to King Charles II – especially not at a time when he was terrified that a pro-Catholic party might attempt to unseat him. The air was thick with intrigue, with plots and counterplots. Men were being paid to go round the coffee houses spreading rumours, in order to stir up as much discontent as possible. In 1675 the King sought to deal with the problem by closing them down. In his *Proclamation for the Suppression of Coffee Houses* he stated, quite correctly, that they were 'the great resort of idle and disaffected persons', and that 'In such houses divers false, malicious and scandalous reports are devised and spread abroad to the defamation of His Majesty's Government, and to the disturbance of the peace and quiet of the realm.' The proclamation was issued on 29 December 1675; the coffee houses were to close by 10 January 1676. But the proclamation led to public hostility on so large a scale that the King quickly realized that he had blundered. On 8 January 1676, two days before the proclamation was due to come into effect, another proclamation was issued by which the first was recalled.

It was not long before any threat that the London coffee houses might have posed to the Government disappeared. Their customers became less serious-minded, partly as a consequence of the belief that, not only was coffee a sober beverage, but that by drinking it people who were drunk could become sober again.* 'There is nothing more effectual than this reviving drink to restore their senses that have brutified themselves by immoderate tippling heady liquors,' claimed one pamphleteer. The supposedly sobering qualities of coffee drew many undesirables from the taverns after they had closed at 9 p.m.; the sober reputation of the coffee houses suffered as a result. By the early eighteenth century James Douglas, a physician who wrote a history of the medical and social uses of coffee, was able to complain that 'At London we can hardly go into a coffee house . . . but we are either stunned and deafened with the noise of dice and tables in all corners of the room, or see the whole company watching the events of a party at ombre or a game of chess, with the same eagerness as if their own welfare depended upon it.'

In France, however, the coffee houses continued to pose a threat to the government in the eighteenth century. The agricultural writer Arthur Young, who visited Paris during the meeting of the Estates-General in 1789, confessed to astonishment at the spectacle at the coffee houses of the Palais-Royal. 'They are not only crowded within, but other expectant crowds are at the doors and windows, [craning their necks to see] certain orators, who from chairs or tables harangue each his little audience: the eagerness with which they are heard, and the thunder of applause they receive for every sentiment of more than common hardness or violence against the present government, cannot easily be imagined. I am all amazement at the ministry permitting such nests and hot-beds of sedition and revolt, which disseminate among the people, every hour, principles that by and by must be opposed with vigour, and therefore it seems little short of madness to allow their propagation at present.' Young had good reason to be amazed. It was from the coffee houses of the Palais-Royal that the French Revolution was initiated; it was from the coffee houses that the Revolution was led. It was from the Café de la Régence that Camille Desmoulins first inspired the crowds to take up arms to overthrow the *ancien régime*. The failure of the government to act against the coffee houses had led to its downfall.

*The idea that coffee sobers up people who are drunk prevails today. If it has this effect, it is for psychological and not pharmacological reasons.

Authoritarian governments were afraid of their subjects when they drank coffee, and they were afraid of them when they smoked tobacco. This new substance was first encountered by the privateer Sir John Hawkins and his men on a voyage to the West Indies and Florida in 1564–1565; it is possible that they were also the first people to introduce the practice of smoking tobacco – then in pipes – to England. Alternatively, it was introduced a generation later, by Sir Francis Drake. Popular tradition may attribute its introduction to Sir Walter Raleigh, but popular tradition in this, as in so many other cases, is wrong. Although Raleigh is a famous figure in the history of smoking, the traditions associated with him are without foundation: that Raleigh's servant, on first seeing his master smoke, poured water over him to put out the fire, and that Raleigh persuaded Queen Elizabeth I to smoke a pipe, which made her ill. What is true is that Raleigh was instrumental in popularizing the practice of tobacco-smoking at the end of the sixteenth and beginning of the seventeenth century and that Elizabeth's successor, King James I, hated him for it. Indeed, it is perfectly possible that James's opposition to the practice originated in its association with Raleigh, for whom James entertained a sufficient dislike to have him held prisoner in the Tower of London for most of his reign.

In 1604 James, who imagined himself as something of an intellectual, published anonymously a pamphlet entitled *A Counterblast to Tobacco* in which he described smoking as 'a custom loathsome to the eye, hateful to the nose, harmful to the brain, dangerous to the lungs, and in the black stinking fume thereof nearest resembling the horrible Stygian smoke of the pit that is bottomless.' It was not, however, on account of his hatred of Raleigh nor of the unpleasantness or unhealthfulness of tobacco-smoking that James sought to prohibit the practice. In the same year as he published his pamphlet he sent an order to the High Treasurer of England instructing that the import duty on tobacco be raised from a nominal 2d a pound to a prohibitive 6s 10d, explaining that tobacco, which had previously been 'taken by the better sort . . . only as physic to preserve health, is now at this day, through evil custom and toleration thereof, excessively taken by a number of riotous and disordered persons of mean and base condition, who, contrary to the use which persons of good calling and quality make thereof, do spend most of their time in that idle vanity.' He was concerned, in other words, that tobacco made his subjects lazy, that it encouraged them to spend their time sitting around talking, that it made them more inclined to conspire. He hoped that, by raising the import duty by four thousand per cent, he would put an end to the recreational use of tobacco by his subjects and ensure that it was smoked only by 'the better sort', in moderate quantities.

This was not what happened. The imposition of a prohibitively high duty simply led to tobacco being smuggled into England and evading customs duty altogether. So in 1608 James reduced the duty to 1s a pound, and farmed out the right to collect it to one of his favourites, in return for a large annual fee. Then, distributors and retailers took to stretching their stocks by adulterating their tobacco with ground-up stalks and leaves of other plants, forcing James to introduce a system of inspection, and thus to set himself up as the guardian of the purity of a drug that, a few years earlier, he had tried to suppress.

The English experience was repeated across the rest of northern Europe. In the first half of the seventeenth century most northern European countries had adopted laws forbidding trading in tobacco, or smoking it, or both; in most cases the penalties were relatively small fines, but Russia tried more severe measures, prescribing at various times whippings, slit noses, torture, deportation to Siberia, and death. These measures did not work. Instead, the English experience was repeated: prohibition of tobacco did not work, so why not legalize it and tax it instead? By the end of the seventeenth century, tobacco was legal throughout Europe.

Another new drug that was popularized in Europe at the same time as coffee and tobacco was spirits. Whereas wine, beer and cider are the natural produce of fermented fruit, spirits are the artificial concentration of that natural produce. Instead of evolving naturally as fermented drinks had done, they had to be invented. It is a matter of dispute among historians whether spirits were invented in the Near East at the beginning of the Christian era, and used for ritual purposes, or whether they were invented more than a thousand years later, in Italy in the twelfth century, and used as medicines.* Certainly, there is little evidence of the

---

*This will be discussed in the Conclusion.

consumption of spirits for recreational purposes before the seventeenth century, when gin became increasingly popular in England, the Netherlands and Germany, brandy in France, vodka in Russia, and whisky in Scotland and Ireland. They were not necessarily drunk neat, however. In England gin was often combined with beer, to make a drink then known as 'purl'. It was with purl that, according to legend, the future King Charles II was fortified at a country inn during his adventurous escape after the Battle of Worcester.

The use of spirits steadily increased during the course of the seventeenth century but they were not yet generally consumed in harmful quantities. This began to happen only at the beginning of the eighteenth century, in London. The landed interest in Parliament having reduced taxes on gin and having removed restrictions on its manufacture and sale in order to dispose of a glut of corn and raise money for a war with France, spirits were now made freely available to the inhabitants of a city that had been destabilized by a century of mass immigration. So great was the influx of unskilled labourers, the poor and the destitute into London during the seventeenth century that the population trebled; by 1700 London, with six hundred thousand inhabitants, was twenty times the size of any other town in England, and the largest city in Europe. Overpopulation brought unemployment, overcrowding, insanitary living conditions, adult disease and infant mortality. Sold at the strength it came off the still – much greater than today's watered-down version – and drunk neat, without the support of food, gin provided an anaesthetic, in many cases a permanent one. The death rate soon exceeded the birth rate; despite continuing immigration, the population was hardly any higher in 1750 than it had been half a century earlier.

'A new kind of drunkenness, unknown to our ancestors, is lately sprung up amongst us,' wrote the novelist and magistrate Henry Fielding in his *Enquiry into the Causes of the Late Increase of Robbers* in 1751, 'which, if not put a stop to, will infallibly destroy a great part of the inferior people. The drunkenness I here intend is that acquired by the strongest intoxicating liquors, and particularly by that poison called gin, which, I have great reason to think, is the principal sustenance (if it may be so called) of more than a hundred thousand people in the metropolis. Many of these wretches there are, who swallow pints of this poison within the twenty-four hours, the dreadful effects of which I have the misfortune every day to see, and to smell too.'

In the same year the Ministers, Churchwardens, Vestrymen and Inhabitants of the Parish of St Martin's in the Fields petitioned the House of Commons to take measures to remedy the situation, saying, 'That by the frequent and excessive use of spirituous liquors religion is scandalously profaned, the health of the people destroyed, their strength and substance wasted, their lives shortened and the human species lessened and decreased; and that idleness and disorder take the place of industry and morality among the labouring and common people; and that numberless robberies in the streets and elsewhere, and even murders are committed by the use of low-priced spirituous liquors; and that if an immediate restraint is not put to this pernicious vice, it will not only increase the above-mentioned evils, but also tend to the destruction of the trade and powers of the kingdom.'

This petition – which resembles some of the comments made about the effects of narcotic drugs among the underclass of major cities today – was supported by a number of others, and between them they persuaded Parliament to pass an Act in 1751 in which the duty on gin was increased, and distillers, grocers and chandlers (who sold bread, cheese and weak beer) were forbidden to sell it by retail. This solved the worst of the problems.

The Government had thus reacted very differently to the mass consumption of spirits from the manner in which it had responded to the arrival of coffee and tobacco. It had wanted to close down the coffee houses; it had sought to prohibit the smoking of tobacco, and had only come to accept it when it was found that tobacco could not effectively be prohibited and that it suited the Government's economic interests to tax it instead. The mass consumption of spirits, on the other hand, had originally been encouraged by the Government, in furtherance of its economic interests; it was not until several decades later that it was eventually forced by popular pressure to introduce some measure of control.

The reason why the Government should have been concerned about the consumption of coffee and tobacco by its subjects, and should have preferred them to consume alcohol, was made explicit in the 1840s, when the leaders of the Chartist movement accused the authorities of conspiring to make the working classes drunk;

they had good evidence for their allegation, since the Government had recently reduced the price of beer and gin, encouraged the development of gin palaces and beer shops, and rejected radical demands for the Sunday opening of museums as alternative attractions. In the 1860s, in a debate on the Representation of the People Bill, the Liberal peer Viscount Goschen accused the Tories of being 'more afraid of the working classes when they think than when they drink'; he enunciated the principle that the working classes 'are more likely to combine if they are sober than if they have spent all their money on beer'.

Authoritarian governments have had good reason to be more afraid of the people when they think than when they drink. This is demonstrated, not only by the part played by the coffee houses in sedition in Ottoman Istanbul and Restoration London and in revolution in eighteenth-century Paris, but also by the events that followed the introduction of Prohibition in Russia at the beginning of the First World War. In 1891 the Russian novelist Count Leo Tolstoy had written an article in the *Contemporary Review* in which he claimed that people drank alcohol 'not merely for want of something better to do to while away their time, or to raise the spirits, not because of the pleasure they receive, but simply and solely in order to drown the warning voice of conscience.' After vodka was prohibited in Russia in 1914, they were no longer able to silence their consciences in alcoholic drink. It may not altogether have been a coincidence that they rebelled and overthrew the government three years later. Certainly this claim was made by the English prohibitionist Arthur Mee. 'The truth about Russia is almost too incredible to believe,' he wrote in 1917. 'It is prohibition that made the Revolution possible; it was stopping drink that made one hundred and seventy million people free.'

This conclusion was supported by the more practically-minded commissioners who were sent round Britain later in the same year in order to inquire into the causes of the industrial discontent that had broken out in the spring and summer. The discontent had followed a reduction in the supply of beer as a result of switching grain supplies from brewing to food production. According to the account given by His Honour Judge Parry, the chairman of the commission in the north-west area, 'The two main sources of trouble appeared to arise from the self-sufficiency of bureaucracy and the insufficiency of beer. Bureaucracy in the absence of the anaesthetic of vodka seems to have been the moving cause of Bolshevism in Russia.' In Britain, at least, the supply of alcoholic drink was increased, and the dangers that might have been posed by an increase in unrest were averted.

Governments may, in the past, have had good reason to believe that the social order was better maintained by encouraging their subjects to drink than by trying to prevent them from doing so, but it was not on account of their sedative qualities that they also refrained from attempting to prohibit them from taking narcotic drugs. If there was no prohibition of the consumption of narcotic drugs in England, Scotland, Wales or Ireland in the sixteenth, seventeenth, eighteenth or nineteenth centuries, it was not because these drugs were unavailable, and that therefore such a prohibition would have been meaningless. Certainly opium was taken in the seventeenth century; the first known opium-addict writer was the Restoration dramatist Thomas Shadwell, who took it to treat the symptoms of gout and appears to have died from an overdose in 1692. But Shadwell, like the more famous literary opium addicts of the late eighteenth and nineteenth centuries, did not take opium for its pleasurable effects, but for medical reasons. Narcotic drugs were not prohibited because they were for long believed to be medically beneficial. It might seem that the reasons for which opium was taken by the two most celebrated opium-eaters in British history – Thomas De Quincey and Samuel Taylor Coleridge – militate against any argument that it was consumed principally for medical reasons. After all, it was De Quincey who, in 1822, in his *Confessions of an Opium-Eater*, first publicized the vision-inducing potential of the drug, while it is a commonplace of literary history that Coleridge's most celebrated poem, *Kubla Khan*, was inspired by the opium that he had taken. But their opium habits, at least in the beginning, were medical in their explanation. De Quincey started to take opium in order to counteract stomach pains and to ward off tuberculosis, of which it was thought he was beginning to show symptoms. Coleridge began by taking opium for toothache; in 1797, when he wrote *Kubla Khan*, he was using it to mitigate the pain of dysentery as well as to free his mind from financial worries. Other writers of the period, too, took opium, not so much in order to encourage literary creativity but in order to treat the illnesses or suppress

12

the anxiety that threatened to stifle it. Thus, Sir Walter Scott wrote *The Bride of Lammermoor* in 1819 during the course of a painful illness for which he was being heavily dosed with opium; Wilkie Collins wrote *The Moonstone* in 1868 under the influence of the opium that he took to treat rheumatism and acute pain in his eyes and to suppress the anxiety caused by the terminal sickness of his mother; Charles Dickens turned to opium after suffering both psychologically and physically on his reading tour of America, and wrote about the drug's effects in 1870 in his unfinished novel *The Mystery of Edwin Drood*. Among non-literary figures, Florence Nightingale resorted to opium on her return from the Crimea, partly to treat severe back pain; many people took the drug for sleeplessness, and (according to the Duke of Wellington) King George IV, who consumed alcoholic drinks in large quantities, occasionally took opium to 'calm the irritation which the use of spirits engenders'.

Admittedly, it was not always possible to distinguish the medical use of opium from its use for pleasurable purposes. People began to take opium to treat disease but then found that they could not do without it. A similar confusion in the motivation for opium consumption can be found in working-class consumption in the Fens, the one part of Britain where opium-eating became a popular Saturday night activity among all classes; indeed, it was so popular that the brewers put opium in the beer. But here, too, the use of opium could be described as quasi-medicinal, since the region was damp, chilly and prone to malaria, all the marshes not yet having been drained.

Coca, too, was popularized in the nineteenth century only for medical reasons. The principal medicine of which coca formed a constituent part was a wine tonic called Vin Mariani – Bordeaux with an infusion of coca leaf, which was supposed to be taken in a dosage of one glass before or after every meal. This had been invented in 1863 by a Corsican chemist called Angelo Mariani, who devoted his life to the study of coca and the development of means of capturing its essence in an appetizing and marketable form. As well as Vin Mariani, he produced Mariani's elixir, Mariani's lozenges, Mariani's pastilles and Mariani's tea – but it was Vin Mariani that was the most popular, as was evidenced by the testimonials that Mariani obtained for his product from Pope Leo XIII, Queen Victoria, Thomas

Edison, Emile Zola, Sarah Bernhardt and Buffalo Bill Cody, among others.

Although Vin Mariani may have been forgotten today, it provided the inspiration for the best-known of all modern drinks. Many imitations of Vin Mariani were produced in the 1870s and 1880s, among them a French Wine Coca, which was manufactured in Atlanta, Georgia, by a druggist called John Pemberton. It has been suggested that Pemberton was attracted to coca by the claim that it could cure opium and morphine addiction, and that he used his own French Wine Coca in an attempt to break his own morphine habit. In November 1885, however, Atlanta voted to ban alcohol. The ban was due to begin in July 1886, and with it, it appeared, the days of wine-based medicine would come to an end.* So Pemberton modified his Wine Coca formula, retaining the coca leaf† and the kola nut but removing the wine and replacing it with distilled fruit oils. The result was marketed as 'a valuable brain tonic and a cure for all nervous afflictions: sick headache, neuralgia, hysteria, melancholy, etc.'; it was called Coca-Cola.

At the same time as coca-based tonics such as Vin Mariani and Coca-Cola were being popularized in Europe and North America, the practice of medicine was being revolutionized as a consequence of the discovery of alkaloids – alkaline substances of plant origin which exerted a pronounced physiological effect on animal organisms. One of the first of the alkaloids to be discovered was morphine, which was isolated from opium in 1803. It was followed by strychnine, quinine, caffeine, nicotine, codeine (also from opium) and atropine. Cocaine was not isolated until slightly later, in the late 1850s, because it was not until this period that there was any significant medical interest in the coca plant.

Now, it was believed at the time that these alkaloids were simply the active principles of the plants from which they had been isolated: that is to say, they exerted precisely the same effect, but in a more concentrated form. It therefore seemed self-evident to doctors that it would be absurd to ask a patient to chew coca

---

*As it turned out prohibition of alcoholic drinks did not include medicinal ones, and Pemberton was able to continue to sell his Wine Coca. But he had not known this at the time he invented Coca-Cola.
†Coca was removed from the recipe for Coca-Cola in 1903; the company has subsequently attempted to deny that its drink ever contained this substance.

leaves or take a spoonful or two of a solution of opium in alcohol* when it was possible to give him accurately measured doses of what they then considered to be their essential ingredients. So first morphine and then cocaine replaced opium and coca in medical practice. For a while, they proved very effective. Before long, however, it became clear that people who were given morphine and cocaine for medical purposes were unable to stop taking them when they recovered: that they were both highly addictive. It was hoped that the problems of morphine addiction might be solved by the isolation in 1898 of another opium derivative, which it was believed carried no danger of addiction. Unfortunately this new substance – heroin – proved no less addictive than morphine had been.

It was in order to prevent people from becoming addicted to morphine, cocaine and heroin that the Government first introduced legislation severely to restrict sales of narcotic drugs. Initially, controls on drug sales were introduced as an emergency measure during the First World War. In 1916, following a highly-publicized case involving the sale of cocaine to Canadian troops in barracks in Folkestone by an ex-convict and a prostitute, opium, cocaine and coca were regulated as narcotic drugs that could only be sold on prescription. In 1920, these wartime restrictions were made permanent, and control was extended to morphine and heroin, in the Dangerous Drugs Act, which was passed in an atmosphere of public panic about a 'drugs menace' – generated principally by excited newspaper reaction to the sudden death in November 1918 of the beautiful twenty-two-year-old actress Billie Carleton, just after attending a Victory Ball at the Albert Hall. Carleton's death was widely attributed to an overdose of cocaine; it is true that she had been taking cocaine just before her death, but in fact it was never proved that this had been the cause of it.

There was no good medical reason why the Government should have tarred opium or coca with the same brush as morphine, heroin and cocaine. The fact that the latter are extracted from the former does not mean that they simply represent them in stronger

---

*Opium was taken by those who could afford it in the form of 'laudanum', an alcoholic solution for which there were various formulae, the most popular being Sydenham's Laudanum: two ounces of opium, one ounce of saffron, one drachm (an eighth of an ounce) each of cinnamon and cloves, and one pint of wine.

and more measurable form. They affect the system in different ways. Indeed, in his apology for coca, *History of Coca: the 'divine plant' of the Incas*, the American doctor W. G. Mortimer went so far as to claim that cocaine, which was no more than one constituent of the coca leaf, 'no more fully represents coca than would prussic acid – because found in minute quantities in the seeds of a peach – represent that luscious fruit'. As for opium, as Sir George Birdwood, a former Professor of Materia Medica in Bombay, had stated in a letter to *The Times* in 1881, this was 'almost as harmless an indulgence as twiddling the thumbs and other silly-looking methods of concentrating the jaded mind.'

If opium and coca were tarred with the same brush as morphine, heroin and cocaine in 1920, it was because there was no lobby speaking out in their favour, no group sufficiently interested in their continued availability. Doctors and chemists were largely unconcerned because there was less need for over-the-counter sales of opium now that new drugs had been developed that fulfilled the same function with less risk: instead of taking opium as an analgesic, it was now possible to take aspirin, which was first marketed in 1899; instead of taking opium as a sedative, it was possible to take barbiturates, the first of which had been marketed in 1906.

And the public were largely unconcerned about the introduction of the ban on the recreational consumption of opium and coca because they did not take them for recreational purposes. The banning of the recreational use of opium and coca can be compared with the continued legality of tobacco. This, too, had had an alkaloid isolated from it, nicotine. And nicotine was even more addictive than morphine, heroin or cocaine. But tobacco had already been established for hundreds of years; it was taken for recreational, rather than medical, purposes; its adherents had not converted from smoking tobacco to ingesting its derivative, nicotine. If coca and opium had been consumed over many centuries in Europe, as they had been in South America and Asia, if they had become integrated into the local culture, then it would have been difficult for any government to ban them. But they had not, so it was not.

Admittedly, sales of alcohol, the longest-established drug in Western society and the one that was most deeply embedded in local cultures, were also banned during the First World War in a few countries, such as Russia; while, in Great Britain, not only was beer hard to come by but sales of spirits were severely restricted by force of law. Permitted hours for the sale of spirits for home consumption were limited to between midday and 2.30 p.m. on weekdays, and the supply of spirits in quantities of less than a quart was prohibited. These measures, however, were directed specifically at the need to maintain good order and efficiency in the wartime economy: they were intended to discourage the home drinking of spirits at weekends, which was the cause of much absenteeism on Monday mornings, and to prevent people from carrying small flasks into their place of work. They were tolerated by the population because they were justified by the exigencies of war. After the war, more or less normal service was resumed.

One Western country where the total prohibition of sales of alcohol was imposed, not during the turmoil of the war, but in the peacetime conditions that followed, was the United States of America. Far from contradicting the argument that Western governments have generally proved unable to ban the preferred social drug of its citizens, however, the experience of American Prohibition in the 1920s demonstrated the impossibility of doing so. It is notorious that Prohibition did not work, that people went on drinking alcohol all the same, that they just did so illegally, without paying any taxes to the government for the privilege.*

The experience of Prohibition also demonstrated the fact that Westerners have generally preferred to take alcohol rather than narcotic drugs for recreational purposes. Since this was a period when the trade in alcoholic drinks was no less illicit than the trade in narcotic drugs, there was no reason for responsible citizens to prefer drink to drugs on grounds of legality. Certainly the 1920s was a decade in which a ban on the sale of alcoholic drinks coincided with an increase in the consumption of cannabis, opiates and cocaine, and certainly it was believed by many people at the time that these two developments were related: that now that the trade in alcohol was illegal, people would be less inclined to choose it in preference to narcotic drugs. For example, in 1929, during the debate in Congress on a bill which proposed tougher penalties for bootleggers, Senator James A. Reed of Missouri, the

---

*The ineffectiveness of Prohibition will be discussed in detail in Chapter 7.

leader of the pro-alcohol faction, stated it as a fact that drug addiction had increased as a result of Prohibition. The fact that narcotic drug use increased during Prohibition, however, does not mean that the two were connected. There is no evidence that people started taking narcotic drugs as a direct result of the ban on the trade in alcohol. The recreational use of opium and cocaine had been banned only a few years before, in 1914. If people had not consumed opium in significant numbers when it was legal before the First World War, then it is hard to see why they should have chosen to do so just because alcohol was made illegal in 1919. Moreover, even during Prohibition, alcohol was still consumed by large numbers of otherwise respectable people – a significantly smaller stigma attached to it than to the consumption of opium or cocaine. As is suggested by the experience of America in the 1920s – and indeed by that of much of the Western world since then – it is not so much the banning of alcohol that increases consumption of narcotic drugs as the banning of the recreational consumption of the drugs themselves. This is partly because it forces the user to find his supplies in the criminal underworld, in whose members' interest it is to encourage addiction, and partly because – in the case of some drugs at least – it is the banning that makes them attractive.

Given a straight choice between alcohol and narcotic drugs, Westerners have generally preferred alcohol. It might seem that an exception to this rule can be found in the experience of the late 1960s and early 1970s, when a thriving culture surrounded the consumption of cannabis*. In fact, this is the exception that proves the rule. Alcohol is the preferred, socially acceptable drug of Western culture, while other types of drugs are generally regarded as deviant. Therefore the consumption of these other drugs is in itself an act of rebellion. One of the main reasons why cannabis became so popular in Britain in the 1960s was that the police had just started to clamp down on its consumption. Until then, its use had been restricted almost exclusively to immigrants from the West Indies; after the clamp-down, taking cannabis became a favourite symbol of rebellion among white teenagers. Similarly, the popularity of Ecstasy in the 1980s can be attributed

*The terminology can be confusing. The plant is hemp, its Latin name *cannabis*. The other three terms that one encounters are simply those used in different continents: ganja in India, hashish in the Middle East and marijuana in America.

in part to its having been made illegal in 1977. No wonder an authority as eminent as the head of the criminal intelligence branch of the Metropolitan Police, Commander John Grieve, has suggested that the Government should look into the possibility of licensing the sale and consumption of narcotic drugs. It would take away much of their appeal.

The differences in the effects of alcohol and cannabis are obvious to anyone who takes the trouble to compare them. They have been clearly documented by the researches of G. M. Carstairs, who spent 1951 living in a large village in the state of Rajasthan in northern India. The ruling caste in the village, the Rajputs, were fighting men, with certain special prerogatives, notably the right to eat meat and drink alcohol, the latter in the form of a spirit called *daru*. They were taught to put great stress on individual bravery in the face of danger. This danger was seldom met, but every young Rajput lived with the anxiety that he might not prove adequate to the occasion when it finally came. He was therefore inclined to assuage his anxieties in the convivial relaxation of a drinking party.

The members of the other top caste group in the village, the Brahmans, denounced the use of *daru*, which they said was utterly inimical to the religious life. 'The result of eating meat and drinking liquor,' said one of them, 'is that you get filled with passion and rage, and then the spirit of God flies out from you.' The Brahmans were often intoxicated, but with *bhang* (an infusion of cannabis leaves and stems), which they believed enhanced the spiritual life. They said that it gave good *bhakti*, this being their word for the sort of devotional act which consists in emptying the mind of all wordly distractions and thinking only of God. The Rajputs did not denounce *bhang* as fiercely as the Brahmans condemned *daru*, but, as one of them pointed out, *bhang* 'makes you quite useless, unable to do anything. *Daru* isn't like that, you may be drunk but you can still carry on.'

Carstairs suggested that Westerners should be compared to the Rajputs, since they too were committed to a life of action, were brought up to regard individual achievement as important, and found the experience of surrendering their powers of volition (through cannabis) to be threatening and distasteful. Moreover, these observations help further to explain the popularity of cannabis among white British teenagers in the 1960s and 1970s.

Not only was it illegal, making consumption in itself an act of rebellion, but the way in which it affected its consumers caused them to rebel against the values of Western society by becoming passive instead of aggressive, by dropping out, tuning in and turning on. No wonder it so offended the authorities.

If the difference between alcohol and narcotic drugs such as cannabis is marked, that between alcohol and hallucinogenic drugs such as mescaline and magic mushrooms is even greater. According to a theory propounded by Aldous Huxley in *The Doors of Perception*, the original function of the brain was not productive, but eliminative. That is to say, it was designed to protect human beings from being overwhelmed and confused by a mass of largely useless and irrelevant memories or sensory information, by shutting out most of what they would otherwise perceive or remember at any given moment, leaving only the very small selection of information that was likely to be of practical use. Certainly this theory helped to explain what had happened to Huxley after he had taken mescaline. In normal circumstances, human beings receive only a small fraction of what is contained in the mind's vast resources. But by taking a vision-inducing drug it is possible to open the doors of perception that are ordinarily closed.

The effect of alcohol is very different. Indeed, it has been argued that alcohol and hallucinogenic drugs are antithetical: that while alcohol allows a person to relate to others by being more sure of himself, a hallucinogen acts not by emphasizing a person's own self but by expanding it into the selves of others – creating a state of empathy, as it were.

It may appear that an argument of this kind could only be made by a person who is himself under the influence of drugs. But the theory that alcohol and hallucinogenic drugs are antithetical is supported by anthropological investigations of the primitive communities that have been encountered by visitors from 'civilization' ever since Columbus's voyage to the Americas five centuries ago. Many of these communities have had their medicine men, witch doctors or shamans, who have been supposed to be able to communicate with the spirits. In order to visit the spirit world, the shaman enters a trance, usually with the help of drugs. He emerges from his trance with information for his tribe, such as news of what will happen in the future, and often imparts this information by 'speaking in tongues': appearing to be possessed and describing what he has seen or heard in a voice that is not his own. When the shaman is introduced to alcohol, however, he loses his powers of divination. When the Russians began the conquest of Siberia at the end of the sixteenth century, they determined to put down shamanism by banning the consumption of the hallucinogenic fly-agaric mushroom – but this regulation was completely ignored. What put an end to shamanism in Siberia was the introduction of vodka by traders. Not only was vodka cheap, but it was readily available all year round, unlike mushrooms. So shamans tried it. Unfortunately, vodka failed to provide the shaman with the visions that mushrooms had done; instead, it blocked the visions, and came to be regarded as an antidote to the mushrooms' effects. Their ability to induce trances having been destroyed by alcohol, shamans took to fakery instead, and deluded their customers with conjuring tricks.

The argument that Europeans have generally preferred the stimulating and confidence-boosting effects of alcohol to the more passive and mind-altering effects of narcotic drugs might seem to be contradicted by the fact that they took with such alacrity to tobacco which, when discovered being used by Indians in the New World, was employed as a hallucinogen in order to induce visions. But the Europeans moulded tobacco in their own image: they transformed it into a drug that is much more closely comparable in its effects to alcohol than to hallucinogenic drugs such as mescaline or magic mushrooms.

Of the two principal varieties of tobacco that grew in the Americas, *Nicotiana rustica* and *Nicotiana tabacum*, the one that was smoked by the natives of Mexico and North America was the more potent *Nicotiana rustica*, which was more readily capable of inducing visions. It is unlikely that Europeans could have used this stronger form of tobacco in order to achieve a trance-like state, even if they had wanted to. The virtues of tobacco, as far as Europeans were concerned, lay in the fact that, when inhaled in short puffs, it acted as a mild stimulant; if they took deeper draughts, they obtained a tranquillizing effect, but without any accompanying visions. Accordingly, the type of tobacco that grew wild in Virginia – *Nicotiana rustica* – was ignored by its English settlers, who established the fame and fortune of the colony in the seventeenth century upon the cultivation and processing of the milder variety, *Nicotiana tabacum*, which was not native to that part of America but had been imported from Spanish plantations in the West Indies or South America in 1611. The more potent *Nicotiana rustica* may still be cultivated today in some parts of the world, but in the United States of America only *Nicotiana tabacum* is grown for commercial use.

The ability of a society to mould a drug in its own image, and to obtain from it the effect it chooses, is demonstrated not only by the history of tobacco but also by more recent experiments with placebos which show that people's reaction to a drug is principally determined by their expectations of how it will affect them. These experiments have been successful not only among the lay public but also when performed on doctors who might have thought that they would be immune to deception because they would know from training and experience how to recognize a drug's effects. In the late 1960s some members of the staff of the Department of Psychological Medicine at Glasgow University carried out a placebo experiment on their colleagues. They gave some of them dexamphetamine and others placebos, and asked each of them to guess which one he had taken. According to the doctor who later wrote up the experiment, 'their guesses were scarcely better than chance'. One experienced psychiatrist recognized his symptoms as coming from dexamphetamine. 'During the next few hours he became more "high", and the following morning announced that participation in the experiment had considerably enhanced his enjoyment of a party the previous evening.' In fact he had taken a placebo. Other members of the staff, equally convinced that they had taken placebos, were told that they had taken dexamphetamine.

In a more recent and less clinical experiment, Dr Tim Stockwell, an Exeter psychologist, served non-alcoholic lager at a party at his home, but switched labels so that people thought they were getting alcoholic lager. Not only did everyone behave 'in a very jolly way, as though they had been drinking', but one of the people there was even convinced that he had gone over the limit for driving and could not believe it when a breathalyzer test proved negative.

This experiment can easily be repeated by anyone who is interested in doing so, although it is probably unwise to serve non-alcoholic lager, which is not a wholly convincing imitation of the real thing. A better choice might well be to give some guests vodka and tonic with a squirt of lime juice, and others just tonic water with a squirt of lime juice – drinks in which the presence or absence of alcohol is considerably more difficult to detect. This was what was done with sixty-four people in the late 1970s by two psychologists at the University of Wisconsin. Half of the people were social drinkers and half were alcoholics. The psychologists told some of the people who were given alcohol that they were being given alcohol and others that they were being given tonic water, and they told some of the people who were given tonic water that they were being given this and others that they were being given alcohol. It was found that both alcoholics and social drinkers drank more when they thought they were drinking alcohol than when they thought they were drinking tonic water, regardless of what they were actually drinking. Some of the alcoholics, having been required to abstain from alcohol for at least eight hours before their appointment in the laboratory, arrived suffering from 'the shakes'; it was found that these physical symptoms of alcoholism were alleviated among those people who thought they were drinking alcohol but not among those people who thought they were drinking tonic water – whatever they were actually drinking.

In reporting their findings, the psychologists referred to other, similar studies which had found that men became less anxious and women more anxious when they thought they were drinking alcohol, that men became more aggressive when they thought they were drinking alcohol, and that both men and women said they felt more sexually aroused when they thought they were drinking alcohol. Again, it made no difference whether they were actually drinking alcohol or not. What mattered was perception, not reality.

The fact that men tend to become more aggressive when they think they have been drinking alcohol gives the lie to those people who would seek to put the blame on alcohol for various acts of violence, ranging from wife-beating to 'lager loutism'. The latter term was coined in the second half of the 1980s in order to describe an apparently unprecedented outbreak of acts of violence by young men in quiet country towns when the pubs closed on Friday and Saturday nights. They had been drinking lager, hence the name. The suggestion that young men become violent as a result of drinking too much lager is certainly one that the young men would themselves prefer to believe. But might they not have drunk the lager because they intended to become violent? The Oxford Polytechnic psychologist Dr Peter Marsh has studied the matter in some detail. He is not convinced that there is a direct connection between alcohol and violence. 'More often than not,' he has suggested, 'being drunk is simply an excuse for violence and belligerence. We expect people who get drunk to get aggressive, so that's what they do.'

Alcoholic drinks do not cause people to loosen their inhibitions; they *encourage* people to loosen their inhibitions. Or rather, they encourage men to loosen their inhibitions. If, as placebo experiments demonstrate, men tend to become less and women more anxious when they have been drinking alcohol or believe that they have been doing so, it is at least in part because alcohol encourages men to become more relaxed and more confident, whereas it encourages women to feel that they have to become more wary of their ability to resist carnal temptation. As generations of men have discovered to their advantage, it is often easier to persuade a woman to indulge in sexual activity if she has first been plied with alcohol. In a survey of 520 American college students in 1978, 70 per cent of male drinkers said that they had used alcohol in order to make a woman sexually more responsive, and 73 per cent of men and women reported that alcohol either sometimes or always increased their sexual activity.

Many manufacturers advertise their wares by linking them with sex, but alcohol producers have more reason than most to do so. Only in the last few years have advertising regulations on both sides of the Atlantic been tightened sufficiently for it no longer to be permitted to market an alcoholic drink by referring to its seductive qualities. Before that, it was possible to indulge in the most blatant attempts to sell an alcoholic drink by referring to its usefulness as a tool of seduction. One such advertisement in the United States, for a brand of tequila called Two Fingers, featured an attractive woman and the slogan, 'Two Fingers is all it takes'.

1

THE CIVILIZATION OF BRITISH TASTE

HEAVY DRINKING HAS ALWAYS BEEN PART OF THE BRITISH character – and one that has differentiated the inhabitants of these islands from their neighbours on the Continent of Europe. The eighth-century missionary and reformer Saint Boniface had been born in Devon but spent most of his life working on the Continent. In his old age, he wrote a letter home to Cuthbert, the Archbishop of Canterbury, in which he referred to a report that 'In your dioceses the vice of drunkenness is too frequent. This is an evil peculiar to pagans and to our race. Neither the Franks nor the Gauls nor the Lombards nor the Romans nor the Greeks commit it.'

Boniface's comments were echoed by those of the historian and chronicler William of Malmesbury in his *History of the Kings of England*, written four hundred years later. Among the English at the time of the Norman conquest, William asserted, 'Drinking in particular was a universal practice, in which occupation they passed entire nights as well as days . . . They were accustomed to eat till they became surfeited, and drink till they were sick.' William even went so far to attribute the success of the Normans at the Battle of Hastings partly to the drunkenness of their English opponents which led them to engage the Norman army 'more with rashness and precipitate fury than with military skill'. After the Conquest, he added, it was not long before the English habits of eating and drinking to excess were adopted by their Norman conquerors.

Although the comments of a biased, Norman source such as William of Malmesbury should properly be regarded with a certain degree of scepticism, there is no doubt that the new Anglo-Norman nation that was formed by force in the eleventh century retained the reputation for drunkenness that had been created by its purely English predecessors. A century after the Conquest, the intellectual and ecclesiastic John of Salisbury, who like Saint Boniface before him had been born in England but had spent much of his life on the Continent, wrote in a letter to a friend that 'The constant habit of drinking has made the English famous among all foreign nations'.

In the sixteenth century, the long-established tradition of heavy drinking was compounded by the growth of a money economy in which an increasing number of people were paid in cash rather than in kind, and of new patterns of work, with fewer employees living in the same place as they worked. When men had drunk at home, they had done so in front of their wives, children and employers, and so were obliged to behave with some restraint. But now an increasing number of them took to going to alehouses to eat and drink. Here, they could do what they liked: there was no-one to stop them from drinking as much as they wanted. In his famous *Anatomy of Abuses* the pamphleteer Philip Stubbes – admittedly a Puritan and therefore a biased source – described how the alehouses were 'haunted with malt-worms' who sat drinking 'all day long, yea, all the night, peradventure all the week together, so long as any money is left, swilling, gulling* and carousing from one to another, till never a one can speak a ready word . . . How they stutter and stammer, stagger and reel to and fro, like madmen, some vomiting, spewing and disgorging their filthy stomachs, othersome pissing under the board as they sit . . .'

At the same time, it was claimed by a number of writers that the practice of heavy drinking was a new introduction into

*Guzzling.

England, having been learnt from Dutch soldiers by Englishmen who had fought beside them in their wars against their Spanish oppressors in the late sixteenth century. For example, it was stated by the author Thomas Nash in 1592 in his celebrated satire on contemporary society, *Pierce Penniless's Supplication to the Devil*, that 'superfluity in drink' was 'a sin that, ever since we have mixed ourselves with the Low Countries, is counted honourable, but before we knew their lingering wars was held in the highest degree of hatred that might be.' Obviously this was untrue – but Nash was far from alone in blaming an increase in drunkenness on the influence of the Dutch wars. And it is true that the English involvement in these wars did last for a long time – the first English soldiers arrived in the Low Countries in 1572 as mercenaries; in 1585 Queen Elizabeth I agreed to furnish troops on an official basis; some of them remained there until well into the next century. It is also true that the intercourse affected English culture in various ways: it influenced seafaring methods, and gave impetus to the draining of the Fens. It also introduced a number of new words to the English language. Previously the English had spoken of 'brewhouses' but this was supplanted by the Dutch term 'brewery'. It is quite likely, therefore, that the Dutch experience further compounded the English vice of heavy drinking, that the contemporary claims were not entirely without foundation.

It was not just that people were drinking more beer and wine than they had been but that they began to consume a new, stronger form of alcoholic drink – spirits. Although these had long been used as medicines, the practice of drinking spirits for recreational purposes did not originate until after another Dutch war – this time against the Dutch – in the mid-seventeenth century. It was observed, wrote Daniel Defoe, 'that the captains of the Hollanders' Men of War, when they were to engage with our ships, usually set a hogshead of brandy abroach, afore the mast, and bid the men drink lustick*, then they might fight lustick; and our poor seamen felt the force of the brandy, sometimes to their cost.' After peace was signed in 1654, the spirits that (it was supposed) had contributed so significantly to the Dutch war effort became popular in England.

The new fashion for brandy-drinking was supported by

*Merrily.

doctors, who were already in the habit of prescribing it as a medicine. Unfortunately, the growth in the popularity of brandy in the second half of the seventeenth century created substantial problems for those doctors who wished to continue to prescribe spirits for the sick. In *Health's Grand Preservative* the philosopher and dietician Thomas Tryon complained that 'Of late years many English women have betaken themselves to the drinking of brandy and other spirits, and have invented the black-cherry brandy which is in great esteem, so that she is nobody that hath not a bottle of it at her elbow, or if ever so little qualm or disorder be on the stomach, or perhaps be merely fancied, then away to the brandy bottle; so that when such people come to be sick, which most of them are very subject unto, the physicians do not know what to administer, they having in their health used themselves to such high fiery drinks that their cordials seem like water to them.'

The enormous social, medical and moral damage caused by these 'high fiery drinks' in London in the first half of the eighteenth century has already been described. Foreigners who came to the English capital took pains to try to understand why they should have come to be consumed in such quantities. In the 1720s the young Swiss César de Saussure was told that the spirits were 'necessary because of the thickness and dampness of the atmosphere'. A similar observation was made by the German visitor Baron d'Archenholz towards the end of the century. Because of the foggy air, he wrote, it was 'necessary to drink strong liquors in England. Those who use water often lose their health, and sometimes their lives. The same effects would attend the use of the English regimen in Italy, where the burning heats require sherbets, cooling liquors and other customs.'

It might appear that those middle- and upper-class men who did not consume spirits or drank them only in small quantities, preferring to drink wine instead, were following a more civilized, Continental regimen. The wine that they drank, however, was not a type that was popular elsewhere in Europe but a uniquely English style that had been fortified by the addition of spirits. Port had begun its life in the late seventeenth century as an unfortified red wine – a sort of Portuguese burgundy – but it was not long before its producers were adding brandy to it after fermentation. They claimed that this was necessary in order to enable it better to survive the journey to England. But it also offered other advantages. They knew that the English preferred the wines to be strong and alcoholic; indeed, in vintages in which port itself was not robust enough for English tastes it was fortified by the addition of appropriate wines from elsewhere. According to the port shipper John Croft, the port wines of the 1732 vintage were not thought strong enough and were therefore mixed with Benicarlo and Alicante, 'strong heavy, sweet and thick Spanish wines, like bullock's blood.' Certainly it was suggested by foreign observers that the English* preference for port – which in most vintages was a strong wine – over lighter wines such as claret and hock should be attributed to the popularity of spirits, and especially of gin. According to Baron d'Archenholz, 'It is their attachment to strong liquors that makes them so very fond of port wine . . . In London they like everything that is *powerful* and *heady*.'

In an attempt to encourage English wine drinkers to convert from port to claret, producers of the latter wine adulterated it in order to make it taste as much like port as possible. They developed a technique called *travail à l'anglaise*, which consisted of adding to the wine during the summer following the harvest some stronger wine from a warmer climate as well as some wine whose fermentation had been stopped before all the sugar had turned to alcohol (stum wine). This caused the claret to referment and, as a result, to become more alcoholic. Sometimes brandy was also added. In the case of the best clarets, the stronger wine that was added came from Hermitage in the Rhône valley; for lesser wines, wine from Benicarlo or Alicante in Spain was employed instead. As was pointed out by a correspondent to the French vine-growers' newspaper, the *Moniteur Vinicole*, the palates of wine-drinkers in England and other northern countries 'are generally spoiled by drinking spirits and strong beer. Consequently they find our wines, the chief merit of which consists in the finesse and delicacy of the bouquet, too light. What they want is something that is rough, strong, and catches in the throat. Talk not to them of flavour, of softness – the terms are, to them, incomprehensible: for them, the stronger the better . . . What must

*Claret remained the national drink of Scotland. When, in the eighteenth century, it became so expensive and so difficult to obtain that only the upper classes were able to continue drinking it, the rest of the population turned to whisky instead.

our wine merchants do if they hope to compete successfully with the wines of the [Iberian] Peninsula? They must assuredly make our wines as strong. The intelligent merchant studies and follows the taste of his customers, however strange and bad it may be.'

Certainly there were good commercial reasons for French wine-makers to adulterate their produce in order that it should conform to the vitiated tastes of English consumers, for the amount of port that was drunk by the middle and the upper classes in the eighteenth and early nineteenth centuries was so great as to appear almost incredible. In his memoirs the old Welsh soldier Rees Howell Gronow, a veteran of the Battle of Waterloo, recalled that it had been standard practice at this time for gentlemen to drink two or three bottles of port after dinner, that some men regularly drank four or five bottles, and that three lords of the realm, Lords Panmure, Dufferin and Blayney, 'wonderful to relate, were six-bottle men.' Another six-bottle man was the Regency sportsman John Mytton, who consumed between four and six bottles of port every day, without fail. He did so by drinking gradually. While he shaved in the morning he had a bottle of port by his elbow; he drank three or four glasses during the morning, a bottle with his lunch, several more glasses in the afternoon, at least a bottle with his dinner, and several glasses after dinner; and when he went to bed he took another bottle up with him. He assisted the absorption of the port by consuming a great quantity of nuts. It is hardly surprising that Mytton died young, at the age of thirty-seven. After his death one of his oldest friends, 'a regular pot-companion', signed an affidavit to the effect that Mytton had been drunk throughout the last twelve years of his life.

Admittedly, Mytton was an extreme figure: a man so reckless of his health or safety that on one notorious occasion he set fire to his nightshirt in order to 'frighten away' an attack of the hiccoughs. But the most respectable politicians of the day were also heavy drinkers: men such as William Pitt the Younger, who fortified himself with the better part of a bottle of port before going to the House of Commons to deliver a speech, and Henry St John, Viscount Bolingbroke, who was reputed to work for long hours during his time in office, being so conscientious as to arrive very early in the morning. The truth of the matter was that 'He used to sit up all night, and not having been in bed, he used to put a wet napkin on his forehead and eyes to cool the heat and headache occasioned by his intemperance, and then he appeared and attended to business with as much ease as if he lived the most temperate life.'

Dr Johnson, who was a teetotaller for most of his adult life, nevertheless told Boswell of having drunk three bottles of port at a dinner at University College, Oxford, 'without being the worse for it.' He also said that when he was a young man, in his home town of Lichfield in Warwickshire, 'All the *decent* people got drunk every night, and were not the worse thought of.' Nor was Boswell especially temperate in his behaviour. Lord Eldon, who served for twenty-five years as Lord Chancellor, told in his *Anecdote Book* of an occasion when both he and Boswell had been serving as barristers at assizes at Lancaster. One night, Eldon (himself no mean drinker) and some of his colleagues found Boswell 'lying upon the pavement, inebriated. We subscribed at supper a guinea for him, and half a crown for his clerk, and sent him, when he waked the next morning, a brief with instructions to move for what we denominated the writ of *Quare adhesit pavimento*, with observations duly calculated to induce him to think that it required great learning to explain the necessity of granting it to the judge, before whom he was to move. Boswell sent all round town to attornies for books that might enable him to distinguish himself, but in vain. He moved, however, for the writ, making the best use he could of the observations in the brief. The judge was perfectly astonished, and the audience amazed. The judge said, "I have never heard of such a writ: what can it be that adheres *pavimento*? Are any of you Gentlemen at the Bar able to explain this?" The Bar laughed. At last, one of them said, "My Lord, Mr Boswell last night *adhesit pavimento*. There was no moving him for some time. At last he was carried to bed, and has been dreaming about himself and the pavement." '

The large consumption by the middle and upper classes in the eighteenth century of a uniquely English style of strong red wine was complemented by the amount that was drunk by the working classes of a new kind of strong dark beer. The gin problem declined in the middle of the eighteenth century not only because of governmental action but also as a consequence of the development and marketing by the London breweries of porter. This beer, which, according to tradition, was first brewed by

Ralph Harwood, a partner in the Bell Brewhouse in Shoreditch, in the autumn of 1722, probably acquired its name, not out of any correspondence with port, but on account of its popularity among porters at London markets. Certainly, it was consumed in very substantial quantities by those who were engaged in physical labour. In his autobiography, the future American revolutionary Benjamin Franklin recalled travelling to England in 1724, at the age of eighteen, and finding employment in a printing house in London. Choosing to drink only water, he was nicknamed the 'Water-American' by his colleagues, who were 'great guzzlers of beer'. His companion at the press drank six pints of strong beer every day: 'A pint before breakfast, a pint at breakfast with his bread and cheese, a pint between breakfast and dinner, a pint at dinner, a pint in the afternoon about six o'clock, and another when he had done his day's work.'

Another foreign visitor, César de Saussure, described porter in a letter he sent home from his lodgings in East Sheen in 1726 as 'a thick and strong beverage', adding that 'The effect it produces if drunk in excess is the same as that of wine'. Although porter was not in fact quite as strong as wine, at about 7 per cent alcohol it was double the strength of the two most popular beers of the present day, bitter and lager. From a modern perspective, it is impossible to tell precisely how the porter of this period would have tasted – but it is possible to make an educated guess as a result of the discovery in the late 1980s of five hundred bottles of porter, still tightly corked, by divers investigating the wreck of a sailing barge that had sunk off Littlehampton in Sussex in 1825. Dr Keith Thomas, a microbiologist at the Polytechnic of North London, heard about this discovery, and obtained two of the bottles. Their contents gave little indication of how porter would have tasted, since their flavour now resembled that of 'old, wet boots' – but they did contain some yeast that was still alive. Thomas isolated and cleaned the yeast, and persuaded it to grow. He then obtained a porter recipe dating from 1850 in the archives of the brewers Whitbread. Using the yeast to ferment the ingredients listed in the recipe, Thomas successfully produced a recreation of historic porter: a beer that tasted something like a cross between a stout and a strong ale, with the hop bitterness and some of the dark colour of the stout and the sweet maltiness and alcoholic strength of the ale. This he commercialized under the label of Flag Original.* Even this beer, however, is significantly less alcoholic than the original, being a little over 5 per cent alcohol.

The eighteenth and early nineteenth centuries, when the upper classes drank themselves stupid on port and the working classes consumed excessive amounts of porter, may well mark the high-point of alcohol consumption in Britain – although there are no statistics to indicate whether this might indeed be the case. What they do mark, however, is the point at which the most popular forms of alcoholic drink were at their strongest and fullest-flavoured. Since that time, there has been a gradual transformation in the nature of the principal types of wine and beer drunk in Britain in the opposite direction: a general trend to lighter drinks, in terms of colour, taste and alcohol content. In the case of wine, the preference of the majority of consumers has been transferred from alcoholic, dark port in the eighteenth century to less alcoholic but dark claret in the later part of the nineteenth and early twentieth century and then to light-coloured white wines in the later part of the twentieth century; in the case of beer, consumers have converted from drinking alcoholic, dark porter in the eighteenth century to less alcoholic, lighter-coloured bitter in the nineteenth and early twentieth centuries and even less alcoholic, even lighter-coloured lager in the late twentieth century.

Although Englishmen certainly did develop a taste for port in the eighteenth century, it was not one that they had originally acquired of their own choosing. It had effectively been imposed upon them in 1703 when Queen Anne signed the Methuen Treaty with Portugal, which stipulated that at no point during its operation would more than two-thirds as much duty be charged on the wines of Portugal as on the wines of France; in return, the Portuguese agreed to lift their ban on the importation of English woollen goods.

Just as the major impetus for the adoption of port had come from the application of a preferential rate of duty on Portuguese wines in order to promote trade with Portugal, so the conversion

*A number of other breweries have begun to produce versions of porter in the 1990s, but none of them as authentic as Flag Original.

from port to claret received its impetus from the application of a preferential rate of duty on French wines in order to further trade with France. First, in 1831, the Methuen Treaty was abandoned, and duties on all European wines were equalized at 5s 6d per gallon. Then, in his Budget of 1860, William Ewart Gladstone, the Chancellor of the Exchequer, reduced the level of duty to 3s; in the following year, he introduced a new system of duties that differentiated between wines according to alcoholic strength for the first time. The duty on stronger wines such as port and sherry was further reduced to 2s 5d per gallon, but the duty on light wines below 15 per cent alcohol was reduced even more substantially, to 1s 9d; the following year, the duty on light table wines was reduced further still, to 1s per gallon.

'Immediately after the introduction of Mr Gladstone's budget the attention of wine merchants was attracted to claret,' wrote the wine merchant Charles Tovey. 'Wine consumers seemed to care for nothing else. The Englishman's favourite port was neglected, and abused as a vile compound unfit for general consumption.' If his comments were intended solely to refer to the middle and upper classes at whom his book was directed, then Tovey was quite correct. As well as altering the system of duties, Gladstone introduced a 'single bottle' Act, which enabled shop-keepers to obtain a licence to sell wines by the bottle for consumption off the premises. Previously, people who wished to buy wine for drinking at home had been obliged to choose between purchasing it in wholesale quantities – hardly a method likely to appeal to the occasional or novice wine-drinker – and trying to find a pub that sold wine that was drinkable – at a time when the pub had developed into an institution from which the middle and upper classes were effectively excluded.*

The combination of the reduction in the duty and the introduction of the 'single bottle' Act therefore led to a great expansion of the claret-drinking habit among the middle classes. The wine importing firm of Walter and Alfred Gilbey, who had originally set themselves up in business in 1857 selling South African wine by mail order, saw that the new legislation offered them a great opportunity to undercut traditional wine merchants who continued to regard claret as a luxury for the rich and therefore made

*The development of the pub will be discussed in Chapter 4.

no attempt to reduce their prices in line with the reduction in duty. The Gilbeys now offered decent claret to the middle classes for 1s 6d a bottle. They also took advantage of the new legislation to establish a network of grocers in provincial towns and cities through which they could sell their claret and other wines on an exclusive basis at fixed prices. By the 1870s they were selling more than nine million bottles of wine a year, nearly 10 per cent of total British wine sales. Not only did their success give rise to the term 'grocer's claret', but it gave credence to the story that Gladstone was a partner in Gilbey's, or at least had a commercial interest in the progress of the firm. This may not have been true, but it was widely believed at the time.

It would be wrong, however, to infer from Tovey's statement that port was abandoned altogether; after all, it too had benefited (as had sherry) from the duty changes, albeit to a lesser extent than claret, and sales of both port and sherry, far from declining after Gladstone's budgets, continued to rise until the mid-1870s. Port and sherry may largely have been abandoned by the middle and upper classes, but they were taken up with great enthusiasm by some of their social inferiors. Indeed, the new-found popularity of port and sherry among the working classes helps to explain the eagerness with which the middle classes turned to claret. Having appeared only recently on the social scene, for the most part as a result of industrialization, the middle classes felt insecure: their position in society was unclear. Therefore they sought to distance themselves from the working classes, from which they had risen; accordingly, once the working classes had taken up port and sherry, the middle classes opted to become claret-drinkers instead.

This social differentiation in taste in wine lasted, by and large, until after the Second World War. Australian and South African wines may have become popular among the working classes in the 1920s and 1930s but these were simply alternative versions of port and sweet sherry that replaced them because they were cheaper.* The period between the wars also saw sherries, in a drier form, regain something of their old popularity among the middle and upper classes. These changes, however, are as nothing when compared with the wine boom of recent times, which has

*The history of 'Empire' wines will be covered in Chapter 5.

seen the majority of the population take up the habit of drinking unfortified table wines.

There are a number of reasons for this transformation, not least the growth in size of the middle class – which has also been described as the development of a 'classless society'. As people have moved up the social scale, they have abandoned their old preference for sweet fortified wines and converted to dry unfortified ones. In many cases, they have done so not because they prefer the taste of dry wines, but because they have been taught to regard them as more sophisticated; learning to like the taste comes afterwards. They have not, however, taken up drinking the red wines that are preferred by traditional wine-drinkers because these taste much too 'dry' to them: that is, they are put off by the mouth-puckering tannins. The wine boom of recent times, therefore, has been characterized by a dramatic growth in the consumption of white wines, and a much more gradual growth in the consumption of red ones – to which some people have converted after first acquiring a taste for dry white wines. It is not known how much red wine was drunk relative to white in the 1960s as figures of this nature were not collected in this period, but it is probable that most of the wine that was imported into Britain was red; in 1970, 49 per cent was white and 51 per cent red and rosé; by the mid-1980s the figures had changed to 70 per cent white and 30 per cent red and rosé.

In the case of beer, as in that of wine, the original impetus for the abandonment of the preference for dark-coloured strong drink that had been manifested in the eighteenth century came partly for economic reasons. Brewers began to convert from the manufacture of porter to that of paler ales at the end of the eighteenth century, following the introduction of the saccharometer (a hydrometer calibrated for measuring the specific gravity of beer). With this instrument, brewers were able to see that pale malt had a greater potential alcoholic degree than brown malt and was therefore more cost-efficient to use. This became especially significant at the end of the century, when malt prices increased greatly as a result of the French wars.

Of course, the beer brewed with pale malts tasted different. At first, the brewers tried to hide the changes in production from the public, but this was not necessary for long. One of the great unknowns of beer history is to what extent the change from strong dark beer to a lighter and milder version occurred spontaneously among the public – a change to which the brewers responded – and to what extent the change was induced by the brewers themselves. Certainly it was in the interest of the brewers of Burton-on-Trent that such a change should occur since during the first quarter of the nineteenth century they converted – principally as a result of international political developments – from producing a strong dark beer for export to the Baltic to making a pale ale to send to India. They were eager also to sell their beer in the English market, and especially in London, which contained only 10 per cent of the population of the country but accounted for between 20 and 25 per cent of the consumption of beer. Before 1839 it was more cost-effective for them to export their beer to distant countries by sea than to send it overland to London, but this ceased to be the case when the railway link between Burton and the capital was completed in that year. To a substantial extent, the conversion in the taste of the population of London should be attributed to the marketing skills of the Burton brewers, notably Samuel Allsopp and Michael Thomas Bass.

On the other hand, there is plenty of evidence that public taste was moving towards milder beer of its own accord and that the brewers simply changed their recipes to meet it. The fashion appears to have begun among the upper classes in the West End of London. In 1817 John Martineau, a partner in Whitbread, observed that, 'generally speaking, at the West End of town, they drink their beer very mild.' The abolition of excise duty on glass in 1845, which encouraged both the bottling of beer for home consumption and the substitution of glasses for pewter tankards in pubs, made clear, sparkling beers more desirable.

The switch from porter to lighter, paler beers occurred only gradually, however. In one late-nineteenth-century account of the rise of the famous Burton brewery Bass, it is stated categorically that Bass acquired its hold on the London market as a consequence of its pale ale having been served in the refreshment rooms of the Crystal Palace at the Great Exhibition of 1851. This would certainly have been a sufficient explanation had it been true, since the exhibition was seen by more than six million visitors at a time when the population of London was less than two and a half million. Unfortunately, it is pure fantasy. No Burton ale was served in the refreshment rooms of the Great

Exhibition because, following pressure from temperance campaigners, alcohol had been banned. Nor indeed did the Burton brewers take advantage of the great number of visitors who came to London to see the exhibition in order to promote their beer. Benjamin Disraeli, then Chancellor of the Exchequer, was informed 'officially' that the foreigners who came to the city to see the exhibition 'drank nothing but London porter'.

The Great Exhibition could hardly have brought on the success of Burton beer in the capital because as late as 1863 porter still held three-quarters of the London market. It was the next two decades that saw the decisive swing from porter to Burton pale ale – which, in its draught version, came to be called 'bitter'. And porter did not disappear altogether until the First World War, when fuel restrictions were imposed that made it impossible to fire the malt to the extent that was required; the limited amount of beer that was brewed during the war was pale in colour and light in taste.

It is the gradual conversion from porter to bitter during the course of the nineteenth century that explains why England did not take up lager, which had swept across Europe and America during this period.* Lager-brewing also conquered Scotland, where brewing practices had been closer to Germany than to England ever since the German system of brewing was introduced in the twelfth century by the monastic orders. Continental lager was being imported into Scotland in small quantities from the 1870s onwards, appearing in up-market licensed grocers in Glasgow. Tennent started brewing it at its Well Park Brewery in Glasgow in 1885 and has done so ever since. Some English brewers did try producing lager. Allsopp began brewing it in 1899 with the intention of trying to compete with imported German lagers which had become fashionable as a result of the growing popularity of the German spas that the Prince of Wales frequented. But this popularity was short-lived.

Lager did not conquer England because the English were already in the process of turning from a darker, heavier style of beer – porter – to a lighter, sparkling one – bitter. In fact, the success of lager on the Continent, and the growing popularity of

*The same period also saw the rise of mild, essentially a weaker (and less bitter) form of porter. This has all but disappeared now but was the most popular style of draught beer among the working classes in the first half of the twentieth century.

imported bottled beers in Britain, hastened this process. British brewers responded to the challenge of lager by producing not only draught bitter but also relatively inexpensive, artificially carbonated, light bottled beers. These bottled light ales continued to grow in popularity for more than half a century, until the 1960s. They were more consistent than draught beers and they catered for an increased demand for beer to drink at home, especially once television ownership began to spread in the 1950s. There was also the question of packaging. In June 1954 *The Brewing Trade Review* stated that the public had become 'more "container-conscious" . . . To [younger people today] a bottle of something conveys an impression of unadulterated cleanliness and virtue.' By this time bottled beers accounted for 40 per cent of all beer sales.

Thus, as a result of the replacement of porter by bitter and the invention of artificially carbonated light bottled beer and its growth through the first half of the twentieth century, it is only in the last thirty years that lager has become really popular in England. The rise of lager in England had in fact begun soon after the end of the Second World War, when the Danish lager brewers Carlsberg and Tuborg began a determined assault on the English market. By the mid-1950s they were selling enough beer to convince the home brewers that it was time to move in. Charrington stepped up the promotion of Carling Black Label; Ind Coope launched Skol with a heavy advertising campaign; Guinness, Courage, Bass and Scottish & Newcastle joined forces to brew and market Harp.* Yet, despite massive advertising, by 1967 lager accounted for no more than 3 per cent of total beer sales. So far lager had proved most successful with younger drinkers and with women; most of it was served with a dash of lime cordial.

What seems to have held back sales of lager in England was the fact that it was still seen as a Continental drink. It only began to take off after it was introduced on draught: this not only made it acceptable to male drinkers but ensured that it was no longer regarded as an expensive imported drink that many people considered to be a rip-off. The first draught lager to be introduced was 'Keg Harp' in 1966; the brewers had been given the idea by

*Harp is brewed and marketed today by Guinness alone.

the fact that it was served on draught successfully on the ship *The Queen Elizabeth*.

During the 1970s British lager-brewers succeeded by means of advertisements in implanting the idea into the minds of beer-drinkers that, if they wanted their beer to be refreshing, they should choose lager. Lager was indelibly associated with refreshment by an advertising campaign in which it was claimed that Heineken refreshed the parts that other beers could not reach. This campaign led to an enormous growth in sales, not just of Heineken but of lager in general, during the hot summers of 1975 and 1976. During these two years lager increased its share of the beer market by nearly 50 per cent; at the end of 1976 it accounted for nearly a quarter of all the beer drunk in Britain.

Advertisements also played a major role in ensuring that lager became not merely acceptable to young men but the drink with which they most wanted to identify, by portraying lager as the laddish thing to drink. The lager-drinker as Jack-the-Lad was invented by a campaign for Harp in which drinkers were told to 'Stay sharp to the bottom of the glass'. This was followed by advertisements for Hofmeister in which George the Bear fulfilled young men's fantasies, and for Fosters in which Paul Hogan gave the lager drinker a harder, more cynical edge. By the late 1980s it was calculated that 83 per cent of lager was drunk by men, two-thirds of them under thirty-five. At the same time, however, the term 'lager lout' was coined to describe unruly young men who supposedly identified themselves with the characters portrayed in lager advertisements. The association of draught lager with loutism led many of the people who had taken up drinking lager in the 1970s or early 1980s to turn back the clock and start drinking expensive bottled lagers with lime in them. The only difference was that the lime was now a fresh one and was wedged in the neck of the bottle rather than poured into the beer.

One factor that links the growth in the popularity of lager and the increased consumption of wine, especially white wine, is the gradual Europeanization of British taste. This has also been evidenced in a great increase in sales of mineral water, and in a tendency to prefer coffee to tea. All of these are Continental tastes which would have been regarded as decidedly strange by the majority of the population half a century ago. To a substantial extent, the adoption of these drinks by the British public can be traced to its introduction to them when travelling abroad.

The explosion of European travel since the last war is well known. Mass-market air travel was introduced as a result of a surplus of wartime Dakota aircraft. The first airborne package holiday was sold in 1950; by 1978 the number of holidays sold per year had reached four and a half million; it peaked at twelve and a half million in 1988. In 1989 a market research survey found that 45 per cent of package holidays were being taken on the Spanish mainland, the Balearics and the Canaries.

This was not, however, the first time that European travel had exerted a fundamental influence on popular taste. Beginning hundreds of years before package holidays were introduced, Britons returning from Europe have brought back new types of drinks, and new manners of consuming them, that have rapidly been adopted at home. Moreover, European influence has almost invariably been in the direction of the civilization of British taste by introducing lighter or less alcoholic drinks better suited to the manners of a refined society. The only exception has been the encouragement that was given to the pre-existing practice of heavy drinking and to the nascent popularity of spirits as a result of the Dutch wars of the late sixteenth and mid-seventeenth centuries. And already, by this time, the influence of overseas travel was beginning to exert a sobering effect. The first coffee house in England was opened in Oxford in 1650, by a Jew named Jacob, at the Sign of The Angel; according to the source of this information, the antiquary Anthony à Wood, coffee was drunk here 'by some, who delighted in novelty'. It is not known from where Jacob came or what gave him the idea of opening a coffee house in England. Certainly, the presence of coffee houses in the great cities of the Ottoman Empire, notably Istanbul, had been widely reported by travellers, and anyone who opened a coffee house in Western Europe would have been following an Ottoman model.

Much more is known about the first coffee house in London, which was opened two years later, in St Michael's Alley in the City, at the Sign of the Greek's Head. The Greek was one Pasqua Rosee, the servant of an English merchant called Daniel Edwards. The former had become accustomed to making and the latter to drinking coffee while they were living at Izmir (then called

41

Smyrna) in Turkey. On their way back to England they had stayed for a while at Livorno (then called Leghorn) in Italy, where they had discovered that the coffee house was already an institution. When they finally returned to England many of Edwards's old friends and acquaintances took the opportunity to call upon him; they were served coffee by Rosee and so enjoyed the experience that they took to visiting Edwards on a regular basis. Soon Edwards was receiving so many visitors that he was finding it difficult to do any work. He solved the problem by setting up Rosee in a coffee house of the kind that they had encountered at Livorno, where the callers could go instead. Thus, coffee was introduced to London indirectly from Turkey, via Italy.

Tea was also introduced to Britain from the East at the same period and in a similarly indirect manner. The tea-drinking habit came to Britain from China via Holland, where it had become fashionable among high society in the 1640s. The first teas to be imported into England, in 1657, had been brought to Europe by Dutch trading vessels, and when tea-drinking spread throughout high society in London in the 1660s it was in conscious imitation of the best Dutch practice. When tea had been encountered by English travellers in the late sixteenth and early seventeenth centuries they had called it by the name by which it was known in Mandarin Chinese, *ch'a* (whence the cockney word 'char'), but when it was first made fashionable in the second half of the seventeenth century, the word that was employed was the one that had been adopted by the Dutch – *te* – the name used by the merchants from Amoy in China who had brought tea to the Dutch trading post of Bantam on the western end of Java. Not only was the Dutch word adopted by early English tea-drinkers but also the Dutch pronunciation: until the middle of the eighteenth century, 'tea' was pronounced 'tay' by the English and was sometimes spelt phonetically as well.

The manner in which tea was introduced into high society was described nearly a century later in a famous history of, and diatribe against, tea written by Jonas Hanway. 'Lord Arlington and Lord Ossory were the persons who brought [tea] from Holland in 1666,' he explained; 'their ladies then became passionately enamoured with it as a new thing: *their* example recommended it to the fine women of those days.' The appeal of the new drink lay not so much in its taste – which was generally mitigated by the addition of sugar* – as in the cachet of an imported luxury and in the ritual of the tea ceremony – which was performed with china dishes and pots that had been imported from China along with the tea. According to popular tradition, this ceremony was introduced to Britain, not from Holland, but from Portugal, through the medium of Charles II's Portuguese wife Catharine of Braganza.

The role of the hostess in the tea ceremony was paramount; it was she who brewed and served the tea in the drawing room in the presence of her guests, boiling the water in a specially-made copper or silver urn† that fitted over a small brazier; the fact that the object of the ceremony had been purchased for an extortionate price only served to increase her social standing. The ritual of the tea ceremony helps to explain its eventual victory over coffee, but that was not until the eighteenth century: in the late seventeenth century it was coffee that was the more popular of the two. Together, they exerted a profound effect in softening English manners. In 1684, in his celebrated social and political survey *Angliae Notitia, or the Present State of England*, Edward Chamberlayne, having repeated the story that 'the foul vice of drunkenness' had been brought home by English soldiers returning from service in the Netherlands 'in our fathers' days', added that 'It may truly be affirmed that at present there is generally less excess in drinking (especially about London since the use of coffee, tea and chocolate)'.

At the same time as coffee and tea were being introduced into England, the upper classes were developing a taste for the fine wines, such as champagne and claret, that had been enjoyed by Charles II and his court when in exile in France. The period immediately following the restoration of the monarchy in 1660 saw French influence in polite English society reach a level that it had not attained since the Norman Conquest six centuries earlier. The French language was commonly spoken at court; French music, plays and ballets were performed; French doctors, cooks and whores were employed. In effect, the court of Charles II, then in Whitehall, was a satellite of the court of Louis XIV at Versailles.

---

*Milk was not generally added until the middle of the eighteenth century.
†In the early eighteenth century the tea urn was succeeded by the tea kettle.

The new wine, champagne, and flûte glasses in which to drink it, were introduced to the English court by Marguetel de St Denis, Count of St Evremond, who had arrived in 1660 as a member of the French embassy sent to congratulate King Charles upon his accession, and had returned on a permanent basis the following year after a disagreement with the French court. Claret was marketed in a more commercial manner. In 1663 Samuel Pepys described in his diary how he had drunk 'a sort of French wine, called Ho Bryan, that hath a good and most particular taste that I ever met with.' This Haut-Brion was the prototype of the château wine: the first wine from Bordeaux to be sold under the name of the estate where it had been made, the purpose being to indicate that it was a wine of superior quality. The idea of commercializing his wine in this way was the invention of the château's owner, Arnaud de Pontac. In 1665 he sent his son François-Auguste to open a tavern more luxurious than any seen before in England, just behind the Old Bailey, under the sign of 'Pontac's Head'. This tavern, which has been called London's first restaurant, charged very high prices both for food and wine. Haut-Brion sold for 7s a bottle when other perfectly good wines could be purchased for a quarter as much. According to John Locke, who visited the château in 1677, the cost of the wine if purchased direct from the estate had virtually doubled within a few years because rich Englishmen ordered it to be bought at any price.

Yet, for all its refinement in other respects, the eighteenth century turned into a 'dark age' as regards the sophistication of drinks. This had a great deal to do with England being cut off from the Continent in a series of wars, during which the importation of French wines such as claret and champagne was either horrendously expensive or was forbidden altogether. Maybe the strong wine and heavy drinking of the eighteenth century should be regarded as an aberration, the result of men having forced upon them for commercial and political reasons a type of wine from which they could gain no pleasure and which they therefore drank solely for the purpose of getting drunk. Or maybe the heavy drinking of the period served to demonstrate that, regardless of the introduction of sophisticated non-alcoholic drinks such as tea and coffee, brutish behaviour remained the norm, not least among male members of the upper class.

It was not until around 1770 that this behaviour began to

improve. In his *Memoirs of the Life of Sir Joshua Reynolds*, Joseph Farrington recalled that 'At this time a change in the manners and the habits of the people of this country was beginning to take place. The coarse familiarity so common in personal intercourse was laid aside, and respectful attention and civility in address gradually gave a new and better aspect to society. The profane habit of using oaths in conversation no longer offended the ear, and bacchanalian intemperance at the dinner-table was succeeded by rational cheerfulness and sober forbearance.' This improvement was inspired in large part by the revival of European travel, particularly to France and Italy.

Travel on the Continent declined with the onset of the Anglo-French wars of the late eighteenth and early nineteenth centuries, but greatly increased afterwards. A similar pattern can be seen after the two world wars in the first half of the twentieth century. The link with war was not so much physical as psychological. People who had spent these wars at home in Britain had been preoccupied with their progress on the Continent; this inspired in them a great curiosity, once peace was re-established, to visit those places of which they had read and thought so much. According to the food historian Christopher Driver, 'The sudden freedom to travel on the Continent after an interlude of isolation played a significant role in the cultural conquest of the conqueror by the conquered.'

Certainly this was the explanation that was offered in the nineteenth century for the abandonment of the practice of men sitting at table after dinner and each drinking several bottles of port. In 1852 the wine merchant Thomas George Shaw attributed the change in taste from fortified to natural wine to 'the numbers who now visit the Continent, and no-one can do so for even a month without finding all our wines, scarcely excepting our claret and other kinds from France, disgreeably heavy and loaded.' He described the habit of sitting at table drinking port after dinner as an 'old custom [that] is peculiar to ourselves and [that], like other singularities of individuals and natives, is falling before civilization and the influence produced by greater intercourse with others.'

Travel on the Continent, and the comparison between British and European uses of alcoholic drink, contributed significantly to the growth of the temperance movement in the second quarter of the nineteenth century. Indeed, the first temperance society was founded in Greenock, Renfrewshire, by John Dunlop, a magistrate who had visited France and had concluded that the reason for the better behaviour of the working classes there compared with their counterparts in Scotland was that they were more moderate in their drinking habits. It was said at the time that a man could land at Ostend and visit Brussels, Antwerp and Liège without seeing as many drunken men on the way as he could see in London in half an hour. Protestant missions in France were discredited by the drunken English navvies who helped build French railways in the 1840s, and by reports of English habits brought back by French visitors. Evidently the reputation that has recently been created by English football hooligans and 'lager louts' is not a new one.

The experience of overseas travel was made accessible to many more Britons by the development of organized tours, beginning with Thomas Cook's first railway tour in 1841. By the end of the century it was possible to attribute the impetus for the conversion to light bottled beer to overseas travel. In the *Journal of the Institute of Brewing* in 1896 it was stated that 'The rapidly increasing demand for a bright, sparkling beer of low gravity . . . is partly due to the altered conditions under which we are at present compelled to live and transact our business in large towns, and partly to the introduction of light German beers into this country. Owing to the enormously increased facilities offered during recent years by various railway and steamship companies, much larger numbers than formerly of our countrymen have visited Germany, Belgium and the United States.'

Before the introduction of airborne package travel for the masses, however, a no less substantial influence in introducing Continental tastes in drink to the generality of the British population was the experience of troops who were fighting or stationed abroad. Service on the Continent in two world wars in the twentieth century has played a major role in extending the habit of wine-drinking to the mass of the population. A very substantial proportion of the vast numbers of soldiers who fought in France in the First World War drank wine during their time there; indeed, the word 'plonk' is thought to be derived from 'plink-plonk', the military slang of the period for the French *vin blanc*. If the habit of drinking light table wines failed to take off in Britain in the 1920s and 1930s, it was not so much because soldiers who returned home readily abandoned their new foreign tastes for their old British ones as because the elevated level of duties on European wine imported into Britain rendered it prohibitively expensive. As a result, it was the experience of soldiers who fought on the Continent during the Second World War, rather than the First, that led directly to the belated adoption by the majority of the British population of a predilection for light table wines. The troops who had acquired a taste for wine during the liberation of Italy, and during their service in the army of occupation in Germany* after the war had ended, retained their taste after they returned home – not least because imported wines became cheaper after the duty was reduced in 1949.

Significant influence on British taste in drink has also been exerted in the past by those expatriates who have lived abroad for lengthy periods without ever abdicating their British tastes. One might have thought that the heat of India would discourage heavy drinking but, at least during the first two centuries of the British presence there, just as much alcohol was drunk by the British in India as by the British in Britain. In the seventeenth century in the communal dining hall at the British factory (trading post) at Surat the individual ration was set at a quart of wine and half a pint of brandy per meal. At the beginning of the nineteenth century it was accepted that servants would drink at least a bottle of wine a day and gentlemen four. Men would demonstrate their prowess by piling the empty bottles on the table, like trophies. If there was to be a ball or reception, people generally had a drinking session in their houses first, arriving in loud and dishevelled groups.

Taste in drink among the British in India seems to have been governed more by the requirement for drinks to survive the voyage from England than by what was suitable to take in the Indian climate. In other words, strong drinks were favoured because they alone could survive the journey. The popularity of madeira is an example; it was so much stronger than ordinary table wine that it was not drunk neat with meals but was generally diluted with water in the ratio of one to three.

*It has been suggested by the German wine expert Stuart Pigott in *Life Beyond Liebfraumilch* that this accounts for the popular preference for Liebfraumilch, but this is *a priori* improbable.

The local spirit, arrack, was usually distilled from the fermented sap of palm trees. This was a very crude liquor which had to be mixed with other flavourings in order to be made palatable. Although ordinary British soldiers drank it neat, the upper classes drank it only as an ingredient of punch. Seventeenth-century India was the great age of punch, which was drunk by every European expatriate and to excess by many of them. Punch may be thought of today in the context of West Indian drinks such as rum punch, but the fact remains that it was introduced to England from the East, not the West, Indies. According to Indian tradition, punch had existed for two thousand years. The name was derived from the Hindi word for five (*panch*), this being the number of ingredients: alcohol, sugar, citrus juice, water and spices.

Punch was introduced by East Indian merchants to Britain where it became extremely popular during the eighteenth century, not least because it satisfied the contemporary predilection for spirits. César de Saussure observed that 'A light punch in summer time is a most acceptable and refreshing drink, and slakes thirst much more efficaciously than wine would' – but he also cited a recipe according to which it was supposed to contain the same quantity of arrack as of spring water. Knowledge of this drink was then carried from Britain to the American colonies and the West Indies. Punch fell out of fashion in India in the middle of the eighteenth century but remained popular in Britain until a hundred years later. Being then considered too intoxicating for contemporary tastes, it was – according to Mrs Beeton – replaced by wine. It is still popular in the West Indies.

In the nineteenth century, the major contribution of expatriates in India to British taste in drink lay in the development of India Pale Ale. This was conceived as a compromise between the need to produce a beer that was strong enough to survive the journey through the tropics and the demands of drinkers in the hot Indian climate for a beer that was pale and bright. As one Calcutta merchant put it, 'The ale adapted for this market should be clear, light, bitter pale ale of a moderate strength.'

Before the nineteenth century, imported English beer was considered too 'liverish' for India and was often watered down with a mixture of toddy (fermented palm sap), brown sugar, ginger and lime peel. The first person successfully to produce and market a beer that suited the demands of the Indian market was

Mark Hodgson, who brewed at the Bow Brewery in East London. By the early nineteenth century, Hodgson's India Ale had become a generic term in the trade for a pale, sparkling bottled ale. Among Hodgson's best customers were the commanders and officers of the Indiamen (ships of the East India Company), to whom he generally gave between twelve and eighteen months' credit. In 1824, however, he insisted on cash, and as a result many of these customers deserted him. This enabled a number of other brewers to enter the market, among them the two Burton-based companies of Wilson and Allsopp (now part of Allied Breweries) and Bass and Ratcliff (now simply Bass).

It is easy to understand why the Burton brewers should have wanted to export their beer to India. They had established their businesses upon the export of their beers to the Baltic, and especially Russia, via the Trent Navigation Canal and the port of Hull. In 1806, however, Napoleon blockaded the Baltic ports as a means of commercial warfare against Britain. At the time at which Napoleon introduced his blockade, Thomas Allsopp had been on a business trip in Hamburg; according to one account, he fled out of one gate of the city as the French army entered through another. From that point on, the Burton brewers were looking for new markets in which to sell their beer. It might be thought surprising that they did not think to look at India until the 1820s. But Hodgson had the Indian market tied up, and the strong, sweet, nut-brown ale that they brewed for the cold climate of the Baltic hardly suited the tastes of consumers in India.

Although a number of stories of how a Burton brewer first developed a pale ale for the Indian market were subsequently written by chroniclers, each claiming the glory for his favoured brewery, the earliest and apparently most reliable record is to be found in a history of Burton and its breweries by J. S. Bushnan, which was published in 1853. According to this account, in 1822 when on a visit to London, Samuel Allsopp was invited to dinner by a director of the East India Company called Marjoribanks. The latter, on hearing of Allsopp's troubles, recommended him to try the Indian market. He said that Hodgson had sold his ale very successfully but had 'given offence to most of our merchants in India'. Then he told Allsopp, bluntly, that 'Your Burton ale will not suit our market'. He had his butler bring out a bottle of Hodgson's ale which had been to India and back. Allsopp tasted it and said that he could manage to brew something similar. On his return to Burton, Allsopp received a gift of a further twelve bottles of Hodgson's ale from Marjoribanks. Allsopp called for his maltster, and instructed him to dry a pale malt, the colour of the sample of Burton ale; they then brewed the first specimen of Burton pale ale in a teapot.

The means whereby Burton-brewed India Pale Ale was introduced to the British market are not known for sure. According to one account, published two generations later in an otherwise reliable history of Burton, in about 1827 an India-bound ship containing approximately three hundred hogsheads of pale ale was wrecked in the Irish Sea. A number of casks were salvaged and these were sold in Liverpool for the benefit of the underwriters. Instead of being re-exported to India, they were consumed locally; they were greatly enjoyed and soon India Pale Ale was being sold in substantial quantities in north-west England and Ireland. The author of a rather less reliable account – the same one as stated that Burton pale ale had been served at the Great Exhibition – repeated this story, and claimed that the beer in question was Bass.

According to Bushnan, on the other hand, Burton-brewed pale ale was introduced into the British market quite deliberately and at the same time as it was introduced into India. The defeat of Napoleon may have brought an end to the Baltic blockade but consumers there had lost their taste for Burton ale and now preferred spirits. Russia, moreover, had imposed a prohibitory tariff on Burton ale in order to protect her domestic agriculture and her own black beer. In 1820, this tariff was removed. After visits to St Petersburg and Moscow, Samuel Allsopp brewed extensively to meet the anticipated demand, but in 1822 Russia restored the prohibitive tariff. Allsopp therefore made efforts to sell the beer that he had brewed for Russia into the British market. He achieved a fair deal of success, and a number of Burton Ale houses were established in London and other places. 'But those who admired its flavour and its purity, and who wished to drink more of it,' wrote Bushnan, 'found it too heady, too sweet, and too glutinous, if not too strong. Indeed it was so rich and luscious that if a little were spilled on a table the glass would stick to it . . . In the October season of 1822 Mr Allsopp brewed the first specimen of the improved Burton ale now so universally drank and admired.' According to Bushnan, the first place in which it was sold was Liverpool.

Depending on which of the above accounts one believes, either the Burton pale ale that became popular in India in the early 1820s was the same beer as that which later became popular as 'bitter' in England, or two different styles of pale-coloured, bitter-tasting ale were brewed independently for the two different markets. It is quite possible that both accounts are correct: that Allsopp and Bass introduced their respective pale ales to the British market by different routes, that Allsopp brewed a different, slightly darker ale for the British market but that Bass commercialized, at least at first, exactly the same beer as it exported to India. Even if the shipwreck story were to be shown to be apocryphal, it is likely that some of the Bass India Pale Ale was sold in Britain in the normal course of events. Bass used the Trent and Mersey Canal to ship its pale ale from Burton to Liverpool for transportation to India; it is probable that it would have taken advantage of this form of transport to sell some of this beer in the Potteries.

By whatever means India Pale Ale had been introduced into the British market, by the middle of the nineteenth century the version that was brewed for domestic consumption had developed along different lines from the export version: despite its name, bitter was less bitter, as well as lower in alcohol, than India Pale Ale (IPA). This divergence is easily explained: whereas bitter was designed for almost immediate, local consumption, IPA was intended to survive the long journey to India, at the end of which its bitterness would have substantially diminished. Although modern IPAs are much lower in alcohol than their nineteenth-century predecessors,* the difference between them and bitter is retained today: there is a clear distinction between the richer, smoother and rather sulphurous flavours of draught Bass bitter and the cleaner, more bitter and hoppy character of the company's bottled IPA, Worthington White Shield. If the latter is generally to be preferred, it has more to do with the poor cellarmanship of the majority of publicans and the greater

---

*This is not true of the recreations of nineteenth-century British IPAs that are produced commercially by a number of American micro-breweries: these tend to taste excessively bitter and alcoholic, having been denied the maturation process that the journey to India used to represent.

reliability of bottled beer than with any inherent superiority.

The final contribution of the Indian Raj to British taste in drink was gin and tonic. It may be imagined that the alliance of gin and tonic is a long-established middle-class tradition, but in fact it is a relatively recent introduction to Britain. The combination was conceived by colonists in India, Africa and the Far East, who had been instructed to take quinine as a prophylactic against malaria. Aerated quinine tonic water in the form that is known today was invented in 1858 by Erasmus Bond, and was first produced by Schweppes in the 1870s. Originally it was drunk neat, but it was not long before it was being mixed with gin to make it more palatable.

Gin and tonic enjoyed several decades of popularity in the colonies before it was introduced to Britain. Before the Second World War, gin in Britain was almost exclusively a woman's drink and was mixed with orange or peppermint ('gin and pep') or sweet Italian vermouth ('gin and It'). Men who could afford to do so drank whisky. After the war gin came off ration in 1949, several years before whisky. At the same time, the taste for gin and tonic was brought back to Britain by the hundred thousand or so expatriates who returned from India, Burma and Malaya after these countries became independent. If gin now became popular with people who had never had to worry about catching malaria, it was because it tasted relatively bland: it appealed to a new generation of drinkers who did not like the taste of mature, wood-aged alcohol. By the 1950s Gordon's, which had been only the third-best-selling gin between the wars, accounted for over half of all gin sales. According to Johnny Holbech, who began working in the gin trade as a salesman for Gordon's in 1950, this brand was successful because it was blander in taste than any of its rivals. Other gins were more aromatic; indeed, Booth's, which had previously been the best-selling brand, was yellow-coloured, having been aged in oak. As a result of Gordon's success, other gin manufacturers changed their formulae in order to make their gins resemble Gordon's as closely as possible. Today, according to market research, 57 per cent of the gin that is consumed in Britain is drunk with tonic.

Clearly, then, the experience of British rule in India has exerted a significant influence on British taste in drink. On the other hand, it has not directly exerted a profound influence on British taste in food. Only one restaurant in Britain, Chutney Mary in Chelsea in London, professes to cook the hybrid Anglo-Indian style of cuisine that was consumed by British settlers in India, and food in this style is not generally produced in private homes. Yet Indian cuisine, cooked not by British returnees from India but by Indian immigrants into Britain, has now become the most popular kind of restaurant food in Britain. Indeed, it is commonly said that there are now more Indian restaurants in London than in Bombay and Delhi put together, and more in Britain than there are fish and chip shops.

It is inconceivable that the explosion of Indian restaurants in Britain should not have affected taste in drink. They have made eating out a much less formal experience in which it is permissible to consume lower-class lager rather than higher-class wine. People who would have considered going into a pub and ordering a pint of lager to be inappropriate to their self-image have thought it perfectly acceptable to drink lager in an Indian restaurant. Doubtless it is as a result of drinking lager in Indian restaurants that many people have become lager-drinkers at all.

What is true for lager may well also be true for wine. The wine boom, like the lager boom, has certainly been inspired in part by the experience of foreign travel and by the consumption of these drinks in the places in which they were produced, but equally many British people have become wine-drinkers because they have acquired the habit of eating out in relatively inexpensive European-style restaurants, principally Italian pizzerias and trattorias, French bistros and brasseries, and Spanish tapas bars, in which wine has been regarded as the appropriate thing to drink. Certainly, many people have drunk wine in restaurants before starting to do so at home.

The same is true of coffee, which was popularized as a result of the invention of the *espresso* machine in Italy by Achille Gaggia in 1946. The principle of the *espresso* machine is that hot water is forced through the coffee at pressure, producing a strong cup of coffee at great speed; hence the name *espresso*. There had been Italian *espresso* machines before the Second World War but they had used steam pressure and the drink that was produced by forcing steam through ground coffee was too bitter even for Italian palates. What Gaggia did was to design and market the first *espresso* machine to work without steam, the water being forced through the coffee at pressure by use of a hand pump. This produced a coffee that was strong and bitter, but not excessively so. Gaggia's name has since served as something of a generic term for an *espresso* machine.

The *espresso* machine was introduced to Britain at the beginning of the 1950s by an Italian dental mechanic called Pino Riservato who travelled round the country selling dental mirrors and other equipment. His travels afforded him the opportunity for extensive investigation of British snack bars. His experience of the coffee that they sold led him to understand why the British were so fond of tea. Hoping to persuade the snack bars to invest in the new *espresso* machines, Riservato imported five of them into the country and set one up in his flat in London for demonstration to various British caterers of Italian extraction. They told him that they had already seen or heard of *espresso* in Italy but that there was no reason to introduce it into Britain since they were already perfectly capable of making good coffee; in any case, they added, British people would not be interested in it.

It was not Italian caterers who introduced *espresso* machines to Britain, but British entrepreneurs. Instead of inserting the machines into pre-existing snack bars, new bars were created around the machines. The first of these was the Moka Bar, which was built by a Scotsman called Maurice Ross on the site of the bombed-out Old Charlotte Laundry at 29 Frith Street* in Soho in 1952. It was designed along clean, contemporary lines, using a great deal of Formica, then a most up-to-date material. Intended to appeal both to the Italian population of Soho and to people on their way to, or back from, the cinema or theatre, the Moka Bar was an immediate success, selling 300,000 cups of coffee in its first three years of operation. By the middle of the 1950s coffee bars were opening up all over London; by 1960 there were five hundred of them in London and more than two thousand in the country as a whole.

The new coffee bars appealed for a number of reasons. Ironically, the coffee was not one of them. British consumers did not drink the new *espresso*, but *cappuccino*†, which was *espresso*

---

*Now the site of a sex shop.
†*Cappuccino* was so called because its colour resembled the habits of the Capucin friars.

with hot creamed milk on top. It tasted more of milk than of coffee, and therefore appealed to those British people who had previously been put off coffee by the taste.

The coffee bars reflected a post-war fashion for Italian cool. The take-off of the coffee bar in the mid-1950s coincided with the popularity of the new Italian motor scooters (Vespas) and the new-wave Italian cinema. The design of the coffee bars was not strictly Italian, however. In 1955 *The Times Educational Supplement* explained that 'The appeal and success of the coffee bars are due to the first designers, who evolved a style of decoration which exactly suited the mood of post-war younger England. They brought the jungle back into catering. There was greenery everywhere. Cacti and ivy and a few low-lit tobacco plants seemed to offer luxury on a scale not to be found outside the most lavish nightclub. There were warmth and colour, an emphasis in the *décor* on places like Italy and Mexico, where life is supposed to be fuller and hotter. It was no coincidence that the first bar was opened during the Italian Film Festival of 1952 by Miss Gina Lollobrigida, for however popular America may once have been among the young it is no longer fashionable. Sometime during the past ten years one of those scarcely perceived shifts have [sic] been occurring which have brought popular taste back from the New World to the Old. It is this change that coffee bars have been cashing in on. They represent the triumph of bamboo over chrome [and of] coffee over Coke.'

The coffee bars may not all have been 'European' in style; some of them may have offered a mish-mash of 'Latin' culture, such as the Cubano in Knightsbridge, with its Jamaican staff and its doorman in a Spanish-style cape standing beside an electric brazier, but it was clear that they represented a rejection of North American in favour of European culture. They demonstrated the truth of the theory that the aftermath of a major war sees the cultural conquest of the conqueror by the conquered.

The movement back to the Old World that the coffee bars represented was a significant one because the period between the wars had seen the high point of American influence on British taste in drink. The 1920s and 1930s saw a craze for the 'modernity' that American culture was supposed to represent. The growth in the popularity of jazz music and cocktails* in the 1920s is well known; there was also a fashion for cocaine, again in imitation of American practice. The period between the wars also saw many people in London copy the practice of their counterparts in big American cities by moving from old houses into new flats. It saw the adoption of practices that people witnessed in Hollywood movies, such as eating some meals in the kitchen and couples sleeping in twin rather than double beds – which was not in fact a reflection of real life in America but rather of the Hayes Code that sought to eliminate 'immorality' from American films. And it saw the spread of mechanization to a wide variety of everyday things, with the introduction of escalators and ticket machines on the London underground, and cigarette and fruit machines in the streets.

Some department and chain stores installed versions of the new American mechanized restaurant – the cafeteria – expecting them to appeal to people who wanted to eat a quick snack in modern surroundings, but they did not catch on as rapidly as milk bars did. Not only were these the last word in design, fitted out in glass and chrome and equipped with the latest American machines for mixing milk cocktails, but the fact that their customers perched on stools at counters added to their image of speed and efficiency. Someone who went to a milk bar could be in and out within two minutes, rather than having to hang around for ages as he would have to if he ordered a glass of milk in a restaurant. In the first twenty years of the century milk had been drunk only by invalids and children; but the modern, American appearance of milk bars made them popular among the young and fashionable in the second half of the 1930s. Milk bars did not remain popular for long, however. By the 1950s the sort of young people who had knocked back cold milkshakes in milk bars had gravitated to lingering over hot, milky coffee in coffee bars.

Apart from the brief fashion for milk bars, British taste in drink has generally been much more influenced by Continental than by American practices. Coca-Cola has been imported into Britain since the beginning of this century but it did not even begin to be sold in significant quantities until the 1970s. Despite the determined efforts that were made to market it in the 1950s and 1960s,

*These will be described in the next chapter.

many young people rejected it precisely because it served as a symbol of American political, military and economic imperialism.*

Colas apart, it would be hard to identify any unique, quintessentially American drink that could have been successfully introduced into Britain. On the whole, American drinks have been copies of European originals, produced by European immigrants. For example, most American beer has been a less flavoursome version of European lager ever since the American brewing industry was taken over by German immigrant families in the 1860s. The best American wines, Chardonnays and Cabernet Sauvignons from California, Pinot Noirs from Oregon, and Merlots from Washington and New York States, are not only made from Bordelais and Burgundian grape varieties but are vinified according to Bordelais and Burgundian techniques. Similarly, the currently fashionable style of cookery, 'Cal-Ital', is – as its name suggests – a Californian interpretation of an Italian original.

The major American influence has been in the area of refrigeration. The American preference for ice-cold drinks cannot be missed by any British traveller who eats in a restaurant and is automatically offered a glass of iced water. This preference is part of a national obsession with cryogenics – which may or may not be explained by a tendency to employ technology in order to distance the user as far as possible from the primitive and brutal life of the frontier and from the insecurity and discomfort experienced by European immigrants into the big cities. Certainly, in his book *America: a user's guide*, the (then) foreign reporter Simon Hoggart suggested that, if Americans often invert the temperature of their homes to an excessive extent – chilling them to 15°C in summer and heating them to 25°C in winter – it is because they have never rid themselves of their fear of poverty and hunger and climatic extremity and therefore exaggerate their response to these dangers.

---

*Resistance to attempts to market Coca-Cola after the Second World War was even greater on the Continent. In France, the Communist Party pressed for a Bill to ban Coca-Cola as a poison, and the newspaper *Le Monde* compared its advertisements to Nazi propaganda. In Italy, the rumour was put about that Coca-Cola turned the hair white and caused the disease called cocacolitis, while one Milanese newspaper reported that 'only a few people succeed, when first drinking Coca-Cola, of getting rid of the unpleasant impression of sucking the leg of a recently massaged athlete'.

There is also the simple fact that, in many parts of the United States, it can become very hot in summer. A Creole from the French West Indies who spent four years in Philadelphia in the 1790s observed that 'During hot weather thirst is so widespread and irresistible in all American cities that several people die each year from drinking cold pump water when hot . . . Printed handbills are distributed each summer to warn people of these dangers. Strangers especially are warned either to drink grog or to add a little wine or some other spirituous liquor to their water. People are urged to throw cold water on the faces of those suffering from water-drinking, and bleeding is also suggested. Sometimes notices are placed on the pumps with these words: "Death to him who drinks quickly." But all these teachings are ignored.'

Given these attitudes, it is hardly surprising that the domestic refrigerator – or rather ice box, since it was then cooled with ice rather than by chemical means – was an American invention. The first ice box was produced in 1803 by Thomas Moore, a Maryland farmer and the son of a cabinet-maker, in order to keep his dairy produce fresh. It took some time for ice boxes to become popular, however; at first the ice was expensive, as it had to be hacked by hand. Ice boxes were popularized as a result of the invention of the ice plough in 1827. This so reduced the cost of ice that eleven years later it was commented in the *New York Mirror* that, although 'it is but a few years since it came into use, [the ice box] is now justly considered as much an article of necessity as a carpet or dining-table.' The spread of ice boxes across America in the nineteenth century may help to explain the great popularity of plain water on that side of the Atlantic. Certainly, British visitors to America in the second half of the century often expressed their amazement at the fact that Americans appeared to drink nothing with their meals except iced water.

Substantial efforts were made by American ice merchants to sell their produce to the British. In the early 1840s a consortium of merchants built several ice houses on Wenham Lake, six miles north of Salem, Massachusetts. In 1844 this consortium sent over to Britain the first ever consignment of American ice. It proved an immediate success. The next year Queen Victoria and Prince Albert directed that a supply of Wenham Lake ice should always be made available to them, and the Wenham Lake Ice Company opened its main office in the Strand in London. In the window was displayed a single block of ice a foot thick and of such clarity that people would enter the shop to touch it and check that it was not glass. In London and the suburbs deliveries were made by liveried staff; for consignment elsewhere in the country, ice was wrapped in blankets and sent by train. This service was not cheap. The ice cost a penny a pound, and the ice boxes that the Wenham Lake Ice Company sold its customers required fifty-six pounds of ice a week to keep provisions cool. This would have required an annual expenditure on ice of £12 – roughly the equivalent of the annual salary of one domestic servant. In 1855 the American magazine *De Bow's Review* contrasted the general use of ice for household purposes in the United States with the limited use of ice in Europe where it was 'confined to the wine cellars of the rich'.

Admittedly, refrigeration with natural ice is not an American invention; in fact, it long predates the colonization of America from Europe. Drinks have been cooled in warm weather with snow and ice that has been stored in ice houses built for the purpose ever since the first recorded ice houses were built in Mesopotamia almost four thousand years ago. The technology was simple enough: snow was brought down from the mountains in winter, pits were dug and lined with straw, the snow was then packed into them, and branches placed on the top. The knowledge of ice houses, like that of water mills and windmills, was transmitted from the Middle East to Western Europe by the Greek and Roman empires. Ice houses were introduced into both France and Britain by the Romans. In France, they survived throughout the Middle Ages; in Britain, they did not. Ice houses, like tea and champagne, became fashionable in Britain during the reign of Charles II as part of the King's attempt to make the court as elegant as that of Louis XIV. Ice houses were built in Green Park in 1660 'as the mode in some parts of France and Italy and other hot countries, for to cool wines and other drinks for the summer season.' Members of the aristocracy soon followed suit, leading to an orgy of ice-house construction.

What was significant about the American ice that was imported in the mid-nineteenth century was that it made ice available to houses in parts of Britain which did not enjoy access to sources of natural ice, or which were short of ice as the consequence of an unusually mild winter. With the coming of the railways, ice importation firms such as the Wenham Lake Ice Company were able to boast that they could deliver to any part of the country within twenty-four hours. Moreover, American ice was much cleaner than the domestically-produced version. It was not a matter of chance that the arrival of American ice into Britain coincided with the adoption by the better-off of the American habit of throwing ice directly into wine, milk or water. Indeed, putting ice into wine, and chilling wine to a point of insensibility, became very Victorian ways of showing off. In his famous record of his wine-drinking career *Notes on a Cellar Book*, published in the early twentieth century, the literary critic and historian George Saintsbury recalled having lived through three different phases of attitude to the temperature at which claret should be drunk; the first of these was the 'Ice Age' of the mid-nineteenth century, 'a barbarous time' when people used 'marsupial claret jugs with a pouch for ice'. This was followed by a period in which claret was heated in front of an open fire; eventually good sense prevailed, and the wine was allowed to reach room temperature of its own accord. But even then it remained common practice to ladle bits of raw ice into a glass of champagne at dinner – another habit that Saintsbury described as 'barbarous'. He suggested that the best method of cooling wines without altogether numbing their flavour was to wrap the bottles in a cloth dampened with water fresh from the tap and place them in a draught for a while.

In Britain, the fashion for drinks that were very cold declined in the early twentieth century, reappearing only as a result of the spread of domestic refrigeration after the end of the Second World War. Although machines for producing ice artificially had been developed as early as the 1850s, they were used solely for industrial purposes, and it was not until the beginning of the present century that an economical chemically-cooled domestic refrigerator was produced. In America, self-cooling domestic refrigerators were common in homes by the 1920s but in Britain they were not generally found even in middle-class homes until the end of the Second World War. The last thirty years have seen not only the almost universal adoption of domestic refrigeration in Britain but also the introduction of central heating into most homes. The fact that there is no longer any reason why refreshing drinks such as lager and white wine should not be drunk chilled throughout the year helps to explain their new-found popularity.

Not only has the development of artificial refrigeration encouraged the consumption of larger quantities of the sort of drinks that are best drunk cold, but it has made these same drinks easier and cheaper for their manufacturers to produce. Indeed, improvements in the means of cooling beer and wine during their fermentation go a long way to explain the transformation that has taken place in popular taste from porter to bitter to lager and from port to claret to white wine.

The limitations of brewing technology in the past are demonstrated by the development of porter in London in the 1720s. The need for a stable beer that could be produced on a large scale to fulfil the demands of the London market had existed ever since Tudor times. This need had not been satisfied because, if beer was brewed in large quantities, the temperature in the fermentation vats would rise to such a level as to cause the beer to spoil. According to a theory that has been put forward by the historian Peter Mathias in his account of the development of the brewing industry in the eighteenth century, the solution was discovered only by accident, when an unknown maltster, probably in Hertfordshire, happened to burn a parcel of normal brown malt. It was found that this new type of high-dried dark brown malt produced a beer that was delicate neither in colour nor in taste, and was therefore not spoiled by the high temperatures of an industrial-sized brewing vat. According to this theory, porter was 'the first beer technically suited for mass-production at contemporary standards of control'.

One of the reasons why the dominance of porter was brought to an end can be found in the introduction of a temperature control mechanism (the attemperator) in the 1780s: lengths of coiled copper piping were placed in the mash tuns and brewing vats and cold water circulated through them. This made it possible to brew ordinary brown ale in large quantities without the danger that the temperature in the fermentation vat would rise too high and spoil the beer. It was the attemperator that made it possible for a type of brown ale – bitter – to replace porter in the nineteenth century.

Like the invention of porter in the eighteenth century, that of lager in the fifteenth had been a response to the problems of spoiled beer within the confines of contemporary technology. At that time, the only yeasts known to brewers were the type that rose to the surface during fermentation. Beer that had been 'top-fermented' had to be skimmed before sale and often turned sour in warm weather. The reason why this spoilage occurred was not understood at the time, and in Switzerland it was blamed on 'beer witches'. But then brewers in Bavaria discovered that if they stored the beer at a low temperature, in caves packed with ice, it would not go off during the summer. Moreover, the yeast gradually settled to the bottom rather than having to be skimmed off the top. In German, *lager* means 'a store'; what is popularly known as 'lager' is described by brewers as being 'bottom-fermented'.

The drawback of the Bavarian system of lager production was that it required caves in which to store the beer and a plentiful supply of ice to keep it cool during its storage period. This became a major problem following the development of the Pilsener (or Pils) method of lager production in the 1840s. The name that is given to this method arises from its origin in Pilsen in what is now the Czech Republic in 1842. Previously, lagers had been as dark in colour as ales because they had been made from dark-coloured malts. But then maltsters at Pilsen developed a procedure for air-drying malt so that it remained light in colour and brewers could use it to produce a pale lager beer. The fame of the new golden-coloured Pilsener lager spread rapidly across Europe, and it became widely available thanks to the development of the railways and of an economic union between German-speaking countries.

Brewers in other countries wanted to produce this new style of lager for themselves but many of them were hampered by a lack of access to natural ice, or by its cost. For bottom-fermentation, it was necessary to hold the beer at a temperature of between 7 and 9°C for a minimum of two or three weeks. It was calculated by Louis Pasteur that, from the cooling of the malt to the day on which the beer was drunk, more than a pound of ice was needed to produce every pint of beer. The expense of natural ice was a significant factor in the refusal of English brewers to follow their Continental counterparts in converting to Pilsener lager production in the third quarter of the nineteenth century.

The problem was solved by the development of machines that

made ice artificially. The first practical, if not very efficient, ice-making machine was designed by James Harrison, a Scottish emigrant to Australia, in 1850. This used liquid ether. A better machine, using compressed ammonia gas, was developed by the French engineer Carré ten years later. It was no accident that these machines were first used in Australia, a country with no natural ice of its own and far away from any country that produced ice for export. Thanks to the development of artificial ice-making machines, in the second half of the nineteenth century lager came to dominate the brewing industry in Australia, on the Continent of Europe and in America – and eventually, in the second half of the twentieth century, to dominate the brewing industry in England.

In the light of the vital part played by temperature control in the development of the brewing industry, it seems extraordinary that it was not used to any significant extent in wine production until after the Second World War. Deprived of any form of temperature control, wine-makers in regions that were warm at harvest time, such as the Douro Valley in Portugal, were restricted to producing naturally sweet wines or fortified wines – or else risk the danger of their wines refermenting and possibly spoiling while they were transported to the place where it was intended that they should be drunk. This helps to explain why port gradually developed into a fortified wine during the eighteenth and nineteenth centuries. It was a style of wine that, under the prevailing standards of technological control, the Douro Valley was best suited to produce. The fact that fortification with brandy developed at least partly as a response to technological difficulties also explains why wine writers continued for more than a century to wonder whether, if port were left unfortified, it would not be a better wine. In the first edition of his *Wine and Wine Countries* in 1862 the wine merchant Charles Tovey suggested that port would be improved if it were treated in the same way as the light wines of France and sent to England in its natural condition. By the time the second edition appeared, fifteen years later, he had changed his mind. If port were not fortified, he decided, it would be nothing more than a second-rate burgundy, whereas fortified port was unique. He accepted that necessity had mothered invention.

While Tovey was dithering over the appropriateness of

fortification with brandy as a means of mastering the fermentation of port, the first temperature control systems were being introduced in Australia. Although it seems improbable that the attemperator was used at all widely before the end of the century, the technique of cooling fermenting grape juice by running cold water through a coil in the vat was certainly known to Australian wine-makers as early as the 1860s. Alexander Kelly, a Scottish doctor who had emigrated to South Australia in 1840 and established a vineyard there, published a book in 1861 in which he referred to the use of the attemperator by Australian wine-makers and its abandonment for fear that the metal used to make the coil would taint the wine. After specifying his own, improved design, Kelly commented that 'It is surprising to find so little attention paid to temperature in the fermentation of wine in these colonies . . . This arises, doubtless, from the difficulty, and I may say, the supposed impossibility of counteracting the excessive heat of the climate.' Yet – in his opinion – the construction of attemperators need be neither difficult nor costly, and their use would certainly improve the quality of Australian wines, most of which were fermented at too high a temperature.

Although it is not known whether any of Kelly's fellow wine-makers followed his advice, nor indeed whether he acted upon it himself, by the end of the nineteenth century cooling mechanisms such as the one he advocated were being used to good effect in wineries in several parts of the world, not only in Australia but also in California, Algeria and Palestine. So why, then, was it not until the second half of the twentieth century that such systems came widely to be employed?

There are several explanations for this. One is that wineries have not generally been situated in places that have large supplies of water available to them; in Europe, at least, vines have usually been planted in remote and barren areas that are ill-suited to the cultivation of food crops. Breweries, on the other hand, tend to be situated in major centres of population and they all have access to large supplies of water because they need it to make their beer. Also, wine enterprises have usually been much smaller operations than breweries and have therefore been unable to justify the cost of expensive new equipment on grounds of economies of scale, as breweries have done. Nor could refrigeration equipment necessarily have been used by wineries in many parts of Europe which would only have been connected to mains supplies of electricity after the Second World War. Furthermore, wine-makers in the majority of European wine regions have been producing wine for hundreds of years without the benefit of temperature-control techniques so it would not have occurred to them that it was necessary. They have produced their wines according to an agricultural ethos rather than according to an industrial one. Not only do they harvest only one crop a year, compared with brewers who produce beer continuously, but they regard their wines – whether correctly or not – as the natural products of their soil rather than the man-made products of their toil. They have therefore shrunk away from installing temperature-control equipment because it seems to them to be too much like cheating. This may well explain why, when the celebrated Russian-born American wine-maker André Tchelistcheff brought cooling machinery into California at the end of the 1930s, it was regarded as a matter for secrecy and the refrigerators were placed out of sight.

It is therefore not surprising that the impetus for a general introduction of refrigeration into wineries after the Second World War came from wine-makers in the New World who not only were required to vinify fruit from warmer regions and under warmer conditions than their counterparts in many regions in Europe but were also a little less hide-bound in their adherence to tradition.

The belated introduction of temperature-control techniques by wine-makers in California and south-east Australia has contributed significantly to the wine boom of the post-war period. Previously, it had only been possible to produce clean, fresh white wines in regions that were relatively cool at harvest time, such as the vine-growing districts of Germany and Burgundy. Not only were these regions relatively cool, but they were also frequently damp; the combination of mildness and dampness encouraged pests to breed, and there was always the risk that the crop would be damaged by rain at harvest time. These problems added to the expense of production, and thus to the cost of purchase. White wines that were produced in other parts of Europe, perhaps at lower cost, were often quite dark in colour and had lost their flavour as a result of oxidation. No wonder red wines were more popular than white in the past. Many people drank cheap red wine not necessarily for positive reasons but because it was less likely to be spoiled than cheap white; unlike white wines, red wines were fermented in contact with the grape skins, and these imparted tannins to the wines that protected them from contamination during fermentation and while in bottle.

The introduction of temperature-control techniques into wine-making has changed all that. It has made it possible to produce reliably clean and fresh white wines at a lower cost in warmer and more reliable climates; it has both fuelled the boom in white wines and satisfied the demands of consumers for white instead of red wine. If much lighter drinks, in terms both of colour and of flavour, are consumed in Britain today than was the case one hundred or two hundred years ago, it has as much to do with changes in technology as with changes in taste.

2

FOOD, DRINK AND
SENSUAL PLEASURE

THE ENORMOUS CONSUMPTION OF PORT IN THE EIGHTEENTH AND early nineteenth centuries was made possible by the length of time that was taken over drinking it. In the opinion of Captain Gronow, the only thing that saved the men who drank four, five or even six bottles of port after dinner was 'drinking very slowly and out of very small glasses'. Dinner was taken in the middle of the afternoon; at the end of the meal the women withdrew into the drawing room to drink tea or coffee while the men remained at table where they drank port until late in the night. Often, they drank themselves under the table. In recalling Scottish manners of this period Dean Ramsay told the story of a Mr Mackenzie, who 'had been involved in a regular drinking party. He was keeping as free from the usual excesses as he was able, and as he marked companions around him falling victims to the power of drink, he himself dropped off under the table, among the slain, as a measure of precaution, and lying there his attention was called to a small pair of hands working at his throat. On asking what it was a voice replied: "Sir, I'm the lad that's to loosen the neckclothes." ' It had been deemed necessary to employ a servant to untie the guests' cravats in order to prevent them from suffocating themselves in the course of their alcoholic stupor.

These habits came to an end in the nineteenth century partly as a result of industrialization and the consequent development of an industrious middle class. They did not have the time to spend seven or eight hours in company as had been the case in the eighteenth century when dinner began at about 3.45 p.m. and ended at 11 p.m. or midnight. They could not afford to have only four hours of day available for work: between the end of breakfast at 11 a.m. and the time at which people began to dress for dinner, at 3 p.m. It was in their interests that breakfast should be taken earlier, dinner taken later, and sustenance provided in the lengthening gap between them. It was probably no more than fortuitous, however, that the interests of the hard-working bourgeoisie happened to coincide with a new fashion that had been adopted by leisured ladies. The practice of taking lunch began as an indulgence among upper-class women in the second and third decades of the nineteenth century; it was many years before it came to be accepted by their husbands. According to the author of *Real Life in London*, a guide book that appeared in weekly parts in 1822, it was fashionable for women to eat luncheon and then to delay the service of dinner until as late as eight in the evening; their husbands, rather than fall in with such new-fangled notions, would arrive famished and fasting, having eaten practically nothing since breakfast. For a decade or more, upper-class men and women conducted their days according to conflicting timetables. Men regarded luncheon as a destructive rather than recuperative force; according to his biographer, it was not until his health began to fail in the 1850s that the essayist and historian Lord Macaulay, 'instead of writing . . . straight on from his late and somewhat lazy breakfast until the moment of dinner found him hungry and complacent, with a heavy task successfully performed, was condemned, for the first time in his life, to the detested necessity of breaking up the labours of the day by luncheon.'

By this time, the conflict over meal times had generally been resolved in favour of ladies of leisure and the new industrious bourgeoisie. The new midday meal had come to be accepted; dinner had moved as a consequence from its eighteenth-century position at around 3.45 p.m. to the hour at which it is eaten today, most commonly between seven and eight in the evening. The transformation of dinner – which remained the main meal of the day – into an evening rather than an afternoon occasion was of psychological as well as social and gastronomic significance. 'When business was moderate,' wrote Thomas De Quincey, 'dinner was allowed to divide and bisect it. When it swelled into that vast strife and agony, as one may call it, that boils along the tortured streets of modern London or other capitals, men began to see the necessity of an adequate counterforce to push against that overwhelming torrent, and thus maintain the equilibrium. Were it not for the soft relief of [an evening] dinner, the gentle demeanour succeeding to the boisterous hubbub of the day, the soft glowing lights, the wine, the intellectual conversation, life in London is now come to such a pass that in two years all nerves would sink before it . . . Dinner it is which saves the modern brain-working man from going mad.'

Although the introduction of lunch served to fill the gap between breakfast and dinner, the increasing lateness of the dinner hour led in its turn to the insertion of a further meal, that of afternoon tea. Hitherto, tea had been drunk by women at breakfast or after dinner, and, if they had taken a snack in the middle of the afternoon, it was one of cake and wine. The practice of taking tea in the afternoon was introduced by certain great ladies in the 1840s, principally by the Duchess of Bedford at her country seat at Woburn and at her town house in Bedford Square. The ladies of the Paget family also liked to take afternoon tea but were forbidden to indulge in it by their father. They continued to do so, however, hiding the tray under the sofa if his footsteps were heard in the passage. Male resistance to the practice of taking tea in the afternoon did not last as long as opposition to the introduction of lunch; within a few years, men as well as women were prepared to indulge in the habit without shame.

Not only did it become the custom to dine later, and to fill up the gap with lunch and afternoon tea, but the practice of women withdrawing at the end of dinner and men then sitting around the table for several hours drinking port fell into abeyance. This change had a great deal to do with the arrival on the throne of Queen Victoria, who required gentlemen to join her in the drawing room shortly after the ladies had left the dining room.

Later in the century, the abandonment by gentlemen of the practice of sitting around over the port after dinner was ensured by the growing popularity of smoking, and especially of cigarettes. In the first half of the century, when gentlemen had smoked, they had smoked only cigars and never in the presence of ladies or in the streets. 'Many was the evening in winter,' recalled Sir Algernon West, 'when the smoking brigade was sent across a sloppy yard to smoke in the harness room; when there were less bigoted hosts we were allowed to remain in the servants' hall.' Men put on smoking caps and jackets in order to prevent their hair and dress-coats from being tainted by the smell of smoke – which would have been considered ungentlemanly.

Attitudes to smoking began to change in the latter part of the century, when it became fashionable to take tobacco in the less pungent form of cigarettes – a habit that supposedly was introduced into Britain by officers returning from the Crimean War, where they had learnt it from their French counterparts. Smoking after dinner was made respectable some years later by the Prince of Wales. Looking back, at the end of the century, on the changes in attitudes to smoking during it, Lady Dorothy Nevill declared that 'There can be no doubt that the cigarette-smoking now practically universally prevalent after lunch and dinner has been a considerable factor in the direction of temperance, and has ended the practice of consuming large quantities of wine, which in the old days was more or less universal.' Gentlemen, she added, no longer sat in the dining room over their wine but now moved quickly after dinner to join the ladies, 'whose society they very naturally prefer to the mineral waters in which so many of them indulge instead of wine.'

The fact that men abandoned their old practice of sitting a long time over the port out of volition, and not because dinner was now held so late that they had no time to do so, is demonstrated by the change that occurred in the manner in which dinner was served. By the end of the nineteenth century, dinner was over much more rapidly and the men could perfectly well have lingered over their port if they had wanted to do so. Before this period, meals had followed the same format as they had in Roman times, and as they do in China (and in Chinese restaurants in Europe) today. Two or three courses were served, each of them comprising a number of different dishes, all of which were laid on the table at the same time. This system, which was known as *service à la française*, was replaced between the 1850s and the 1870s by the system that still prevails in restaurants today, which was then known as the *service à la russe*. Dishes were composed in the kitchen or on the sideboard and handed out by the servants ready-prepared. A major explanation for the change was precisely the fact that, because the dishes no longer had to stand on the table waiting for people to help themselves, dinners were over much more quickly; this was, as the social historian John Burnett has pointed out, very much in tune with the new age of speed and progress. With the conversion to *service à la russe*, men had less opportunity to drink copiously during the meal; they could have compensated by drinking more afterwards but they chose not to do so, preferring to smoke instead.

Furthermore, they did not drink before meals. In the eighteenth century, they had not had any reason to do so because they could start drinking at the beginning of dinner, in the middle of the afternoon. But now they had to wait until the middle of the evening. Guests for dinner were expected to arrive half an hour before the time appointed for the meal; it was generally acknowledged that the next thirty minutes were spent in some discomfort. Mrs Beeton cited a poem:

> How sad it is to sit and pine,
> The long half-hour before we dine!
> Upon our watches oft to look,
> Then wonder at the clock and cook.

It might have seemed the obvious thing for the hosts to have offered their guests something to drink before dinner. The more sophisticated among them may have known that this was done in some other countries, but they regarded the practice as somewhat barbarous.

The practice of taking a drink before dinner had begun in Sweden, where the *smörgasbord* was originally a pre-prandial snack of herring, cheese, bread and aquavit, laid out on a separate 'aquavit table'. This practice spread to Russia from the late seventeenth century, where it was known as *zakuski*; then, at the end of the eighteenth century, it arrived in France. Here, it was known as the *coup d'avant*: according to the gastronome Grimod de la Reynière, it consisted of 'a large glass of vermouth, absinthe or rum, or even a simple glass of brandy which is presented to every guest to get their appetites going.'

The practice of taking a drink before dinner may have arrived in France around the time of the Revolution, but it was not until a century later that it became widespread. It was not generally accepted until people convinced themselves that it did them good. This belated acceptance was connected with a change in the name, from *coup d'avant* to *apéritif*. The latter term had previously been used only as an adjective, in a medical sense, referring to the opening of pores and veins, but now it appeared as a noun, referring to the idea that the ability of diners to digest their meals was enhanced if they took a glass of wine to prepare their stomachs beforehand.

Despite its now being accepted in France, the country from which many British gastronomic habits were derived, it took quite some time before the practice of taking an *apéritif* became established in Britain. At the end of the nineteenth century the port shipper Lorenz Feuerheerd, in a guide to the choosing of wines for dinner, stated that the serving of *hors d'oeuvre* at the beginning of a meal had been introduced in imitation of Scandinavian and Russian practice, but that their 'nasty habit' of washing down these *hors d'oeuvre* with spirits had not yet been introduced in Britain. There were, admittedly, a few people in the early years of the twentieth century who 'whetted' or 'tickled' their appetites before a meal with drinks such as sherry and bitters, gin and bitters, gin and Italian vermouth, or gin and lime-juice cordial. Before the First World War, however, the pleasure of the *apéritif* was restricted to a minority; it was much more common to drink sherry with the soup course of a meal than to drink it as an *apéritif*.

What popularized the consumption of *apéritifs* was the First World War. Some years later, in a history of the wine merchants Justerini & Brooks, the thriller-writer Dennis Wheatley suggested that 'Perhaps it was the nerve-strain of the war which led to a great increase in the consumption of spirits and the general desire to put away not one but several drinks before dinner; or it may have been that the fashionable hour for dining had been growing later and later, causing a hiatus in the day which called to be filled in sociably.' It now became quite common for a man to take a drink in his club before luncheon, usually before his guest arrived. It was still not the custom to have drinks before luncheon at home, however.

Cocktails* were not a new invention. The Victorians knew cocktails such as 'Corpse Reviver', 'Gum Tickler' and 'Eye Opener', and punch had been the height of fashion in the eighteenth century. But cocktails became all the rage among young people in the early 1920s because they were regarded as new and American, and because by drinking cocktails they were able to outrage their elders. The period of outrage did not last for long, however. By the late 1920s, the cocktail party had replaced the after-dinner party in respectable London life.

Just as the Burton brewers of the mid-nineteenth century competed with each other for the glory of having been the first to brew pale ale for India and the first to introduce it back into England, so hosts of the mid-twentieth century competed for the honour of having been the first to introduce the cocktail party. Allegedly the idea was first tried in 1924 by the painter C. R. W. Newison and his wife, who complained of the difficulty of finding anything to do in London in the winter between tea and dinner. They sent out a number of invitations to an 'At Home' from 5 to 7 p.m.; they made a large jug of a cocktail of which rum was the chief ingredient, but only two guests arrived. The experiment was then repeated the next year by the author Alec Waugh, except that, not wanting to alarm his friends, he told them that he was inviting them to tea. He served a rum swizzle, mixed by a friend from New York. According to his own account, this party was a success, and within eighteen months the cocktail party had become an established form of entertainment. It is not clear, however, that Waugh's claim that he invented the cocktail party should be believed; according to other accounts it was introduced into London by the American-born hostess Madame Alfredo de Peña, or by a group of American undergraduates at Oxford. The likely explanation is that a number of people came up with the same idea at more or less the same time. Certainly, it is easy to understand why cocktail parties became so popular. They were both cheaper and easier than inviting people to dinner.

The popularity of cocktails only served to increase the damage

*The etymology of 'cocktail' remains an unsolved mystery.

that was being done to the sherry trade. People no longer drank a glass of dry sherry in the middle of the morning; they ate shorter meals, often omitting the soup with which dry sherries would normally have been drunk, and the introduction of smoking after meals meant that they drank fewer dessert wines, such as sweet sherries. Now the cocktail habit meant that people were not even considering drinking sherry as an *apéritif*. A number of sherry shippers decided to pool their money for a generic advertising campaign in which they pointed out that sherry was a flexible drink, with a clean taste, and that it offered good value for money; they also claimed that it was more healthy than cocktails. They succeeded. People began to give sherry parties instead of cocktail parties, and at the majority of the latter it became the practice to offer sherry as an alternative. The new sherry parties might not have been as much fun as cocktail parties had been but they were a darn sight cheaper. They also suited the new mood of the times. In about 1937 the cocktail age came to an end: cocktails now seemed unnecessarily flippant. Those people who still drank them rejected the more outrageous mixes of the 1920s and returned to classic gin-based cocktails.*

The transformation that had occurred in drinks tastes during the period between the wars had been a profound one. Soon after the end of the Second World War, Ernest Cockburn, a member of the famous port-shipping family, observed that 'Up to the war of 1914–1918 . . . the habit of drinking wine with the meal was almost universal . . . but *tempora mutantur*! and it is the practice nowadays to indulge all too largely in other habits . . . The 1914–1918 War had left young people with money such as they had never known before, and it seemed to have bred in them an overwhelming desire never to sit down and rest in their own homes. This encouraged them to be everlastingly in search of excitement and amusement, coupled with a desire to dine hurriedly in restaurants . . .'

Another reason that Cockburn gave for the decline in drinking wine with meals was a shortage of domestic servants, which made it difficult to entertain at home. Not only was it cheaper to hold cocktail and sherry parties than to invite people to dinner but it could be done with a much smaller domestic staff. During the

---

*The same was true after the Second World War, the period when gin and tonic established its supremacy.

period between the wars middle-class families were no longer able to employ the number of servants necessary for the organization and service of large-scale dinner parties. They did, however, manage to retain one or two live-in servants who cooked for them and waited at table. And they did continue to drink wine at home with dinner. Indeed, it has been suggested by Alan Jackson in his memoir of middle-class life in the first half of the twentieth century that the ritual consumption of four or five meals a day, including a dinner of six or seven courses, was perpetuated principally in order that the servants should be kept busy. This ritual may have been modified after the First World War but it did not disappear until the 1940s.

Thus, although the development of new attractions and the economic difficulties of the period between the wars did lead to the decline of the habit of drinking wine with meals, the practice was not killed off until after the Second World War. Like the heavy consumption of *apéritifs* and cocktails after the First World War, this development was attributed to the psychological effect of the war itself. 'Came the last war,' wrote Robin McDouall in an article in *The Compleat Imbiber*, 'with the cutting off of supplies from Europe and the greater desire for drink which fear and insecurity engender, drink became more and more a thing in itself and less an accompaniment to a meal.' Soon after the end of the Second World War it was stated in an article in *The Times* that 'The people of this country have almost given up the habit of drinking table wine with their meals.' The author of a basic primer on wine-drinking, published at this same time, found it necessary to disabuse his readers of 'the belief held by many that drinking with meals is injurious to the digestion'.

Given that the decline in the availability and the increase in the expense of maintaining servants in the first half of the twentieth century had led to a diminution in home entertainment and to the replacement of dinner parties by cocktail or sherry parties, it is ironical that it was the disappearance of the last of the live-in servants at the end of the Second World War that caused the middle classes to learn to cook for themselves and to start to become interested in food and wine. Much has been said about the important role played by the cookery books written by Elizabeth David in the early 1950s in evoking Continental plenty in a country which was only beginning to emerge from rationing and wartime deprivation but their significance was much wider than this. They became famous partly because they attracted a new audience of middle-class men and women who were interesting themselves in food for the first time.

Since the 1950s, interest in food among middle-class households has continued to grow, partly for the same reasons as the revival of interest in, and consumption of, wine. Before the Second World War, middle-class families generally took their holidays in Britain. Not until the 1950s did they begin to travel in large numbers to the Continent of Europe, partly out of curiosity engendered by the war, and partly because increasing numbers of working-class people were holidaying in the British resorts that they had previously frequented. On their visits to Mediterranean countries they found people who cooked exactly the sort of food that Elizabeth David had described and who all drank wine with their meals. Indeed, at this period it was generally believed in both France and Italy not only that a family meal was incomplete without wine but that to consume wine outside the context of such a meal was bizarre and even unhealthy. This habit of drinking wine with meals had spread sufficiently to Britain by 1988 for one survey to find that 53 per cent of middle- and upper-class households* usually drank wine with a meal at home or in a restaurant, and that more than 40 per cent of the population as a whole did so.

Thus, in the course of two centuries, social and economic changes have led to the appearance, disappearance and reappearance of the practice of drinking wine with food. Heavy drinking after dinner in the late eighteenth and early nineteenth centuries was replaced by drinking with dinner in the second half of the nineteenth century, by drinking before dinner in the first half of the twentieth century, and by drinking with dinner again in recent times. The type of wines that are chosen, however, and the manner in which they are matched with the food, differ greatly from the practice of the late nineteenth century, and – superficially, at least – even more greatly from what was done in earlier times.

The food that was consumed in classical Rome has been compared to some of the oriental cuisines of today, partly because

*Socio-economic classes A and B.

some of the ingredients and dishes are similar, and partly because the seasoning was more important than the primary flavour. Certainly the seasoning was a strong one. One vital ingredient of Roman meals was *liquamen*, a fermented fish sauce whose nearest modern equivalent is the Thai sauce *nam pla*; but even *nam pla* is not as fishy as *liquamen* would have been. It was the Roman habit, moreover, to combine powerfully savoury tastes of this kind with every sort of sweetening, including sweet wine. Indeed, the wine that the Romans most commonly drank with their meals, *mulsum*, was actually a mixture of wine and honey. The Roman dinner, which began at about 2 or 2.30 p.m., was divided into three parts: the *hors d'oeuvre*, which was usually accompanied by *mulsum*, the main course, and the dessert course of pastry and fruit which was also sometimes accompanied by *mulsum*. *Mulsum* was also sometimes drunk at public banquets, so that in Roman life it performed the triple function of *apéritif*, luxury wine and dessert wine. As well as honey, the Romans also added a wide variety of spices and flavourings to their wines, including absinthe, rose petals, violets, mint and pepper, to produce what have been described, with some reason, as 'the forefathers of our vermouths'.

Not only did the Romans drink sweet and savoury wines with their sweet and savoury food, but these matching tastes may have served one single end. As many theories have been offered to account for the decline of the Roman Empire as have been propounded to explain the fall of the dinosaurs; one of the most popular, and most eccentric, attributes the collapse to chronic lead poisoning. Whatever its consequences may have been, it is certainly true to say that the Romans absorbed lead from their water pipes, from cups and cooking pots, from women's cosmetics, and from wine. Two symptoms of lead poisoning are loss of appetite and a metallic taste in the mouth. It is quite possible that the Romans needed their wine and food to be strongly flavoured in order to stimulate their appetites and to kill the taste of lead.

Consciously or unconsciously, the food and drink that people consumed in Britain and much of the rest of Western Europe in the Middle Ages resembled what had been eaten and drunk in Roman times. Although the art of making *liquamen* had been lost, medieval chefs continued to rely on strong flavourings: they still sweetened their food with sugar and honey and enlivened it with spices. They did so at least partly because their patrons and customers liked the taste. Sugar and spices had been encountered by Crusaders when in the eastern Mediterranean; they attached themselves to these expensive commodities, and demanded them when they returned home because they wanted to maintain a link with the more sophisticated world that they had seen on their travels. Thus, medieval chefs used spices and sugar from choice when cooking fresh food – but they also used them from necessity when cooking preserved food.

Since it was both difficult and expensive to keep food animals alive during the winter, most of the meat that was intended for consumption during the winter and spring had to be preserved by salting or smoking. It was also more or less impossible, in places inland, to obtain fresh fish. This was unfortunate because the Church required everyone to fast on three days each week, Wednesdays, Fridays* and Saturdays, as well as on major saints' days, for three days at each of the Quarter Days, and for the forty days of Lent (excepting Sundays) – amounting to approximately half the year. Fasting was enforced, not because the Church actively wanted to encourage the consumption of fish, but because it wanted people to eat less meat, considering that their carnal passions were inflamed by too carnivorous a diet. For the most ascetic, fasting meant living on bread and water; for the rest of the population, it meant making do with fish – usually salt fish. Evidently, a diet that was based on salted and smoked meat, and salt fish, was neither pleasant nor varied. Chefs did their best to disguise the flavours of salt and smoke with mustard, vinegar, spices and fruit, and they cut up the meat and fish, or ground them in mortars, so that the largest pieces were no greater than could be eaten with a spoon – forks not yet having been invented. The result was a sweet-and-sour cuisine that combined a great variety of flavours in a single dish.

The popularity of spicy foods was complemented by a preference for spiced wines. These, too, served to vary the monotony of everyday tastes – which, in the case of wine, was mostly that

---

*The custom of eating fish on a Friday originated with the Romans, for whom Friday was *dies Veneris*, the day sacred to Venus, the goddess who sprang from the foam of the sea. The Christian Church simply adapted the pagan Roman custom, decreeing that the purpose of eating fish on Fridays was now to commemorate the events of Good Friday.

of claret, pale red wine (*clairet*) from Bordeaux, not then part of the Kingdom of France but, until the middle of the fifteenth century, belonging to the English Crown. At feasts and special occasions those people who could afford to do so drank spiced wine, of which the most popular and most famous was Hippocras, a mixture of red wine, sugar or honey, cinnamon, ginger and pepper. This was not drunk with food but with the dessert or after the meal.

Spiced wines may not have been drunk with food, but sweet wines were – as they had been by the Romans. In a period when sugar was scarce and expensive and when foods were dominated by salty and smoky flavours, it was both a matter of preference and a mark of prestige to be able to afford to buy wines that were sweet. Sweet wines were more expensive than claret, not least because they came from rather further afield. Known generically as Malmseys, they came originally from Monemvasia in the Peloponnese and later from Crete. It was not until the sixteenth century that they were obtained from Madeira, which is the source of a roughly comparable style of Malmsey today. It was thus in a butt of Malmsey from the eastern Mediterranean, rather than from Madeira, that the Duke of Clarence was popularly supposed to have been drowned on the order of his brother, Richard III – in order, it has since been suggested, to put more body in it.

In the sixteenth century, the most popular wine was no longer Malmsey, but sack. It was sack that the legendary John Falstaff of Shakespeare's plays consumed in excessive quantities, on its own or with a capon or with anchovies. In one of his most celebrated perorations, he declared that, 'If I had a thousand sons, the first humane principle I would teach them should be, to forswear thin potations and to addict themselves to sack.' Sack was usually, but not invariably, sherry, in what would now be described as an oloroso style. It is not known for sure whether sack was dry or sweet; some sources describe it as one, some as the other.* The most likely explanation of this conflict is that sack was sometimes dry and sometimes sweet. What is clear is that

*No support for the argument that sack was a dry wine should be derived from the statement in the *Oxford English Dictionary* that 'sack' was derived from *seco*, meaning 'dry', since this is in all probability wrong. It is likely that the word was derived from the Spanish *sacar*, meaning 'to draw out', indicating a wine that was intended for export.

sack, when the term referred to sherry, was not naturally sweet. If it was sometimes exported to England as a sweet wine, this was because it had been sweetened by the addition of unfermented grape juice, which had been concentrated in colour, flavour and sweetness by simmering it over a slow fire. In other words, sherry, which was naturally a dry wine, was often made sweet in order to satisfy the taste of English consumers for sweet wines.

It did not matter so much whether a particular consignment of sack was sweet or dry because its appeal lay not only in its sweetness but also in its strength. Before the fortification of wine with brandy was known, indeed before the potential was known of spirits as a pleasurable drink rather than as a form of medicine, the wines that were most esteemed were not only those that were sweetest but also those that obtained the highest natural alcoholic strength – not least because these were the wines that were most likely to survive the rigours of transportation without spoilage. In most cases, they were one and the same: they were the wines from the warm countries around the Mediterranean, made from grapes whose natural ripeness was often accentuated by drying them in the sun before turning them into wine. These wines fermented to a high alcoholic strength and retained a good deal of unfermented sugars, thus remaining sweet. The contemporary term for these strong, sweet wines was 'hot'.

By the sixteenth century, it was becoming recognized that these hot wines were not altogether suited to drinking with all sorts of foods. Andrew Boorde, a famous physician who had lived for many years as a Carthusian monk but had been compelled by his philandering to leave the order, published one of the first English books on diet, the *Dietary of Health*, in 1542. In it he wrote that 'Mean wines, as wines of Gascony [and] French wines, is good with meat, especially claret wine. Hot wines, as Malmsey wine, Greek wine* [and] sack, be not good to drink with meat, but after meat, and with oysters, with salads, with fruit, a draught or two may be suffered.'

Boorde's comments about the ordering of wine are complemented by the observations of William Harrison later in the

---

*This did not mean wine from Greece but rather a sweet white wine that had been made in the same style as some of the wines of the Greek islands. Ironically, it usually came from the Italian peninsula.

century, in his celebrated *Description of England*. 'We commonly begin with the most gross food, and end with the most delicate,' he wrote. 'We also use our wines by degrees, so that the hottest cometh last to the table.' It seems that the reason why the strongest wines were served last was that it was these that were the most esteemed. 'The stronger the wine is, the more it is desired,' wrote Harrison. In other words, the modern order of wines, from most delicate to strongest, was established, not because that makes gastronomic sense, but because the everyday wines were served first and the finest wines were served last.

The observation that more substantial food was generally served before the lighter was a reference to a belief in the virtues of economy: that if grosser and cheaper cuts of meat were served before more delicate and expensive ones, then diners would consume more of the former and less of the latter, and so the cost of the meal would be less. As is implied by Boorde's reference to the consumption of oysters after meat, fish also conformed to this rule, and, when it did appear at a meat-based meal, it was served with the lighter meats towards the end. Fish, however, was rarely served on days on which meat was permitted; people were tired enough of all the fish that they were forced to eat on fast days. The modern practice of serving fish at the same meal as meat, and before it, is supposed to have originated as a result of a sumptuary law enacted by Elizabeth I in the 1560s. The practice of fasting had fallen into decline after England had adopted its own form of Protestantism, and the Wednesday fast day had fallen into abeyance. But Elizabeth wished to reimpose it for political reasons: to encourage the development of the fishing industry upon whose members the Navy would be able to draw in time of war. So she passed a law reimposing the Wednesday fish day, but with two possibilities of avoiding its provisions. Those people who could afford to do so were able to buy exemption from the new law by paying a sum of money to the poor box of their parish, while people who did not wish, or could not afford, to buy exemption were given permission to serve on Wednesdays one meat dish alongside every three fish dishes, providing that the fish dishes were put on the table for *bona fide* consumption and not just for show. It is possible that the manner in which housekeepers ensured conformity to this provision was by putting the fish dishes on the table at the beginning of the meal so that diners were unable to eat the meat before they had consumed the fish.

At the same time as something closer to the modern sequence of dishes at meals was being introduced, making them more compatible with the sequence in which wines were already being served, the dishes themselves were changing in such a way as to be less likely to conflict with dry wines. In the Middle Ages, England, France and Italy had shared a similar cuisine, which relied heavily on the availability of large amounts of spices, imported by Genoese and Venetian merchants from the eastern Mediterranean. At the end of the fifteenth century, however, the spice trade was captured by the Portuguese. This led to a substantial increase in the price that Italian chefs had to pay for their spices. They responded by developing a new, subtler style of cooking in which they sought to express the flavour of the individual ingredients rather than to blend them into a hotch-potch of meat, vinegar, fruit and spices. Supposedly the new Italian cookery was introduced to France by the chefs who accompanied Catherine de'Medici on her journey from Florence in 1533 to marry the future Henri II; in fact, there is no hard evidence to support the tradition that French cuisine grew out of Italian, and it is just as likely that it developed along similar lines on its own.

It was at this period that English and French gastronomic traditions diverged. Certainly, English cooks followed their Italian and French counterparts in abandoning heavy spicing and the mixture of contrasting ingredients in the same dish. But while in France chefs now turned their attention towards the creation of delicate and complex meat dishes, in England they concentrated on the production of plain roast meats. The large part that was played by plain meat in the English diet of the seventeenth and eighteenth centuries was frequently commented upon by foreign visitors. Pehr Kalm, a Swede who passed through England on his way to America, pointed out that English dinners differed from those of other nations in that butcher's meat formed the greater part of the meal and its principal dishes. He applauded the quality of English meat, which he said had 'a fatness and a delicious taste', but was less complimentary about English skill in cooking. 'The English understand almost better than any other people the art of roasting a joint,' he wrote, 'which is not to be wondered at, because the art of cooking as practised by most Englishmen does not extend much beyond roast beef and plum pudding.'

The same period saw a conversion in sophisticated English taste from sweet to dry wines. This was intimately connected with a fall in the price of sugar, made possible by the development of sugar-cane plantations in the new West Indian colonies. In the eighteenth century, not only was sugar more affordable but it was regularly consumed by all classes of society as a necessary addition to a new drink called tea that was being taken in ever-increasing quantities. As a result, it was no longer a mark of sophistication to prefer sweet things. Already, at the court of King Charles II, fine new French dry wines, single-château claret and champagne, were introduced; the reigns of King William III and Queen Anne saw the arrival of another new wine, port. It is from this period that the first use of the word 'dry' to describe a wine that was not sweet appeared, in the doggerel of one Richard Ames who published an account of his travels in 1691 round London's taverns in search of 'a bottle of good old dry orthodox claret'; he was unable to find it, since all that he was offered was port or madeira.

Although port is a sweet wine today, its popularity during the eighteenth century manifested not only a continuation of the English taste for strong wines but a new preference for dry ones. Indeed, in one of the first English-language wine books, *The History of Ancient and Modern Wines*, published in 1824, Alexander Henderson went so far as to describe the taste for port as a manifestation of the decline of sweet wines. Referring to 'the rough vintages of Portugal,' he says that 'From the long continued use of these strong dry wines, which were made doubly strong for the English market, the relish for sweet wines, which was once so prevalent, has gradually declined; and several kinds, such as Canary, Mountain, etc., which, as several of my readers may be old enough to remember, were drunk very generally by way of "running whet", are now scarcely ever met with.'

The reason why port was a dry wine in the eighteenth and early nineteenth centuries while it is a sweet wine today is because it was made differently in the past. Today, port is made sweet by adding brandy during the fermentation; this causes the fermentation to stop, leaving some of the sugar unfermented and thus a wine that tastes sweet. In the eighteenth century, brandy was sometimes added, but generally after the wine had fermented out to dryness; the purpose was not to produce a sweet wine but a stronger, more alcoholic dry one. The process whereby port was transformed from a dry into a sweet wine occurred gradually during the course of the nineteenth century, the turning-point coming as a result of the 1820 vintage, a very hot year in which the grapes were naturally so ripe and so rich in sugar that they never succeeded in fermenting fully and some sugar was left in the wines. When these were shipped to Britain they caused a sensation; they were so greatly enjoyed by the mass of consumers that port shippers tried to replicate their taste in subsequent, cooler vintages. This could only be done by adding brandy during the fermentation in order to produce an artifically sweet wine.*

The popularity of port in the eighteenth century therefore lay not in sweetness but in strength. It satisfied the demands both of drinkers who wanted a wine for drinking after meals that would make them drunk, and of diners who called for a strong dry wine to wash down the vast quantities of meat that they consumed. One might have imagined that simpler English cookery would have made the matching of food and wine easier to manage. But it did not. There is simply no evidence of attempts by English hosts or diners to match individual dishes and wines before the nineteenth century. Nor was this a subject in which those people who consumed substantial quantities of port in the eighteenth century – largely, it seems, for the purposes of inebriation – would have been interested.

In the first half of the nineteenth century, port fell out of favour and was replaced by sherry. This had been popularized in the early years of the century by the future George IV, who became Prince Regent in 1810 on account of the illness of his father, George III. In his *Practical Treatise*, one of the first English-language wine books, Richard Shannon describes it as 'the present fashion to run upon pale white wines, particularly pale sherry'. By the middle of the nineteenth century, sherry was so popular in Britain that it accounted for over 90 per cent of all the sherry that was produced and for 43 per cent of the nation's total wine

---

*The famous campaign that was conducted against adulterated port in the 1840s by the port shipper Baron Forrester, which has generally been written off by wine writers as a hang-over from the previous century, should in fact be regarded as a contemporary response to this development.

imports. This enormous consumption of sherry is to be explained by the fact that it was not drunk as an *apéritif* as it is today but was consumed throughout the meal.

The consumption of sherry with food might have been perfectly justifiable in modern terms had it been the sort of dry sherry that is drunk today.* But the sherry that was so popular in the early years of the century was not a dry wine, and, even when drier sherries became popular from the middle of the century onwards, they were not as dry as dry sherries are today. Indeed, the sherry shippers were faced with a conundrum: consumers believed that drier drinks were more sophisticated, so demanded that they should have drinks that were dry, but they did not actually like the taste of dry drinks, so even 'dry' sherries had to be sweetened for the British palate.† The sherry that came to dominate British wine consumption in the middle of the nineteenth century differed from the sack that had been so popular in the sixteenth century not because it was drier but principally in that it was now fortified by the addition of some brandy, the better to preserve it on its journey to England, and was therefore an even stronger wine than it had been in the past. How strong was a matter of dispute. Certainly, there were many complaints in nineteenth-century wine literature of sherry shippers who over-fortified their wine in order to compensate for its lack of natural flavour. It appears that sherry in the nineteenth century, although it might have been lighter in colour and taste than port, is unlikely to have been much lighter in alcohol.

The usual alternative to port or sherry with meals was beer. Restaurants did not exist for most of this period; instead there were cook shops, later chop houses, where men of all social ranks, from peers and gentry to merchants and tradesmen, would eat together and where the food was simple in the extreme and beer was the usual drink. Henri Misson de Valbourg, a Frenchman who visited England at the end of the seventeenth century, described what was served in the cook shops: 'Generally four

---

*Dry sherry may not be drunk with food in Britain today, but in its home of Andalucia it is usually accompanied by *tapas*.

†The same is true today, when it explains the cunning creation of Dry Sack, a medium sherry that satisfies the demands of consumers for the title 'dry'. Since sack was at least sometimes a sweet wine, the name is quite correct: it is not a dry sherry, but it is a dry sack.

spits, one over another, carry round each five or six pieces of butcher's meat, beef, mutton, veal, pork and lamb; you have what quantity you please cut off, fat, lean, much or little done; with this, a little salt and mustard upon the side of a plate, a bottle of beer and a roll; and there is your whole feast.'

The situation had not changed much by the time that Queen Victoria came to the throne. According to an account given by Walter Besant fifty years later, at this time very little light table wine was drunk. Instead, 'Beer was universally taken with dinner; even at great dinner parties some of the guests would call for beer. Even among the upper classes, claret was absolutely unknown, as were burgundy, Rhône wines, Sauternes and all other French wines. In the restaurants every man would call for bitter ale, or stout, or half-and-half with his dinner, as a matter of course, and after dinner would either take his pint of port, or half-pint of sherry, or his tumbler of grog. In the family circle [champagne] never appeared at all, except at weddings, and perhaps on Christmas Day. When people spoke of wine in those days they generally meant port.'

Another thirty years, however, and the situation had changed completely. In the 1860s the wine merchant Thomas George Shaw recalled the habits of the early years of the nineteenth century from a high moral standpoint. 'The dinner hour was early and, among many, the hour of rising from the table was late . . . Those who recur to the period cannot have forgotten that when gentlemen dined alone they seldom left the table before eleven o'clock, and were generally tipsy. So it was also, at public dinners, where at least two bottles were drunk by each. Port was the invariable wine after dinner, and anyone drinking white wine was then considered peculiar. Now, *tempora mutantur, et nos mutamur in illis**; and a jolly good change it is. There are, of course, many jolly drinking parties still; but the late hour of dinner now in general renders it impossible, even if it were desired, to remain long at table afterwards; and almost all that is drunk during dinner is sherry, champagne and other white wines.'

Attitudes had changed in part, at least, because food had become lighter. In his reminiscences of his youth in the early nineteenth century Captain Gronow recalled that 'Even in the best

*Times change, and us with them.

houses . . . the dinners were wonderfully solid, hot and stimulating
. . . The wines were chiefly port, sherry and hock; claret and even
then burgundy being designated "poor, thin, washy stuff".' This
was no longer the case by the 1860s. As Shaw observed, 'It is
often stated, probably with a great deal of truth, that heavy joints
require heavy wine, and that nothing will have a more powerful
influence in inducing a taste for light or neutral wine than lighter
and more scientific cookery.'

One explanation for the conversion to lighter dishes is evident
from the abandonment of the practice of drinking beer with meals.
As was pointed out at the time, beer was a nutritious drink that
was suited to people who indulged in physical labour or took
plenty of exercise, but not to people whose work required them
to sit at a desk all day, and who exercised little. Thus, the
introduction of the railways, which reduced the necessity of taking
exercise by riding horses, and the growth in business as a
consequence of the Industrial Revolution, which increased the
need for lawyers, accountants and clerks of all kinds, enlarged
the proportion of the population for whom beer was not appropriate and whose new styles of life were better suited to the
consumption of light table wines.

Linked with the growth of cities and the development of office
work was the general change in eating habits, with a later dinner,
the introduction of lunch and tea and the abandonment of the
practice of drinking port after dinner; these, in their turn,
encouraged the consumption of lighter meals. And the consumption of lighter wines to accompany these lighter meals was
encouraged by the changes in duties: the equalization of duties
on all European wines in 1831, their reduction in 1860, and the
introduction of a system of preferential duties for lighter wines in
1861–1862. While the last of these changes was being introduced,
The Times published a leading article in which it described how,
'A very few years ago, claret was an expensive luxury, only
brought to the table after the company had been previously well
soaked with port, just as school children are economically
crammed with pudding before they begin at the meat . . . The
regular wines were port and sherry, religiously produced in
couples, so much so that decanters were manufactured and sold
"by the pair". Wine was not a beverage but a liqueur. It was both
too strong and too dear.'

The practice of serving claret with the dessert* did not help to encourage its consumption. As was pointed out by a doctor writing in *Dublin University Magazine*, under these conditions claret tasted 'acid and poor, and John Bull shook his ponderous head and complacently pitied the poor French . . . who did not know what good wine is . . .' The reductions in duty made all the difference. The majority of the English middle class now turned away from port and (to a lesser extent) sherry and became drinkers of claret. The former wines were not, however, abandoned altogether; rather they were moved to what would appear, from a modern standpoint, to be their proper places in a meal: sherry was restricted to the beginning of the meal and served with the soup or fish course, while port was kept for the end, when it was drunk in moderate amounts with the pudding, savoury or cheese. In between, lighter table wines appeared, notably claret and champagne.

Thus, in the second half of the nineteenth century, the old habit of drinking just one wine – be it port or sherry – with (and indeed after) the meal was replaced by a habit of drinking various different wines with the different courses. This change was made possible by the replacement of the *service à la française* by the *service à la russe*. There had been no point in attempting to combine specific dishes with particular wines when meals were conducted according to the *service à la française*; since different kinds of food were placed on the table at the same time, a formal matching of food was hardly feasible.

It was not merely that diners would be eating the same dishes at different times but that no two diners would have eaten precisely the same meal. Rather than eating all the dishes in each course, the diners restricted their attention largely to the few dishes that were placed in the immediate vicinity of their places. It was permissible to ask a servant to pass a helping of something placed a distance away, but it was not done to ask too often. It was not guaranteed that one would be able to obtain a portion of any particular dish on the table – as is demonstrated by a tale concerning the ruffs and reeves that were served at a grand dinner

*This practice did not fall into decline until the end of the century, and then not because of the intervention of gastronomic good taste but as a result of the growing popularity of smoking after dinner in its stead. And it survived for several more decades at traditionally-minded institutions, such as Oxford and Cambridge colleges.

at the home of the Archbishop of York at Bishopthorpe towards the end of the eighteenth century. Ruffs and reeves were wild birds that tasted good only if they had been captured alive and fattened on boiled wheat or bread and milk mixed with hemp seed for about a fortnight before being killed. They were therefore something of a delicacy. At this dinner 'A dish of ruffs and reeves chanced to be placed immediately in front of a young divine who had come up to be examined for priest's orders . . . Out of sheer modesty the clerical tyro confined himself exclusively to the dish before him, and persevered in his indiscriminating attentions to it till one of the resident dignitaries (all of whom were waiting only the proper moment to participate) observed him, and called the attention of the company by a loud exclamation of alarm. But the warning came too late: the ruffs and reeves had vanished to a bird, and with them, we are concerned to add, all the candidate's chances of preferment.' Incidents such as this one help to explain why the *service à la française* disappeared.

As long as the *service à la française* had persisted, even the most eminent of cookery writers had appeared generally to be unconcerned about giving precise directions as to the matching of wines with foods. The most celebrated of these were two Frenchmen: the gastronomic philosophers Grimod de la Reynière and Brillat-Savarin. The former did propose a few associations of particular dishes with specific wines in the *Almanach des Gourmands* that he published at the beginning of the nineteenth century, such as a recipe for spit-roast ham with which he recommended serving a rustic wine from the south of France, and oysters, which he said had to be washed down with Chablis. He also commented that red burgundy was too delicate to be served with the *entremets* (the third course in the *service à la française*) and should rather be served with the roast (the second course). But all that Grimod's more famous successor, Brillat-Savarin, had to say on the subject of matching wine with food in his *Physiologie du Goût* was that the dishes at a dinner should progress from the most substantial to the lightest, and the wines from the simplest to the most sophisticated, from the mildest to the headiest and most perfumed; he had, in other words, little to say on the subject that had not been said by Harrison 250 years earlier.

All this changed during the course of the nineteenth century. The introduction of meals at which each of the diners ate each of the dishes at the same time led to the beginnings of the modern principles of matching wine and food. These principles were first enunciated in print at the beginning of the 1850s by the essayist Abraham Hayward in a book called *The Art of Dining*. 'The wines which may be deemed to be indispensable at a complete English dinner,' he stated, 'are sherry, champagne, port and claret.' A decade later, after the excise duties on light French wines were reduced, it became more common to serve the claret before the port, as is done at formal dinners today.

Champagne, however, remained central to the meal and was served with the principal courses – a practice that does not at all accord with modern taste. The reasons for this were quite logical, however. In the early part of the nineteenth century champagne had been a rare and expensive wine; it became much less expensive as a result of the development in 1836 of a means of measuring the amount of sugar that was present in a bottle of champagne before it started fermenting for a second time, which finally brought some control to the breakages of bottles that had made champagne so expensive to make and to buy. The cost of champagne in the early nineteenth century was such that hosts did not want their guests to consume too much of it. So they often served it at the end of a meal. This practice was discountenanced by a number of gastronomes, notably the independently-minded food critic Thomas Walker, who described it as 'an absurd contrast of calculation and display'.* Despite such criticism, the consumption of champagne with the dessert in the early nineteenth century could be justified on gastronomic grounds – even if the reasons for the combination in question were not entirely, or even principally, gastronomic. At this time, champagne was a sweet wine whose service with the dessert was not wholly inappropriate; it was only in the second half of the century that champagne was transmuted from a sweet sparkling drink into the dry one that we know today.

It is not known precisely why the transformation of champagne from a sweet to a dry wine took place. It did not occur in France,

---

*Walker was a great advocate of simplicity in dining, in which he was out of step with the general practice of his time. He also went against contemporary attitudes in insisting on the virtues of fresh air. This led him to go out in bad weather in winter without wrapping up properly, contract pulmonary consumption, and die at the age of fifty-two in 1836.

where sweet champagne was still preferred at the beginning of the twentieth century. In 1903 the restaurant reviewer Colonel Newnham-Davis described having participated in a shooting lunch organized by a syndicate of some of the big champagne shippers at which he was offered a dozen of the leading brands of champagne. He asked his host for '*du vin brut*'. '*Ah! Vous buvez ce poison-là,*' exclaimed his host in reply. Thus champagne was transformed into a dry wine in order to meet the demands of the English market. The port shipper Feuerheerd was told by one of his friends that champagne was wanted dry because it had become popular as an alternative to brandy and soda. Maybe so. It is perfectly possible, however, that the champagne that was produced for the British market was turned from a sweet into a dry wine because it was wanted to be taken with food.

In the second half of the nineteenth century, champagne was generally drunk at formal dinners in Britain as an accompaniment to the course in which roast meat was served. From a modern perspective, it might have been expected that gastronomes would have been as critical of this practice as they had been of the consumption of sweet champagne at the end of the meal in the first half of the century. But they were not. Indeed, they condemned those people who were so careless as to serve champagne at another stage in the meal. In his guide to the choice and service of wines Feuerheerd criticized those people who had taken to serving champagne throughout the meal 'because the drinking of champagne with all kinds of food is not commendable . . . Dry champagne should only be offered with the roast.' The idea that champagne might have been drunk with roast meats seems so strange to modern tastes that in a recent book on champagne the wine writer Serena Sutcliffe has attempted to argue that 'Not much can be gleaned from menus of the period with regard to how and when champagnes were served.' She suggests that just because the printer placed a particular wine alongside a particular food it did not mean that these were served at the same time. Yet at the end of *Notes on a Cellar Book* the literary critic and historian George Saintsbury set out, very carefully, thirteen model menus of dinners that took place between 1884 and 1905. In twelve of them champagne was served, usually as an accompaniment to poultry or mutton.

As well as drinking champagne with roast meat, Victorian

diners differed from their present-day descendants in their belief that wine should not be served with cheese. According to a manual for butlers written in the early nineteenth century, 'Wine is seldom drunk with the cheese, only porter, ale or something of that kind . . .' This advice was repeated by another manual for would-be butlers written a generation later, which instructed that when the cheese was served the wine glasses should be removed from the table, 'the company seldom drinking wine with their cheese. Ale or beer, toast and water, or soda water, etc., is taken by some.'

These Victorian attitudes towards combinations of wine and food may seem absurd to modern palates. It would be a mistake to assume, however, that they indulged in these combinations simply because their tastes were inferior to those of the present day. Certainly there were many people whose dining habits, and whose choice of food and wine, were dictated more by social requirements and by a desire for conspicuous consumption than by any good taste that they might or might not have possessed, but the rules about matching wine and food were established by gastronomes who devoted considerably more time and attention to their task than their counterparts do today. If Victorian tastes in combining food and wine differed from modern ones, it was largely because their food and wine tasted different, even when they bore the same names as the food and wine that are consumed today. Although champagne, for instance, was drunk with food, it was not simply because the *apéritif* did not exist then. The dry champagne that was imported into Britain in the second half of the nineteenth century tasted different from the champagne that is imported today: it was made from lower-yielding vines and generally contained a higher proportion of the black grape Pinot Noir; as a result it was a fuller-bodied wine, better able to stand up to food.

Similarly, it would be naïve to criticize Victorian attitudes towards wine and cheese, since these reflected the different nature of the cheese that they consumed. They consumed hard cheeses which had been made entirely from unpasteurized milk (pasteurization not yet having been invented) and which were generally kept for longer than cheese is today. Soft, creamy cheeses may have become popular in France precisely because of their suitability for eating with wine, but French soft cheeses were not imported into England in the nineteenth century. Moreover, not only was cheese in the nineteenth century generally older and harder than it is today, but beer was stronger. Burton pale ale was 7 per cent alcohol compared with 4 or 5 per cent today, and much more capable of standing up to strong, hard British cheese. This was demonstrated by the batch of India Pale Ale that was brewed by the Bass Museum at Burton in the summer of 1993 at historic strength according to a historic recipe. Not only was it richer and more alcoholic than modern bitters but the flavour was much more intense also. It is also possible that Victorian beers were more acidic than modern ones because wild yeasts from the Brettanomyces family would have been present in the vats.* Since it is the presence of acidity in wine, and its absence from beer, that is the principal explanation for the modern preference for drinking wine rather than beer with food, it is likely that Victorian beers would have been much better suited to drinking with cheese than modern ones.

It is a development common to all European countries that drinks have become milder and less astringent as food has become less strongly flavoured. It can be seen not only in beer but also in cider. Traditionally-made English farmhouse cider, a product that is nearing extinction but is still produced on a few farms in Somerset, Herefordshire and Devon, has become much less tannic than it used to be. At the beginning of the 1990s the Somerset cider-maker Henry Perry recalled that before the Second World War his customers ate fat bacon and strong cheese. So they called for a style of cider that would break down the fat. Half a century later, this was no longer necessary. 'Everyone,' said Perry, 'is going for milder drinks in today's world.'

Possibly the most significant explanation for the tendency of food to have become less strongly flavoured lies in the introduction of better transport and refrigeration. The effect of this development on the taste of wine can be seen most clearly in the changing style of red burgundy, a delicate yet malleable wine, whose character has evolved in various different ways over the last three hundred years in order to suit the demands of its consumers across Europe. 'Before the Second World War,' says Gérard Potel, manager and part-owner of the celebrated Domaine

---

*These yeasts have since been eliminated from British beers but the acidic character that they impart is evident from the few surviving traditionally-made *lambic* and *gueuze* beers that are produced in and around Brussels in Belgium, notably by the Cantillon brewery.

de la Pousse d'Or in the village of Volnay, 'people did not have refrigerators. They ate game that was high and fish that was not fresh. They cooked heavy sauces to hide the taste of decay, and drank solid, tannic, acid wines.' In the 1960s and 1970s red burgundy became a lighter, fresher, more delicate style of wine. This change attracted a lot of hostility from English consumers but it reflected a transformation in the prevailing style of food that was served in restaurants in France, with the advent of *nouvelle cuisine*. As a consequence of this change, most modern red burgundy is too delicate to be drunk with the food with which it has traditionally been associated: peasant dishes such as *boeuf bourgignon* and *coq au vin*. Nor does it stand up any longer to strong Burgundian cheeses such as Epoisses and Cîteaux.

Food has changed, and so have people's attitudes to it. In the nineteenth century, to be fat was a mark of prosperity, a sign that one could afford proper nourishment. Not until the mass of the population was able to feed itself sufficiently – a development that occurred to a certain extent after the First World War and to a greater degree after the Second – did it then become a mark of sophistication to be thin. Thinness has come to be esteemed because it shows a self-restraint, an ability to rise upon the common gratifications of the table; it shows that one can afford to consume expensive, delicate food rather than relying on a simple calorific diet based on starch and fat. So sophisticated tastes have tended towards the consumption of food that is delicate in flavour, and to more delicate wines to go with it.

Not only have tastes changed, but so have lifestyles. Thanks to the development of mechanized transport, and of labour-saving devices in homes, people take vastly less exercise than they did in the first part of the nineteenth century, and considerably less than they did in the second part – so much less, indeed, that they have found it necessary to conceive of contrived means of exercising by jogging and going to gymnasia and swimming pools. And, thanks to the introduction of central heating in homes, people no longer have such a need for internal fuel. As the gastronome and wine writer André Simon pointed out in his autobiography in the 1960s, young people before the First World War 'had appetites and digestive organs far superior to those of the present time'.

*   *   *

The multi-dish dinners served *à la française* in the earlier part of the nineteenth century and the multi-course dinners served *à la russe* in the later part of it have disappeared and have been replaced by shorter meals, featuring simpler dishes. To a certain extent, this transition can be seen as a conversion from French to Italian attitudes. In the late nineteenth century, the composition of dinners in English restaurants, and the ordering of their service, was reorganized by the French chef Georges Auguste Escoffier according to the best French custom of the time. Indeed, the sequence of dishes served in Anglo-French restaurants today – *hors d'oeuvre* or soup, fish, meat and vegetables, sweet, savoury, dessert – is a legacy of Escoffier's influence. In the 1980s and 1990s, however, the food that has become most fashionable reflects what would be regarded as more traditionally Italian attitudes. If there is a fundamental distinction between established attitudes to food – and indeed wine – in France and Italy, it is that in France wine and food are both forced to bow to a culture that believes in turning them into something more complex, something greater than the sum of its parts, while in Italy what is valued above all is simplicity: that wine and food should express their own flavours, unadorned and unhindered. In Britain, since the early 1980s, fashions in food and wine have developed along the latter course. Along with the replacement of butter by olive oil, roasting by grilling and mushy vegetables by crisp ones, elaborate, long-cooked dishes have been replaced by simpler, more quickly prepared ones.

At the same time, there has been a movement from drinking complex, high-class, mature, expensive French wines to drinking young, fruity wines with fresh, simple, grape flavours. Admittedly, the reasons for these developments are as much financial as gastronomic; but they have taken place together. Admittedly, too, the simple, fruity wines that are now widely preferred do not very often come from Italy; they may do so in restaurants but, for consumption at home, they have tended to come from Australia. A boom in Italian wine for home drinking has been presaged for many years but it has not yet occurred. A combination of wine scandals, poor promotion, overpriced 'boutique' wines and a myriad of confusing names and regions have served to repel consumers. Instead, Australian wines, with a nomenclature that is much easier to understand, have grown markedly in popularity. Although they have been produced on the other side of the world, the simple, fruity flavours they offer serve to satisfy an Italian or, as it is often described, a 'Mediterranean' taste.

The other major gastronomic change of the second half of the twentieth century has been the rise in popularity of oriental cuisines, or at least of a British interpretation of the cuisines of parts of India and China and, most recently, of Thailand. It is no accident that this development has occurred at the same time as the transition from classic 'French' restaurant food to an Italian version. They are both essentially manifestations of multi-culturalism, products not so much of the experience of travel abroad as of a desire to travel abroad without leaving home. Sometimes they are combined, in a magpie attitude to foreign cultures, demonstrated most notably by Stephen Funnell, chef at The Black Chapati in Brighton. In terms of wine, however, the two developments are quite distinct, since one links food with wine and the other does not.

Consumers of oriental, or orient-derived food, have tended to reject wines altogether. The part played by the popularity of Indian restaurants in making lager more widely acceptable has already been mentioned. The drink that is most widely consumed in Chinese restaurants is Jasmine tea. These can hardly be regarded as attempts to indulge in an undiluted cultural experience, since lager is hardly a typical Indian drink – and what Chinese tend to drink, at least at banquets, is cognac. If wine is not generally drunk with Indian, Chinese or Thai food, it is principally because these are considered to be in-expensive, everyday types of food with which a high-status drink such as wine is inappropriate. Also, it is believed that Indian, Chinese and Thai food is too hot or too spicy to combine with wine.

This is not what people thought in the Middle Ages, when they also consumed what could be regarded as a Western interpretation of Eastern cuisine, or at least a Western cuisine that relied heavily on the use of Eastern ingredients. Certainly, the comparison has been made between medieval European and modern Indian or Arab cookery, not only because of their generous use of spices but also because of their tendency to heighten flavour with sweet and acid ingredients and because of their practice of serving highly flavoured meat dishes with bland porridges or purées of grains or legumes.

There is no reason not to combine wines with oriental foods; it simply requires a certain amount of thought. Suitable wines for drinking with particular foods can be selected according to one of two principles: that of harmony, or that of contrast. If harmony is the aim, then it is necessary to find wine and food of a similar weight and a similar style, be it spicy wine with spicy food or more delicate wine with classic *haute cuisine*. This principle might lead to the choice of rich, warm, spicy red wines from the south of Italy or maybe Australia or California for drinking with Indian food, or ripe, fresh, slightly spicy white wines such as New Zealand Sauvignons and Alsace Rieslings with Chinese. The fact that this principle is not invariably successful is demonstrated by Alsace Gewürztraminers, the wines that are generally thought to be best suited for drinking with Chinese food: they can be excessively spicy, so that they fight with the food rather than harmonize with it. The alternative principle, that of contrast, is more difficult to apply successfully, since it is not similar features that are being sought in the wine and the food but rather ones that will balance each other. Examples of the successful application of contrast are drinking a tired old claret with spicy Indian food, in which case the spiciness of the food enhances the flavour of the wine, and a young light red burgundy or New World Pinot Noir with hot Thai food; again, the seasoning of the food brings out hidden flavours in the wine.

If people do not make the effort to combine good-quality wines with oriental foods, it is partly because experimentation with wine, unlike experimentation with food, takes place at home, and oriental foods are generally consumed in restaurants. Indeed, the rapid rise in the popularity of oriental restaurants serves to demonstrate the fact that experiments with food are more often made in restaurants than at home. It is less likely that people should experiment with food at home because those who eat the food will not necessarily be prepared to give the chef their honest opinion, especially not if the food is bad; if they do voice their distaste to the chef, the latter is likely to feel insulted. In a restaurant, they may not be inclined to voice complaints, either, but they are not obliged to visit it again.

There is no such problem in the case of wine: there is no barrier to the conducting of experiments at home because the product is simply bought from a shop; the producer who might take offence is not present. Nor is it likely that experiments with wine will take place in a restaurant, partly because the mark-ups that are imposed by most restaurateurs render such experimentation prohibitively expensive, and partly because diners-out are generally cautious about their choice of wine and look to tradition rather than to pleasure. The boom in Australian wines began at home; it was only after they were established that restaurants began to list them.

Even when dining at home, in matching wine and food people are generally more concerned with perpetuating a cultural tradition than with devising what might best suit their pleasure. This can be seen, for example, in the survival of the rule that white wine should be drunk with fish. In fact, there is no reason why fish should necessarily not be eaten with red wines – and not just fishes that have been cooked in dark, red-wine-based sauces but darker-coloured, oily fishes such as salmon, tuna and sardines. It used to be said that it was not possible to drink red wine with fish because the mouth-puckering tannin that preserves red wines reacts with fish to leave a metallic aftertaste. But in fact the tannins in red wines are offset by the proteins and fats that are present in flesh that has not been overcooked; this explains not only why tannic red wines combine well with rare beef or lamb but also why they can be drunk with great pleasure with lightly-cooked salmon or tuna steaks. Moreover, red wines are much less tannic than they used to be. It might be ridiculous to drink a robust red wine from the Rhône valley or California with white fish but there is no reason not to choose a light, relatively acidic style of red wine that can be served cool, such as a red wine from Burgundy, the Loire Valley or New Zealand.

The British tendency to combine wine and food according to tradition rather than according to pleasure can partly be explained by the terror of making a mistake, especially when dining in a restaurant – of being laughed at by a waiter for making such an eccentric choice as selecting, say, a red burgundy to drink with a hot Thai curry or a New Zealand Pinot Noir to drink with salmon. But there is also a deeper explanation. In following tradition rather than pleasure, it seems that little has changed since 1862 when the cookery writer Charles Francatelli, who had once been chef to Queen Victoria, criticized the order in which wines were served at many tables, on the grounds that 'Custom and fashion have ever had more to do with this practice than any real consideration for health or taste.' The connection with the nineteenth century is not accidental. The development in the last century or so of traditions of matching wine and food has coincided with the development of an ethos that does not permit the taking of any pleasure in the process.

Before the nineteenth century some consumers, at least, took a very open pleasure in what they ate and drank. The different attitudes of the nineteenth and eighteenth centuries to food and drink are epitomized by a comparison between the manners of Dr Johnson, who died in 1784, and of Robert Browning, who was born in 1812. 'When at table,' wrote Boswell, Johnson 'was totally absorbed in the business of the moment; his looks seemed riveted to his plate; nor would he, unless in very high company, say one word, or even pay the least attention to what was said by others, till he had satisfied his appetite, which was so fierce, and indulged with such intenseness, that while in the act of eating the veins of his forehead swelled, and generally a strong perspiration was visible.' Browning, a man so fastidious that he would not go out of doors without putting on a pair of gloves, and so ignorant of matters sexual that he included the word 'twat' in his poem *Pippa Passes* in the mistaken belief that it referred to an item of nun's attire, regarded eating as such a private act that he could not bear anyone to see him indulging in it.

In a history of the relationship of food and sexuality in England, *Consuming Passions*, Philippa Pullar suggested that it was the Puritans of the seventeenth century who established the association of guilt and appetite, but this is no more than another of the myths with which the word 'Puritanism' will forever be cursed. The idea that food, like sex, is something necessary, but definitely not to be enjoyed by the virtuous, is a product, not of seventeenth-century Puritanism but of nineteenth-century non-conformism. It was the new Victorian Protestant sects that prevented their adherents from taking sensual pleasure in food or drink. Their most important doctrine, according to the social historian E. P. Thompson, was 'Thou shalt not!'

In Victorian England, people did not show open sensual pleasure in food and drink. They were too closely connected with other, unmentionable functions of the body – sexual and excretory – to be polite. Obviously, this posed a problem when it came to dinner parties, at which a great deal of food and drink would inevitably be consumed and would, in the natural course of things, have been enjoyed. It was necessary for the diners to distance themselves from the physical sensations they were experiencing. Eating was such a private act that it could only be performed in public if the people who did so pretended to ignore it. One American commentator of the period stated that it was incorrect to comment on the food before one, even in praise, on the grounds that such remarks would be too naked an expression of 'animal and sensual gratification' over mankind's 'intellect and moral nature'. No matter how much the food might have been handled during the preparation of the meal, in the dining room servants and guests participated in elaborate rituals of purity. Although neither group wore gloves, each waiter wrapped a napkin around his thumb in serving so that his hand never touched the surface of the plates. It was partly in order to minimize the carving of meat in the presence of guests, the passing of dishes at table, and the sight of leftovers shared in common, that the Victorian upper and middle classes converted the ordering of their dinner parties from *service à la française* to *service à la russe*; it enabled them better to protect their social sensibilities.

In the light of these sensibilities, it is hardly surprising that respectable people in early Victorian England shrank away from eating or drinking in public. Gentlemen rarely went to public houses and when they ate out in public in town they did so in eating houses that were provided with compartments that shielded them from contact with their fellow diners. Ladies did not eat out at all; it was considered that their presence in eating houses 'would have been considered fast, if not disreputable'. Nor did they need to dine in public since they had plenty of time for shopping and paying calls on their friends and acquaintances between breakfast and the dinner they took at home in the middle or at the end of the afternoon. When, however, the dinner hour changed in the middle decades of the nineteenth century, the absence of eating places suitable for ladies began to pose a major problem. With the introduction of lunch, it became necessary to provide places where ladies could eat in town. Since it was not considered respectable for them to take their lunch in private, curtained apartments, this need could only be fulfilled by the creation of a new kind of eating place that combined the openness of dining in public with the refinement that their sensibilities required. The solution lay in the construction of large rooms in which it was possible to maintain an essential degree of privacy by providing wide spaces between tables.

The term 'restaurant' had been used in France since the 1760s, where it had emerged in reaction to the power of the guild of the *traiteurs*. The latter enjoyed exclusive rights to sell cooked meats, which they would only sell as whole cuts, not as individual helpings. However, the stock that was produced in the cooking of the meat fell outside the monopoly, and so this was sold by soup kitchens under the name of *restaurant* ('pick-me-up'). In 1765 the owner of one of these soup kitchens, Boulanger, decided to extend his repertoire by offering sheep's feet in white sauce. The *traiteurs* took him to court. They lost; the restaurant had been created. By the time of the Revolution, a fair number of restaurants had already opened in Paris, but the main impetus for their growth came from the Revolution itself. It led to the arrival in Paris of large numbers of revolutionary deputies from the provinces who lodged in boarding houses and needed somewhere to go out to eat; the new source of customers encouraged the former chefs of aristocratic households to set themselves up in business in restaurants. By 1815, Paris was full of restaurants. This is the date at which the first reference to London 'restaurateurs' appeared, in *The Epicure's Almanack*, a guide to eating out in the capital. But all that 'restaurant' seems to have meant at the time was an eating house that served French food. The restaurant in the modern sense of a stylish and sophisticated public eating house did not develop until after the change in the dinner hour in the middle of the century. Although a number of the early London restaurants have long since disappeared, and others – such as the Café Royal which opened in 1865 – have since been rebuilt, it is still possible for visitors to London to appreciate the spaciousness of these new premises by visiting the Criterion at Piccadilly Circus, which opened in 1874.

The development of restaurants that were smart enough and large enough to enable ladies to dine in public led diners further to divorce the practice of eating from the experience of sensual pleasure. This was especially true of the restaurants that were established in the last two decades of the century in a number of new hotels, notably the Savoy, which was opened in 1889. Soon after its opening the management was entrusted to César Ritz, the most celebrated hotelier of his time, and the food to Auguste Escoffier, the most celebrated chef. 'When Escoffier and Ritz began their careers together,' wrote Ritz's widow Marie Louise, 'the *tempo* of life was increasing and even more important than that, perhaps, was the fact that the epoch of the "New Woman" had begun. Women were beginning in the Eighties to demand equal rights with men – even in such matters as food! They were beginning to assert their right to appear in public places with men, and to share some of their worldly pleasures. When Ritz decorated and furnished his hotels he always considered *first* the requirements and taste of ladies, and Escoffier was the first great chef to esteem their taste in food or cater for it.'

The Savoy and the other new hotels of the time were not simply hotels with restaurants: they were part of fashionable life, places where men took women in order that the latter could show off their clothes. The new hotel restaurants, wrote Escoffier, 'allow of observing and being observed, since they are eminently adapted to the exhibiting of magnificent dresses.' Their customers, he added, 'only had eyes for one another.' They were not interested in paying serious attention to large amounts of different kinds of food and wine, or to problems of combining the one with the other. They simply ordered champagne and got on with it. As Colonel Newnham-Davis pointed out in his guide to London's restaurants, 'In Paris, no man dreams of drinking champagne, and nothing but champagne, for dinner; but in London . . . ladies as a rule will consider a dinner at a restaurant incomplete without champagne. Ninety-nine out of a hundred Englishmen, in ordering a little dinner for two, turn instinctively to the champagne page of the wine-card. It is wrong, but until we . . . give up taking ladies out to dinner, champagne will be practically the only wine drunk at restaurants.' Indeed, champagne became so popular in this period that by the end of the nineteenth century total annual consumption of champagne in Britain had passed seven million bottles, a figure not again achieved until 1982.

Once it had become fashionable for both sexes to dine in public, to dress up in order to do so, and to drink champagne, it was not long before the hotel or restaurant dinner developed into a ceremony at which social standing was displayed. The high quality of the food that was produced, and the wine that was drunk, served not as a focus in themselves but as a means to an end: a public demonstration of status, of sophistication and of good taste. The elaborate rules that were developed in order to add to the ceremony of the occasion – such as the wearing of long gloves by women and white bow-ties by men – served to establish the restaurant dinner of the fifty years before the Second World War as a ceremony that was suited to the rulers of a great empire: a visible expression of their civilization and of their superiority over the peoples they governed – people whom they disparaged for regarding eating, like sex, as a simple and open expression of sensual pleasure.

Some wags have suggested that it was fortunate that diners concentrated on ceremony in this way because it distracted them from the necessity of eating the poor quality food. This cannot be correct. There was no difference between the restaurant food produced under the supervision of Escoffier in England and what he produced for Ritz's hotel ventures on the Continent. The poor reputation that is enjoyed internationally by British food today is a product, not of the incompetence of late Victorian and Edwardian chefs, but of the lack of interest shown in the taste of food by their customers, who wished to preserve their own social sensibilities and to emphasize their country's imperial grandeur. Certainly, no such reputation had existed before this period, despite the excessive concentration of British chefs on plain roast meat. Indeed, the first grand restaurant to be opened in Paris, in the 1780s, was named in homage to the quality of the food that was produced in the London taverns of this period – La Grande Taverne de Londres.

It is a moot point whether these Victorian values have altogether been abandoned today. There may no longer be an empire to rule, nor natives to lord it over, but the open expression of sensual pleasure is still not a British characteristic. On the face of it, it might seem that the popularity of oriental cuisines, with their sensual, spicy flavours, is a manifestation of a rejection of food as status in preference of food as pleasure. But in fact oriental-style cuisines enjoy a relatively lowly status compared with European cooking: the prices that are generally charged for Indian, Chinese and Thai food are much less than those for French or Italian food of equivalent or even lower quality. The British regard Eastern highly-spiced food as inferior to Western savoury cuisine partly because they have been taught by tradition to do so, but partly also for the very reason that the flavours are openly exciting and sensual.

The British also continue to shy away from the expression of open sensual pleasure in drink. It may appear to be contradictory that a nation whose inhabitants take care to avoid public indulgence in sensual pleasure has been able to acquire the international reputation of being the home of wine con-noisseurship. But what the British have done is to treat wine as an intellectual rather than a sensual pleasure: as something to be analysed rather than something to be enjoyed. This may well explain why British wine-connoisseurs in the twentieth century have tended to prefer clarets to burgundies. Clarets can be understood in terms of their structure, balance, weight and length; burgundies cannot be studied in this way: they are sensual wines, which exist to be enjoyed, openly and without shame.

Moreover, in order that the taste of fine wines should be enjoyed most fully, it is necessary to suck in air in order to aerate the wine in the mouth. This is done by wine-tasters at professional tastings, but if they were to extend this practice into a social context it would be condemned – because sucking is a sexual act. Lips are sexual organs as well as being the part of the mouth through which a human being first feeds – a fact that led the sexologist Havelock Ellis to equate breast-feeding with sexual intercourse. 'In both cases,' he wrote, 'we may observe the phenomenon of detumescence in an organ which has momentarily swelled and which, through the expulsion of a precious liquid, leads to the complete, physical and psychic satisfaction of the persons involved. The swollen breast corresponds to the erect penis, the avid, humid mouth of the child to the palpitating, humid vagina.' Freud, too, described the sucking of the infant as the first sexual act of the human being. This sexual pleasure is at first bound up with the action of feeding at the mother's breast but the child soon learns to separate the two. It is presumably because of its sexual connotations that adults have abandoned sucking – at least in public – with the result that professional wine-tasters take care not to indulge noisily in extracting maxi-mum pleasure from the consumption of fine wine.

The British avoidance of public display of sensual pleasure goes a long way to explain why attitudes towards the matching of food and drink are founded in the traditions that were established in the late nineteenth and early twentieth century rather than being based on contemporary experimentation. But then, given the choice, the British will usually prefer the old to the new.

3

NOBLE ROT

IT IS GENERALLY BELIEVED TODAY, BOTH IN FRANCE AND BRITAIN, that French food is superior. This may or may not be true. The quality of the food that is served in the majority of French restaurants has declined significantly in recent years, with an increasing reliance on pre-prepared dishes and microwave ovens. There are many fine restaurants still, but there are an increasing number of those in Britain. Moreover, the kind of food that is currently fashionable in restaurants in France is the same as that which is fashionable in Britain. It is not so much a French but an Italian style of food, a simpler cuisine that seeks to emphasize the flavours of individual ingredients; it is French only in so far as it is made in France using largely French ingredients. The most prominent exponent of this new French 'Mediterranean' style and its tireless promoter is the thirty-five-year-old Alain Ducasse, chef at the Louis XV restaurant in the Hôtel de Paris in Monte Carlo, for which he was awarded three stars by the Michelin guide within three years of opening.

If French food is generally regarded as superior, it is partly because the French have made a better job of promoting their cuisine than other countries. In considering why England, a richer country than France with a vastly richer aristocracy, failed to create the reputation for its food in the nineteenth century that France managed to do, the historian Theodore Zeldin suggests that one explanation lay in the fact that 'The French have put much more effort into propaganda about their food and they exported a very large number of cooks, whereas the English sent abroad more colonists, missionaries and administrators.'

The myth that French cuisine is superior to that of other countries is paralleled by a similar myth of the superiority of French wine. This myth is widely believed, not only by the majority of French people, wine-makers, wine-drinkers and tee-totallers alike, but also in what continues quaintly to be described in wine circles as the New World.

A hundred years ago, Californian wines had to pass under phony French labels in order to be accepted by American wine-drinkers. Retailers in Boston and New York sold their lesser European wines with Californian labels, and their better Californian wines with European ones. Moreover, substantial quantities of Californian wines were exported to Europe, and it was claimed that some of them were re-exported to America bearing French labels. American wine-makers may no longer pretend that their wines come from Europe, but they still dignify them with French names such as champagne, burgundy and chablis.* Schramsberg, which was established in the Napa Valley in 1965, has enjoyed an international reputation ever since President Nixon had thirteen cases flown over to Peking in order that they could be served at his historic banquet for Premier Chou En-lai. In the American market, Schramsberg is sold as 'champagne'. The reason for this, explains its owner Jack Davies, is that consumers would not expect a bottle labelled simply 'sparkling wine' to be of high quality – that, in other words, an American sparkling wine can only attain an up-market reputation if it accretes to itself some of the trappings of France.

Some producers have found ways of identifying their product even more closely with champagne than Schramsberg has been. The first winery to be established at Hammondsport in the Finger

---

*They use these names for the wines they sell domestically, but not for the ones that they export to Europe, since this would be forbidden by European Union law. Thus, Gallo Hearty Burgundy is sold in Britain as Gallo Dry Red.

Lakes in New York State was the Pleasant Valley Wine Company, which was founded in 1860 in order to produce a sparkling wine in the French style. In order that the French connection should be made as obvious as possible, it obtained the post office address of Rheims, which it used on its letterhead for the next hundred years. The Rheims post office may long since have been closed, but the tiny village of that name still exists. In 1991 a dozen French wineries filed suit in the Federal District Court in Rochester in an attempt to stop Philippe Guermonprez from selling the produce of his Finger Lakes winery under the label 'Château de Rheims'. Guermonprez argued that, because he lived in the village of Rheims, the law was on his side. It was not. When the case was decided at the end of the year Guermonprez was ordered to cease using the name 'Château de Rheims' and to destroy all existing labels within six months. It is easy enough to determine what was Guermonprez's reasoning in all this. As a native of France, he perfectly well understood that American consumers prefer that their domestic wines should be as French as possible.

The American conception that French wines are superior derives from the fact that French wines came first, and that American wine-makers began by copying them. They planted French vine varieties, notably the Cabernet Sauvignon and Merlot of Bordeaux and the Chardonnay and Pinot Noir of Burgundy and Champagne, and they employed French wine-making techniques. Not only do the most prestigious American wines today continue to be made from French vine varieties, but many American wine-makers continue to copy French techniques. It is believed by many connoisseurs that the best Pinot Noirs in America are being produced, not in the Napa Valley in California, but in the Willamette Valley in Oregon, where the first vineyards were established by emigrants from California in the late 1960s. On the principle that the climate of the Willamette Valley was closer to that of the Côte d'Or in Burgundy than to that of the Napa Valley, many of these immigrants adopted Burgundian wine-making methods. For example, Pat Campbell, co-owner and wine-maker at Elk Cove, planted the Burgundian vine varieties Pinot Noir and Chardonnay in 1974 because, she says, she loved burgundies. She visited Burgundy in 1976 during the harvest before making her first wine in 1977; she freely admits that she 'tried to learn by copying Burgundian techniques.' A decade later,

Russ Raney set up Evesham Wood after corresponding with Henri Jayer, the most celebrated wine-maker in Burgundy. Raney, who describes Jayer as his mentor, even fermented some of his Pinot Noir grapes in the 1989 vintage with the yeast taken from the sediment in a bottle of Jayer's wine – and released the result as a separate 'Cuvée J', at nearly twice the price of his ordinary Pinot Noir. 'I'm not ashamed to admit that we would like to emulate Burgundy,' he explains.

Every summer since 1987 Oregonian wine-makers have organized a Pinot Noir Conference, which they have paid Burgundian wine-makers to fly over to attend. In 1989 Philippe Senard of Domaine Senard in Aloxe-Corton came over and spoke about his trendy new method of macerating the grapes in their juice at a low temperature before fermentation. Two months later, most Oregon wine-makers were trying it out. Because this method extracts more fruit and colour from the grapes, it can be useful in Burgundy where red wines made from the Pinot Noir grape have often been found to be lacking in these qualities, but it is not necessary in Oregon where Pinot Noirs are naturally deep-coloured and fruity. There is, indeed, no good reason why Burgundian methods should be the ideal ones for Oregon. The climate may be closer to that of Burgundy than to that of California – indeed, the average growing temperature during the season is very similar to that of Burgundy – but this does not mean that the climate is practically the same as far as the vines are concerned. Oregon is warmer than Burgundy during the day and colder at night so the vines grow differently. They are also trained in a different way. It is therefore not surprising that the grapes they produce differ from those in Burgundy, from which it would logically follow that they should be vinified in a different way. But, in general, they are not. 'People follow Burgundy,' says one Oregonian observer, 'because they don't know any better. Americans have no cultural heritage, so they have to have someone to imitate.'

The extent of French cultural heritage is undeniable, and the French make great use of it in selling their wines. The international reputation of the fine wines of Champagne and Bordeaux dates back to the seventeenth century when the Count of Saint Evremond introduced champagne to the English court, and François-Auguste de Pontac opened the Sign of Pontac's Head in the City of London to sell Château Haut-Brion for seven shillings a bottle. The reputation of the fine wines of Burgundy dates back further still, to the Valois Dukes of the fourteenth and fifteenth centuries. In the early fourteenth century, red burgundy (then known as 'Beaune') and a wine that has been all but forgotten today – that of Saint-Pourçain-sur-Sioule – shared the same status, and appeared alongside each other on the dinner tables of the French King and of the Pope. The significance of Saint-Pourçain-sur-Sioule was that it was the most prestigious of the wines produced within the domain of the French royal house of Bourbon. A new Duke of Burgundy, Philip the Bold, was determined that the wine that was produced within his domain should be the most prestigious within France – especially after his marriage to Margaret, daughter of the Duke of Flanders, added a major wine-consuming country to his possessions. In 1375, when at Bruges with other great French nobles to meet the envoys of the King of England and also the Pope to discuss the possibility of ending the war between France and England, Philip took care to ensure that substantial quantities of Beaune were consumed; on several occasions he sent large amounts of Beaune both to his father-in-law the Count of Flanders and to his nephew King Charles VI of France; and in 1395, when staying at his palace in Paris, he held splendid festivities at which he dispensed the contents of two hundred casks of Beaune of the best quality.

More significant than this, however, was the wine that Philip sent to the Pope. In 1308 a papal quarrel led Clement V, the former archbishop of Bordeaux, to move the site of the papacy to Avignon. The new papal court was encouraged to acquire a taste for the wines of Beaune, and did so readily. By 1364 it had become necessary for the Avignonese Pope Urban V to issue a bull (an edict) forbidding the Abbot of Cîteaux to send any wine to Rome on pain of excommunication. In 1366 the celebrated Italian poet and scholar Petrarch, then nearing the end of his life, wrote to Urban V urging him to return the seat of the papacy to Rome, adding that the cardinals were unwilling to go back because there was no Beaune in Italy: they did not believe they could lead a happy life without Beaune, which they considered as though it were the fifth element.* By the fifteenth century, not

---

*It was believed in the Middle Ages that all substances were composed of four elements: fire, air, water and earth.

only had the wine of Saint-Pourçain-sur-Sioule disappeared from the list of wines served at the most brilliant festivals, but it was generally believed that the position of Beaune at the summit of the hierarchy of wines was no less contestable than that of the Pope at the summit of the hierarchy of mankind.

The fact that burgundies today are sold at least in part on their medieval heritage is evidenced by the deliberately antiquated labels that most bottles bear – and is admitted by Robert Drouhin, one of the most respected of Burgundian merchants and certainly the one with the highest profile. 'We don't sell wine,' he said, 'we sell luxury. We sell the image of the cobbled streets of Beaune.'

The French have come increasingly to rely on their cultural heritage to sell their wines as a result of comparative tastings in which clarets (red Bordeaux) and burgundies have been out-performed by wines from California and Oregon. The latter state was put on the world wine map by two such tastings in 1979 and 1980. The first of them, the Gault-Millau 'Wine Olympiad', had in fact been won by an Australian wine, Tyrrell's Pinot Noir 1976; the 1975 Eyrie Vineyards Pinot Noir Reserve from Oregon had come third. Drouhin said that the reason why red burgundies had not done as well as expected was that the tasting had not been a fair one: that the best red burgundies had not been chosen to compete with the best of the New World wines. He organized a rematch in 1980, with red burgundies selected from his own cellars. This time, the 1975 Eyrie Reserve came second, behind Drouhin's Chambolle-Musigny 1959 but ahead of his *grand cru* Chambertin-Clos de Bèze 1961.

These tastings exerted less influence, however, than one held in the American Bicentennial Year of 1976, which first put Californian wines on the map. This tasting had been organized by Steven Spurrier, an English wine merchant who owned a wine shop in Paris called Les Caves de la Madeleine; the purpose of the tasting was to publicize the shop. Wary of possible French reaction, Spurrier had (in his own words) 'rigged' the tasting so that the French wines would win. Against the Californian Cabernet Sauvignons and Chardonnays he pitted first-growth clarets and *premier cru* and *grand cru* white burgundies, all from good or very good vintages; and all the tasters were French. In fact, Stag's Leap Wine Cellars 1973, from California, came out top of the Cabernet Sauvignon class, ahead of Château Mouton-

Rothschild 1970; and Château Montelena 1973, which (despite its name) also came from California, came out top among the Chardonnays, ahead of the Meursault *premier cru* Les Charmes from Guy Roulot.

The French judges at this tasting pointed out, quite rightly, that the Californian wines were big and fruity and showed especially well in their youth; they claimed, more dubiously, that they won the tasting, not because they were better, but because they were ready to drink, while the wines with which they were competing were not. When, however, at the instigation of Warren Winiarski, owner of Stag's Leap Wine Cellars, Steven Spurrier organized a repeat tasting of the same wines ten years later, it was not the Stag's Leap Wine Cellars 1973 that came top of the Cabernet Sauvignon class but Clos du Val 1972, which (despite *its* name) also came from California; second was Ridge Montebello Range 1971, again from California; the top-placed French wine was Château Montrose 1970, which came third. 'This seems to prove,' commented Spurrier, 'that California Cabernets do age.'

The response that French wine-makers have now offered to the results of tastings such as these has been to introduce an element of mysticism into the equation – to talk up their soil (*terroir*). Wines from the New World cannot possibly be compared to the best clarets and burgundies, they say, because, however good the grape-growing and wine-making might be, they do not have the French soil. In particular, they do not have limestone. California can never produce Chardonnay to rival Burgundy, say French wine-makers, nor Oregon such good Pinot Noir, because the vines do not grow on limestone subsoil, as they do in Burgundy. The superiority of limestone, they add, is demonstrated by experience. It is not, however, demonstrated by science. No expert is able adequately to explain in what way the presence of limestone might affect the flavour of the wines that have been made from the vines that grow upon it. Bailey Carrodus, who produces some of the finest wines in Australia at Yarra Yering in the Yarra Valley, used to work for the government as a plant physiologist. Yet, when asked how soil types affected wine flavour, he replied that he had no idea. 'Soil science,' he explained, 'is not well advanced. We do not yet understand the underlying principles.'

Despite the lack of evidence to explain the link between the two, the circumstantial connection between the quality of red and white burgundy and the presence of limestone subsoil has led several major vine-growers in California and Australasia to plant their Chardonnay and Pinot Noir vineyards on limestone subsoil. Josh Jensen of Calera and Dick Graff of Chalone have gone so far as to plant vineyards in the inaccessible heights of the Gavilan Mountains in central California because that is where they have been able to find limestone. Their adherence to the importance of limestone has led Jensen, Graff and their like to be described as '*terroiristes*' – believers in the importance of *terroir*.

It is not only the French who fall into this obfuscation. Many British connoisseurs of burgundy have been taught to recognize as the taste of the *terroir* what is in fact a product, not of peculiarly Burgundian soil, but of peculiarly Burgundian wine-making defects. 'There is something animal, often something erotic about great burgundy,' wrote the wine merchant Anthony Hanson in his seminal book on the region. He added, in a phrase that will live for ever, 'Great burgundy smells of shit.'

This 'animal' character is a product of wine-making methods that are practised in Burgundy, which – despite the adoption by Oregonian wine-makers of the majority of Burgundian techniques – differ in a few important respects from those used in the New World. In Burgundy, many growers continue to produce their red wines in essentially the same way as they have for centuries, bringing the grapes in from the vineyard, pouring them into open wooden vats and leaving them there until they start to ferment. During fermentation, the grape skins tend to settle and form a cap on the top of the juice. The cap needs to be mixed back into the juice in order to maximize the extraction of colour and tannins and to stop vinegar from developing. The operation of punching down the cap is called *pigeage*. Traditionally, it was performed by the wine-maker climbing into the vat. According to one story, before the French Revolution, at the then monastic vineyard of Clos de Vougeot, the monks who used to make the wine climbed naked into the vats on three occasions during vinification. 'It was the only occasion in the year when the monks had a bath and for many years after this unhygienic stirring was abandoned it was said that a real burgundy expert could declare by taste whether a wine was pre- or post-*pigeage*.'

In general, wine-makers who produce red wines in America and

Australasia from Pinot Noir, the grape that is used to produce red burgundy, pour the grapes into stainless steel rather than wooden vats, and add a cultured yeast strain in order to induce fermentation artificially. The difference between New World Pinot Noirs and red burgundies should be attributed in part to the fact that burgundies are fermented with naturally-occurring vineyard and cellar yeast strains. When, in 1989, Russ Raney fermented a batch of his grapes with yeast that he had taken from the sediment in a bottle of Henri Jayer's burgundy, the wine turned out to be softer and richer than wine from the same vineyard fermented with a selected, commercially available yeast strain. In Raney's opinion, 'It has, compared with the other yeast types, a definite Burgundy "barnyard" character.' Growers in Burgundy describe this 'barnyard character' as being *le goût du terroir* – the taste of the soil. If it has come into the wine as a result of fermentation with the natural vineyard yeasts, then this description is probably appropriate.

There are other means, however, by which red burgundy can develop animal, not to say faecal, aromas. It may well be that bacteria are responsible. John Middleton, the owner of Mount Mary vineyard in the Yarra Valley in Victoria, makes some of the most Burgundian Pinot Noirs and Chardonnays in Australia yet condemns many of the wines made in Burgundy as 'crap'. The problem, he believes, is that they go through their malolactic fermentation – in which harsh malic acid is converted into softer lactic acid – when they are already very low in acidity. In these conditions, a bacterium called *Pediococcus* often gets to work on the malic acid, and 'he can really shit in your wine'. Jean-Pierre de Smet, the wine-maker at Domaine de l'Arlot in Nuits-Saint-Georges, agrees that bacteria are involved, but believes that it has less to do with the action of bacteria during the malolactic fermentation than with the effect of the bacteria that are present in the lees – the dregs that settle at the bottom of the cask during maturation. 'Burgundies,' he says, 'acquire a gamey taste from spending too long in contact with their lees in cask. It is a defect. I do not want it in my wine.'

If bacteria are the cause of faecal aromas and gamey tastes, then it is simple enough to explain why these characteristics become more pronounced during ageing in bottle. The bacteria attack the acids and other constituents of the wine and break them down.

Although it has not been proven that bacteria play an important role during ageing in bottle, this would certainly explain the effect of cellar temperatures on the ageing of red burgundies. At under 10°C, a wine ages too slowly; at 15°C or over it ages too fast. This may well be related to the speed at which the bacteria work. It is certainly the reason why a cellar should be between 10°C and 14°C.

The introduction of defects into Burgundian wine-making techniques may also serve to explain much of the difference between New World Chardonnays and white burgundies. In America and Australasia, wine-makers like to work with clean, healthy grapes; if they need more ripeness, they simply leave the grapes longer on the vines before picking them; if they need more acid, they simply add it to the wine during or after fermentation. The tradition in Burgundy is very different. According to Roland Rapet, a leading producer of the *grand cru* Corton-Charlemagne, vine-growers in Burgundy have traditionally picked a mixture of one half ripe, healthy grapes, one quarter unripe grapes, to give the wine more acidity, and one quarter 'nobly-rotten' grapes, to give it more body.

Now, 'noble rot' is the term that is used in the wine business to describe the effect of the *botrytis cinerea* fungus on ripe grapes; it is responsible for producing the world's finest sweet white wines, Sauternes from Bordeaux in south-west France and the Auslesen, Beerenauslesen and Trockenbeerenauslesen of the Rhine and Mosel valleys in south-west Germany. 'Noble rot' is an oxymoron, because normally, if the rot fungus is allowed to develop, the grapes are ruined. But in the autumn in Sauternes, the Rhine and the Mosel, if it is foggy in the morning and dry and sunny in the afternoon, the rot fungus simply shrivels the grapes and concentrates their flavours, allowing delicious sweet wines to be produced. Burgundy, on the other hand, does not generally enjoy weather conditions such as these. It is true that in the unusual 1983 vintage the weather was hot and humid at the same time, and *botrytis* did develop in Burgundy on ripe grapes. But in most years there is nothing noble about the rot other than the fact that it has been produced in Burgundy. It is grey rot, the term that is used by wine-makers to describe the effect of the *botrytis* fungus on *un*ripe grapes, and which is responsible for ruining many vintages of red burgundy. If it does not ruin the white wines as it does the red, it is because white grapes are not fermented in contact with their skins. In 1975 the vintage was disastrous for red wines but some of the white wines, although they were no less badly infected with rot, turned out very well: they were fragile but the rot made them richer and softer than they would otherwise have been. Grey rot also contributed an exotic aspect to the bouquet of many 1986 white burgundies, a vintage that was acclaimed in its youth but whose potential for long-term maturation is now generally considered to be doubtful.

The strange aromas that are produced by allowing rot-infected grapes to be fermented by naturally occurring yeast strains have led many Californian and Australian wine-makers to condemn burgundies as defective. Not only is James Halliday Australia's most prominent wine writer and a leading wine show judge but he also makes an excellent Chardonnay at his Coldstream Hills vineyard in the Yarra Valley in Victoria. He has collected a large range of white burgundies over the years but now, he says, he is selling them off. Much of his life has been devoted to criticizing wines and seeking out their defects; he can no longer drink white burgundies without noticing the defects and being upset by them.

It is true that Burgundian wine-makers sometimes allow too many defects into their wines, and ruin them. But on other occasions the defects are small enough to ensure that their effect is to make the wines more complex and more exciting. Clean, technically perfect wines are boring. Burgundies may have defects, which may sometimes destroy them; but, to make great wine, it is necessary to live dangerously.

Even if defects do serve a positive function, however, it is essential to their purpose that French wine-makers should continue to insist that all the unusual characteristics of their fine wines should be attributed, not to wine-making techniques, but to the soil of the vineyard. The French emphasis on *terroir* serves not only to combat competition from wine-makers in America and Australasia, but also to create an aura around the most famous French wines: to establish them as natural phenomena, beyond the control of man. According to Comte Henri de Vaucelles, the owner of Château Filhot in Sauternes, 'A luxury product must never say that it is manufactured: it must be a miracle of climate and soil.' That is why, he says, each region has invented its own legend: this enhances the miraculous, and thus inimitable, nature of its wines.

The vineyards of Côte-Rôtie, one of the three most prestigious red wine *appellations* of the Northern Rhône valley – Hermitage and Cornas being the others – are generally regarded as being divided into two slopes, the Côte Brune and the Côte Blonde, which produce wines of very different character: more profound from the Côte Brune, more showy from the Côte Blonde. This division and the village as a whole have attracted a great deal of attention in recent years thanks to the efforts of Marcel Guigal, the wine merchant who commercializes one third of the entire production of the *appellation*. In particular, Guigal has been successful in obtaining high ratings from wine writers and high prices in the marketplace for his three single-vineyard Côte-Rôties, La Mouline, La Landonne and La Turque – a success that has reflected a considerable amount of glory on the region as a whole. Now, Guigal describes La Mouline as quintessential Côte Blonde, La Landonne as classic Côte Brune, and La Turque as a Brune with Blonde characteristics. On tasting, it is evident that La Mouline is more perfumed and elegant, and La Landonne richer and more powerful but dumber in its youth, while La Turque combines the best elements of the two. These prosaic distinctions are brought to life by the local legend, that of a nobleman who owned the hillside in the Middle Ages and who had two daughters, a blonde and a brunette. For their inheritance, he divided the vineyard between them. The slope inherited by the blonde produced wine which was pretty in its youth but faded quickly; wine from the slope inherited by the brunette was shy at first but developed splendidly.

In Alsace, too, the reputation of the most prestigious single-vineyard wine is assisted by a local legend. It was in the vineyard of Brand in the village of Turckheim that in the Middle Ages (according to the legend) a battle took place between the sun and a local dragon. Not surprisingly, the dragon lost; he was burnt to the ground, leaving nothing more than a brand in the earth. As the legend has it, the battle infused the soil with a heat so fierce that the grapes would ever afterwards have great colour and extraordinary ripeness. Certainly, the village of Turckheim is one of the few places in Alsace capable of producing a decent red wine from the Pinot Noir grape. Once upon a time, the village was planted entirely with black varieties and was famous for a red wine known as 'Turk's Blood'. Although some red wine is still produced here, it is the full-bodied white wine from the Tokay-Pinot Gris, a mutation of the Pinot Noir, that is the finest product of Brand today.

The name Tokay-Pinot Gris is the product of a compromise. Elsewhere in France, this grape is simply called Pinot Gris; one might therefore have expected that it would pass by this name in Alsace also, especially since it arrived in the region from Burgundy and bears no relationship to the grapes that are used in the manufacture of the Hungarian wine called Tokay. Yet, until a recent ruling by the French authorities, wines that were made from the Pinot Gris grape in Alsace were not even labelled 'Tokay-Pinot Gris' but simply 'Tokay'. The origin of the name derives from the legend that in the 1560s a colonel in the imperial army called Baron Lazare de Schwendli led a regiment in an expedition against the Ottoman Turks. Having attacked and captured the Turkish fortress at Tokay, Schwendli then expelled its defenders and seized four thousand vats of Tokay wine as booty. He enjoyed this wine so much that he took back cuttings of the vine from which it had been made. Unfortunately for the Alsatians, this legend is disproved not only by the dissimilarity of Tokay-Pinot Gris and the grapes that were (and are) used to produce Hungarian Tokay, but also by the fact that there is no evidence that this grape was growing in Alsace before the mid-seventeenth century nor that it was called 'Tokay' before the mid-eighteenth. It is likely that the story was invented at some point during the eighteenth century, at a time when Tokay was the most famous wine in the world, the choice of monarchs such as Peter the Great of Russia and Frederick I of Prussia; that the Alsatians were simply hoping that some of the glory of Tokay would rub off on their own, humbler produce.

Tokay enjoyed an elevated reputation partly because it was believed to contain gold. This story was originally propagated at the beginning of the sixteenth century by the Italian humanist author Marzio Galeotto who, following a visit to Hungary, claimed that the hills contained strains of gold ore, that their sands contained grains of gold, and that there were golden shoots on some vines in Tokay. The famous physician and alchemist Paracelsus of Basel came to Hungary in order to find out the truth of this story for himself. Despite performing prolonged experiments on the grapes and wines, he failed to extract gold from them, but he was not downhearted: he offered the opinion that 'The vine of the Hegyalja region is the most magnificent plant because in that country vegetals are allied to minerals, and sunshine, like a thread of gold, passes through stock and roots into the rock.' This verdict was sufficiently obscure, and sufficiently promising, to ensure that the myth about the gold content of Tokay was kept alive for centuries. The myth, in turn, helped in the marketing of the wine. In his *Travels in Hungary*, published at the height of the wine's fame, in the late eighteenth century, Robert Townson observed that 'Tokay is no doubt a fine wine, but, I think, no ways adequate to its price: there are few of my countrymen . . . who would not prefer to it good claret or burgundy, which do not cost one-forth the price.' Forty years later, the English wine writer Cyrus Redding described the high price put on Tokay as an 'example of the caprice of taste or fashion in wine', adding that 'The peculiar flavour in the wine of Tokay . . . has nothing more than its singularity to recommend it.'

Tokay might not have justified its high price by containing gold, but it was made from nobly-rotten grapes. Indeed, it was at Tokay – again according to legend – that the suitability of apparently spoiled grapes for making fine sweet wine was first 'discovered'. This was in 1650, when Prince Rákóczi, the ruler of Transylvania, delayed the harvest in Tokay until late November because he was expecting the Turks to attack. It is unlikely to be a coincidence, however, that Rákóczi's father had acquired the castle of Tokay and the vineyards that surrounded it only three years earlier; it would not be surprising if he had sought to claim the credit for a discovery that had in fact been made some years previously.

Nevertheless, if tradition is to be believed, until the late eighteenth century Tokay was the only wine in the world to be made deliberately from nobly-rotten grapes. According to a standard account of events that has been reproduced in a large number of wine books, the properties of noble rot were unknown in Western Europe before they were discovered, again by accident, at Schloss Johannisberg in Germany, in 1775. At this time this estate was owned by the Bishop of Fulda, whose permission was needed before the harvest could begin. In the year in question, as the grapes were reaching ripeness, a messenger was sent from the estate to Fulda, a hundred miles away, to ask for permission to start picking, but for some reason his return was delayed by a couple of weeks. In the meantime, the grapes had been contaminated by rot. They were picked, but the wine made from them was kept separate in case it spoiled the rest. It turned out to be marvellous. From this point on, whenever the season permitted, sweet wines were deliberately produced in the Rhineland from nobly-rotten grapes. If legend is to be believed, however, it was not until half a century later that the secret of this technique was brought from Germany to Sauternes, by a gentleman called Focke, a native of the Rhineland, when he purchased Château La Tour Blanche.

This may be the generally accepted account, but it is easy to pick holes in it. The fact that a similar story about delaying the harvest should be told of Schloss Johannisberg as was told of Tokay is in itself suspicious. And if Sauternes was not made from nobly-rotten grapes before the 1830s, then what were the 'rotten wines' for which the region was already esteemed in the seventeenth century? And why was the story about Schloss Johannisberg not known to the great American wine connoisseur Thomas Jefferson who visited the estate thirteen years after the event was supposed to have taken place?

According to Comte Henri de Vaucelles, the reason why Jefferson had not heard the story was that it was made up half a century after the event, after the French Revolution, when the estate had passed from the hands of the Church into those of a secular owner, Prince Metternich. Sweet wine had been made from nobly-rotten grapes in France and Germany since the Middle Ages. But its manufacture had had for several centuries to be concealed from its consumers because clerics would have regarded it as heretical to have admitted that their sacramental wine was made from diseased grapes. Instead of describing it as 'nobly rotten', the term used today, they called it '*crème de tête*', meaning 'the cream off the top'. Only when European states were secularized in the nineteenth century could the truth be revealed. It was then that legends were invented to account for the apparently sudden appearance of wine made from nobly-rotten grapes.

Another legend that was developed as a consequence of the French Revolution was the most famous wine legend of them all, that of

Dom Pérignon, who is known to posterity as a blind monk who invented sparkling champagne. During the French Revolution, the Abbey of Hautvillers, where Dom Pérignon had done his work at the end of the seventeenth century, was destroyed. One of the monks who witnessed the destruction of the abbey was Dom Grossard. Thirty years later, when the monarchy had been restored, Dom Grossard went out of his way to exaggerate Dom Pérignon's achievements, in order to emphasize the damage to French culture that had been caused by the Revolution. He attributed to Dom Pérignon all the advances in vine-growing and wine-making that had occurred in his lifetime – including the invention of sparkling champagne.

Now, it is true that Dom Pérignon was a monk who did a great deal to improve the quality of champagne by perfecting the art of blending together wines from different vineyards. But he did not invent sparkling champagne. Indeed, he devoted his energies to blending in order to ensure that the champagne he made would always be a still, white wine. Not only was sparkling champagne something that Dom Pérignon would have regarded as undesirable, but it had already been invented by 1668, the date at which Dom Pérignon arrived in Champagne. And it had been invented, not in France, but in England. This is easily explained. The climate of Champagne was a cool one by viticultural standards, and the harvest late, so the wine did not always finish its fermentation before the winter set in. Some unfermented sugars therefore remained in the wine at the end of the winter, when it was exported to England. When the weather warmed up again in the spring the wine awoke and finished its fermentation. If it had been kept in a cask, as other wines were at the time, the carbon dioxide gas that was given off during the fermentation would have escaped through the staves of the wood. But champagne was kept in bottle, because it was too delicate to survive in cask. The gas was trapped in the bottle, and the wine sparkled. Because the gas applied great pressure on the sides of the bottle, a new type of stronger glass was required. As it happened, just such a type of glass was invented in England at this time, as a by-product of the needs of the Navy. Admiral Sir Robert Mansell had been concerned at the destruction of forests by glass-makers and had persuaded King James I to prohibit the use of wood in glass-works furnaces. Coal was employed instead, and found to be better.

The introduction of coal-fired furnaces in glass-making led to the invention of lead crystal bottles. The introduction of these stronger bottles explains why sparkling champagne became popular in England whilst wine-makers in France were still trying to ensure that it stayed still.

Not only did Dom Grossard make up the story that Dom Pérignon invented sparkling champagne but he also added an extra element of romance to Dom Pérignon's genuine achievement, the selection and blending of the best qualities of grapes from different vineyards, by devising the story that Dom Pérignon was blind. The idea of a blind monk who could identify wines from different vineyards purely by taste immediately took hold on the popular imagination. And the story that it had been invented at an abbey lent respectability to sparkling champagne, which in its early days had been associated exclusively with dissipation and seduction.

The legend of Dom Pérignon has contributed greatly to the image of champagne as a whole, and especially to that of Moët et Chandon, the company that purchased the site of the Abbey of Hautvillers, reconstructed it, and turned it into a museum. Wine made from the grapes that continue to grow in the vineyards around the abbey, although no longer of the very highest quality, contributes to the blend of Moët et Chandon's most expensive and most prestigious champagne, 'Dom Pérignon'. Nor is it unlikely to be a coincidence that the person who has done most in recent years to perpetuate the legend of Dom Pérignon – Patrick Forbes, the author of *Champagne: the wine, the land and the people* – was for a number of years the director of Moët et Chandon's London office. In his book, which, although it was published as long ago as 1967, has as a general account of champagne still not adequately been superseded, Forbes included a chapter entitled, 'Dom Pérignon: the legend and the truth'. The truth, as far as Forbes was concerned, was that Dom Pérignon was a blind monk who 'almost certainly was the first man to produce sparkling champagne in France'.

This said, Forbes does admit that the English were bottling champagne so that it would sparkle some years before Dom Pérignon began his work – and one of the most significant aspects of the creation of the legend does lie in the fact that it took away from the English the credit for inventing the most famous of all

French drinks. Indeed, the principal effect of the legend of Dom Pérignon is rather more prosaic than that of the various stories of the discovery of noble rot. Far from enhancing the miraculous, God-given nature of the wine, it focuses on the fact that it is man-made – that, in this instance, man has been able to improve on nature. This poses a problem for its present-day manufacturers, however. Since even they admit that the reputation of champagne depends as much on the skill of the people who make it as on the soil in which the vines grow, they are less easily able to defend themselves against competition from copies of champagne in other parts of the world by pointing to the uniqueness of their *terroir*. They do use the soil argument – but they support it in this case by defending the good name of champagne with great ferocity. They may not have always been successful in their efforts in this direction in the United States, but they have been successful in Europe, and especially in their most important European market, that of Great Britain.

The 'Costa Brava champagne' case arose as a result of the discovery by a young English student called Michael Grylls of Spanish sparkling wine when on holiday on the Costa Brava in the 1950s. With the assistance of a wealthy Spanish businessman, Grylls founded the Costa Brava Wine Company and imported Perelada sparkling wine, which he then advertised as 'Spanish champagne'. In 1958 the champagne industry launched a criminal prosecution against Grylls for fraudulent mislabelling under the Merchandise Marks Act. The judge summed up in the industry's favour but the jury sympathized with the young man and found in favour of the Costa Brava Wine Company.

Grylls's acquittal caused a great deal of anger in France, where it was popularly believed that the British government had engineered the result as part of a plot to sabotage French wine exports just when France and five other countries were about to start operating the European Economic Community. Some bars in Paris refused for a time to serve Scotch whisky, and a consignment of 'Spanish champagne' on its way to England was turned back by French officials at the Spanish border in the Pyrenees. The French Embassy was concerned that the dispute might escalate, and tried to persuade the champagne producers to drop their action. But they refused. In 1960 they sued Grylls in the civil courts, alleging that he was seeking to 'pass off' as champagne a wine that had neither been produced in the Champagne region of France nor had been made by the champagne method. In this case, which was later described by some French newspapers as 'the Second Battle of the Marne', no jury was involved. The judge found in favour of the champagne industry and ordered the Costa Brava Wine Company to obliterate all mention of the name 'champagne' from its labels within forty-eight hours.*

Ever since the Costa Brava case, the use of the name 'champagne' on wines on sale in Britain has been exclusively reserved to producers of sparkling wine by the champagne method in the Champagne region of France. But the champagne manufacturers have sought to extend their domain considerably further than that. In 1975 they obtained an injunction forbidding the manufacturers of Babycham from describing it as 'champagne perry', and even succeeded in having the use of the name 'Babycham' itself prohibited – although this latter ruling was reversed by the Court of Appeal on the grounds that the champagne industry had not been able to produce a single witness who had been confused by the Babycham label.

Then came the 'elderflower champagne' case. This began in April 1992, when the champagne industry applied to the High Court for an injunction to prevent Guy Woodall, owner of Thorncroft Vineyard in Surrey, from selling a non-alcoholic artificially carbonated elderflower drink as 'elderflower champagne'. Woodall opposed the application, claiming that he too had tradition on his side. 'Thorncroft Elderflower Champagne', he declared, was a traditional English drink, made according to his grandmother's recipe: it appeared from his comments that he wished to give the impression that he was defending English gastronomic culture against a foreign aggressor. In the first instance, the judge did not agree with him. While admitting that 'not even a moron in a hurry would confuse the product with French champagne', Justice Robert Reid granted the injunction, pending a full hearing. The full hearing – that is, a civil action for passing off – took place in the High Court in February 1993, before Sir Mervyn Davies. The judge ruled that the elderflower

---

*Grylls subsequently involved himself in politics, and since 1974 has served as the Conservative Member of Parliament for North-West Surrey.

champagne, which was packaged in champagne-style bottles with wired corks, was indeed a 'misrepresentation calculated to deceive'. But he did not find in favour of the champagne industry. He said that it was unlikely that many members of the public would be deceived by the misrepresentation and that the champagne industry was not likely to suffer substantial damage as a result. He therefore found in favour of Thorncroft Vineyard. After the case, on the steps of the court, Woodall declared that 'The spirit of Agincourt lives on'. As in the first of the Costa Brava cases, it seemed that a young English David had defeated the Goliath of the champagne industry.

In some legal quarters, however, Sir Mervyn Davies's ruling was regarded as rather bizarre. The champagne producers appealed, and in June 1993 the Court of Appeal overturned the decision of the High Court. The Master of the Rolls, Sir Thomas Bingham, ruled that to allow the elderflower drink to be sold as 'champagne' would 'debase and cheapen' the image of genuine champagne. Thorncroft Vineyard was ordered to pay costs, amounting to at least £200,000. The case had been lost in part because – as was also pointed out in the Court of Appeal by Lord Justice Peter Gibson – the suggestion that 'Thorncroft Elderflower Champagne' was a traditional drink was a 'creative interpretation of what was known to Dr Woodall'. Traditional English 'elderflower champagne' was a naturally sparkling, alcoholic drink, produced by marinading elderflowers for twenty-four hours in a mixture of water, sugar and lemon juice, and bottling the resulting liquid in a strong stone vessel. The yeasts from the elderflowers caused the dissolved sugar to ferment, producing a sparkling, alcoholic drink. Modern non-alcoholic sparkling elderflower drinks, such as Thorncroft's, have been made possible by the development of filtration and pasteurization technology. They are produced by adding sparkling water to a bacteriologically sterile cordial made from elderflowers, sugar and lemon juice.

Admittedly, in claiming that his new invention – which he had first produced in 1991 – was in fact a traditional drink Woodall was in very good company. For example, German wines are generally regarded by British consumers as being sweet. Indeed, the production and marketing of inexpensive sweet German wines such as Liebfraumilch has played a major part in encouraging a new generation of Britons to take up drinking wine for the first time. In Germany, however, there were growing demands among consumers in the 1980s for native dry white wines that were suitable for drinking with food. So producers converted from making sweet wines to vinifying dry ones. They sought to justify their conversion from the style of sweet German wines that had proved commercially so successful in Britain by referring to evidence that indicated that in the eighteenth and nineteenth centuries, and maybe even in the first half of the twentieth, the vast majority of German wines were dry. For all that time, sweet wines were an exception, the produce of nobly-rotten grapes in abnormally warm summers. The manufacture of sweet German wines on a commercial scale was only made possible by the development of sophisticated filters after the Second World War. By removing yeasts from the wine, these filters made it possible to bottle a low-alcohol sweet wine without any danger of its refermenting. From then on, wine-makers concentrated on producing sweet wines. If they returned to dry wines in the 1980s and 1990s, it was not because they had suddenly discovered that these were the wines that their forebears once produced. It is not for reasons of authenticity that wine-makers have returned to the production of dry wines after two generations of making them sweet. They have simply wanted to give an historical underpinning to the creation of dry wines in order to satisfy the demands of German consumers. They have also been hoping that, if they propound the idea that German wines were traditionally dry, they might succeed in overturning the down-market image of German wines among British consumers as inexpensive sweet wines for novice drinkers. As yet, this message has been lost on the British market.

Similarly, many French wine-makers go out of their way to describe as traditional their practice of maturing their produce exclusively or almost exclusively in new oak casks, rather than using a preponderance of old oak casks and only renewing a few of them each year. Certainly, there is some evidence that wines were matured in new oak casks in the past, such as in Côte-Rôtie in the northern Rhône valley. Having been renowned in the nineteenth century, Côte-Rôtie fell into decline after the First World War and began to be revived only in the 1980s. The major player in the revival has been Marcel Guigal, whose three single-vineyard Côte-Rôties, La Mouline, La Landonne and

La Turque, have already been mentioned. These wines are all matured entirely in new oak; Guigal himself insists that in doing so he is simply following tradition. 'Last century,' he says, 'top-quality Côte-Rôtie was matured in new oak. Other people stopped it because it was too expensive. We kept it up.' However, Marius Gentaz, who has been making top-class Côte-Rôtie at Domaine Gentaz-Dervieux since the end of the Second World War and who says that he makes his wine in essentially the same way as his father-in-law did before the First World War, avoids new oak altogether. When asked what he thinks of Guigal's wines, Gentaz replies that he sells wine, not oak. 'I experimented with new oak ten years ago and did not like it,' he adds. In his wonderful book *Adventures on the Wine Route* Gentaz's American importer, Kermit Lynch, condemns the popular approbation of Guigal's Côte-Rôtie, which he describes as 'a very anonymous-tasting wine, easily mistaken for a big, oaky Gigondas or even a Bordeaux. It reminded me of an acquaintance who always seemed to have a new girlfriend. His girlfriends all had two things in common: huge breasts. His choice might be pretty or not, interesting or not, intelligent or not. Nothing seemed to matter to him as long as the breasts were enormous.'

Guigal may mature his wines in new oak casks because he believes it improves them, but his ability to sell these wines at high prices and the ability of American wine merchants to sell them at considerably higher prices depend on the fact that the new oak enables them to be appreciated immediately after purchase by consumers whose experience of fine wines is limited and whose storage facilities are nil. This is because wines that have been matured in new oak casks appear much more aromatic and rounded in their youth than comparable wines that have been matured in older casks, the reason being that there is more exchange between the wine inside and the air outside if new casks are used. Also, new casks impart a spicy, toasty, vanillin flavour to the wines that are stored in them. Certainly the taste of new oak is very pronounced in Guigal's single-vineyard wines in their youth, not least in La Landonne. Moreover, those other producers of Côte-Rôtie who have been persuaded by Guigal's success to follow him and begin maturing their own wines in a substantial proportion of new oak casks are in no position to justify themselves by referring to tradition, because in adopting the practice they have simply responded to modern commercial pressures. If they mature their wines in new oak, it is in order that they should taste attractive in their youth, regardless of whether or not they conform to the general understanding of the character of Côte-Rôtie. The decision is a purely commercial one. If the tradition of long ago is invoked, it is in order to legitimize what is patently, in modern terms, an innovation.

In addition, those wine-makers who stored their produce in new oak casks last century did not do so because they liked the taste, but for reasons of hygiene. As is pointed out by Laurent Ponsot, wine-maker at one of the most prestigious and most genuinely traditional estates in Burgundy, Domaine Ponsot in Morey-Saint-Denis, 'New oak is used in the search for artificial aromas. For this reason it is not traditional.' This is especially true in Burgundy, where – as in Côte-Rôtie – there is certainly some historical evidence for the maturation of wines in new oak in the late nineteenth century, but where the raw material in the 1980s and 1990s is completely different from what it was a hundred years earlier. The selections of the Pinot Noir grape variety that were grown then were different ones, the yields were lower, and the grapes were fermented for a longer period. As a result, the wines were more concentrated and tannic, and thus better able to stand up to the taste of the oak. In the late nineteenth century, the effect of maturation in new oak was not totally to dominate the natural flavours of red burgundies. In the late twentieth century, it often is. Indeed, Alain Ambroise, the manager of the Domaine Clos Frantin in Vosne-Romanée, does not believe that people can have used new oak casks in the past, because they matured their wine in casks for more than eighteen months and, in his experience, wine that spends any longer than eighteen months in new oak casks loses its fruit and dries out. Ambroise's grasp of history may be incorrect, but his point is a valid one. Modern red burgundies are generally too delicate to withstand long maturation in new oak. This was not true in the past.

Not only in Burgundy is the good name of tradition used in order to justify the adoption for commercial reasons of the practice of maturing wines in a substantial proportion of new oak casks, but it is also invoked in order to add credibility to what is patently an innovation. The most controversial figure in the region is an oenologist called Guy Accad, who has persuaded a number of wine-makers to subscribe to his method of making red wines by macerating the grape skins in the juice at a low temperature for up to two weeks before fermentation is allowed to begin,* and then fermenting the wine for a very long time at a low temperature in order to extract as much as possible from the grapes.

It might seem absurd for Accad to claim that a wine-making method that depends on modern temperature-control techniques could possibly be traditional, but that is precisely what he does. He points out that in the past, if the weather was cool at harvest time, the grape skins often macerated in the juice of their own accord for a few days before the yeasts had multiplied sufficiently in order to start fermentation; he says that he is simply applying modern knowledge and technology in order better to employ a traditional practice. Accad also claims traditional motives for his long, cold fermentation. He delights in citing 'an old broker' who told him that 'He found in my wines the quality that existed at the start of the 1950s'. Accad explains that these traditional full-bodied red burgundies have been forgotten in the subsequent obsession with modernization, and in the headlong rush in the 1960s and 1970s to produce bigger crops of grapes and lighter, more delicate wines. It would be impossible, says Accad, simply to recreate the wines of the 1950s. 'I use different methods from those employed then because the grapes are different. I have changed the method in order to find the same quality.' Whether Accad has achieved his aim is a moot point. Certainly, he has persuaded some prestigious estates, including Domaine Senard in Aloxe-Corton, Domaine Grivot in Vosne-Romanée and Château de la Tour de Vougeot, to adopt his techniques. They did so only in the late 1980s, however, and, since Accad's methods are supposed to produce wines for long-term maturation, it will not be possible until early in the twenty-first century to arrive at a mature judgement.

Just as in France the good name of tradition is falsely invoked in order to add credibility to new styles of the national drink, wine, so in Britain attempts have been made to enhance the image of

---

*The method that was described earlier as being adopted in Oregon in 1989, in slavish adherence to the latest Burgundian fashion.

new versions of its most traditional drink, beer. In 1988 Guinness launched a new type of canned beer that replicated the creamy head and taste of draught Guinness. It had taken fifteen years and cost £5 million to develop. It involved the insertion of a plastic widget, with a minute hole in it, at the bottom of the can. Beer containing dissolved carbon dioxide and nitrogen gas was then filled into the can at greater than atmospheric pressure. This caused the widget to become partially filled. When the can was opened the fall in pressure forced the mixture of beer and gas through the small hole, thus creating small, relatively stable bubbles. As the bubbles surged through the beer they created a creamy head. The invention of this device won Guinness the Queen's Award for Technological Achievement in 1991.

Other brewers soon followed Guinness's lead, developing similar systems for insertion into a wide range of canned beers, bitters as well as stouts. These new 'canned draught' beers are an undoubted improvement on traditional canned beers. In fermentation, beer produces only one gas, carbon dioxide. When beer is pulled up from a cask in the cellar of a pub to the bar by means of a hand pump, the pump action introduces air into the glass of beer. The nitrogen in the air enhances the texture and head of the beer in the glass because it produces smaller bubbles than those produced by carbon dioxide. Traditional canned beers, which are served without the benefit of a hand pump, contain only carbon dioxide. The new 'canned draught' beers, on the other hand, have nitrogen introduced into them as well, by means of the widget. Not only does the nitrogen make these beers more creamy and give them a better head, but it also protects against oxidation. The brewer can therefore permit these beers to contain less carbon dioxide, and as a result they no longer suffer from the excessive 'gassiness' of canned beers in the past.

The most widely publicized of the new 'canned draught' bitters is Boddingtons, which was launched in this form by Whitbread in April 1990. Partly as a result of an extensive television advertising campaign, in which it has been promoted as 'the cream of Manchester', within five years of its launch sales of 'canned draught' Boddingtons have surpassed fifty million cans a year. The Whitbread 'Draughtflow' system differs from that patented by Guinness in that Whitbread do not inject a mixture of nitrogen and carbon dioxide into the beer but only nitrogen. Steve Philpott,

Whitbread's marketing director, explains that by this means the total amount of carbon dioxide contained in 'canned draught' Boddingtons bitter is much the same as that in cask ale, so it does not taste at all 'gassy'; he also claims that 'the canned Boddingtons "draught" is very similar to the way the Boddingtons is served in its homeland, Manchester'.

This is a matter of considerable controversy. The use of a widget system to produce 'canned draught' stout is understandable. Neither Guinness nor its rivals Beamish and Murphys is served on draught in cask-conditioned form, in which the conditioning – a more complex flavour, and some bubbles of carbon dioxide – is produced by the natural secondary fermentation of the beer in cask, and the beer is brought up to the bar by means of a hand pump; instead they are filtered (and in Britain, but not in Ireland, pasteurized) and forced up to the bar by the pressure of added carbon dioxide. They are given a creamy head by the addition of nitrogen to the carbon dioxide in the dispense system. Thus, there is no qualitative difference between the system used to produce 'canned draught' stout and the means by which the draught version is served.

Draught bitters, on the other hand, are – or should be – cask-conditioned. Filtered, pasteurized and artificially carbonated keg beer had its day in the 1960s and 1970s but has gradually been in decline since then, thanks largely to the efforts of the consumer group the Campaign for Real Ale (CAMRA). Keg beer has proved unpopular partly because the pasteurization destroys much of the flavour. In this respect, lighter-coloured bitters are simply not as robust as dark-coloured stouts. Because 'canned draught' bitter is based on pasteurized keg beer it is inevitably inferior to the cask-conditioned draught version.*

'Canned draught' bitter is also drunk at the wrong temperature. It is essential to serve 'canned draught' beer no warmer than 8°C, in order to prevent the gas from escaping too vigorously.† In the case of stout, this is not very different from the temperature at which the draught version is now served. Draught bitter, on the

*Since 1994 the major brewing companies have been trying to reverse the decline in keg beer sales by introducing 'nitrokeg' beers, essentially 'canned draught' beers on draught.
†At the end of 1994 Bass relaunched its 'canned draught' Worthington Best Bitter with a new type of metal widget, which it claimed would obviate the need to chill the can before opening.

other hand, should be served at 13°C. Finally, there is the north-south divide, to which Philpott obliquely referred. Whereas in the south of England draught beer has traditionally been served fairly flat, in the north of the country it has a thick creamy head. This is produced by a sparkler, which causes turbulence in the beer as it flows through the pump, forcing some of the gas out of solution and into the head. Since the gas that is forced into the head in this manner is carbon dioxide, it is hard to see how Philpott can be correct when he claims that the system that Whitbread uses for 'canned draught' Boddingtons reproduces the northern style of draught beer. The use of nitrogen alone means that 'canned draught' Boddingtons has an even denser, creamier head than the cask-conditioned draught version. As for the creamy head of the 'canned draught' version of southern beer such as Courage Directors, which is brewed in Bristol, this is clearly an aberration.

Whitbread, it must be admitted, has not gone so far as to claim that 'canned draught' Boddingtons is identical to the draught version, nor that it has actually been filled from a hand pump into the can. For its 'canned draught' beer, Bass has stretched the truth a little further. In one advertisement it showed a can of 'Draught Bass' being filled with beer from a traditional hand pump; in 1992 the packaging was redesigned in order actually to feature a hand pump on the can. This and other claims led CAMRA to allege that drinkers were being 'conned'; it said that it had been told by other brewers that they were embarrassed by Bass's misleading advertisements; it cited Peter King, managing director of the Sussex brewery King & Barnes, as saying that 'It's important that the misuse of the term "draught" is stopped. Claiming that the beer in these new cans is the same as the draught version is a serious misrepresentation.'

As a result of CAMRA's accusations, trading standards officers launched an investigation into the labelling of 'canned draught' beers. In February 1993 the Local Authorities' Co-ordinating Body on Food and Trading Standards (LACOTS) issued a consultative paper in which it said that it considered that it was 'inappropriate' to apply the term 'draught' to canned beers, as 'the term "draught" must relate only to the way the beer is delivered and not to its taste or appearance'. This led CAMRA to call for the brewers that produced 'canned draught' beers to be prosecuted for fraud. In the summer of 1993, however, LACOTS backtracked on its earlier advice, stating instead that 'Where canned beer is of the same composition and has the same properties as its bulk-dispensed equivalent, no consumer prejudice arises through describing it as "draught".' This advice is obviously wrong. The brewers may have shied away from stating that their canned draught beer is identical to the draught version, but they have certainly encouraged consumers to believe that this is the case. There are undoubtedly many beer-drinkers who think that there is no difference between canned draught beer and draught beer except that one comes in a little container and the other in a big one. The differences, as have been pointed out, are in fact considerable.

The usurpation of the good name of draught beer by brewers for the labelling of an improved version of their canned beers may be compared to the misleading practice of displaying hand pumps on the bar of a pub when in fact the beer to be dispensed is the filtered, pasteurized and artificially carbonated product of a keg. The presence of a hand pump leads consumers to expect that this pump will be used to draw cask-conditioned beer from the cask, and not merely employed to enhance the status of keg beer. In the February 1987 issue of *What's Brewing*, the CAMRA news-paper, pubs owned by Eldridge Pope, Camerons of Hartlepool and Greenall Whitley were cited as serving keg beer on hand pumps. A spokesman for Greenall Whitley was quoted as having replied that 'Careful market research shows that the majority of the public prefer their beer to be drawn through a hand pump.'

This spokesman had exposed the real reason for the marketing of keg beer on hand pumps, and more recently of canned draught beer. The heritage of British beer is a valuable marketing tool that is ignored by the major brewers at their peril. At the end of the 1980s a marketing psychologist called Thornton Mustard carried out research into the psychology of the British beer-drinker in order to develop a new packaging for cans of Hall & Wood-houses's Tanglefoot Traditional Ale and Badger Country Bitter. The men taking part in the research were asked to select pictures they associated with 'ale' and ones they associated with 'bitter'. The pictures they picked out suggested that the ale drinker is buying into an eighteenth-century rural fantasy, the bitter drinker into a nineteenth-century industrial one, but going back in both cases to the days when men were men, and women provided food and foaming tankards.

Not only are these fantasies exploited by the manner in which beer is packaged but they are also capitalized by the appearance of the places in which beer is served. Pub design has undergone several vicissitudes in recent years. In the 1960s and early 1970s – the age of the Watneys 'Red Revolution' – the insides of many pubs were ripped out and plasticized. Then, in the late 1970s and early 1980s, brewers were sufficiently persuaded by theories of market segmentation to adopt the concept of the 'theme pub' – altering pubs to conform to a number of pre-conceived themes. This was the era that produced disco pubs, sports pubs, American saloons and pubs in an 'old colonial' style. Some of these themes were immediately unsuccessful, others were successful for a while – but not for long enough to repay the capital investment of their owners.

By the 1990s it was evident that the only one of the themes to have proved durable, and to have won widespread acceptance, was the theme of the 'traditional British pub'. That this was a modern theme rather than an attempt genuinely to conform to tradition was evident from the manner in which the redecoration was performed. The method by which a 'traditional British pub' is created today is no different from the system used to produce the more exotic themes of the 1980s. The interior of the pub is ripped out and then filled with a pre-arranged assortment of items that are considered to be conducive to the creation of the desired image, such as wooden beams that are not integral to the structure, horse brasses a century and a half after they were rendered redundant by the coming of the railways, oil lamps and coal scuttles that ignore the introduction of electricity and gas, books that are bought by the yard and old shop signs that are purchased by the van-load. No attention is given to how rural pubs might actually have looked in the eighteenth century, nor urban ones in the nineteenth. No effort is made to reinstate traditional table service nor to restore the succession of individual 'snug' bars that characterized the genuine Victorian pub. All that matters is to fit in as many pseudo-historical references as possible. In the report of the judges of the Pub Design of the Year Awards in 1994, jointly sponsored by CAMRA and English Heritage, it was complained that 'Once again, the majority of pubs submitted for the awards have been provided with brand-new open-plan interiors couched in fake Victoriana. These travesties bore little resemblance to the style of the age they were pretending to evoke. Incorporating half a forest, "Playschool" stained glass and grotesque "tart's knickers" curtain displays into a gutted arena and then calling it a refurbishment is not in the interests of the pub or the customers who have had to endure these dismal depredations.'

The current obsession of pub companies with the recreation of a form of Victoriana means that the development of a contemporary form of pub design has been almost entirely neglected. A comparison, for example, of Barcelona, with its variety of modern bars, with London, would tend only to the detriment of the latter. In London there are hardly any modern, let alone post-modern, interpretations of the public house. It is no accident that the two most notable exceptions – the Market Bar and Beach Blanket Babylon* – were designed by the same person within two years of each other (1989 and 1991 respectively), and are both situated in Notting Hill, where many architects, designers and self-consciously trendy people live. Elsewhere, few pub customers would feel comfortable about patronizing places that looked so ostentatiously fashionable. For the judges of the Pub Design of the Year Awards to have stated that the 'Victorian' theme was not in the interest of pub customers could well be regarded as naïve. It is precisely because the majority of their customers feel safest in reliving a fantasy of the days when – they believe – their place in society was secure that pub designers have generally made no attempt to enhance the present or to look forward to the future, but have retreated to the past. Pseudo-Victorian pubs can be compared to supermarkets done up in the style of gigantic country cottages, or industrial heritage museums where people made redundant by the collapse of traditional industries are employed to masquerade as their own forefathers for the benefit of tourists and day-trippers. If a drinks company wants to make sure of commercial success in the 1990s, it joins the heritage industry.

*Named after a bar that featured in a series of books by Armistead Maupin about life in San Francisco in the 1960s.

4

BARS AND BOOZERS

IN THE EARLY HOURS OF SATURDAY 12 OCTOBER 1991 GROUPS of youths in the town of Cáceres in western Spain went on the rampage. Wearing Balaclava helmets and armed with rocks and stones, they smashed a number of shop fronts and attacked three banks before breaking into offices of the central government and setting fire to the main hall. The riot ended only after the police fired rubber bullets at several hundred protesters as they tried to storm the offices of the provincial Civil Governor, Alicia Izaguirre. 'They tried to raze Cáceres to the ground and, if they could have done so, they would have,' the governor later declared. It had in fact been in response to one of the governor's edicts that the riot had occurred. Following countless complaints about noise late at night from people living in the vicinity of bars, Izaguirre had introduced closing hours in the city for the first time. Having been brought up to regard it as their inalienable right to drink till dawn, the youths were protesting at the requirement that bars now close at 3 a.m.

No such event could possibly occur in Britain. Far from considering it their right to go out for a drink whenever they want to, Britons have been taught to accept that they cannot drink after about eleven in the evening, and are lucky to be allowed to drink in the afternoons or at any time on Sundays. It was not until 1976 in Scotland and 1988 in England and Wales that pubs were permitted to open on weekday afternoons, and, although limited Sunday opening has always been allowed in England, it was not permitted in Wales until 1961 nor in Scotland until 1976 nor in Northern Ireland until 1987.

It might be wondered why such repressive laws, so different from those that apply on most of the Continent of Europe, should have existed. The closing of pubs in the afternoon and early at night has not in fact served any practical purpose since the second decade of the twentieth century: from that point on, its only function has been to serve as reminders of the response of the authorities to the changing social circumstances of the Industrial Revolution and to the pressures of the First World War.

The English licensing system, in which public houses require licences from Justices of the Peace, was introduced by Edward VI in 1552.* This Act placed a limit on the number of taverns (which sold wine) in each town and forbade most people from keeping wine in their houses for private consumption. It said nothing about opening hours, however. The licensing justices only began to impose restrictions on opening hours in the late eighteenth century, when in many areas they started to make it a condition of granting or renewing licences that alehouses (which sold beer) should close at a specified time in the evening, generally 9 p.m. in winter and 10 p.m. in summer. In introducing evening closing the justices were responding to the changing nature of work patterns consequent upon the Industrial Revolution. They were concerned that heavy drinking in alehouses was obstructing the introduction of more regular, systematic work practices in factories and workshops. The justices also wanted to control the activities of the casualties of industrial reorganization, agricultural improvement and demographic growth. It was in alehouses that unemployed labourers chose to meet, and sometimes planned crimes, such as the wave of robberies that swept London during the 1780s.

Certainly, it was difficult for agricultural workers to adjust to

*It was extended from England to Scotland in 1756.

the new environment of industrial society. Agricultural workers had been at the mercy of the weather, and had resorted to alcohol for warmth. Their work was sporadic and seasonal, and they had tended to fill in the gaps with drink. They did not take regular holidays, but indulged in random drinking sprees. All this changed with the transfer of the place of work to indoors, in large towns. People worked standardized hours and took standardized holidays. Compared with agricultural labour, working in industry required less physical effort but greater sobriety, both in front of machinery and in the cramped living conditions of the towns. However, by increasing the monotony of the work, industrialization replaced physical with psychological strain. Industrialization fostered drunkenness by forcing migrant labourers into a strange environment and weakening traditional sanctions on conduct.

By the early nineteenth century a major problem was being posed in the newly industrialized cities by the behaviour of people who had spent all Saturday night out drinking. On Sunday mornings there was chaos and turmoil outside gin palaces, with people swearing, fighting and bawling obscenely, and others lying on the pavement dead drunk. In London, this problem was solved by the 1839 Metropolitan Police Act, which prohibited the opening of public houses in the metropolis before 1 p.m. on Sunday (except for travellers*). This Act having brought about a 35 per cent reduction in the number of people apprehended for drunken and disorderly conduct in London, in the course of the 1840s it was extended to the rest of the country. The introduction of Sunday morning closing not only improved the social order but also made a great deal of difference to the standard of living of many working-class households. Men had to go home; they became sober and hungry and with the money they had left found food for themselves and the family; they were able to begin work on Monday morning. The custom of 'Saint Monday', of adding an unofficial day off on Monday to an official one on Sunday, disappeared.

The introduction of Sunday morning closing having proved effective, it was extended to weekdays. First, all-night drinking on weekdays was ended by the 1864 and 1865 Public House Closing Acts, which forbade public houses to sell liquor between

---

*The issue of what constituted a 'bona fide traveller' is discussed below.

1 a.m. and 4 a.m., except to lodgers. Then, in 1872 the Liberal government introduced a Licensing Act which fixed the weekday closing time at midnight in London and 11 p.m. elsewhere. This applied to the pubs that were frequented by the working classes – but not to the clubs that were generally patronized by the better-off. In Liverpool publicans deliberately fomented riots by telling their customers that there was 'one law for the rich and another for the poor'; in Coventry a club was attacked by a mob singing, 'Britons never shall be slaves'; at Ashton-under-Lyne ten thousand people demonstrated outside the home of the leader of the local teetotal movement, and troops had to be called out in order to disperse them.

Members of the Conservative Party might have sympathized with the measures that the Liberal government had introduced, but they were happy to let the latter take the blame for the popular hostility these measures had attracted, and to accept the support of disaffected publicans. In the general election of 1874 the Liberal government was soundly defeated; Gladstone, who had been the Liberal Prime Minister, wrote to his brother that 'We have been borne down in a torrent of gin and beer'. One of the first acts of the new Conservative government in which Benjamin Disraeli was appointed Prime Minister in Gladstone's place was to reward the publicans for their support by giving them an extra half-hour's drinking in London, moving the closing time forward to 12.30 a.m. After that, neither the Conservative nor the Liberal Party thought it politically expedient to meddle with the opening hours until the First World War.

In 1914, within a few weeks of the outbreak of war, earlier closing hours were being introduced in some areas at the request of the naval and military authorities, largely in order to prevent servicemen from being treated by their civilian friends. The evening closing hour in London was brought forward in September from 12.30 a.m. to 11 p.m. The effect was beneficial. According to *The Brewers' Gazette*, 'A transformation of the night scenes of London has followed from the closing of the public houses at 11. Great traffic centres, like the Elephant and Castle, at which immense crowds usually lounge about until 1 a.m., have suddenly become peaceful and respectable. The police, instead of having to "move on" numbers of people who have been dislodged from bars at 12.30 at night, found very little intoxication to deal with, the last hour and a half [from 11 p.m. to 12.30 a.m.] being responsible for much of the excess of which complaint is made. Many of the houses were half-empty some time before closing time. Journalists, who are necessarily out late, have quickly noted the effects of the change upon public conduct, and have been spared the sounds of ribald songs, dancing and quarrelling which have hitherto marked "closing time" since war began.'

There was nothing, however, to prevent people from starting their drinking at 5 a.m. in London or at 6 a.m. in other towns, and nothing to prevent them from continuing to drink all day until closing time. The introduction of morning closing and that most famous of the anomalies of the English licensing laws, afternoon closing, was effected by the Liquor Control Board that was set up by the Government in May 1915 in response to claims that production in the munitions and shipbuilding industries was suffering as a consequence of the excessive consumption of alcohol by many of the workers.* The Control Board was given the authority to impose whatever controls might be thought necessary in whatever areas it thought fit. It used this authority to impose even earlier closing at night, to introduce a closed period during the afternoon, and to prohibit drinking before midday. This last measure was more important than it might seem today. It had been the practice in the industrial centres of the north (and especially the shipyards) for men to call at the pub for a glass or two of spirits on the way to work. Matutinal drinking had also contributed a good deal to intemperance among women living at home, who used to slip out to the pub halfway through the morning.

The restrictions imposed by the Control Board proved effective. Convictions for drunkenness in England and Wales fell from 183,828 in 1914 to 29,075 in 1918. Since the greatest fall occurred between July 1915 and May 1916 – the period during which the restrictions on opening hours were increased – it would be logical to attribute the fall to the conditions imposed by the Control Board. According to Arthur Shadwell, the author of the standard work on the licensing legislation of the First World War, 'There can be no doubt that the beneficial effect of the

*These claims will be discussed in Chapter 7.

reduced hours was the main factor in effecting the improvements ascribed to controls.'

The fact that the controls that were introduced during the First World War were generally effective and beneficial during abnormal wartime conditions does not mean, however, that there was good reason to retain them during peacetime. But retained they were. The 1921 Licensing Act that re-established peacetime licensing legislation was seen at the time as a compromise between demands for the restoration of pre-war conditions and demands for the retention of wartime restrictions. In fact, it retained the wartime measures of early morning and afternoon closing, and its attempted extension of the opening hours was soon overturned by licensing justices, who were under the impression that early closing would exert the same beneficial effect on public order in peacetime conditions as it had during the war.

The Royal Commission on Licensing that sat in 1929 and 1930 saw no reason to recommend that opening hours be extended. It was told by Sir Edgar Sanders, who had been the general manager of the Carlisle and District State Management Area and was later to become the Director of the Brewers' Society, that 'The present opening hours have met with extraordinary acceptance by the British public . . . The earlier closing hour has been a reform of the first magnitude for the whole country. The last hour in the evening is always the worst, whatever the period of opening is, and to get the streets cleared at least an hour earlier than used to be the case has been an enormous benefit. The health of the working classes must also have benefited through getting more sleep.' These comments, however, ignored the fundamental defect behind the principle of early closing – which was pointed out to the Royal Commission by a Mr Arthur Reade, who told them that during the last few minutes before closing time 'customers may be seen clamouring at the bar to gulp down two or three drinks where, in a free country across the channel, they would have been perfectly content to sit at their leisure over one.' Early closing, in other words, was counter-productive.

The veracity of Mr Reade's argument was demonstrated by the *reductio ad absurdum* of the closing hour that was introduced during the war in Australia and New Zealand. In February 1916 there occurred a riot among troops who were stationed at Casula and Liverpool in New South Wales. The riot was provoked by an increase in the number of hours that the troops had to spend in training. It was inflamed by the alcohol that the troops looted from the Commercial Hotel at Liverpool: they drank not only every bottle they could find in the bar but also the contents of eleven hogsheads of beer, wine, rum and whisky that they found in the cellar. The rioters fought with the staff at Liverpool railway station: twenty shots were fired, seven men were injured and one was killed. Then the rioters drove trains to Sydney, where they marched through the streets, smashing shop windows and looting the contents. The New South Wales Cabinet responded by blaming enemy agents and holding a referendum asking people what time they would like the pubs to close. The people voted overwhelmingly for a closing time of 6 p.m. The governments of Victoria and South Australia, fearing that their own troops would riot as those in New South Wales had done, soon followed suit.

Or so goes the traditional explanation for the introduction of 6 p.m. closing. This explanation is still the one that is generally believed: it is repeated, for example, by Jan Morris in her recent book on Sydney. Unfortunately, it is wrong. The riot was not the cause of the introduction of 6 p.m. closing; it merely happened to coincide with it.

The background to the 6 p.m. closing of pubs lies in the 6 p.m. closing of shops, which was introduced at the turn of the century. Temperance campaigners argued that bars should be closed at the same time as shops. They did not really think that they would be: they simply took up 6 p.m. as a bargaining position. They would have been prepared to accept any closing time that was sub-stantially earlier than the 11 p.m. that then applied in New South Wales, and the 11.30 p.m. that then applied in Victoria. Had the politicians been prepared to compromise, and accepted a closing time of, say, 9 p.m., the temperance campaigners would have accepted it. But the politicians took a different course. In 1913 the South Australian government decided that a referendum on closing hours would be held after the next general election, expecting that the temperance campaigners would find insufficient popular support. But the election was not held until 1915, by which time war had broken out. A combination of temperance sentiment with patriotic fervour led the electors to plump for 6 p.m. The governments of Victoria and New South Wales now sought to placate the temperance reformers by offering to adopt

9 or 10 p.m. closing, but it was too late. The South Australian referendum had given the temperance movement the initiative. At the beginning of 1916 a by-election was held at Parramatta in New South Wales in which the early closing of bars was the central issue. The by-election was won by the Liberal candidate Albert Bruntnell, a long-standing advocate of early closing. The results of the by-election came out on the same day as the troops rioted; it was the electoral defeat rather than the riot that caused the New South Wales Premier W. A. Holman to decide to hold a referendum on the issue of early closing. As in South Australia, the referendum was a defensive tactic: Holman had expected the electorate to reject 6 p.m. closing. But they voted for it, overwhelmingly.

Whatever the explanation for its introduction, the fact remains that, from the First World War until the 1960s, pubs in much of Australia – and in all of New Zealand – were forced to close for the night at 6 p.m. One reason why this measure, like afternoon closing of pubs in England and Wales, not only outlasted the First World War but also most of the men who had fought in and survived it, was that it suited the liquor trade rather well. After all, people did not drink any less, but they did drink more quickly, so that landlords' overheads were reduced.

The social consequences of 6 p.m. closing were disastrous. The bars were transformed. Anything that interfered with the fast dispensing of drink between 5 and 6 p.m., such as dart boards or billiard tables, was removed. The Six O'Clock Swill, the hour of frantic drinking after work, was a disgusting spectacle. The walls of many bars were tiled so that it was easier to clean off spilt beer and vomit. Any idea of bars as a social centre, any possibility of conversation with the landlord, was abandoned.

The closing time of 6 p.m. had been introduced in New Zealand in 1917, as a compromise between the prohibitionists and the liquor trade. In 1945 W. H. Woodward, a magistrate and chairman of two licensing committees, described the closing time, and the licensing laws in general, as 'the results of a battle between greed and fanaticism, in which the interests of ordinary sensible citizens have been ignored. The outcome is a system in which said citizens drink, jowl by jowl like pigs at a trough, what they are given instead of what they want, and, like pigs, gulp down more than they need of it while they can get it; and, for the privilege of doing so, pay many times the cost of the hogwash they swallow.'

In England and Wales, as in Australia and New Zealand, the licensed trade was perfectly happy with a system that encouraged heavy sales in the period immediately before closing time while at the same time exempting publicans and their staff from the necessity of working late into the night. In the nineteenth century, some publicans had put collecting boxes for teetotal associations on their bars because the latter were campaigning for shorter hours, which most publicans secretly favoured. Indeed, the anti-alcohol campaigner James Parker revealed that he had been refused permission to approach customers in only six out of the two thousand pubs he had visited. Once the shorter hours had been introduced during the First World War, it was in the interest of publicans to see to it that they stayed that way. This may well help to explain why the licensing hours that had been introduced in order to deal with the extraordinary conditions of the First World War were not altered to any significant extent before 1988.

Certainly, the licensed trade played a part in scuppering the first serious attempt that was made by the government to reintroduce drinking hours in England and Wales that were appropriate to peacetime conditions, at the beginning of the 1970s. Public and political opinion had moved towards licensing law liberalization during the course of the 1960s, a decade when several liberal reforms were introduced, such as laws legalizing abortion and homosexuality. The tourism industry, which was growing in importance, was pressing for liberalization. Also, a 1969 Monopolies Commission report on the brewing industry – which the Department of Trade and Industry had accepted – had recommended relaxation in the law so as to promote greater competition and efficiency. In 1971 the Home Secretary Reginald Maudling appointed a Departmental Committee on Liquor Licensing under the chairmanship of Lord Erroll of Hale. Maudling was quite clear about his position. He stated in the House of Commons that 'I think the laws are archaic. If the committee comes up with the view that they are perfect, I and many others will be surprised.' Maudling was not surprised. When the Erroll Committee reported in 1972 it recommended several significant changes to the existing licensing laws, notably that on-licence hours should be extended and the afternoon break abolished, that the legal minimum drinking age should be reduced from eighteen to seventeen, and that children should be allowed into bars under certain circumstances. These recommendations received a generally hostile reception, especially from the medical press. The Government shelved the report.

Scottish licensing laws being different from English and Welsh ones, the Government's review of liquor licensing was undertaken by a different departmental committee, under the chairmanship of Dr Christopher Clayson. This reported in 1973, and, like Erroll, it recommended a significant relaxation of the laws. This report was accepted by the Government, which introduced in 1976 many of the reforms that Clayson had recommended.

Two principal explanations account for the Government's acceptance of the Clayson, yet rejection of the Erroll, report. In the first case, the Clayson Committee had been cleverer: it had claimed that relaxed licensing laws would reduce the problem of alcohol misuse, such as by reducing the pressure to drink within a restrictive time period. The Erroll Committee, on the other hand, had failed to attach sufficient weight to public health considerations, and had justified its recommendations on consumer and trade grounds. Its report was therefore received by the medical press in a much more hostile manner than the Clayson one. No less significant, however, was the attitude of licensees. In England and Wales they were generally satisfied with the existing regime, and opposed reform on the grounds that it would lead to increased competition and longer working hours. Scottish licensees, on the other hand, supported most of the Clayson Committee's recommendations because they faced a much more restrictive licensing regime than their counterparts in the south.

It was not until 1988 that some of the recommendations of the Erroll Committee were implemented, and their belated implementation had a great deal to do with the success in Scotland of the introduction of the measures that the Clayson Committee had recommended. As it happened, the effect of the 1976 Licensing Act was to relax the laws in Scotland more than the Government had intended. Permitted hours were extended by one hour in the evenings, from 10 to 11 p.m., and local licensing authorities were given the power to grant licensees an extension to licensing hours through the afternoon and late at night. What the Government had not intended was that the authorities should use this power quite as frequently as they were to do. When, however, in the mid-1980s several scientific assessments of the effect of the changes introduced as a result of the Clayson report were published, they came generally to the conclusion that the liberalization of the Scottish licensing laws had not led to any increase in alcohol-related harm.

Within England and Wales, once it had become obvious that the Government was not prepared to implement the Erroll report, a number of backbench Members of Parliament began to show an interest in promoting their own legislation along these lines. The first serious attempt was Kenneth Clarke's Licensing (Amendment) Bill in 1976, which proposed that the law should be changed in order to allow pub licensees to apply to the licensing justices for permission to extend their opening hours to a maximum of 10 a.m. to midnight. 'I take the view,' Clarke said, 'that our licensing laws are among the most complicated, archaic, uncivilized and restricted parts of our legal system.' The (Labour) Government officially adopted a neutral stance on this Bill, but in practice took pains to provide adequate parliamentary time to discuss it; the Home Office supported the Bill and assisted in its drafting. But the Bill failed. During the debate in the House of Commons, the anti-alcohol campaigner Sir Bernard Braine read out a telegram he had received from the National Association of Licensed House Managers which claimed that the Bill, if passed, would cause pub prices to increase and many pubs to close down, and was therefore 'a retrograde step'. The Labour Member of Parliament David Weitzman added that he had 'received very strong protests from many constituents against the possibility of the Bill's becoming law'. The Bill failed, in other words, largely because elements of the licensed trade still opposed reform.

It was only after the formation in 1984 of FLAG, the campaign for flexible licensing hours, that licensees changed their attitude to reform. They may well have been opposed to longer hours, but they were all in favour of flexible ones. By espousing flexibility rather than extension FLAG succeeded in uniting the interests of licensees with those of the brewing, leisure and tourism industries, as well as dividing those other groups that had previously opposed reform but were prepared to consider the introduction of more flexible, as opposed to longer, hours. The combination of pressure from FLAG and the favourable reports on the effect of the implementation in Scotland of the recommendations of the Clayson Committee persuaded the Home Office to back the cause of reform in 1986. Douglas Hurd, then the Home Secretary, made a statement to this effect, and the Conservative Party included the liberalization of licensing in its manifesto for the 1987 General Election. In the autumn it introduced a Licensing Bill, which Hurd described as 'a common-sense Bill designed to remove an absurdity that has come into our law as a result of history rather than logic'.

The 1987 Licensing Bill did not, however, propose a very substantial liberalization. There was too much opposition for that. The Bill was introduced at a time of substantial medical disquiet about the harmful effects of excessive alcohol consumption on the national health. Indeed, in September 1987 representatives of all the medical colleges urged the Government to scrap its plans to extend opening hours and to increase alcohol prices instead. The Bill did not propose an extension of opening hours in the evening – but it did move for the abolition of the quaint seventy-two-year-old tradition of afternoon closing, which had caused mirth and frustration in equal measure to millions of visitors from the Continent of Europe. It was passed without too much difficulty. However, for fear of offending the temperance lobby any more than it had done already, the Government avoiding publicizing the day on which all-day opening was to begin: it came in quietly on 22 August 1988, ten days earlier than expected.

The fears of those who had opposed the Bill did not turn out to have been justified. Chief Superintendent Peter Stevens of the Kentish Town Division of the Metropolitan Police carried out a survey covering the month before and the month after the introduction of the reforms. He found that there were fewer drink-related arrests and emergencies in the two hours after 11 p.m. than there had been before. 'People either have only so much to spend, or tend to drink only so much,' he explained. 'If they've been in the pub all afternoon they'll leave before closing time. What you don't have now is the two big turn-outs at 3 p.m. and 11 p.m. There are fewer people leaving at night and so there's less likely to be trouble.' In 1987 the government-funded pressure group Alcohol Concern had opposed the Licensing Bill, saying that, if it was passed, it would lead to a rise in alcohol consumption and therefore necessarily to a rise in alcohol-related social problems. If, however, market research surveys carried out for the Office of Population Censuses and Surveys (OPCS) are to be believed, average weekly alcohol consumption fell from 9.5 units* in 1987 to 8.8 units in 1989. In 1993, Alcohol Concern admitted that the all-day opening of pubs had not caused an increase in drunkenness.

By removing the anomaly of afternoon closing the 1988 Licensing Act had gone some way towards the introduction of sensible licensing hours. But the introduction of weekday afternoon opening made very little difference to people's drinking habits. The period between 3 p.m. and 5.30 p.m. on a weekday afternoon was not when many people wanted, or were able, to drink alcohol. Only 6 per cent of the people who had taken part in the OPCS's 1989 survey said that they had taken a drink on licensed premises between 4 p.m. and 5 p.m. the previous week. If the Government had really wanted to liberalize the licensing laws, it would have allowed pubs to stay open throughout Sunday afternoon – the one afternoon of the week most people had free. According to a survey that was published during the passage of the 1987 Licensing Bill, 55 per cent of regular pub-goers wanted pubs to stay open on Sunday afternoons.

One effect of the liberalization of 1988, therefore, was to accentuate the restrictions that were placed on drinking on a Sunday – the day on which people's pleasures had always been more closely circumscribed than during the rest of the week. Indeed, Sunday hours were the first to be legislated. In 1618 James I issued a proclamation ordering the closure of alehouses during the hours of divine service. During his Protectorate Oliver Cromwell insisted on total Sunday closing. Then the laws appear to have become lax again, and it was not until the justices made their first efforts to impose closing times on alehouses in the late eighteenth century that the issue was again addressed. They imposed severe restrictions on Sunday opening, especially outside London.

Sunday opening hours were relaxed again after 1830 as a consequence of the creation of a new category of beer shops, which were allowed to sell beer without the requirement of

---

*Glasses of wine, half-pints of beer or single shots of spirits.

obtaining a licence. Parliament had introduced controls on the opening and closing times of beer shops during the week, but had made no special law as to Sunday hours. The justices therefore had no option but to relax their rules and allow the licensed pubs, like the beer shops, to be open all Sunday, provided that they respected the general prohibition on drinking during the hours of divine service. In fact, this prohibition was widely ignored. The amount that people were drinking on Sundays in the middle of the nineteenth century is evident from a survey of Manchester in 1854, which counted more than 200,000 going in and out of the city's pubs on a given Sunday. The population of Manchester was 300,000.*

The middle of the nineteenth century saw a substantial growth in Sabbatarianism.† In England and Wales, a number of restrictions were placed on working-class leisure, among them the closure of parks, museums and art galleries; there were even attempts to stop trains from running on Sundays. In Scotland, from 1853, all the pubs were closed on Sundays; this measure had little to do with a belief in temperance – improving the manners and morals of the working classes by encouraging or compelling them to drink less alcohol – but arose from the conviction that all enjoyment on a Sunday was wicked. The legislature in England and Wales did not go quite so far as this. A Commons Select Committee that met in 1853 and 1854 recommended that Sunday opening hours be restricted to between 1 p.m. and 2 p.m. and 6 p.m. and 9 p.m., saying that working men need not suffer, because the publicans could perfectly well provide them with stone bottles and jars in which to take beer home with them on Saturday night for Sunday use. 'If it is well corked down . . . so as to keep it airtight,' stated the Committee in its report, 'the beer will drink equally well on the following day.' The 1854 Sale of Liquors on Sunday Act implemented the Committee's recommendations.

This new law took the public unawares; the first that many of them heard of it was when they tried to enter their local pub at

---

*Some people would have visited several pubs in the course of the day, and would therefore have been counted several times.

†Strictly speaking, Sunday is not the Sabbath. The Sabbath is the seventh day of the week, on which God rested after creating the world; Sunday is the first day of the week, on which Christ rose from the dead. To call Sunday the Sabbath is a seventeenth-century Puritan invention.

ten or eleven on a Sunday evening and found that an Act had been passed to prevent their admission. Public discontent at the new measure fermented over the winter, then erupted the next summer, when the wealthy Sabbatarian Member of Parliament, Lord Robert Grosvenor, introduced a Bill to prevent shops from trading on Sundays. On Sunday 24 June 1855 thousands of working people converged on Hyde Park in the centre of London, 'to see how religiously the aristocracy is observing the Sabbath'; groups of demonstrators gathered outside the houses of Members of Parliament who had supported the Bill, and wealthy people taking their afternoon drive along the Serpentine were abused. The next Sunday, an even larger crowd collected, supposedly 150,000 in number. This time, they pelted the carriages of people driving in the park with stones, and the mob had to be broken up in the evening by police, who 'used their staves with considerable freedom'. The next Sunday detachments roamed through the West End, smashing windows as they passed. The Hyde Park riots frightened the upper and middle classes sufficiently for a new Commons Select Committee to be appointed; this immediately recommended that Sunday opening hours be extended to 1 p.m. to 3 p.m. and 5 p.m. to 11 p.m.; by the middle of August an Act had been introduced to this effect.

In England, no further restrictions were introduced on Sunday opening hours until the First World War. On its Celtic fringe, however, Sunday closing was made complete. In 1878 Sunday closing was imposed on most of Ireland, with the exception of the five cities of Dublin, Cork, Limerick, Waterford and Belfast. When the country was divided in 1921, total Sunday closing became the law in Northern Ireland, including Belfast. In Wales, Sunday closing had been introduced in 1881.

The fact that Sunday closing measures were introduced, however, does not mean that people were prevented from drinking on Sundays. The introduction of Sunday closing in Wales led to the invention of special tin vessels, so shaped as to fit closely to the body under the clothes, with the intention that their carriage could not be detected. These 'belly-cans' were kept by publicans under the bar counter, for surreptitious sale to their customers on Sundays. In the industrial south there was a mass exodus on Sundays across the border into Monmouthshire; the law was also evaded, within the confines of Wales itself, by the creation of licensed clubs whose sole purpose was to enable people to drink on Sundays.

In 1889, after the failure of the legislation had been admitted even by Lord Aberdare, the man who had guided the Sunday Closing Bill through the House of Lords, the Government set up a Royal Commission to look into the matter. This found that the legislation was not working but, instead of advising its repeal, recommended more rigorous enforcement. So the Act stayed on the statute books until 1961, by which time 60 per cent of adult men belonged to licensed clubs and so were not prevented from going out to drink on Sundays. Now, at long last, it was recognized by the Government that the law was not working – and would not work unless it was actively desired by the local population. So local option was introduced: each locality was given the chance to vote once in every seven years on whether it wished to stay 'dry' or go 'wet' on Sundays. The industrial south voted to go wet at once; parts of the rural north and west took rather longer. In the fifth of the local option polls, in November 1989, Ceredigion in Dyfed finally voted to go wet; this left Dwyfor in Gwynedd as the one remaining place in Wales where Sunday opening was forbidden.

It was one of the consequences of the ineffectiveness of Sunday closing in Wales that the measure was not extended into England. Indeed, Wales had deliberately been selected as a testing-ground for a measure that, had it been more successful, might well have been applied to England as well. In 1889, in the same month as the Government appointed a Royal Commission to look into the effectiveness of Sunday closing in Wales, a Bill for enforcing Sunday closing in England obtained a majority in favour of its second reading. This led *The Times* to publish a leading article in which it described the Bill as 'an invertebrate measure, supported by flabby arguments, based upon a narrow, vulgar and retrograde theory of ethics, and condemned by our experience of analagous enactments . . . To hedge people round with petty restrictions instead of teaching them nobility of conduct and a worthy use of liberty is the perennial resource of shallow and incompetent reformers. A small minority occasionally injure themselves with bad liquor on Sunday, and these reformers can think of nothing better than to forbid the entire community to drink on Sunday at all. To punish the swindlers who supply poisonous liquor, to provide alternative resorts to the public house, and to give men better employments and amusements for their leisure than idle talk in front of a bar, would be worthy objects for a paternal government. But these things are too hard and not sufficiently sensational for the mechanical moralists who provide the grandmotherly legislation of the present day.' The Bill was not passed.

The rejection of the English Sunday Closing Bill was a wise one, since even the limited restrictions that had been imposed on Sunday opening in England had proved ineffective. The 1854 and 1855 Acts had excepted 'bona fide travellers' from the restrictive Sunday licensing hours. It did not take long for this clause to become a national joke. It led, for example, to individual day-return train tickets being passed round pubs to enable people to buy a drink out of hours. There is a story from *The Diary of a Nobody*, which was published in *Punch* in 1892, of how Mr Pooter and his three companions walked on a Sunday afternoon from Holloway in North London across the Heath to a pub a couple of miles away in Hampstead. 'We arrived,' recounted Pooter, 'and as I was trying to pass, the man in charge of the gate said: "Where from?" I replied: "Holloway." He immediately put up his arm, and declined to let me pass. I turned back for a moment, when I saw Stillbrook, closely followed by Cummings and Gowing, make for the entrance. I heard the porter say: "Where from?" When to my surprise, in fact disgust, Stillbrook replied: "Blackheath," and the three were immediately admitted.'

The exemption of 'bona fide travellers' from the restrictions on Sunday opening hours was abolished as one of the extraordinary provisions that were introduced during the First World War; at the same time, Sunday opening hours in England were further reduced, to five hours in all, two at lunchtime and three in the evening. These measures were perpetuated by the 1921 Licensing Act; with minor changes, they remained in force for another three-quarters of a century.

Now, at long last, the Sunday licensing laws have been modernized, and Sunday-afternoon drinking has been introduced.* The reasons that were given by the (then) Prime Minister,

*In Scotland, England and Wales (except Dwyfor), but not in Northern Ireland, where, since the ban on Sunday opening was lifted in 1987, pubs have been allowed to trade for only five hours a day.

John Major, when announcing at the beginning of 1995 his intention to liberalize the English Sunday licensing laws, were that they were 'old-fashioned, out-of-date, patronizing, Government-knows-best regulations and they should go.' Undoubtedly, he was right. But, if it was as simple as all that, then it is difficult to understand why it took the Government so long to come to its senses, and why, specifically, Sunday-afternoon drinking was not introduced together with weekday-afternoon drinking in 1988.

It may reasonably be wondered, indeed, whether the English Sunday licensing laws would have been modernized at all, had they not been rendered untenable by the development of anomalous distinctions between English and Scottish legislation in respect of Sunday trade in general. In the past the population of Scotland was, on the whole, much more religiously observant than that of England. That is why pubs and off-licences were prohibited from opening on Sundays in Scotland, whereas in England limited opening was permitted. That is also why no law was ever passed prohibiting food shops from opening in Scotland on Sundays: it was simply assumed that their proprietors would refrain from opening them and their customers from patronizing them on that day. In England, on the other hand, people might well have wanted to buy and sell foodstuffs and other goods on Sundays, so a law had been passed prohibiting them from doing so in 1936.* By 1993 these legislative anomalies had produced a ridiculous situation in which it was legal for supermarkets to open in Scotland on Sundays (and they did) but illegal for them to sell alcoholic drinks alongside the food, while it was illegal for supermarkets to open in England on Sundays (although they did) but legal for them to sell alcoholic drinks alongside the food that they sold in contravention of the law, provided that they respected the hours that had been set down in the liquor licensing regulations.

The anomalousness of Scottish legislation went even further than that. Following the recommendations of the Clayson Committee, the 1976 Licensing Act made it legal for pubs to open on

---

*It was permitted to sell certain goods, essentially those that were considered to be 'perishable'. Notoriously, it was illegal to sell a Bible (because it was a non-perishable book) but legal to sell a soft-core pornographic magazine (because if was a periodical with a limited shelf life).

Sundays. Similar hours were set to those applying in England – 12.30 to 2.30 and 6.30 to 11 p.m. – but in 1990 the provision was introduced that pubs might apply to local licensing boards for their Sunday hours to be extended. A year later, two-thirds of all pubs were open in Scotland on Sunday afternoons. Since now not only shops but also pubs were open all day, the Government was in no position to refuse requests that off-licences be allowed to trade normally in Scotland on Sundays, and in 1994 legislation was passed to that effect.

Thus Scotland had acquired a much more liberal set of Sunday trading and licensing laws than applied south of the border. In part, this was because efforts to liberalize the laws in England had been blocked. An attempt by the Conservative government in 1986 to deregulate Sunday trading in England and Wales had led to the only parliamentary defeat of Mrs Thatcher's premiership, when eighty-six Conservative backbenchers – some hard-core Sabbatarians, some incurable romantics, others more concerned that shop-workers might be exploited by their employers – had defied a three-line whip and sided with the Opposition. As a result, although the Government had originally intended to include Sunday afternoon opening in the 1988 Licensing Act, it did not dare to do so. One small step forward was taken, however: the afternoon closing time was extended from 2 to 3 p.m. In its 1960 Licensing Bill the Government had proposed to move the afternoon closing time on Sunday back from 2 to 3 p.m., but complaints from publicans, and a desire to appear non-controversial, had led it to drop the measure. This time it was cleverer. The Government did not propose in its Bill to move the afternoon closing time on Sunday back to 3 p.m.; instead this extension was introduced as an amendment by a Conservative backbencher. The Home Office minister in the House of Lords, Lord Ferrers, was due to object to this amendment but failed to do so because, he said, he thought his Whips were going to perform the job. Ferrers's 'mistake' was demonstrated to have been more of a conspiracy than a cock-up by the fact that, when the Bill returned to the Commons, the amendment was accepted, in spite of the earlier assurances of Home Office ministers that they would oppose any backbench effort by a Member of Parliament connected with the drinks industry to insert a clause extending Sunday hours. It was with good reason that the extra hour's drinking on Sunday afternoons came to be known as the 'Ferrers hour'.

The Conservative Party had included in its manifesto for the 1987 General Election not only the introduction of weekday-afternoon opening of pubs but also a commitment to make another attempt to reform the Sunday trading laws. It was at a loss how to proceed, however. So it did nothing – until the problem grew so great that it had no choice but to act. By the beginning of the 1990s not only were corner shops and DIY stores trading illegally on Sundays but supermarkets and department stores as well. Those companies that continued to obey the law complained that they were losing business and demanded that the Government find a solution. The Government offered Members of Parliament a choice of three regulatory schemes; the Members voted to allow large shops to open for a maximum of six continuous hours on Sundays between 10 a.m. and 6 p.m. and small shops to trade without restrictions.

This new legislation, which came into effect in the summer of 1994, created anomalies of its own. Supermarkets were now permitted to sell food on Sundays from 10 a.m. to 4 p.m. or from 11 a.m. to 5 p.m. but had to rope off their off-licence departments before midday and after 3 p.m. Not surprisingly, they now put pressure on the Government to liberalize the Sunday licensing laws.

At this point, the attention of the Home Office had just been drawn to the question of the Sunday-afternoon closing of pubs as a result of is consultations with interested parties on a proposal to allow children into pubs.* Several of the organizations consulted had replied that the issue of children in pubs was not one about which they felt very strongly; they were much more concerned about Sunday-afternoon closing. The Home Office promised to consult further on the matter.

As yet there was no certainty that the Home Office would introduce a Bill to permit pubs to open on Sunday afternoons – nor, if it did so, whether it would take a long time to act. After all the trouble it had encountered over the issue of Sunday trading, the Government was in no mood to risk alienating Conservative Members of Parliament and Conservative Party supporters in the

---

*This will be discussed later in the chapter.

country. But then, out of the blue, not in the House of Commons but in a speech at a dinner given by the British Retail Consortium, the Prime Minister made his announcement. Legislation was to be introduced to allow pubs to stay open throughout Sunday afternoon and to permit off-licences to trade all day, from 10 a.m. to 10.30 p.m. On the radio the next morning the Director of the Keep Sunday Special Campaign, Michael Schluter, described the proposals as a cheap attempt by the Government to win popularity; in a newspaper interview the following day he stated that 'The Prime Minister is sending a signal to the public that consumer interests are more important than family life.'

Although Schluter's assumption that family life should necessarily preclude a visit to a pub on Sunday afternoon was patently absurd, in one respect he was quite correct. Among the most dedicated opponents of Sunday-afternoon opening had been the National Association of Licensed House Managers, which represented 8,500 pub managers in England and Wales. Sunday afternoons were the only time that its members could guarantee to have off with their families; if the laws were changed, they feared that their employers would force them to work on Sunday afternoons as well. Their opposition had been instrumental in persuading the Home Office to proceed cautiously with its investigation of the possible reform of the Sunday licensing laws.

Now that the Prime Minister had made his announcement, however, the personal interests of licensees need no longer stand in the way. The Government moved a Bill in the House of Commons to liberalize the laws along the lines that the Prime Minister had described. Taking into account past experience and the caution that the Home Office had initially shown about the measure, it might have been expected that the debate would be stormy and the opposition fierce. But they were not. 'In the mid-1990s,' pointed out George Howarth, Labour Party spokesman on home affairs, 'there does not seem to be a great deal of heat left in the arguments about Sundays.' Once the Government had decided to act, sectional interests were no longer in a position to impose their will upon the population at large. With the passage of the Licensing (Sunday Hours) Act in the summer of 1995, the situation that obtained before the passage of the Sale of Liquors on Sunday Acts in 1854 and 1855 has been restored. The rule of Sabbatarianism has, at long last, been brought to an end.

*   *   *

This does not mean that the liberalization of the licensing laws has been completed, however. Nothing has yet been done (at least not at time of writing*) to take up the recommendation that was made by the Erroll Committee in 1972 to extend the closing time beyond the hour of 11 p.m. that was originally imposed at the beginning of the First World War. Yet an examination of their history does not demonstrate that restrictive closing hours have proved successful. It is one thing to outline the history of official opening and closing hours, and the reasons that were given for introducing them at the time; it is quite another to know whether they actually worked. It may seem laudable that evening closing hours were introduced in the nineteenth century, but the police were powerless to enforce them without the support of public opinion; in many slum districts this public support simply did not exist. The police, moreover, relied on publicans for information about the criminal world. Publicans had been forbidden to entertain policemen by the 1829 Metropolitan Police Act, but half a century later police constables were still accepting free drinks from publicans and bottles of drink offered to them in the streets by members of the public.

Furthermore, there is a great deal of evidence that the imposition of restrictive closing hours simply leads to the provision of alternative, illegal facilities. When, in 1904, the closing time in the major cities of Scotland (Edinburgh, Glasgow, Dundee and Aberdeen) was brought forward from 11 p.m. to 10 p.m., the principal result was an increase in drunkenness in both Glasgow and Edinburgh, with the opening of many more illegal drinking dens. Within two years of its introduction, the early closing measure was being described in the *Glasgow Record* as 'a miserable fiasco' and in the *Scottish Weekly Review* as 'worse than useless'. Yet 10 p.m. closing remained the law in Scotland until 1976.

In England, during the First World War, early closing was introduced, not only for pubs, restaurants and hotels but also for nightclubs. It was clearly absurd that an institution calling itself

*This book was originally completed in June 1994 but the text was amended in June 1995 in order to take account of the major changes that had occurred in the intervening year.

a 'nightclub' should have been forced to close, from November 1915, at 9.30 p.m. In response, the clubs went underground. By the end of 1915 there were 150 illegal nightclubs in Soho in the West End of London alone. After the war, in London in the 1920s, the further growth of nightclubs was stimulated by the early closing hours of pubs. According to the 1921 Licensing Act clubs were supposed to stop serving alcoholic drinks at the same time as the pubs closed, but they did not. Therefore they were frequently raided by the police. The raids encompassed the haunts of the most famous and respectable members of society; apparently many members of the aristocracy enjoyed the thrill of having their names taken by the police. They were masterminded by Sir William Joyson-Hicks ('Jix'), a reactionary teetotal Conservative Member of Parliament who notoriously had supported General Dyer's conduct in ordering the Amritsar massacre in 1919. As soon as he was appointed Home Secretary in 1924, he set out to destroy London's nightclubs, justifying his ruthlessness by an exaggerated denunciation of the evil he intended to crush. His preoccupation with nightclubs gave them a reputation for orgiastic activities, and the raids made headlines in the Sunday newspapers.

After the police had successfully cracked down on nightclubs people started organizing 'private bottle parties', on the basis that the law had no authority to interfere with the consumption of liquor at a private party. The 'host' of a bottle party was given a generous contribution by his 'guests' towards the cost of holding the party. The early bottle parties were smart affairs, with dance bands, in luxurious premises. They rarely opened before midnight or closed before 6 or 7 a.m. But soon they went down-market. They were too expensive for the young; their customers mainly comprised businessmen, prostitutes and 'adventurers'. There were several hundred bottle parties in the West End of London when war broke out again in 1939.

This situation was resolved, as regards London, by the 1949 Licensing Act, which provided for the grant of 'special hours certificates' to restaurants and clubs that offered music and dancing, up to 2 a.m., with half an hour's drinking-up time after that. This Act also abolished bottle parties by prohibiting the consumption of liquor outside permitted hours at private parties organized for gain. The special hours certificates were extended to the rest of England and Wales by the 1961 Licensing Act.

Thus, the position today is that the 11 p.m. closing time of public houses forces people who wish to drink, or merely to socialize after that time, to go to nightclubs.* There are two consequences of this. In the first case, the atmosphere of nightclubs is generally rather more *risqué* than that of public houses. A nightclub can obtain a licence from the justices to serve drinks until 3 a.m. in London and 2 a.m. elsewhere but only if it has already obtained a music and dancing licence from the local council. This means that it tends to be a discothèque, and a pick-up joint, patronized principally by people under the age of twenty-five. Young people in search of sexual congress are unlikely to be concerned about whether they are drinking in a civilized or controlled manner.

Secondly, nightclubs are generally forbidden to serve drinks after 2 or 3 a.m.†, but they often stay open much later than this. After the end of legal drinking, it is much simpler for nightclub customers to consume easily-transported, easily-swallowed tablets of narcotic drugs than to smuggle in bulky bottles of alcoholic drink.

If nightclubs open very late, they may not consider it worth their while to serve alcohol at all. In 1991 the Ministry of Sound, a large warehouse club based on similar institutions in New York, opened in the unprepossessing area of the Elephant and Castle in South London. Initially, it operated only on Friday and Saturday nights – or rather on Saturday and Sunday mornings, from midnight until 9 a.m. The fact that it was unlicensed did not prevent it from rapidly becoming the most fashionable club in London. Its customers appear to have been quite content to refresh themselves with soft drinks; the management has insisted that they do not narcotize themselves with drugs. But the club can do nothing to prevent its customers from swallowing tablets of Ecstasy or other drugs before they enter the premises. By turning

---

*It is also often possible for the determined drinker to find a pub or restaurant that will sell him drink illegally after hours. A restaurant is permitted to serve alcoholic drinks between 11 p.m. and midnight only to someone who is eating a meal.

†Alcoholic drinks can only be served legally after this time if a 'general order of exemption' has been obtained. This is possible only if the club is intended to cater for people working locally whose jobs require them to work late at night – such as people employed in casinos.

its back on alcohol, the Ministry of Sound has reflected the fashion for narcotic drugs that is central to the 'rave' culture of the 1990s.*

It has become common practice to describe all-night parties in which people take drugs but not alcohol as raves, regardless of whether they are held in nightclubs or in warehouses or halls hired for the occasion. In 1993 the Henley Centre for Forecasting reported that young people made one million visits to raves each week, spending an average of £35, approximately half of that on drugs such as Ecstasy, amphetamines and LSD, and that the total amount of money spent annually at raves was about £1,800 million, equivalent to a quarter of total consumer expenditure on spirits. Richard Carr, chairman of Allied Leisure (part of Allied Breweries), cited the fact that 'youngsters can get Ecstasy for £10 or £12 and get a much better buzz than they can from alcohol' as being 'a major threat to alcohol-led businesses'. The popularity of raves among young people is causing significant damage to the alcoholic drinks industry, not only because people who attend them choose other drugs in preference to alcohol and refresh themselves with soft drinks rather than beer, but also because they are so time-consuming. People who spend up to twenty-four hours each week at a rave obviously have less time (and money) available to them to devote to other leisure activities such as going to pubs or drinking at home. Visits by young people to pubs fell by 11 per cent between 1987 and 1991 and have been forecast to fall a further 20 per cent by 1997.

In the light of the growth of rave culture, it is not surprising that the apparent rigidity of the 11 p.m. closing time in pubs has attracted its critics. Indeed, the issue became the focus of major public controversy just at the time that the 1987 Licensing Bill, which extended drinking in the afternoon but not (except for ten minutes extra 'drinking-up time') in the evening, was passing through Parliament. The years 1987 and 1988 were the years of the 'lager lout', in which a wave of 'rural riots' swept across formerly tranquil country towns and villages. In a report published in June 1988 the Association of Chief Police Officers recorded that in 1987 more than two thousand people had been

---

*In 1994 the club obtained a licence to sell beer and wine (but not spirits) until 2 a.m., on the grounds that this might be useful for private functions.

arrested in more than two hundred and fifty such incidents in country towns and villages, that half of these disturbances had occurred on Friday and Saturday nights, and that almost all of them involved people who had been drinking.

One of the most surprising features of these disorders was that they were not related to social deprivation. As Douglas Hurd pointed out to the Police Federation Conference, the troubles had occurred in affluent areas of the country. 'You do not find much poverty or social deprivation in these parts,' he said. 'What you do find are too many young people with too much money in their pockets [and] too many pints inside them.'

Some people suggested that the solution to the problem of rural riots lay in shutting pubs earlier or in putting up prices so that the young men in question could not afford to drink so much. A more intelligent solution was offered by Peter Marsh, a lecturer in social psychology at Oxford Polytechnic. After spending a number of years studying the behaviour of drinkers at several hundred pubs on behalf of the brewing industry, Marsh reported that the number of pub disturbances had not increased since he had begun researching into the topic in the late 1970s, but they had become more violent. He also found that nearly half of all violent incidents occurred between 11 p.m. and midnight on Friday and Saturday nights. Marsh suggested that the licensing laws served to increase the likelihood of disorder late at night. The 11 p.m. closing time created a problem, because people had to drink faster, and at closing time they had nowhere to go to discharge their energies and were more likely to fight. He recommended that licensees should be allowed to determine their own closing hours, so that the phenomenon of large numbers of people converging on the streets would be replaced by a more orderly pattern of drifting home. He pointed out that 'free closing' had experimentally been introduced in a number of towns in the Netherlands since 1987, with a resulting decline in street disorder.*

Marsh's work has received support from official quarters. The report of the Association of Chief Police Officers into 'rural riots'

*At the time of writing, the Home Office is considering the possibility of extending the closing time on weekday and Saturday nights from 11 p.m. to midnight. Were such a change to be introduced, it would not solve the problem of violence at closing time but simply shift it by one hour.

in 1987 had led the Home Office to commission a more detailed study, *Drinking and Disorder: a study of non-metropolitan violence*, which appeared in 1989. This report suggested two solutions to the problem: the provision of better public transport away from the entertainment centre late at night, and the importance of planning towns for evening as well as daytime use. It pointed out that in the towns it studied there were certain natural 'cluster points' where people gathered in the daytime and evening to wait, meet and gossip, and that there were also obvious 'congestion points' where crowds or groups coming from different directions might collide; it was where 'cluster points' and 'congestion points' coincided that trouble was likely to occur.

The city of Coventry sought to deal with the problem of lager loutism by imposing a ban on drinking in the city centre. The council's press officer Bob Wade later stated that this was not a panic measure against hordes of drunks on the rampage, that the council had been pressuring the Home Office to allow such a scheme for a couple of years, and that it was the Home Office that was persuaded to agree to the scheme in 1988, when 'lager loutism' hit the headlines. The scheme was originally introduced as a two-year experiment, in which the Home Office invited six other towns, of varying shapes and sizes, to participate. In 1990 the Home Office announced that it was satisfied with the results of the experiment, and would make by-laws banning drinking in city centres generally available to local councils. These laws could not, however, be introduced by the councils themselves. First, they had to spend six months canvassing public opinion and investigating whether there might not be other, more appropriate means of remedying city-centre disorder. Then they had to send the results of this survey to the Home Secretary, who would decide whether or not a by-law might be introduced. By 1994 the Home Secretary had given permission for a further ten towns to join the original seven; apart from Coventry, they include Bath, Chester, Salisbury, Bolton and Hereford.

It is a moot point whether, in those towns in which they have been introduced, the new laws have proved effective in reducing the amount of disorder in the streets. It is largely irrelevant, moreover, whether they have been so or not. In 1990 and 1991 a study of the economic, social and cultural life of twelve (other) towns called 'Out of Hours' was financed jointly by the towns and the Gulbenkian Foundation. Researchers who interviewed older townspeople about their use of the town centres were told that they no longer went into town to visit the cinema or theatre nor to eat out because they were afraid of being accosted by gangs of young people. Certainly, these gangs existed: in Swansea there were up to 5,000 young people milling around on Friday and Saturday nights. But few of the older people had actually encountered these gangs, much less been threatened by them. What had made them afraid, and stopped them from visiting the town centre at night, was sensationalist reporting in the local press; one such account, for example, described Gloucester as 'thug city'.

If people did stop visiting town centres because of newspaper reports of 'lager loutism' rather than because of their own experience, then the councils were right to introduce high-profile but practically ineffective laws banning drinking out of doors – because what mattered was perception, not reality. The important battle was taking place in the media, not out on the streets. As Bob Wade of Coventry City Council admitted, the purpose of the ban on street drinking was 'to improve people's perception of the centre, so that they would be more likely to come in after shopping hours.'

The public perception of 'lager loutism' in the 1980s can thus be compared to that of bootlegging during Prohibition in the United States.* The crimes of the bootleggers were never as important or sensational as newspaper reports of the period suggested: they were exaggerated by journalists in pursuit of good stories and especially by those who wished to see an end to the prohibition experiment. Similarly, stories of lager loutism were exaggerated by sensation-seeking journalists and by all of those who wished to find an easy scapegoat for the breakdown of long-established social values, and who were not prepared to accept that the blame for violence among young men lay, not with the alcohol they drank before they committed the acts of violence, but with the young men themselves, and with the society that had moulded them.

*　　*　　*

*Prohibition, like the bans on city-centre drinking, was intended to change public perception as much as to control popular practice. It will be discussed in Chapter 7.

Banning the consumption of alcohol in public may make people less scared of lager louts, but it also serves to marginalize alcohol by dissociating it from the normal social life of the city, and thus to turn heavy drinking by young men into a greater long-term problem. In Bath, which was one of the towns to introduce the experimental scheme, a number of licensees complained that the tourist trade had suffered because the by-law prevented them from putting tables outside on the pavement. This problem was partly solved by amending the by-law to allow drinking on marked-off areas of pavement outside some restaurants. It nevertheless remains the case that in many towns, and especially in London, licensing laws serve to marginalize drink – to hide it from the public gaze – by preventing people from sitting at tables outside cafés in the Continental manner.

People are only allowed to take drinks outside a pub if the pub has had an area of the pavement included in its premises by the licensing justices. There is generally no sign to indicate whether this is the case, although a few pubs do paint a line on the pavement to indicate where their premises end. If the pavement has not been licensed, then it depends on the police. They may turn a blind eye. However, if people drinking outside the pub have caused an obstruction, or if residents have complained, then the police will tell the publican to prevent his customers from taking drinks outside. Pub-goers who drink on an unlicensed pavement could, in theory, be arrested by the police for obstruction.

If bars place tables outside on an unlicensed pavement, it is up to the council to send round an enforcement officer who will tell the publicans to remove the tables and may have them prosecuted and fined. In the West End of London, bars are also required to obtain planning permission and purchase a licence from Westminster City Council before they put tables and chairs outside on the pavement. Only a limited number of bars take the trouble to go through all the necessary procedures. The dubious legality of the practice of placing tables outside on an unlicensed pavement may help to explain why table service in such establishments is so rarely found. If the pavement has not been licensed, then the bars are not permitted to serve their customers with alcoholic drinks, as technically they have sold them in their capacity as an off-licence. British customers may not mind going into a bar and serving themselves but European tourists in those pavement cafés that do exist in London do not understand that the licensing laws and our national unwillingness to provide service make it unlikely that their requirements will be satisfied. Often they sit down, wait half an hour to be served, then leave.

It is frequently said that people are not really interested in drinking out of doors in Britain because the weather is so bad. This is nonsense. The weather is sometimes damp, but it is generally mild. Paris is a city of pavement cafés yet it is scarcely any drier than London: the average rainfall in Paris is 22.3 inches per year and in London 22.9 inches. There are plenty of pavement cafés in Holland and Belgium, where the weather is much the same as in Britain. The fact that the habit of sitting outside at a café is more cultural than climatic is demonstrated by those cafés on the Continent which heat their terraces so that their customers can sit outside in the depths of winter, such as the famous Falstaff brasserie in Brussels.

There are signs of progress, however. In Leeds, in the summer of 1993, the city council sought to encourage cafés to put tables and chairs out in the street by opening its own outdoor café in the city centre. It supported its initiative by publishing statistics showing that the city, which sits in a 'rain shadow' between the Pennines and the North Sea, enjoys a drier climate, not only than London, but also than Paris or Milan. These statistics were slightly misleading, because it actually rains more often in Leeds in the summer than in Paris or Milan; it is simply that, when it does rain, it does so less heavily. Nevertheless, a number of cafés have followed the council's initiative. By encouraging pavement cafés rather than making life hard for them – as some other councils have done – Leeds City Council has helped to improve the life of the city centre.

Another respect in which people are prevented from sitting out and drinking at pavement cafés in England and Wales is that the law draws a distinction between pubs and restaurants. Pubs are predominantly places where people go to drink alcohol, whereas cafés and restaurants are places where they go to eat food. They cannot simply sit and drink at a table in a café or restaurant because it is unlikely to have been able to obtain a full pub licence which would allow it to serve alcohol to people who do not eat. The situation is different in Scotland, where the licensing authorities have in recent years shown a much more enlightened attitude than their English and Welsh counterparts, and have generally been prepared to grant restaurants full pub licences, whether they have a separate bar area or not. By making it possible for Scottish restaurants to serve alcohol, with or without food, at any time during the day or evening, the licensing authorities have encouraged a boom in Continental-style brasseries, of which the best-known is probably Café Gandolfi in Glasgow, and thus stimulated a more relaxed attitude towards drinking.

Since the liberalization of 1976, Scottish law has also offered the possibility of obtaining a 'refreshment licence', which is supposed to enable cafés that mostly serve food and non-alcoholic drinks also to serve alcoholic drinks to people without the latter being required to order food. These licences have not proved highly popular: by 1992, sixteen years after their introduction, there were only two hundred and forty-five of them in the whole of Scotland, accounting for 1.5 per cent of all licensed premises. In this same year, however, Michael Howard, then the Employment Minister, made a policy statement in which he proposed to introduce a similar form of licence in England and Wales, enabling cafés that did not have bar counters to serve alcohol without food provided that food and non-alcoholic drinks were also available. He made this proposal as part of an initiative to encourage tourism, an industry that created 5 per cent of the Gross National Product: he said that he wanted to introduce Continental-style licensing laws in Britain.

As with many of the measures that have been suggested by this minister in his time, this proposal met with substantial criticism from informed sources. An article in *Marketing Week* described it as wholly discreditable that 'The cultural change is to be imposed, not in the mistaken belief that it would be in the interests of the indigenous population, but because it would be good for the tourist industry. We might as well turn ourselves into one huge theme park and be done with it.' Steve Cox, Campaigns Manager of the Campaign for Real Ale (CAMRA), wondered whether foreign visitors really wanted 'fake Continental cafés to go with British fake Continental lagers'. He also pointed out that the proposed new licence was wholly unnecessary, because café-bars already existed in England and Wales: they had pub licences.

Indeed, these café-bars or café-pubs were becoming increasingly popular. Maybe this was the point. Maybe the real motivation behind the proposal to create a new café-bar licence was in fact to encourage publicans to open more café-bars within the scope of the existing licensing legislation. When Kenneth Clarke, then the Home Secretary and a long-term proponent of licensing law reform, repeated Michael Howard's proposal a year later, Neville Marshall of the National Federation of Licensed Retailers suggested that 'What Kenneth Clarke is trying to do is kick the trade up the backside by telling them to clean up their pubs and go out and attract new people.'

Not surprisingly, many pub landlords objected strongly to the proposal. An article on the subject in the CAMRA monthly newspaper *What's Brewing* quoted Richard Ridler, publican at the Cross Keys in Great Missenden in Buckinghamshire, as saying that the 'tourism theory' was 'rubbish', that one of the reasons why tourists came to Britain was to visit traditional British pubs, and that if the Government wanted to make it easier for tourists to understand British licensing laws then it should allow the pubs to open whenever they want, rather than keeping hours that confused the natives, never mind the tourists. Ridler and other opponents of the proposals were supported by a survey of visitors to Britain, carried out for the Brewers' Society, which found that two out of three foreign visitors preferred British pubs to bars in their own country, principally because British pubs had a 'better atmosphere' and were 'more homely' than their own bars.

The atmosphere of pubs may be one of the reasons why tourists come to Britain, but the fact remains that pub culture exerts a detrimental effect on the behaviour of its citizens, by effectively forcing them to drink alcohol. To a substantial extent, people who go out for a drink have no choice but to drink alcohol because there is a lack of alternative drinking-places to the pub. This has not always been the case.

The coffee houses that became so popular in London in the second half of the seventeenth century were everything that the taverns were not. Sobriety and moderation were the order of the day; people went to read the newspapers, or to talk quietly. The coffee house served as a news exchange, and a place to discuss political and literary topics; it was the social centre for the public life of the middle class, a place where the bourgeoisie developed new forms of commerce and culture. The French traveller Henri Misson de Valbourg, who visited England at the end of that century, was very impressed by what he found there. 'These houses,' he wrote, 'which are very numerous in London, are extremely convenient. You have all manner of news there; you have a good fire, which you may sit by as long as you please; you have a dish of coffee; you meet your friends for the transaction of business, and all for a penny, if you don't care to spend more.' At the beginning of the eighteenth century it was estimated that there were nearly three thousand coffee houses in London, the equivalent of one for every two hundred inhabitants.

Not surprisingly, alehouse- and tavern-keepers felt threatened by this new institution and did their best to stifle its development. As has been described, the first coffee house in London was opened in 1652 by a merchant called Daniel Edwards, who set up his servant Pasqua Rosee in business at the Sign of the Greek's Head. Soon this establishment was attracting so much custom that the local alehouse-keepers petitioned the Lord Mayor to have it closed down on the grounds that Rosee was not a Freeman of the City. Edwards dealt with this problem by having his father-in-law put his coachman, who was a Freeman, in charge of the business, as Rosee's partner. Four years later, the second coffee house in London was opened by a barber called James Farr on the site of the old Rainbow Tavern in Fleet Street. It may well have been at the instigation of the tavern-keepers that some other retailers took out a summons against him 'for making and selling a drink called coffee, whereby in making the same he annoyeth his neighbours by evil smells, and for keeping of fire for the most part night and day, whereby his chimney and chamber hath been set on fire, to the great danger and affrightment of his neighbours.' In fact, Farr's Coffee House survived the Great Fire of 1666 – which destroyed not only the Sign of the Greek's Head and many other coffee houses, but a substantial number of taverns as well. It was not the tavern-keepers that eventually killed off the coffee houses but the coffee houses themselves. They were so successful in spawning new institutions – journals, newspapers, insurance companies such as Lloyd's, the Baltic Exchange, auction houses and clubs – that these in time replaced them, and rendered them redundant.

In the eighteenth century coffee houses, which had been the domain of sober, middle-class men, were also replaced to a certain extent in London by tea gardens, which were patronized by both sexes and all classes. Their popularity contributed substantially to the replacement of coffee by tea as a drink – even though their appeal was limited principally to warm, or at least dry, days in summer. Open from April or May to August or September, they provided flowered walks, shaded arbours, a room with music for dancing, skittle grounds, bowling greens, and various entertainments. Bermondsey Gardens offered exhibitions of paintings; Cuper's Gardens, concerts; Marylebone Gardens, carnivals and fireworks; White Conduit House, cricket. The most exclusive were the Ranelagh Gardens, which opened in Chelsea in 1742. These charged 2s 6d for admission, to include tea (or, for those patrons who preferred it, coffee), bread and butter. Ranelagh were the only gardens to offer a substantial indoor space: the celebrated Rotunda, a circular room, 150 feet in diameter, with a fireplace in the middle, which could be used not only in wet weather but also in winter. People strolled around the Rotunda, or sat in boxes around the circumference. The popularity of Ranelagh and the other tea gardens declined at the end of the eighteenth century. Ranelagh's Rotunda was used for the last time in 1803; soon afterwards, it and the other buildings were demolished, and their contents sold at auction. A portion of the grounds was subsequently absorbed into those of Chelsea Hospital.

In the early nineteenth century, coffee houses became popular once again. These differed, however, from those of the late seventeenth century, in that they appealed principally to working-class men, and helped do the work of the temperance movement in turning them away from public houses and alcoholic drinks. In 1840 one coffee-house keeper went so far as to attribute the appearance of working men's temperance societies 'entirely to the establishment of coffee houses, because a few years ago it used to be almost a matter of ridicule amongst working men to drink coffee; now they are held up to emulate each other. I believe that not one third of my customers ever go into a public house at all. I have never heard an indecent expression and, with two exceptions, have never seen a drunken man in my house.' These coffee houses fell into decline in the second half of the nineteenth century, however – partly because coffee was once again replaced in popularity by tea, which this time was consumed almost entirely at home.

During the nineteenth century, other attempts to provide alternative attractions to the pub, in the form of improved public facilities, met with hostility from publicans, who claimed, for example, that the parks that were created in several industrial towns would damage their trade. Indeed, an Act of Parliament of 1850 that enabled towns to support libraries and museums from the rates was opposed in some places by mobs that included 'friends of the beer-house interests'. Thanks in part to the opposition of publicans, the number of alternative attractions remained limited, and the consumption of alcoholic drink remained the principal recreation of the working classes. Indeed, this period includes the decade of British history for which the highest reliable records of drink consumption exist – the 1870s, when it was common for 25 per cent of working-class earnings to be spent on drink. On average each person consumed a hundred and fifty litres of beer and six litres of spirits a year, but the consumption of working-class men must have been at least double that, for it was a time when heavy drinking was going out of fashion among the middle and upper classes, while very few women of any class drank alcohol at all. If, after forty years of the temperance and teetotal movements*, working men spent a very high proportion of their earnings on drink in the 1870s, it was largely because there was little else on which these earnings could be spent. In 1877 Ruskin wrote to a group of working men to say that, 'If I were in your place, I should drink myself to death in six months, because I had nothing to amuse me.' Benjamin Seebohm Rowntree carried out two studies of working-class life in York, in 1899 and in 1935. In the second study he commented that 'Twenty or thirty years ago the main street in York was crowded, night after night, with young people walking aimlessly up and down.'

By the time of Rowntree's second study, however, there was no shortage of attractions. When he interviewed publicans to find out if there was as much heavy drinking as there had been at the end of the nineteenth century, he was told that young people did not generally drink a lot of alcohol because their lives were too

*These will be discussed in Chapter 7.

full of other interests. Foremost among these was the cinema. On average more than twenty million cinema tickets were purchased every week. Of cinema-goers, 80 per cent went in the cheap seats; that is to say, most of those who attended were working class. And many of those who attended were young. It was estimated by Rowntree that in York in the mid-1930s half the customers of cinemas were children and young people, and that many of them went twice a week or more often. One of the tasks undertaken by the researchers who took part in the famous Mass-Observation study of Bolton in 1937–1938 was to count several thousand pub-goers and to estimate their ages; they concluded that only 7 per cent of them were under twenty-five. One of the reasons for the absence of young people from pubs, the report commented, was that young people were interested in courtship, not in drink – which was why they strolled about the streets and went to dance halls and cinemas. As one employer commented in 1931, 'Youths of eighteen to twenty-four go in for smart clothes and are dancing mad. This type never mention public houses.'

It has also been suggested that the introduction of afternoon closing during the First World War proved beneficial afterwards in so far as it served to encourage men to devote their time to other activities, at least on Saturday afternoons. Middle-aged men no longer sat 'soaking' in pubs after having worked a half-day on Saturday morning. Instead, they went out and watched other people exerting themselves in sporting activities. This may well have been the case. But for the authorities generally to have attributed the reduction in drunkenness in the period between the wars to the reduced licensing hours, and to have as a result supported the continuation of stringent restrictions on those hours, was quite absurd. Drunkenness had fallen because drink was out of fashion. People, and especially young people, had better things to do than to spend their free time in pubs. They also had vices other than drink freely available to them, such as machine-made cigarettes, betting on horses, and gambling, principally on the football pools. In 1935 total consumer expenditure on tobacco was £151 million, on alcohol £237 million, on betting and gambling anything between £300 million and £500 million. Beer consumption was only 40 per cent of what it had been in the 1870s and spirits consumption had fallen to as low as 15 per cent of the level of sixty years before. It was even being suggested that gambling, supposedly a similar vice to drink, had taken the place previously occupied by drink in the minds of moralists.

The development of alternative places of entertainment to the pub and alternative vices to alcoholic drink coincided with the development of alternative drinking places. The second half of the 1930s saw a craze for milk bars which lasted through the Second World War. Although these bars became popular because of their modern, mechanized, American appearance, the idea of opening milk bars in England in fact arose from their success in Australia where they had been introduced at the beginning of the 1930s and had led to a great increase in milk consumption, not only in the bars but also at home. The first milk bar in Britain was the Black and White, which was opened by an Australian, the Hon. Hugh D. Macintosh, in Fleet Street in the City of London in 1935. It served about fifty non-alcoholic drinks with milk as the basis. Malted milk, yeast milk, milkshakes, milk punch, milk cocktails, egg and milk, milk soups, milk phosphates (made fizzy with phosphorus) and plain milk, either hot or cold, were all available. Charles (now Lord) Forte read an article in the *Evening Standard* about the Black and White Milk Bar and went to see it. He proposed to Macintosh that they went into partnership and served a variety of foods but Macintosh said that was not the purpose of a milk bar. Forte then went and found himself a site in Upper Regent Street and opened the Meadow Milk Bar. Milk bars were soon all the rage, and not just in London. Two years after the Black and White Milk Bar had been opened there were more than a thousand of them across the country. They were busy in winter as well as in summer. *The Times* wrote in 1936 that 'The first men who stood at milk bars were already victims of taunts from public houses, where "milksop" has actually revived as a term of abuse' but that now 'Stalwart young men think nothing of standing at a milk bar and drinking glasses of milk'. The Mass-Observation survey of Bolton reported that, although there was only a single milk bar in the town, many pub landlords nevertheless saw the milk bars as a threat to their business. A high percentage of the milk bar's clientele was under the age of twenty-five, which was precisely the age group that was seen least often in pubs. The brewers had become sufficiently disturbed by the success of milk bars across the country to have been considering selling milk drinks alongside beer, and indeed had made an approach to the Milk Marketing Board to this effect.

During the war, free milk for schoolchildren was introduced. When these children grew up they retained a taste for milk but a desire for something more sophisticated. Their parents drank tea, so they turned to coffee. The coffee bar craze of the Fifties was thus partly an extension of the milk bar craze of the Thirties. Young people were attracted to coffee bars by the theatrical performance of ornate new *espresso* machines but, having been brought up on milk, they did not drink strong, black *espresso*. They preferred *cappuccino*, essentially frothy milk with a coffee flavour. Indeed, when people asked for *espresso*, what they really wanted, and what they were given, was *cappuccino*. If a person wanted a real *espresso* he asked for a 'Roman *espresso*'. Neither the *cappuccino* nor the *espresso* tasted convincingly like the Italian original. It did not matter. Young people did not go to coffee bars for the coffee, but because these provided a place for them to meet. The *Times Educational Supplement* pointed out in 1955 that 'The majority of the people sitting sipping their *espressos* are not the sort that are found in the saloon bar or the Hammersmith Palais. They have not been tempted from anywhere except their own homes. For the bars really have built up their own public, and taught them to enjoy sitting out late in London over a black coffee and a piece of iced *gâteau*. The majority of them are young city workers, most of whom either have a home in the suburbs or else share a bedsitter in Bayswater or Earls Court. To them the bars bring not only a certain amount of luxury on the cheap. They also bring companionship.'

The heyday of the coffee bars came in the 1960s. Then they declined. By serving large cups of milky coffee that their customers could spoon around for half an hour the coffee bars ensured their own downfall. Italy is still full of coffee bars because people who drink shots of *espresso* standing up stay only five minutes. In Britain, the bars died a slow death during the inflationary period of the early Seventies, when the space became too expensive to rent. Admittedly, the last few years have seen a resurgence of coffee bars in the centre of a few major cities, notably in Soho in the West End of London, centred around the Bar Italia in Frith Street, which has long served the local Italian population. Some of them, such as the Bar Italia itself and the Café Nero opposite, have ensured that customers do not stay too long by offering nothing more comfortable than high stools on which to sit. Those customers who want to sit more comfortably can do so only at one of the tables that the bars have put out, legally or illegally, in the street. Coffee bars have re-emerged because of the 11 p.m. closing time imposed on pubs by the licensing laws, and because Soho is close to the cinemas and theatres of the West End, and home to a number of nightclubs.

Outside a few areas such as Soho, however, young people have nowhere to go out to other than the pub. And pubs are designed for the consumption of alcohol, to the exclusion of everything else. Certainly they serve soft drinks – but these are hardly inexpensive. A survey by the Consumers' Association in 1989 found that the average price of orange juice in a pub was the equivalent of £2.37 a pint, that of bitter lemon £2.03 and that of tonic water £2.02. This compared with 93p for a pint of bitter beer, of which 19p was excise duty. Moreover, even if the prices of soft drinks in pubs were not extortionate, it is unlikely that they would have become significantly more popular among pub-goers. After all, it was not by looking at the provision of a better range of more interesting soft drinks that the big pub-owning brewery groups responded in the late 1980s to the governmental clamp-down on drivers who had been drinking, and to the growing public perception that drinking and driving was no longer acceptable. Instead, they devoted large sums of money to the research and development of low-alcohol and non-alcoholic beers for people who wanted to spend their evenings in the pub and then drive home afterwards. As was explained at the time by Andrew Knowles, who designed White Label low-alcohol bitter for Whitbread, 'Soft drinks break the rules of social intercourse in pubs. You need something that doesn't make you look as though you are cheating.' At least beer from which some or all of the alcohol had been removed looked like the real thing, even if it did not taste quite like it.

The reason why the rules of social intercourse in pubs require a drink to be – or to appear to be – alcoholic can be found in the drinking customs of pre-industrial artisan society. Before the emergence of a purely market economy in the middle of the nineteenth century the workplace was as much a social as an economic community, in which the symbolic acts that established social ties took precedence over productive activity. The most important of these symbolic acts was the consumption of alcoholic drink. Labouring men drank together in order to affirm that they belonged to a group. It was through drink that the loyalty of an apprentice to the group he had joined was ensured. In almost all trades apprentices were expected to pay a drink fine when they began their service and when they completed one of various stages in their learning process. And it was through drink that the principles of equality within the group were affirmed. In many trades any purchase of new clothes by an individual required that they be 'wetted', that is, a drink fine was owed on their account. If a man refused to drink, or refused to contribute to the drinking expenses of his companions, he was ostracized: he had effectively chosen to withdraw from society.

In his *Philosophy of Artificial and Compulsory Drinking Usages*, the Scottish magistrate and early temperance campaigner John Dunlop described in great detail the treatment that was meted out to recusants in the early nineteenth century. They were sent to Coventry; their shoes were nailed to the floor; their tools were hidden. Sometimes, their tools were stolen by their workmates and pawned in order to pay for drink. It was the practice among miners to lay a recusant on his back on top of a coal-rake, with its teeth facing upwards, and hold him there while they placed a crow-bar on his chest and pressed down on it until he yielded.

With the coming of capitalism, the workplace lost its social function. Its purpose now lay solely in maximizing production. The social values of the workplace, and the drinking customs that had affirmed them, were transferred to the pub. The pub afforded a retreat for the working classes from the interference of their social and economic superiors; it was in the pub that, in a world that was being changed without any consideration for working-class interests or the values that the working classes held dear, their old ways could continue. Indeed, it is the role of the pub as the preserver of the past that offers a small crumb of justification for the pseudo-historical pub design of the big brewery groups. For the last century and a half, the drinking customs of the pub, and especially the buying, giving and receiving of rounds of drinks, have preserved the values of pre-industrial artisan culture. Some people do attempt nowadays to perform this ritual with non-alcoholic drinks but it is not the same – not least because they simply did not exist at the time when the custom of round-buying originated.* Pubs perpetuate male artisan and working-class traditions – which in England and Wales has meant the consumption of beer, and in Scotland and Northern Ireland, that of whisky.

Not only does the history of the practice of round-buying explain why people drink alcohol in pubs, but it also helps to account for their drinking more of it than they might otherwise have wanted. After all, social convention requires each person to purchase a round of drinks as soon as one or two members of the company have finished theirs, regardless of whether the person whose turn it is to buy the round has finished his drink from the current or the previous round or indeed the one before that. The ritual significance of the practice of buying rounds of drinks, and the excessive consumption of alcohol to which it tended to lead, was shown most dramatically during the First World War, when the fellowship of those who stayed at home with those who fought at the Front was demonstrated by the purchase of drinks for soldiers who were home on leave. In Lincoln in 1917 a young man, who had been awarded the Victoria Cross for bravery and had returned home wounded, found that the customers of his local pub had paid for a hundred and twenty pints to be waiting for him when he arrived. Apparently, he accepted the offer with such enthusiasm that he 'was nearly dead with it before he was rescued'. In another case at Sheffield, three soldiers, who had been no less lavishly entertained, were found lying incapable on the tramlines. The Government had, in fact, forbidden the treating of soldiers with drinks at the beginning of the war, but evidently this order was widely ignored. More controversially, the Government also forbade members of the general public from buying each other drinks. The explanation for this prohibition lay in the development among groups of workmen of the custom of buying excessive numbers of rounds of drinks 'partly through abundance of money and partly through war excitement', a custom which affected both the quality and the quantity of their work the next day. It led, however, to such unfortunate cases as that of a

---

* Non-alcoholic drinks also lack the symbolic value of alcoholic ones, as will be explained in the Conclusion.

workman in Liverpool who was given three months' hard labour for treating a friend, and that of a husband in Bristol who was fined for buying his wife a drink.

If many pub-goers continue to drink heavily today, this is to be explained not only by the survival of the tradition of round-buying but also by the fact that the rounds tend to be bought, and drunk, quickly – as a result of the tradition of drinking while standing up. Before the early nineteenth century, the only feature that distinguished the pub from the private houses that surrounded it was the signboard that hung over the door. Its ground floor was divided into tap room, public parlour, bar, kitchen and publican's private parlour. The tap room was furnished with wooden tables and fixed wooden benches round the walls; the public parlour was for more genteel customers, and had tables and chairs rather than benches. Drinks were brought to the customers by the pub staff; there was no bar in the modern sense of the word. What was then called the bar was a separate room that the public was forbidden to enter; it approximated to the reception desk and office in a modern hotel.*

The pub changed because of the dram shop. A product of the gin age of the eighteenth century, the dram shop had neither parlour nor tap room but sold spirits and wine across the counter. These were either drunk by the customer standing on the premises or taken away. A dram-shop element began to appear in some public houses in the early years of the nineteenth century. It became the practice to open up one side of the bar with a counter, across which all orders were received and all drinks distributed. With the appearance of the counter, the traditional image of the public house, as a private house that was open to the public, began to disappear. The owner of the house was no longer 'mine host'; his guests were no longer waited on by waiters in the parlour and by pot boys in the tap room. The pub became a shop in which goods were sold over the counter by smartly-dressed shop girls. The pub thus fell victim to the retailing revolution of the 1820s, which had been made possible by the invention of gas lighting and plate glass, enabling the premises to be advertised in the most dramatic way. The gin palaces that were built in

---

*An archaic survival of such a pub is to be found at The Crooked Billet in the village of Stoke Row in Oxfordshire.

the 1830s were simply glamorous-looking shops from which customers bought alcoholic drinks to take away or to drink standing up on the premises.*

The introduction of perpendicular drinking also suited the economic interests of the owners of gin palaces. In order to recoup their investment from customers who had individually little money to spend, they needed the turnover of customers to be as large as possible. The gin palace, observed the German socialist Karl Kautsky, was 'set up so that no-one could possibly feel tempted to linger longer than is necessary to empty a glass . . . In such a place there is not a trace of *camaraderie* or exchange of ideas.'

The gin palaces thus formed part of the Industrial Revolution: the architectural equivalent of distilled spirits. Just as spirits speeded up the process of inebriation, so the bar sped up the process of drinking. Gin palaces with their bars resembled factory assembly lines. Indeed, the bar has been described as 'a traffic innovation', which hurried up drinking just as the railway sped up travel or the mechanical loom sped up textile production.

With the gin palace came class segregation. By the 1830s decent London tradesmen were drinking at home, and private as opposed to public drinking was becoming a mark of gentility. By the 1850s no respectable urban Englishman entered an ordinary public house, and the village inn, where all classes drank together, had become a nostalgic memory. Since his more prosperous customers had left him, the publican provided fewer facilities and the pub became more like a shop; that is to say, it was not only the conversion of pubs into gin palaces that alienated the middle classes but also the departure of the better-off from pubs that led publicans to transform their premises into industrial drinking places.

Now that the middle and upper classes had left the pubs, they lost their personal interest in the maintenance of the institution. By the end of the nineteenth century it seemed that attacks by social reformers and anti-alcohol campaigners on working-class drunkenness might cause the pub to disappear altogether. By the early years of the twentieth century, the then Liberal government

*Unfortunately, none of these survive today in their original form. Glamorous 'gin palaces' such as The Salisbury in St Martin's Lane in the West End of London and The Crown Liquor Saloon in Belfast date from much later in the nineteenth century.

was dedicated to reducing the number of licensed premises, and in some areas to getting rid of them altogether.*

The brewers had very little idea how to face the threat to their prosperity – with the exception of one bright young brewer called Sydney Nevile who had the idea that pubs might be reformed. Nevile greatly surprised his colleagues when, at a meeting of brewers in 1908, he declared that 'Brewers could make more money out of "England sober" than "England drunken"; that they should not leave "temperance reform" to the prohibitionists; and that they should face the problem not merely as a matter of conscience but on the grounds of commercial interest.' He argued that, if, for example, they sold food in their pubs, the profits they took on this would outweigh any decrease in takings resulting from a decline in drunkenness.

It was not, however, until after the First World War had brought in its wake social upheaval and a general propensity to accept change that Nevile's ideas were countenanced by the major brewers and came gradually to be put into practice. Nevile himself, having joined Whitbread in 1919, was instrumental in the improvement of some pubs, and the construction of some new ones. One of the first of the latter was The Welcome Inn at Eltham, built in the early 1920s. 'We decided, having the space, to make a bold experiment,' Nevile later explained. 'Our first plan was to have no drinking at the bar, but to provide waiter service instead; the idea was that the customer should remain seated at table, but this experiment was in the end found to be impracticable. For various reasons, the custom of getting what one needs at a bar is in Britain too deeply ingrained to be easily changed: perhaps this is due to the difficulty of attracting the attention of waiters, or the feeling that it is necessary to tip those who attend to one's needs.'

The Welcome Inn was an entirely new house, to which Whitbread had transferred the licence of The Burrage Arms in Woolwich, which had been demolished because it was standing in the way of road widening. From the beginning of the century until the Second World War those brewers who wished to build new, more salubrious pubs or to improve existing ones were regularly obstructed by licensing justices who refused to allow

*The 'local option' campaign will be discussed in Chapter 7.

existing pubs to be enlarged, seeing the additions only as extra drinking space. They believed that proposals by brewers to improve their pubs were simply a device to enable them to have poor and inconvenient houses rebuilt and thus increased in value, that brewers who promised that they would serve food as well as drink in their improved pubs would soon forget this undertaking, and that the result would merely be a large increase in the sales of beer. The justices were therefore prepared to allow improvements at one pub only if the licence of another was surrendered. This exasperated Nevile. 'It seemed impossible to convince many benches that better conditions would induce a higher standard of behaviour,' he wrote. The desertion of the pubs by the middle and upper classes in the nineteenth century had wrought its consequences. The justices whose role it was to control the licensing of pubs no longer visited them, and knew nothing about what went on inside.

Efforts to improve the quality of pubs were also obstructed by anti-alcohol campaigners. Ernest Oldmeadow, the editor of *The Tablet*, described to the Royal Commission on Licensing of 1929–1930 how he had attended a brewster (licensing) session at which 'An innkeeper sought permission to make his house, which lacked light and air, more healthy for his family and customers. This request was fought so fiercely by the local temperance* organizations that, as a novice, I asked for an explanation and received the prompt answer, "We must make drink stink." I was told that, next to a man lying drunk in the gutter, the best argument for temperance was a squalid public house, and that every attempt by a publican to improve his premises must therefore be resisted to the utmost.'

This suited some of the brewers rather well. Mr B. S. Strauss, the Licensing Justice for the St Marylebone District, told the 1929–1930 Royal Commission that more pubs in London 'on the Continental model' would be welcomed by nine-tenths of the London justices but that 'Brewers do not want to spend a lot of money on increasing the size of premises and putting in tables, etc., when they know that it is going to lessen rather than increase the consumption of alcoholic liquor.' Just as the

---

*The term 'temperance', which properly meant 'moderation', was (and is) widely misused to refer to campaigners who were opposed to the consumption of alcohol in any quantity and in any form.

managers of pubs in the twentieth century have been instrumental in blocking reforms of the licensing hours, so the owners played their part in ensuring that pubs remained insalubrious drinking dens.

Nevertheless, a substantial number of pubs were improved in the period between the wars. In particular, the 1930s saw the development of 'roadhouses': large neo-Tudor or neo-Georgian buildings that were constructed at major road intersections on the outskirts of cities and in the countryside, largely in response to the spread of private motoring. These offered not only large bars but also restaurants, gardens, and entertainment and dance halls. Some also had heated and floodlit swimming pools ('lidos'), tennis courts and bowling greens. They attracted the disapproval of George Orwell, who condemned them as 'dismal sham-Tudor places' that posed a threat to working-class drinking traditions. But this was the whole point. They made pubs respectable once again; they enabled the middle classes to return to them. Even more important, they were frequented not only by men but also by women.

The attendance, and acceptance, of women in pubs has fluctuated markedly since the middle of the eighteenth century when, according to the magistrate Patrick Colquhoun, 'It was thought disgraceful for a woman (except on holiday occasions) to be seen in a public house, and those who would venture to sit down among men in a tap room were considered as infamous prostitutes.' The presence of women became more common in the latter part of the eighteenth and early nineteenth centuries, probably because of the growing popularity of spirits, which were regarded as more of a woman's drink than beer. Indeed, it is possible that the personification of 'Mother Gin' should be attributed to its popularity among female drinkers. Women were among the principal customers of the eighteenth-century dram shops, and appear in the early nineteenth century to have transferred this patronage to the gin palaces. In 1828 the French sociologist Gustave d'Eichthal described these female patrons as 'a sight to be seen as they gulp down their glasses of gin, whisky, toddy and cheap brandy'.

During the course of the nineteenth century, however, women gradually disappeared from the pubs, as the domains of men and women became polarized. Women ran the family home, and if men wished to avoid them they went to the pub. The exclusion of women from pubs was also a product of Victorian notions of propriety: pubs were not places in which women should be seen. These notions culminated in an Act that was passed in New Zealand in 1910 which made employment of barmaids illegal except for members of the licensee's family and barmaids employed before the Act came into force. The purpose of the Act was partly an anti-alcohol measure – to make bars less attractive to young men – but its intention was also to demonstrate that the pub was no place for a young woman, who belonged in the home.

After the First World War, at least in Britain, women began to return to pubs – a process that was accelerated by the creation of clean, modern improved public houses. By the 1930s it was common for a quarter or a third of the customers in town and city centres at weekends to be women. They did not tend to go out alone or in groups, however; they were generally accompanied by their husbands or their boyfriends. The pub remained male territory; it was just that women were no longer excluded from it. This has remained the case in modern times. In 1977, a survey of what the British thought about their pubs was carried out for the *Sun* and only one in three women named the pub as her favourite place for a drink.

The feelings of alienation that were still experienced by women who went into pubs, and the likelihood that they would be regarded as 'fair game' if they stayed there, were the underlying causes of the development of wine bars in the 1960s, 1970s and 1980s. The seminal event of the wine bar boom occurred in 1972, when Julia Carpenter, a former interior designer, opened Wolsey's Wine Bar in the Fulham Road in west London as a place where women could meet for a social drink without their intentions being 'misunderstood'; this was the first occasion on which a woman had been granted a full bar licence. The alienation of women from pubs and their attraction to wine bars have been ensured by the very different architectural styles that have been adopted by the two institutions. The opaque glass and curtained windows and doors of most British pubs serve sharply to separate the inside of the pub from the street; there are rarely tables and chairs outside; it is as though the pub has turned its back on the street. Before someone enters a strange pub he or she has no means of knowing what kind of atmosphere and what sort of people – if any – will be found within. Wine bars, on the other hand, have generally adopted a much more open appearance, allowing the passer-by to see inside and to enter with confidence. They have also used potted palms, framed pictures and tablecloths in order to create a less threatening and more domestic atmosphere. The pubs that have proved most popular with women have generally been those that have incorporated some of the elements of wine-bar architecture.

The other group whose exclusion has helped turn the pub into a male-oriented, heavy-drinking place, is children. They were gradually excluded from pubs during the nineteenth and early twentieth centuries, the purpose being to prevent them from drinking heavily. The 1834 Parliamentary Select Committee on Drunkenness took evidence that showed the enormous extent to which child drinking prevailed in the United Kingdom. Medical testimony was given of disease in quite young children caused by spirit-drinking; reports from Lincolnshire spoke of 'children of twelve or fourteen years of age dead drunk in the streets'. At this time there were no restrictions of any kind upon the sale of liquor to children of any age inside or outside public houses. In 1839 the Metropolitan Police Act prohibited publicans in London from selling spirits to any child apparently under sixteen for consumption on the premises, but there is evidence that in many places this was ignored.

It was not until 1872 that Parliament went so far as to prohibit the supply of spirits to anyone under sixteen anywhere in the country, and even then a clause in the Bill that would have prohibited the sale of beer to anyone under fourteen was rejected. Among those who opposed it in the Commons was a Mr Lock, who asked: 'Why should not children under fourteen who work be allowed to have beer with their meals?' It was not until 1901 that the sale of beer to children under fourteen was finally prohibited, and even then the presence of children in pubs was expressly sanctioned if they had come to fetch their parents' beer in sealed vessels. Indeed, it was alleged that some publicans installed special steps leading up to the bar for children too small to see over the top. After 1908, however, children under the age of fourteen were forbidden from entering a bar, and had instead to fetch their parents' beer from separate 'jug and bottle' departments.* This prohibition remained in force until the 1990s.

It may well have appeared reasonable, at the beginning of the twentieth century, that children should have been protected from the worst excesses of pub life in this way. By the later part of the century, however, the law excluding children from bars† was proving socially detrimental.

It served to marginalize drinking from normal society; it prevented children, while still under parental control, from gradually becoming used to seeing people drink alcohol, and it made pubs seem more desirable and more dangerous to children than they really were. If the phenomenon of 'lager loutism' should have been blamed on any one thing, it was the law that prevented children from going into pubs with their parents. This could have been demonstrated by a comparison of restaurants in Britain and France. Many British visitors to France have commented on the presence and good behaviour of children in restaurants. Many French visitors to Britain have commented on the opposite. French children have been taken to, and tolerated in, restaurants because they know how to behave; British children have not because they do not. British children do not know how to behave because they have not been brought up from an early age in an atmosphere of people eating and drinking around them. If they had been allowed into pubs their behaviour might well have been different.

Permission was not given, however, until very recently. And, as in the case of afternoon opening, it was bestowed in Scotland before it was granted in England and Wales. From the beginning of 1991 Scottish pubs that served meals were enabled to apply for 'children's certificates' that allowed children into their premises until 8 p.m. A year after the introduction of this measure Michael Howard, then the Employment Minister, made a policy statement in which he said that he was proposing to introduce 'children's licences' in England and Wales as part of a package of 'tourist-friendly' measures (including the café-bar proposal mentioned earlier). It took another couple of years for this commitment to be transformed into legislation. Only since the

---

*The minimum age for drinking in pubs was raised to eighteen in 1923, and for the purchase of drinks for consumption at home was increased to eighteen in 1953.
†They were allowed into separate rooms that had specifically been set aside for the consumption of food.

beginning of 1995 have English and Welsh publicans been able to apply for 'children's certificates' to allow children under fourteen into bars before 9 p.m. provided that they are accompanied by an adult and that food and soft drinks are available for sale. In the first few months of the operation of the new law, moreover, there have been complaints that licensing justices have imposed excessively stringent conditions on pubs applying for children's certificates, involving expensive redecoration, and that as a result many publicans have shrunk away from requesting the new certificates or have withdrawn their applications. Nevertheless, the significance of the change cannot be gainsaid.

Indeed, the most important developments in the nature of the pub during the course of the twentieth century have begun to occur at the end of it. The public house is in the process of being transformed from a place that men go to on their own in order to drink into a place that welcomes women and children, into a venue to which families go together, often in order to eat. For the greater part of the twentieth century, not only have pubs generally alienated women and excluded children but they have offered drink without any food to absorb it. During the First World War a number of the state-owned pubs in the Carlisle area experimented with opening outside permitted licensing hours for the sale of snacks and non-intoxicating drinks, but they soon gave up for lack of demand. The general manager, Sir Edgar Sanders, later told the 1929 Royal Commission on Licensing that 'In the majority of houses there is no demand whatever for food, and if the Central Authority put fresh food in those houses they would have to take it away again at the end of the day and there would be an absolute waste.' This remained the case until as recently as the 1970s.

Pubs began to serve food largely because of the growth of competition from, and the experience of, wine bars. The number of these grew substantially in the late 1960s and early 1970s, but between 1973 and 1975 many operators were forced out of business by escalating wine prices and the fact that their novelty had worn off. When wine bars began to re-emerge from 1976 onwards, they did so in a slightly different guise, placing much more emphasis on food. Indeed, many of the new wine bars that opened in the late 1970s and early 1980s were not really wine bars at all: they did not have full pub licences but restaurant licences, according to which they were not permitted to sell wine to their customers unless the latter also ate.

The experience of the wine bars thus alerted publicans to the economic potential of serving food at a time when they were looking for new means of attracting customers, not only because they were losing them to wine bars but, more importantly, because people were deserting the pubs in order to go and drink at home.

This had been a battle that publicans had been fighting ever since the wireless became popular in the 1930s and the television in the 1950s, but the losses increased greatly in the 1980s because of the ubiquity of video recorders and the improvement in the quality of the canned beer that was sold in off-licences for drinking at home following the development of so-called 'canned draught' beer. Also, wine had become very popular, thanks largely to the supermarkets, and good-quality wine had always been a rarity in pubs. If they were going to survive, the pubs had to attract back their customers somehow. So they turned to food. By the early 1990s, catering accounted for an average of 25 per cent of pub turnover; in one survey, 66 per cent of those who told market researchers that they went to pubs said that they were attracted to them by pub food. It was being reported, moreover, that wine bars were in decline. A survey found that the percentage of the adult population visiting wine bars was falling because many former wine bar customers had defected to pubs. Wine bars were in decline because they had fulfilled their role, which was to force pubs to improve: to sell good food (and even drinkable wine) and to make themselves attractive to women.

In the 1980s it was commonly said that the most popular, and ubiquitous, form of restaurant in Britain was no longer the fish and chip shop but the Indian restaurant. By the 1990s, when nine out of ten pubs were serving meals, accounting for 40 per cent of all catering outlets in Britain, the most popular venue for eating out was no longer the Indian restaurant, but the pub.

Not only has the number of pubs that sell food grown enormously in the last few years, but so has the range and quality of the food that they offer. Some restaurant critics, including the influential Fay Maschler of the London *Evening Standard*, have expressed the view that 'The role of the bistro in French life could and should be taken on by pubs in Britain'. This is increasingly the case in Maschler's home territory of London, where a number of down-at-heel, inner-city pubs or otherwise run-down buildings have been converted into open, airy, bare-boarded premises with plenty of tables and chairs, in which the service of traditional cask-conditioned beers is combined with a good range of wines and fashionable, Mediterranean-style food of high quality, all of them served together in the bar area rather than in separate rooms. The Eagle and The Peasant in Clerkenwell, The Lansdowne in Primrose Hill, The Fire Station in Waterloo, The Westbourne Tavern in Paddington and The Paradise by Way of Kensal Green* in Kensal Green, have all been transformed in this way; they may well represent the brightest future for the pub in Britain.

The future of the pub does not, however, lie in food alone. It is also to be found in the provision of alternative facilities, in learning from the experience of alternative institutions in the past, such as the coffee houses of the late seventeenth and early eighteenth centuries, in which the first newspapers were produced. If chains of pseudo-French brasseries such as The Dôme and Café Rouge can offer newspapers to their customers, there is no reason why pubs should not also do so. Indeed, in the light of the decline of publicly-funded libraries, it would be perfectly possible for pubs to provide a private alternative. A number of pubs now offer shelves filled with books as a form of decoration; there is no good reason why these books should not be intended for use. There is no reason, either, why pubs should not sell books and newspapers – as some bars do in France – nor indeed branch out into other areas of retail trade. If pubs are to survive, they must continue to adapt with the times, to provide facilities that people cannot find in their own homes. So far they have been hampered by a lack of foresight, and by the petty restrictions of the licensing laws, a hang-over from the days when pubs were mere drinking dens and their customers had to be prevented from spending all their money on achieving a state of alcoholic stupor. Now that the laws are, at long last, being modernized, there is no longer any obstacle to prevent pubs from responding imaginatively to the changing social circumstances of the late twentieth and early twenty-first centuries.

---

*The name is taken from the last line of G. K. Chesterton's poem, 'Before the Roman came to Rye or out to Severn strode/The rolling English drunkard made the rolling English road.'

5

FOR ALL THE TEA IN CHINA

JUST AS ATTEMPTS TO IMPROVE THE QUALITY OF PUBS HAVE BEEN blocked by brewers, who have seen greater profit in maintaining them as drinking dens, so the heavy consumption of alcohol by the pubs' customers has been encouraged by the Government in the pursuit of revenue from taxation.

Indeed, the worst period of drunkenness in British history arose as a direct result of governmental action. The second half of the seventeenth century saw a substantial growth in the popularity of spirits, especially of French brandy. Following the accession of the Dutch Prince William of Orange to the English throne in 1688, however, war was declared with France, and efforts were made to prohibit the importation of French produce by imposing a very high level of duty. It remained possible to obtain French brandy, but only if it had been smuggled through Portugal, Spain or the Netherlands – in which case it passed as 'German brandy'. The difficulty, expense and dangers of smuggling raised the price of French brandy beyond the level that ordinary people could afford, so they turned to domestically-produced spirits instead.

Not only was the King concerned to prevent the expenditure

of British bullion on French goods, but he was chronically in need of funds to finance his military campaigns. The Worshipful Company of Distillers had been founded during the reign of King Charles I by Sir Theodore de Mayerne-Turquet, the King's physician, and Thomas Cademan, the Queen's doctor, at a time when spirits were consumed principally for medical purposes. From Charles they had obtained a royal charter that awarded their Company a monopoly of distillation within the cities of London and Westminster, and to a surrounding distance of twenty-one miles. One of the first actions of William III after he ascended the throne was to break the monopoly of the Company of Distillers, and to allow anybody to manufacture spirits on payment of a duty.

The desire of the King to prohibit the importation of French brandy and encourage the manufacture of domestic spirits in order to maximize revenue reflected the concerns of the most powerful group in Parliament. This was the landed interest – gentlemen farmers who lived off the revenue from their estates and who were faced with a glut of corn after several large harvests. In the 1690s they voted through a series of statutes that sought to deal with the glut by encouraging the use of the corn for distillation into gin. It was permitted to distil spirits from other materials, but it was impracticable because Parliament imposed high duties on spirits derived from anything other than corn.

Successive reductions in the duties on gin and an increase in the duty on beer meant that after 1694 gin cost less than beer. National gin consumption increased from half a million gallons in the year of the Glorious Revolution in 1688 to 19 million gallons in 1742. That is ten times the amount of gin consumed in Britain today, although the population was then only one-tenth as large.* And most of that was drunk in London, in some areas of which it was claimed that one in every four houses sold gin.

Much of the gin, moreover, was drunk by women. 'We find the contagion has spread among [the female sex] to a degree hardly possible to be conceived,' reported a committee of justices from the Middlesex Bench in 1736. 'Unhappy mothers habituate themselves to these distilled liquors, whose children are born weak

---

*Eighteenth-century gin was also much stronger than the modern version, as it was drunk at the strength that it came off the still rather than broken down with water, as it is today.

and sickly, and often look old and shrivelled as though they had numbered many years; others, again, give [gin] daily to their children, whilst young, and learn them, even before they can go*, to taste and approve of this great and certain destroyer.' Some women treated their children with even less consideration than that. In one case that came before the Old Bailey, a young woman named Judith Dufour had a two-year-old child housed in the workhouse, where he had been given a new set of clothes. The mother came to take him out for the afternoon. No sooner was she clear of the workhouse, however, than she strangled the child, stripped off the clothes, and threw the naked corpse into a ditch in Bethnal Green. She sold the clothes for 1s 4d; with the money she bought gin.

In the circumstances it might not appear surprising that the death rate in London in the first half of the eighteenth century far exceeded the birth rate. The historian Peter Clark has attempted to underplay the part played by gin in causing this deficit, pointing out that the increase in death rate had less to do with adult than with infant mortality, and arguing that the latter should be attributed to smallpox and typhus rather than gin; but this ignores what is suggested by the report of the Middlesex justices and the story of Judith Dufour, that many of the children died because their mothers lived off gin during pregnancy and were more interested in finding the wherewithal to pay for gin than in looking after the children when they were born. 'The diminution of births,' wrote Corbyn Morris (later commissioner of the customs) in 1751, 'set out from the time that the consumption of these liquors by the common people became enormous.' Not only, he explained, did gin reduce the birth rate by rendering fathers impotent and mothers sterile, but it was also responsible for 'the sickly state of such infants as are born, who with difficulty pass through the first stages of life and live very few of them to years of manhood . . . Enquire from the several hospitals in this city, whether any increase of patients and of what sort, are daily brought under their care. They will all declare, increasing multitudes of dropsical and consumptive people arising from the effects of spirituous liquors.'

Whatever the precise extent of the responsibility of gin in

*Walk.

causing degradation, disease and death might have been, it was evident that governmental action had caused severe social and medical problems that needed to be remedied. Yet, more than half a century after the consequences of the excessive consumption of cheap gin had manifested themselves, it appeared that the Government had done nothing to stop them. Admittedly, it had tried – but even then, some of its efforts had been half-hearted, and they had been exceedingly belated in their introduction. As early as 1695 the political economist and former commissioner of the excise Charles Davenant had warned that the consumption of spirits was 'a growing vice among the common people and may, in time, prevail as much as opium with the Turks, to which many attribute the scarcity of people in the East.' He had also expressed the opinion that 'There is no way to suppress the use of it so certain as to lay such a high duty as it may be worth no man's while to make it, but for medicine.'

By the beginning of the 1720s there were public campaigns against the supply of cheap gin, and petitions were being presented to Parliament. Yet the Government did nothing at all to try to solve the problem until 1729 when it passed an Act forcing retailers to take out an expensive licence and imposing a high rate of duty on gin. Whether the Government had been persuaded to delay taking action by the demands of distillers, or whether it had been unwilling to alienate the farming lobby in the House of Commons, is not known. Certainly it was complaints from both farmers and distillers that they were suffering from this new legislation that led the Government, four years later, to repeal the Act. In 1736, however, renewed public agitation about the harmful effects of excessive gin consumption, notably by the Middlesex justices, led the Government to introduce a new Gin Act that imposed such a high duty on gin as effectively to prohibit its sale. This was certainly a drastic measure; unfortunately, its effect was simply to drive gin production underground, and by the end of the decade the Government had abandoned its efforts to enforce the law.

In 1743 the Gin Act was replaced by another Act that sought to suppress the gin shop by making the sale public and respectable. Annual licences costing £1 were to be issued only to those who had an alehouse licence, and distillers were prohibited from retailing. This seemed to be working, but in 1747 the distillers, pleading hardship and discrimination, petitioned Parliament to be allowed to retail; the petition was allowed, and as a result gin consumption rose again. Hogarth's famous *Gin Lane* dates from this period. Another Act was passed in 1751, this time forbidding not only distillers but also grocers, chandlers (who sold bread, small beer and cheese) and workhouse-keepers from selling gin, and further increasing the duty. This succeeded in ensuring that gin was no longer universally available nor excessively cheap. It certainly played its part in ensuring that the gin problem disappeared in the 1750s. But so too did a succession of poor harvests that led to a rise in the price of corn; indeed, in some years distillation was actually prohibited. The gin problem had been solved because the landed interest in Parliament no longer needed to encourage its consumption in order to sell more of its corn.

The morality of the Government's approach to the gin problem was discussed at great length in the debate in the House of Lords in 1743 on the government proposal to introduce a duty that made spirits affordable in small but not large quantities, so that the poor would not be able to drink them to excess. The speeches were reported from memory by Samuel Johnson, then working for the *Gentleman's Magazine*. In the opinion of members of the Opposition, the explanation for the Government's introduction of the Bill was not to be found in any concern for the health or welfare of its people but rather in its need for money to finance the war on the Continent.

Lord Hervey spoke out strongly against the Bill, arguing that 'It is the business of government not so much to drain the purses as to regulate the morals of the people; not only to raise taxes but to levy them in such a manner as may be least burdensome, and to apply them to purposes which may be most useful; not to raise money by corrupting the nation, that it may be spent in enslaving it . . . We have mortgaged almost every fund that can decently be thought of; and now, in order to raise a new fund, we are to establish the worst sort of drunkenness by a law, and to mortgage it for defraying an expense which, in my opinion, is both unnecessary and ridiculous. This is really like a tradesman's mortgaging the prostitution of his wife or daughter, for the sake of raising money to supply his luxury or extravagance . . . The Bill, my lords, is, as it has been termed, only an experiment; an experiment, my lords, of a very daring kind, which none would hazard but empirical politicians. It is an experiment to discover how far the vices of the population may be made useful to the government, what taxes may be raised upon a poison, and how much the court may be enriched by the destruction of the subjects.'

If the Government learned anything from the experience of the gin age, it was how to make use of the vices of the population. By the nineteenth century it was regularly deriving between 30 and 40 per cent of its total tax revenues from customs and excise duties on the import, manufacture and sale of alcoholic drinks. Throughout the nineteenth century, in other words, the economic health of the nation depended on maintaining the consumption of alcoholic drink at a level that was likely to be conducive to the ill health of its inhabitants.

It was not until the First World War that the importance to the Government of the revenue derived from taxes on alcoholic drinks began to decline. Great Britain differed from other belligerent countries in that it stuck to a financial policy of defraying the cost of the war as far as possible out of current revenue. It was impossible to pay for a third of the costs of conducting the war out of the imposition of taxes on alcoholic drinks, partly because this would have necessitated raising taxes to such a level as would end up reducing consumption rather than increasing revenue, but principally because the Government was concerned to prevent, rather than encourage, the excessive consumption of alcoholic drinks by workers in the shipbuilding and munitions industries and by troops who were stationed at home or who had returned home on leave. Therefore, alternative forms of raising revenue were exploited, notably income tax. This had first been introduced by William Pitt the Younger in 1798, but only as a temporary measure; it was not made permanent until 1842. From that point and for the rest of the nineteenth century, income tax remained an insignificant burden on those who were required to pay it. Not until the Boer War did the Government consider it necessary to raise the level of income tax even as high as 1s (5p) in the pound. But during the First World War income tax was raised to such an extent that in 1918 it stood above its present-day level. Standard income tax was 6s (30p) in the pound; high-earners paid a supertax of up to 4s 6d on top of that. The total revenue obtained from income tax had increased from £34 million before the war to £585 million after it; this compared with revenue from customs and excise of £100 million.

The conversion of the Government from relying on indirect taxes, principally on alcoholic drinks, to depending on direct taxes on income, exerted a profound effect on society as a whole. The changes that were effected during the First World War turned the individual into a citizen, upon whose labours the well-being of the state depended. It was now more important for the Government that its subjects should be healthy and hard-working than that they should swell its coffers by the unhealthy consumption of large quantities of alcoholic drink. The new dependence of the state on income tax did not mean, however, that it was no longer concerned to raise revenue from taxation on alcoholic drinks. Customs and excise duties on alcoholic drinks may have been less important than in the nineteenth century, but they still accounted, in the period between the wars, for between 10 and 15 per cent of total taxation revenue; and they have still contributed, since the Second World War, between 5 and 8 per cent of the income of the state. Currently, the Government obtains about £7,000–£7,500 million a year from duty and VAT on alcohol.

Not only do taxes on alcoholic drinks remain an important source of revenue for the Government, but they are an especially convenient one. Demand for alcohol is relatively price inelastic; that is, it is not affected significantly by small rises in price. The Government is able continually to increase taxes on alcohol more or less in line with inflation because – according to Treasury statistics – a 1 per cent rise in price results in less than a 1 per cent fall in consumption, so, each time that the tax is increased, the effect of any decline in consumption on revenue earned is more than offset by the increased revenue from the remainder.

Moreover, not only is increasing alcohol taxation an efficient means of increasing revenue in line with inflation, but it is one that can readily be justified on the most unobjectionable of grounds. The Government can always claim that its real motive for keeping taxes high is not the need for revenue but actually a concern for the health of the population. The Government can say that, if it did not raise duties in Britain more or less in line with inflation each year, the fall in the real price of alcoholic drinks would necessarily lead to an increase in their consumption, and thus to more alcoholism and alcohol-related diseases.*

Certainly these were the terms in which the British government couched its objection to a proposal by the European Commission in 1987 that duties on alcoholic drinks should be homogenized throughout the Union (then the Community) at the average of the levels currently obtaining in all the member states. This would have meant a drastic reduction in the excise duties imposed in Britain on beer, wine and spirits. The duty on spirits would have been reduced by £1.93 a bottle, on wine by 77p a bottle, and on beer by 16p a pint. It was calculated by the Institute of Fiscal Studies that, if this measure were implemented, it would lead in Britain to an increase in average alcohol consumption from 13.9 to 20.3 litres of pure alcohol, and that the proportion of people consuming over thirty-five units of alcohol a week would go up from 12 to 20 per cent and the proportion of those consuming over fifty units a week would rise from 6 to 11 per cent.

It was not really out of concern for the health of its subjects, however, that the Government resisted pressure from the European Commission towards European harmonization, thus encouraging the development of the perception of Britain as an unwilling participant in the European Union. It was also calculated by the Institute of Fiscal Studies that, if the Commission's proposals were implemented in Britain, and consumption remained unchanged, the revenue to the Exchequer from duties on alcoholic drinks would fall by £3,900 million – in other words, by more than half. Even if the reduction in taxation were to cause alcohol consumption to increase to a level at which total consumer expenditure on drink remained the same – which would perhaps be more likely – the revenue would fall by £1,900 million. The Government opposed duty harmonization because it meant a reduction in the revenue that it derived from alcohol – revenue that it would have to find from another source, which would be likely to be politically unpopular within the United Kingdom, even to the extent of causing the Government to lose a subsequent general election.

It was not necessary, however, for the Government to state categorically that it would not be prepared to countenance the homogenization of duties on alcoholic drinks at any time in

*This argument depends on paying lip-service to the Ledermann theory, which will be discussed in Chapter 7.

the future. A more productive strategy was to play for time – and to support the extension of the Community to include the Scandinavian countries. At the time that the European Commission made its proposals, most other member states had lower levels of duty than the United Kingdom, so the harmonization of excise duties in Europe would mean a fall in excise duties at home. But this was likely to change if Sweden, Norway and Finland, countries with very high levels of duty and a far more repressive attitude to alcohol than existed in the United Kingdom, became members of the Community. So the Government encouraged and supported their applications for membership.*

The argument that the true motives of the Government in opposing proposals for harmonization of duties within the Union lie in its reliance on revenue from alcoholic drinks, and that its eagerness for the Scandinavian countries to join the Union can be explained at least in part by their attitudes towards the taxation of alcohol, receives support from the manner in which the Treasury and Customs and Excise have between them sought to obstruct the implementation of the Single European Market, which was introduced at the beginning of 1993. Since then, travellers who have visited one member state within the Union have been permitted to bring back to another member state an unlimited quantity of alcoholic drinks, provided that the requisite taxes and duties have been paid in the state in which they have been purchased and that they are intended for personal consumption. According to the European Commission, it is not even necessary for the purchasers to accompany the bottles on their journey; if they have ordered the goods on the telephone and paid the costs of transportation in advance, then it is perfectly permissible for the goods to be delivered by a courier. Evidently, if people bring home with them to the United Kingdom vast quantities of alcoholic drink on which no domestic excise duty is payable, and especially if they purchase even vaster quantities of alcoholic drink by mail order, the consequence will be a significant reduction in the revenue derived by the Government from the sale of alcoholic drinks. The fact that this was likely to happen as a result of the introduction of the Single European Market was

*In 1994 the Swedes and Finns voted in referenda to join the European Union but the Norwegians decided to remain outside.

evident to anyone who made even the most cursory examination of the difference between British and French rates of duty, which stood at the beginning of 1993 at 94p on a bottle of wine in Britain compared with 2p in France, 22p on a pint of beer in Britain compared with 1p, and £5.55 on a bottle of spirits compared with £2.65.

In order to minimize the loss to the revenue, the Government has gone to battle on several fronts. Firstly, Customs and Excise has prevented people from having alcoholic drinks sent to them from France by courier; it has simply said that it refuses to accept the European Commission's interpretation of the relevant directive. People who attempt to bring alcoholic drinks into Britain by mail order will find that Customs and Excise charges them duty on their purchase. This means that those people who wish to take advantage of the much lower French duty levels have no choice but to undergo the inconvenience of travelling over or under the Channel and bringing the drink back with them. Having taken this trouble, they might imagine that the fact that there was now a Single European Market meant that they would be allowed to bring as much duty-paid alcoholic drink with them on their return from the Continent as they wished or as their car or van might be capable of carrying. But they are not. Travellers are told by Customs officers that each person is permitted to import up to 90 litres of wine, 110 litres of beer and 10 litres of spirits from each visit abroad.

These might seem to be very generous allowances, but evidently they do not cater for a single person travelling by car whose household consumes a bottle of wine a day and who wishes to buy a sufficient quantity to keep it supplied for more than four months, nor indeed a wine connoisseur who has been travelling in Bordeaux, Burgundy or the Loire Valley and wishes to bring home more than ten cases of a particularly good vintage to lay down in his cellar.

These allowances are not finite ones, however; they are Minimum Indicative Levels (MILs) – levels below which the Customs will automatically assume that the person is bringing in the drink for personal consumption only. There is nothing, in theory, to prevent someone from bringing in substantially greater quantities of alcoholic drink than his MIL. In practice, however, he will be required to demonstrate that it is indeed for his personal consumption: someone who brings in twenty cases of champagne and says that it is for a wedding or a party will be asked by Customs officials for proof that a venue has been booked and that people have been invited. The European Commission has attempted to insist that there should be a presumption of innocence in the case of anyone carrying more than his MIL, that 'personal consumption' should be interpreted as generously as possible. The British government thinks otherwise. Gillian Shepherd, when a Treasury Minister, stated that 'Private individuals will be able to bring in goods in excess of these levels, provided that they can demonstrate that the goods are for their own personal use and not for commercial purposes.' That is to say, the onus is on the consumer to prove his innocence.

The reason that has been given for the introduction of MILs is the necessity of preventing smuggling. If that was truly the reason, it has not worked. Now that the borders have been opened, the responsibility for ensuring that people who bring back large amounts of drink from France are doing so for their own personal use and not for resale has been transferred from customs to excise officers; the control is no longer at the point of entry but by investigating leakage into commerce. Evidently, it is much more difficult to prevent people from selling drinks illegally anywhere in Britain than to prevent them from bringing the drinks into the country in the first case. Certainly, the powers of the Excise Verification Officers are superior to those of the police; notoriously, they can enter without a warrant any building in which they have reason to believe that there is an excisable product on which duty has not been paid. But in order to make use of their powers they have first to find the smugglers. They patrol shops, pubs, nightclubs, street markets and car-boot sales in order to find where bootleggers are disposing of their purchases; but it is evident that the majority of illegal sales escape them. Already in 1993 Bill Keen, excise collector at Dover, admitted that cross-Channel smuggling had become a big business, with some people earning as much as £6,000 a week. Vic Bassi, a former policeman who became head of security for the Courage brewery, went further. 'The leaders of organized crime are moving in,' he said. 'We find it incredible that the Government can have created such a crazy situation.' As the Labour Party Treasury spokesman Dr John Marek had warned before the borders were opened, the new regulations have proved to be a 'Smugglers' Charter'.

The prevention of smuggling was not, however, the only reason for the introduction of MILs; it is probable that it was not in reality the principal one either. If the Government is concerned to prevent smuggling, it is not so much because it is in itself illegal as because it diminishes governmental revenues from duty and VAT on alcoholic drinks. In 1992, before the opening of the borders, Customs and Excise carried out a study to find out what the potential loss to the Treasury's revenue from cross-border shopping would be. It arrived at a figure of £250 million for alcohol and tobacco combined, representing only 2.3 per cent of the Treasury's combined revenue from alcohol and tobacco, which totalled £10,400 million. Towards the end of 1993, however, the Wine and Spirit Asociation announced the results of a survey that showed that the loss of revenue to the Government from personal imports had so far been £264 million from wine and spirits alone, that is to say, without counting beer or tobacco. This figure was equivalent to roughly 10 per cent of the current Exchequer revenue of £2,500 million from wines and spirits. Early in 1994, the Brewers and Licensed Retailers Association (formerly the Brewers' Society) declared that during 1993 330 million pints of beer had been imported privately from the Continent, equivalent to seven times the output of a medium-sized regional brewery such as Fuller, Smith and Turner, and claimed that this had resulted in the loss of £160 million in revenue to the Government, the equivalent of the whole of the trade of every pub in the county of Kent.

It might well be wondered why the Government did not prevent this problem from occurring in the first place, by reducing British duties on alcoholic drinks before the borders were opened. This was, after all, what the Danish government had done, by reducing excise duties substantially in 1991 and 1992. In Denmark, the introduction of a Single European Market in 1993 did not lead to an increase in personal imports of beer across the border from Germany. Instead, the proportion of the beer drunk in the country that had been carried in from Germany fell from about 10 per cent to a quarter of that. The explanation for the inaction of the British government lies partly in the Conservative philosophy of leaving it to the market, of being reactive rather than proactive, of seeing what effect market forces will exert, rather than bringing in harmonization first and then seeing how the market reacts to that. But it also lies in hard economic fact. However much fuss the associations representing British wine and spirit merchants and British brewers and publicans make about the loss of revenue to the Government as a result of self-importation from the Continent, they will find great difficulty in persuading the Government of the economic merits of their argument. Even if their estimates of a revenue loss of more than £400 million in 1993 are to be believed – and it is not impossible that these have been exaggerated in a spirit of what is called in German *Zweckpessimismus*, or self-serving pessimism – they come nowhere near the £1,900 million that was the *lower* of the figures calculated by the Institute of Fiscal Studies as being the likely loss in revenue if the Government had reduced taxes on alcoholic drink in response to the proposal of the European Commission that duties be harmonized throughout the Union.

This said, there is some evidence that a reduction in drinks taxation might well lead to an increase in consumption sufficient actually to increase revenue. Indeed, it is surprising that such an argument has not found favour with a Conservative government that has for many years preached the gospel of reducing direct personal taxes on the grounds that this stimulates consumer spending, encourages the growth of the economy, and thus leads to a greater overall yield in taxation. Before the second of the two budgets in 1993 the Adam Smith Institute produced a report in which it argued that, were the Chancellor to cut the duty on spirits by 40 per cent, this could increase the revenue by as much as £1,200 million simply as a result of the extra demand that would be created by the lower prices. The author of the report, tax economist Dr Barry Bracewell-Miles, said that the Government had long been hindered in its alcohol policy by attempting to balance the conflicting interests of raising revenue, satisfying the health lobby and controlling inflation. The report added that 'British Government policy towards excise duties on alcohol can be expected to collapse before long from its own weight and internal contradictions.'

If the Government were to be persuaded to change its policy towards the implementation of the Single European Market in respect of alcoholic drink, it would not be the first time that it would have been compelled by the activities of smugglers to change its policies; nor if, as a result of the change in policy, its revenues were to fall by much less than it might have expected, would it be the first time that this would have happened, either. It was, for example, the smuggling of French wines in the eighteenth century that forced the Government to remove barriers to their importation. English wine-drinkers had developed a taste for fine French wines such as claret and champagne in the late seventeenth century. They did not develop a taste for port. Instead, it was thrust upon them in 1703, when the government of Queen Anne signed the Methuen Treaty with Portugal, and rates of duty of £7 per tun (252 gallons) were imposed on Portuguese wines, and £55 per tun on French.

After the Treaty was signed Queen Anne did buy some port, but the next year she imported claret, burgundy, champagne and Hermitage from France via Holland. War with France did not prevent advertisements for French wines from appearing in the papers. Lady Sunderland was caught trying to smuggle some wines through Holland, and had to pay over £250 in fines. Robert Walpole plotted with his friend Josiah Burchett, the Secretary of the Admiralty, to smuggle a large quantity of claret, burgundy and champagne from Holland. One consignment was interrupted on the way to King's Lynn; another was saved from the same fate only by a timely gift of brandy to a customs officer; a third reached the Pool of London easily enough but Burchett had great difficulty in slipping it past Customs. Eventually he overcame them by using an Admiralty launch.

Members of the Government may themselves have indulged in smuggling without feelings of guilt, but this did not prevent them from trying to fulfil their patriotic duty by ensuring that other people were unable to do so. For example, the Government attempted to prevent smuggling in 1728 by prohibiting the importation of wines in bottle, on the grounds that casks of wine were larger and more conspicuous than bottles. The problem remained, however, that the tax on wine was a Customs and not an Excise duty: that is to say, it was payable only to customs officers on entry into England and not to excise officers when the wine was sold within the country. Once the wine had been brought in nothing could be done to police or prevent its distribution. An attempt was made to deal with this problem by

Walpole in 1733, when he put forward an Excise Bill which proposed to transfer the control of imports from Customs to Excise. Walpole believed that this would help to bring smuggling under control, not least because the division of powers between Customs and Excise, and the keen rivalry between the two departments, had produced large loopholes through which contraband could enter. But for the Excise Bill to be effective it was necessary that increased powers be granted to excise officers; they would probably have to be given licences to enter private houses in searches for contraband. The possibility of this infringement on its liberties aroused such opposition among the electorate that the Excise Bill had to be abandoned. The smuggling of French wines was not effectively checked until half a century later, in 1786, when William Pitt the Younger succeeded where Walpole had failed and transferred the greater part of the duty from Customs to Excise. Those people who wished to continue to consume French wines now had little choice but to pay an exorbitant level of duty.

The smuggling of French wines by the upper classes in the eighteenth century was paralleled by the smuggling of spirits by the rest of the population – notably in Scotland. The Treaty of Union in 1707 had provided that the same duties should be levied in Scotland as applied in England. In 1713, just before signing the Treaty of Utrecht that ended the War of the Spanish Succession, the British government announced a plan to levy an equal duty on malt in England and Scotland, in order to meet the costs of the war. This enraged the Scots, because the Treaty of Union had exempted Scotland from paying for the war. Scottish peers went so far as to move a motion to dissolve the Union, which was defeated very narrowly in the House of Lords, by 71 votes to 68. The Government carried its legislation for the malt tax, but secretly agreed not to apply the tax in Scotland. Then, in 1725, Robert Walpole, the Prime Minister in all but name, proposed to apply the malt tax to Scotland at half the English rate. For the tax to be put into operation, it was necessary for excisemen to survey the existing stocks of malt, but on the appointed day for this exercise rioting broke out in Glasgow. The local Member of Parliament, Daniel Campbell, who had voted in favour of the tax, had his mansion sacked, and eleven people were killed. A large military force had to be called out in order to put an end to the riots.

Customs regulations, however, continued to be treated in Scotland with almost universal contempt. In 1736 two notorious smugglers, called Wilson and Robertson, broke into the Customs House at Pittenweem in Fife and stole £200, in order to recoup the losses they had suffered as a result of seizures by customs. They were captured, tried, convicted and condemned to death. However, during the service at St Giles Kirk in Edinburgh to which malefactors were traditionally taken on the Sunday before their execution, Wilson helped Robertson to escape. Wilson himself was hanged in the Grass Market on 14 April. The crowd that attended the hanging showered the city guard and its unpopular commander Captain Porteous with stones; Porteous ordered his men to fire into the crowd, and six people were killed. This led to Porteous in turn being tried and convicted of murder. He was due to hang on 8 September but pressure from influential people persuaded Queen Caroline to give him a six-week stay of execution. What followed has been immortalized by Sir Walter Scott in *The Heart of Midlothian*. A mob tore Porteous from prison and hanged him themselves, in the late evening of 7 September. The Government in London was furious but was unable to find out who was responsible, so instead it introduced a Bill of Pains and Penalties which proposed to imprison the Provost of Edinburgh and other magistrates (who were in fact blameless). After much argument in the Commons, the most objectionable passages were removed from the Bill, but the Provost, Alexander Wilson, was still prevented from ever again holding office as a magistrate.

In the first half of the eighteenth century, the spirits that were generally the object of smugglers' operations were imported brandy, rum and Dutch gin. The illegal distillation and smuggling of Scotch whisky was given an impetus when, after the general failure of the harvest in 1756, the Government prohibited commercial distillation throughout Britain between 1757 and 1760. Since it remained legal to distil for one's own private consumption, this prohibition simply served to divert home-distilled spirits from legal to illegal channels. In 1781, in an attempt to put an end to smuggling, private distillation was prohibited altogether and rewards were offered for information leading to the discovery of a still, but all that happened was that illegal distillers informed the Excise of the whereabouts of their old stills and used the premiums to buy new ones. This measure having failed, the Government attempted to encourage licit distillation in the poverty-stricken Highlands by setting the licence fee for commercial distillation at a lower level in the north of Scotland than in the south, and prohibiting the exportation of Highland whisky to the Lowlands. In order to make the licence fee easier to collect, stills with a capacity of less than forty gallons were declared illegal. This simply drove small family distillers underground. John Stein of Kilbagie, at the time the greatest distiller in Scotland, told a Select Committee of the House of Commons that sat in 1797–1798 that over half the whisky consumed in Scotland was illicitly manufactured, that illegal spirits from the north had cornered the lion's share of the market in Perth, Stirling, Glasgow and other Clydeside towns, and that as a consequence he had great difficulty in selling any of his whisky.

The main reason for the success of the illicit whiskies was probably that they tasted better than the legal ones.* This again was the result of government tax policy. The amount that it cost to take out a licence to distill spirits was related to the capacity of the still, which meant that the amount that the licence fee added to the selling price of each gallon of spirits could be reduced by working the plant more intensively. Also, the tax that was payable on the malted grain that produced the beer that was distilled into whisky had greatly increased as a result of the Government's need for money to pay for the Napoleonic Wars. This led licensed producers to use a large amount of raw, unmalted grain, leading to a deterioration in quality. John Stewart, a Perthshire innkeeper, told the 1797–1798 Select Committee that his customers would pay double for the illicit spirit rather than imbibe the legal product which 'did not agree with their stomachs; it gave them a great headache if they took the quantity they could take of Highland spirits without that effect.'

The heyday of illegally distilled spirits in Scotland came to an end in the 1820s, partly because of vigorous action by the Army and Navy against the illegal distillers, but principally because the Excise Act of 1823 reduced the duty and standardized the

---

*The same was true in Ireland, where it was said that everyone considered poteen to be 'superior in sweetness, salubriety and gusto to all that machinery, science and capital can produce in the legalized way.'

licence fee, thus making illicit production unattractive both to the distillers and, more importantly, to their landlords. Many illegal distillers now legitimized their operations, notably Captain George Smith*, the producer of The Glenlivet.

There was a great deal of smuggling of spirits in the late eighteenth century in England, too. It was estimated in the early 1780s that upwards of four million gallons of geneva (Dutch gin) were smuggled annually, and about half that of brandy. There were also many private distillers in London and Bristol who made large quantities of spirits without paying any duties. Many unlicensed dram shops sold smuggled brandy and gin, along with home-produced spirits. In Kent there were 1,607 licensed houses compared with 4,821 unlicensed ones. The problem was partly solved by a reduction in the English spirits duty in 1825, and partly by the Beer Act of 1830. This extraordinary measure removed all taxes on beer and permitted anyone to open a beer shop, free of any control by the licensing justices, on payment of a two-guinea fee. That free licensing should have been introduced in this way may appear inexplicable, but the need to take the traffic and sale of drinks out of the hands of smugglers may well offer some justification for the measure. It is possible that the beer shop system was intended as a means of controlling houses that might otherwise have sold beer illegally, as well as of weaning the urban masses off their taste for gin. Given that the urban masses had originally been given this taste as a consequence of governmental action in the 1690s, the Government was trying to solve a problem that was at least partly of its own making.

This said, in England at least, the smuggling of tea was more significant, and on a larger scale, than that of spirits. This could be explained by the fact that tea was more profitable to smuggle than spirits, being lighter and easier to transport. Tea had been smuggled into England ever since it had first become popular, but smuggling had been encouraged at the beginning of the eighteenth century because taxes had had to be raised to pay for the War of the Spanish Succession and as a result the price of tea leaves

---

*The family had formerly been called Gow, but had been compelled to change its name as a consequence of its support for the Young Pretender; it deliberately chose a name that did not sound Scottish.

reached 5s a pound in 1711. In an attempt to put an end to smuggling, in 1723 Walpole introduced a warehousing system, under which no quantity above six pounds could be moved without a permit. This was a complete failure. Indeed, for sheer absurdity this particular piece of legislation should be placed alongside the taxation of tea by liquid measure between 1660 and 1689 (whereby the tea was made for the Customs, then re-heated for the consumer), the 'bona fide traveller' exemption from the Sunday closing laws, and the current Customs and Excise regulations regarding the amount of alcoholic drink that Britons returning from a visit to another member country of the European Union are allowed to bring home with them.

A more successful anti-smuggling measure was introduced in 1745 by Henry Pelham, who reduced the duty on tea to 2s a pound. This brought in more money to the revenue than when the duty had been high: in the first half of the 1740s taxed consumption had averaged 770,000 pounds a year and revenue £175,000; in the second half of the decade, after Pelham had reduced the duty, consumption averaged 1.8 million pounds a year and revenue £318,000.

In the 1750s, however, the Government was again forced to raise taxes on tea in order to pay for the Seven Years' War. This again made smuggling profitable. Then, after the end of the war, smuggling grew to such an extent that it threatened to wipe out the legitimate tea trade altogether. The smuggling trade changed its nature. Small, unarmed boats were replaced by heavily-armed ships, some of them as large as three hundred tons, mounted with twenty-four guns and carrying eighty men. By developing more efficient means of transportation, by taking advantage of international facilities for capital and credit, and by taking over established channels of legal distribution, the new smugglers were able to appropriate a large share of the market. On the one hand, the new system of smuggling posed a serious threat to the legal trade; on the other, the competition between the two groups led to a vastly expanded market for tea.

The success of smuggled tea in the third quarter of the eighteenth century was founded partly on its low price and partly on the fact that – like illicitly distilled whisky in Scotland and Ireland – it was considered to be superior to the legitimately imported version. This had already been true in the first half of the eighteenth century, the reason being that officers on East Indiamen (ships belonging to the East India Company) were given a certain amount of free space on the ship with which to indulge in their own private trade. Since the privilege of private trade was limited by space rather than by weight, it was clearly in the interest of officers to transport only the very best tea. It was also in their interest to evade paying duty and to sell the tea to smugglers, since the profit that was to be made on a ton of tea was equivalent to a year's wages. However, most of the tea that was smuggled into Britain after the end of the Seven Years' War was not diverted from East Indiamen but imported from other European countries, without payment of British tax – just like beer and wine in the 1990s. In this period, Continental countries generally obtained better tea than the British East India Company did. Whereas the East India Company imported from China mostly the basic kind of black tea, called Bohea, Continental companies imported more of the better-quality Congou. They were encouraged in this policy by the attempt in the 1760s of the London wholesalers to defeat the smugglers by bidding down the price of legitimate Bohea at the East India Company auctions. Since the Continental companies were now unable to make a profit by selling Bohea, they dedicated themselves to the importation of Congou, of which the East India Company imported relatively little and which it sold at a relatively high price. The smugglers bought Congou in Europe, and by their efforts turned it into one of the most popular teas in Britain. In Scotland, where there were fewer restrictions on smuggling than in England, virtually all the tea that was drunk was Congou.

By the early 1780s all the tea that was consumed in towns on the south coast of England, and most of the tea drunk in Scotland*, was smuggled. The amount of tea that was smuggled into Britain each year during this period has been estimated at anything between 4 and 7.5 million pounds. This compares with legitimate imports which declined from 7.5 million pounds a year in the late 1760s to 3.5 million by the early 1780s.

It was the effect of smuggled teas on the sales of the East India

*Duncan Forbes, the Lord President of the Court of Session, had suggested in 1743 that the smuggling of tea in Scotland could be prevented by forbidding its use to people with an income of less than £50 a year, who could not afford the legitimately imported version. Nothing had come of this suggestion, however.

Company that led the company to try to dump the surplus of seventeen million pounds of tea that it had accumulated in its warehouses on the American market, thus precipitating the American Revolution. In 1767 the Chancellor of the Exchequer, Charles Townshend, had persuaded Parliament to place duties on tea, paper, lead and paint imported into the colonies. Colonists had responded by boycotting British goods; it became acceptable to drink tea only if it had been smuggled in by Dutchmen. The tea boycott served only to worsen the parlous financial state of the East India Company. Parliament soon repealed the Townshend Acts, but, at the insistence of Lord North, retained the 3d duty on tea. North was concerned that the British government should retain its claim to levy taxes upon the colonies, and was convinced that Americans would drink tea if the price was right, regardless of their principles. By the Tea Act of 1773 the Government also sought to undo some of the harm that had been caused the Company as a consequence of the Townshend Act of 1767. Hitherto the Company had landed all its tea in England, where British tea duty was paid; it was then bought by British and American merchants for marketing in America. The Tea Act gave the Company the right to import tea directly into America in its own ships and sell it through its own agents.

By eliminating British duty the cost to the American consumer would have been halved; the Company would have been able to undercut even the Dutch smugglers. But for the Americans more than money was at stake. The British government, declared Benjamin Franklin, 'can have no idea that any people can act from any principle but that of interest. They believe that 3d on a pound of tea . . . is sufficient to overcome the patriotism of an American.' American patriots campaigned against British tea, on medical, political and moral grounds. Colonists who dared to drink British tea were attacked by the Sons of Liberty; they were stigmatized in the newspapers as betrayers and enemies of their country; their property was often destroyed. In December 1773, the *Boston Broadside* published a statement that the 'worst of plagues, the detested tea, shipped for this port by the East India Company, is now arrived in this harbour. The hour of destruction, or of manly opposition to the machinations of tyranny, stares you in the face.'

In England, the tea smugglers were finally defeated in 1784, when William Pitt the Younger undercut them by reducing the tea tax from 119 to 12.5 per cent on the value of the tea. It had been calculated that this would lead the revenue to fall from £700,000 to £100,000, and the window tax* had therefore been increased by an amount calculated to provide another £600,000. But in fact the fall in smuggling and the rise in duty-paid consumption were such that tea revenues reached almost half their old level. So the Exchequer's revenues were increased overall.

Thanks to Pitt's measure, tea-smuggling ceased to be a problem; but the same could not be said of adulteration. A substantial proportion of the tea that had been consumed in the 1770s had been 'British tea', made from elder buds and such like. In 1777 an Act of Parliament imposed a fine of £5 – or, in the case of non-payment, a prison sentence of up to twelve months – upon anyone who was caught selling or manufacturing 'British tea', the trade in which had greatly increased in recent years 'to the injury and destruction of great quantities of timber, woods and under-woods [and] the prejudice of the health of His Majesty's subjects'. The extent to which the consumption of 'British tea' prejudiced the health of His Majesty's subjects was demonstrated by a recipe that was given in 1784 by Richard Twining for manufacturing 'smouch' from the leaves of ash trees, for mixing with black tea. This stated that the leaves should first be dried in the sun, then baked; 'they are next put upon a floor and trod upon until the leaves are small, then sifted and steeped in copperas† with sheep's dung; after which being dried on a floor, they are fit for use.'

The duties on tea were increased again at the end of the eighteenth century, in order to contribute to the financing of war with France, and remained high until the 1860s. Adulteration not only continued but became organized on a more commercial scale. There existed at least eight factories in London in the 1840s expressly for the purpose of drying used tea leaves and re-selling them to fraudulent dealers; these leaves were then treated with a wide variety of colouring materials, including copper carbonate and lead chromate, both of them poisonous, before being returned to normal commerce. It was not until the 1870s that tea adulteration declined, partly because Gladstone reduced the duty but principally because of the passage of the first Sale of Food and

*A property tax that was rated according to the number of windows a dwelling contained. It was repealed in 1851.
†Iron sulphate.

Drugs Act, which exposed tea to scrutiny not only by Customs on its entry into the country but also by public analysts if its domestic adulteration was suspected.

The beneficial effect of a reduction in duty is shown by the history in the nineteenth century not only of tea but also of coffee. In 1824 the duty on British plantation coffee (mostly from Jamaica) was reduced from 1s to 6d per pound. By the early 1830s there were 3,000 coffee-shops in London serving 2,000 pounds of tea and 15,000 pounds of coffee every day. As the House of Commons Select Committee on Import Duties was told in 1840, a vast number of coffee-shops had opened in London, serving working men at a low price, and some of them were visited each day by hundreds of men who had in the past resorted to public houses for refreshment. The Committee was told that this beneficial change in the habits of working men had come about solely because the coffee could be obtained cheaply, and that any increase in duty that removed this advantage of comparative cheapness would simply serve to send them back to the public houses.

Certainly, coffee was cheaper than it had been. But for some people it was still too expensive. Before the 1840s there were hardly any coffee stalls in the streets of London; what was sold instead was a drink prepared from a powder made from orchid roots, called saloop. If the stalls then began to sell coffee, it was not so much because the price of coffee itself had fallen but that it had been discovered that the coffee could be adulterated with ground chicory. By the mid-1840s the chicory was being adulterated in its turn with baked carrots. In the 1850s between four and five thousand tons of chicory were being produced in England each year, nearly all of it destined for the adulteration of coffee. The mixture, far from being looked down upon by coffee-drinkers, was often preferred. In *The Food of London* George Dodd cited the story of 'a coffee-dealer who conscientiously objected to [mixing] chicory surreptitiously with the coffee sold by him. He gradually found his sale of [coffee] diminish. He was for some time unable to account for the decline; but a lady one day said to him, "You do not sell such good coffee as your neighbour." The dealer examined his neighbour's coffee, and found chicory in it. The next coffee he sold to her he treated with an admixture of a little chicory; and she said, "Now your coffee is very good." He then resolved on experimenting with his own family: he gave them coffee mixed with chicory, whereupon surprise was expressed that he had favoured them with "some of his best coffee"!'

Writing thirty years after Dodd, at a time when coffee had been overtaken again by tea, Peter Simmonds wondered in his book *The Popular Beverages of Various Countries* why it was that Great Britain, which dominated the world's carrying trade and whose tropical colonies grew a great deal of coffee, nevertheless drank so little coffee compared with other countries: less than one pound per head per year, compared with five pounds in Germany and ten in the United States. He attributed the low level of coffee consumption in Britain to its adulteration with chicory, pointing out that the British consumed almost as much chicory as they did coffee.

This will not do. It is no good pointing to chicory as the reason why, in the second half of the nineteenth century, coffee consumption fell off, and tea established itself as the British national drink. Nor would it be a sufficient explanation to point to a fall in the price of tea. Gladstone may have reduced the duty on tea, but he had also reduced the duty on coffee.

One explanation that has been offered is a psychological one. According to the coffee historian Heinrich Jacob, 'Coffee cultivated an excitability and an acuteness which were not, in the long run, accordant with the English character . . . Tea promotes quietude, Buddhist self-absorption. It is a beverage for a taciturn people, and is therefore better suited than coffee to the English.'

It is also true that the quality of coffee that people drank in England in the nineteenth century was generally inferior to that of tea. All other things being equal, and if neither product had been adulterated, a customer in a coffee house, a diner-out in a restaurant or a guest in a private house was likely to do better if he asked for tea than if he requested coffee. Andrew Kirwan, a much-travelled gentleman who wrote a book on the giving of dinners in the 1860s, speaking of London observed that 'There is no spot in this world where coffee is generally so badly made'. He offered three explanations for this: first, that the beans were burned instead of roasted, so the coffee tasted too bitter, secondly, that, instead of being bought by the consumer in the form of beans, coffee was sold ready-ground, and was used up so slowly that its flavour had dissipated long before it came to be made into a drink, and thirdly, that, when making coffee, an insufficient quantity of the ground beans was infused, and too much water was added. Similar criticisms could be made today. Indeed, in a strange café or unknown restaurant, or when visiting a private house for the first time, it remains a much safer policy to ask for tea rather than coffee.

The poor quality of most of the coffee that was brewed in England in the nineteenth century was certainly one of the factors that contributed to the triumph of tea, but equally it was one of its consequences. Kirwan explained that English servants 'are insensible to the true flavour of coffee, and as they do not themselves partake of the beverage, become indifferent to its preparation.'

The fundamental reason why tea came generally to be preferred to coffee by British consumers in the second half of the nineteenth century, came to dominate the market for hot beverages until well after the Second World War, and still accounts for twice the volume of liquid that is consumed in the form of coffee, emerges from a comparison with the experience of other European countries which have established a tradition of preferring coffee to tea.

The occasional bans on coffee consumption in the Muslim world in the sixteenth and seventeenth centuries found a parallel in the banning of coffee in Prussia in the eighteenth century. The difference was that the rulers of the Ottoman Empire feared that the consumption of coffee led men to sedition, while the Prussian king, Frederick the Great prohibited the consumption of coffee for purely economic reasons. An advocate of mercantilism, a philosophy that stressed the importance of a favourable balance of trade, Frederick was concerned to prevent money from leaving the country to pay for coffee. In seeking to ban the consumption of coffee, he appealed to the patriotism of his subjects. Coffee was an unpatriotic drink, not merely because the flow of money out of the country made Prussia poorer, but also because the drink had supplanted the hallowed national beverage, beer. In 1777 Frederick issued a 'coffee and beer manifesto' in which he stated that 'It is disgusting to notice the increase in coffee used by my subjects and the amount of money that goes out of the country in consequence. Everybody is using coffee. If possible this must be prevented. His Majesty was brought up on beer and so were his ancestors and his officers. Many battles have been fought and won by soldiers nourished on beer, and the King does not believe that coffee-drinking soldiers can be depended on to endure hardship or beat his enemies in the case of the occurrence of another war.'

This attempt at prohibition achieved only limited success. In 1781 Frederick tried a different policy, creating a royal monopoly in coffee and forbidding its roasting except in royal roasting establishments. He issued special licences to the nobility, clergy and government officials, permitting them to roast the beans that they had bought at a high price from the government, but rejected all applications for coffee licences from ordinary people. The possession of a coffee-roasting licence thus became a badge of membership of the upper class. The poorer classes either had to obtain their coffee by stealth, or fall back on substitutes, made from barley, wheat, corn, chicory or dried figs. Discharged wounded soldiers were employed to spy upon people day and night, following the smell of roasting coffee to find out if people were roasting without permits. The spies, who were given a quarter of the fine collected, were popularly known as 'coffee-smellers'. This monopoly did not work, either, and it was abolished on Frederick's death in 1787 by his son Frederick William II.

The eventual solution of the foreign exchange problem was found in the development of a coffee substitute, in the form of chicory. To make this acceptable to the population, this too was cloaked in ideological garb. Chicory was portrayed as a healthier drink than coffee. People were persuaded to take to chicory in preference to coffee because, although they enjoyed the taste and aroma of coffee, they were made afraid of its effect. Just as legends were subsequently concocted to account for the discovery of the beneficial effects of 'noble rot' on grapes that were destined to be made into wine, so a legend was created to account for the adoption of chicory as a substitute for coffee. According to this tale, the wife of Major von Heine had been robbed by a party of French cavalrymen. This caused her much nervous suffering, for the treatment of which her doctor prescribed a decoction of chicory root, to be taken for several weeks. The taste of the decoction of the unroasted root was so unpleasant that the patient decided to roast it 'as if it had been coffee'. It is presumably no coincidence that the first chicory powder factory was established by Major von Heine in 1770. Chicory rapidly became popular, principally on account of its price.

The French took to chicory in the early nineteenth century when Napoleon blockaded Europe to keep out English traders as part of his Continental System of 1806–1813. In the eighteenth century, however, the French had seen little reason to drink chicory instead of coffee. Neither had the Dutch. Unlike the Prussian government, they had no need to restrict the consumption of coffee, because they were colonial powers, and were able to satisfy the growing demand for coffee by developing plantations in their colonies, the Dutch in the East Indies and the French in the West.

This said, they experienced some difficulty in so doing. Coffee was native to the countries of the Arabian Peninsula, from where the exportation of coffee plants or cuttings to the West was prohibited; it was even claimed by some sixteenth- and seventeenth-century botanists that the authorities insisted that all coffee beans be boiled or passed through a hot oven before being put on sale, in order to prevent foreigners from buying the beans for the purpose of germination. If such a regulation ever did exist, it was evaded by a Muslim pilgrim from India named Baba Budan, who is supposed to have smuggled seven coffee seeds out of Mecca and brought them back to Mysore in south-west India strapped to his belly in (depending on which account is believed) either 1600 or 1695. From the descendants of these seven seeds plants later spread up and down mainland India.

According to one account, it was only as a consequence of Baba Budan's smuggling venture that the Dutch were able to propagate coffee in their colonies in the East Indies. In 1696 they carried coffee plants from Malabar in India to Java, but these were destroyed by earthquake and flood. In 1699 some more cuttings were brought over, and these were successfully established. These plants were the progenitors of all the coffee plantations in the Dutch East Indies. According to another account, however, the Dutch did indeed establish their coffee plantations at this time, but with cuttings brought directly from the Arabian Peninsula. Some Dutch sailors had anchored off the coast in 1690, gone ashore and cut a few shoots from coffee plants. These were brought to Amsterdam and planted in hothouses, where they flourished. Then they were transferred to Java and Sumatra.

Early in the eighteenth century, some coffee plants were sent back from the Dutch East Indies to Amsterdam, where they were cultivated successfully in greenhouses. The burgomaster of Amsterdam befriended a French soldier called Ressons, and gave him a cutting from one of the coffee plants. Ressons gave it to the botanic gardens in Paris, but it produced neither flowers nor fruit. So negotiations were held at a government level, and in 1714 the burgomaster sent a young, vigorous plant, five feet high, to France; it was presented to Louis XIV at the Château de Marly, then transferred the next day to the greenhouses at the botanic gardens. It grew well, and other plants were propagated from it.

Next, various attempts were made to transport coffee plants from the botanic gardens in Paris to the French West Indies, but the first two of them met with failure. Success was finally achieved by a young naval officer called Gabriel Mathieu de Clieu, who was returning to Martinique after a visit back home to France. His first difficulty lay in obtaining a plant. He eventually managed to do so thanks to M. de Chirac, the royal physician, through the kindly offices (de Clieu later explained) of a Lady of Quality to whom de Chirac could give no refusal. De Clieu and his precious plant undertook their voyage in either 1720 or 1723. He had installed it in a box covered with a glass frame in order to absorb the rays of the sun and thus better to retain the stored-up heat for cloudy days. Another passenger tried to take the tree from him, and tore off a branch, but the plant survived. The ship then narrowly escaped capture by a corsair off Tunis, was threatened with destruction by a violent tempest, and was becalmed. Water ran short and was rationed. For more than a month de Clieu kept his coffee plant alive by sharing his meagre water ration with it. They reached Martinique safely together, and this single brave plant was the origin of the majority of the coffee plants that were subsequently cultivated throughout the Caribbean.

For the rest of the eighteenth century, virtually all of the coffee that was consumed in Western Europe (and indeed America) came from the Dutch East Indies or the French West Indies. Their dominance came to an end after Toussaint Louverture's revolution had brought an end to coffee-growing in Haiti and Santo Domingo in 1791 and after the worsening of the relations between the Dutch and their coolie labourers in the East Indies had given

Brazil the opportunity to play the largest part in the world coffee trade from the 1830s onwards.

It may seem strange that the British did not develop a substantial coffee trade of their own from plantations in their own colonies across the globe. Certainly, coffee was introduced to Jamaica from Hispaniola by the governor Sir Nicholas Lawes in 1728, and the island became the major source of coffee for the British market. But why did the British not begin the cultivation of coffee in India until 1840, when the coffee bush had been smuggled into Mysore in the seventeenth century? It cannot have been because they were concentrating on the production of tea, because no tea was cultivated in India before this period. It was true to say, however, that the British were concentrating on the trade in tea, and might well also have been concentrating on its production if only they had been able to obtain the bushes and work out how to cultivate and process them.

Despite its present-day identity as a quintessentially British drink, tea was in fact introduced into Europe by the Dutch, and was first popularized in Holland. The Dutch East India Company had begun importing tea from Japan as early as 1610, but it was not long before its position in Japan was being made awkward by the messianic activities of Portuguese priests, and the Company turned to importing tea from China instead. According to one contemporary account, the Dutch East India Company was especially eager to develop a taste for tea among the population of Holland, because it had developed a cunning scheme that enabled it to obtain tea from China very cheaply. It rarely bought tea with hard currency, instead exchanging it for goods that it had brought out from Europe. One of these goods was sage, which did not grow in China. The Dutch told the Chinese that sage was able to cure a large number of the illnesses to which the latter were susceptible, and the Chinese believed them. They were quite happy to exchange tea for sage at the rate of two pounds of tea for one pound of sage.* Having thus obtained a large quantity of tea at no great expense, the Dutch East India Company presented it to consumers in Holland as a sought-after and rare merchandise, even in the Orient, and put it on sale at a very high price.

*They also accepted borage, which the Dutch told them would encourage gaiety and calm stomach-ache.

Thanks to the marketing skills of the Dutch East India Company, and the recommendations of doctors – who were handsomely rewarded by the Company for their trouble – tea became in the 1640s a fashionable beverage among high society at The Hague; within a generation it had come into general use in the Netherlands, first in the homes of the gentry and later in the homes of the bourgeoisie and the poor. It was only then that the habit of tea-drinking spread to England. And here it took quite some time for the use of tea to extend beyond the upper classes, largely for reasons of expense: in the 1660s it sold for £3 a pound, much the same price as today.

In England, tea did not fall significantly in price until the second decade of the eighteenth century; it was at this point that it became popular among the middle and lower classes, and it is from this period that the tea trade began to play an increasingly important part in the business of the English East India Company. Thus, it was not at first the English East India Company that encouraged a taste for tea in order to stimulate its trade with China, but rather that there was a growing demand for tea in England that the Company did its best to satisfy.

This demand continued to increase during the course of the eighteenth century. The popularity of the tea gardens served to spread tea consumption among all classes, at least in London, and by the 1740s tea had in many homes replaced ale as the standard breakfast drink. As tea consumption increased in Britain, it decreased in Holland. The Chinese had long since discovered that sage (and borage) were not quite as efficacious as they had been told, and the Dutch economy could no longer afford the loss of the bullion that was now needed in order to pay the Chinese for tea. For the English, this was less of a problem. Gradually, the English East India Company took over the dominance of the tea trade from its Dutch counterpart. The amount of tea carried in the ships of the English East India Company, having passed three million pounds in the late 1740s, had reached nine million pounds by the end of the 1760s, despite the competition from smugglers. By this time, the English East India Company was so heavily dependent for its very existence on the trade in tea that the Government was prepared to provoke its American colony to rebellion in order to enable the Company to rid itself of surplus supplies of tea on the American market. And, after smuggling was effectively suppressed in 1784, this trade increased markedly, to sixteen million pounds a year.

Given the dependence of the English East India Company on the tea trade with China, it was obviously not in its interest that it should encourage the development of tea plantations in British colonies. For much of the eighteenth century, this was really not an issue because it would not have been possible for the British government to have planted tea in one of its colonies, even if it had wanted to do so. The only countries that produced tea were Japan, which was now closed to the West after its unfortunate experience with the Portuguese, and China, which exported tea to the West but only through the port of Canton, and was also effectively closed to Westerners. And it was evidently in the interest of the Chinese government to prevent Europeans from cultivating tea in their own colonies, because its exportation of tea to Europe was part of a grand scheme developed by the ruling Manchu dynasty for an empire based on trade. It was hardly going to kill the goose that laid the golden egg. Thus, the British may have drunk vast quantities of tea in the eighteenth century, but they knew remarkably little about it. They had not actually seen any tea bushes, which may account for the fact that green and black tea were thought to be different varieties of the plant, when in fact they are the results of different methods of processing the same leaf. This misclassification of tea into two distinct varieties, *thea viridis* (green) and *thea bohea* (black) was made by Linnaeus in 1762. It was not until eighty years later, after the British had opened up China by force, that the botanist Robert Fortune was able actually to see some tea bushes and to correct the error. And by that time the British had finally started growing tea for themselves in India.

It is a moot point whether the East India Company did its best to discourage the development of tea plantations in India because it depended on the tea trade with China, or whether it tried to encourage tea cultivation in India but without success. Before 1784 there would have been no reason for the Company to act to the detriment of the Indian economy because it effectively ruled India, and even after this date – when the government of India was transferred to a Board of Control, which was responsible to the British Parliament – the Company would have been inclined to favour the development of agriculture within India because it continued to enjoy a monopoly of the trade between India and Britain. Indeed, in 1788 the Company asked the celebrated botanist Sir Joseph Banks, the President of the Royal Society, to prepare a series of notes on the cultivation of new crops in India. In his notes Banks advocated the cultivation of tea, suggesting that the problem of the lack of knowledge of tea cultivation and manufacture might be obviated by 'the offer of liberal terms' in order to induce Chinese tea-growers and tea-makers to bring their bushes and come to work in India. In 1793 Lord Macartney was sent on the first-ever British embassy to China, along with instructions from the Company to obtain some tea plants. Banks contributed some written advice on how they might best be transplanted. Macartney did what he was told, and sent some tea plants from China to the Botanic Garden in Calcutta, where they arrived in healthy condition.

It is not known what happened after that. Nothing more was heard of the progress of attempts to encourage tea cultivation in India for forty years – a period that coincided with the enormous expansion of the tea trade of the East India Company, and indeed the development within India of an industry to manufacture opium for sale to China in order to fund the purchase of tea. The Company had hitherto paid for its tea mostly in silver, which the Chinese preferred to gold. The French Revolutionary and Napoleonic Wars placed a great strain on British public finances, however, and caused the value of silver (and gold) to rise markedly. Faced with this rise in costs, it made sense for the Company to seek to fund its imports from China as far as possible by turning to the manufacture of a commodity that was desired by the Chinese as much as tea was wanted by the British.*
It would also have made sense if the Company had been, at the very least, disinclined to encourage the development of a tea industry within India. This disinclination may well have been converted into active opposition after 1813, when the Company lost its monopoly of British trade with India but retained its monopoly of British trade with China. But the historical record does not say.

---

*The opium trade became so important to the revenues of British India that, in order to protect it, the British government went to war against China in 1840 – a war that ended with the cession of Hong Kong to the British Crown.

Certainly, circumstantial evidence encourages the belief that the blame for the delay in tea-growing, at least after 1813, should be placed on the Company. It is likely to be more than a coincidence that, when an initiative to encourage the cultivation of tea in India was at long last made, it was in 1834 – a year after the East India Company had lost its monopoly of British trade with China, and was therefore in a position to interest itself in the economic development of India once again. By this time there had been experimental plantings of tea bushes in Penang, Java, St Helena, Brazil and Carolina. Tea bushes grew wild in Assam, and were being plucked, processed and infused by the local inhabitants. Between 1823 and 1831 two independent confirmations had been made of the existence of indigenous tea in Assam, and samples had been sent to Calcutta. The new Governor-General, Lord William Bentinck, who had been appointed in 1828, had hitherto been kept busy on other affairs, but now it occurred to him that the development of tea-growing might help to bring some stability to Assam, which had suffered badly from the incursions of the Burmese and from tribal and dynastic warfare. Accordingly, in 1834, he established a Tea Committee to investigate the possibility of growing tea in India.

This Committee was composed primarily of men of purely administrative experience; the only scientist was Dr Nathaniel Wallach, the Director of the Government's Botanical Gardens at Calcutta. The extent of Wallach's knowledge of tea had been demonstrated in 1826 when the branches of tea bushes found in Assam had been sent to him for identification, and he had said that they were not tea at all. So, instead of investigating the tea plants that were growing wild in Assam, the Tea Committee sent its Secretary, George James Gordon, to China to bring back not only plants and seeds, but also people to make and grow the tea. On his way he learned of the difficulties that had been encountered by the Dutch in their attempts to smuggle tea plants and tea manufacturers out of China, through the agency of a young tea-taster called Jacobus Jacobson. The latter had managed to obtain the raw material without too much difficulty, but it had not been until his fifth trip to China that he had succeeded in bringing out any workmen, a dozen in all, and they had become entangled in a brawl with the coolies on their arrival in Java and some of them had been killed.* So clearly Gordon would have some trouble in fulfilling his task.

At the same time as Gordon had been sent to China, however, Wallach had sent out a questionnaire enquiring about the climate in various parts of India, so that he would know where best to plant the tea bushes that he hoped Gordon would bring back with him. In response to his questionnaire, Wallach was sent tea seeds, tea plants and manufactured tea from Assam. This proved even to him that Assam produced tea. So Gordon was recalled from China, and a scientific sub-committee of the Tea Committee set off for Assam, where tea bushes were duly discovered.

Once it had recovered from its initial excitement, however, the Committee realized that it was one thing to find tea plants but quite another to make tea of the same quality as was produced in China; so Gordon was sent back to China again. This time, he did manage to recruit some Chinese tea-growers and tea-makers – and they did succeed in producing, from the bushes growing wild in Assam, the first tea to be manufactured under British supervision in India. This was sent to London, where it arrived in 1838. It was pronounced by experts to be rather 'burnt' and harsh, but capable of competing on equal terms with China teas.

Once tea production in India was established, in the 1850s, the Government did its best to persuade consumers to convert from the China tea that they had been drinking for well over a century to the new type of tea that was now being produced in its Indian colony. It might have appeared to be a disadvantage that the Indian tea was less delicate than the Chinese product and turned out satisfactorily only if it was fermented in order to turn it black. The China tea to which people were accustomed, on the other hand, was frequently unfermented and therefore green. But this made it possible for doubts about the healthfulness of green tea to be fostered. In *The Chemistry of Common Life*, the first general scientific survey of drugs, James Johnston, Professor of Chemistry at the University of Durham, expressed the opinion that 'Green tea, when taken strong, acts very powerfully upon some constitutions, producing nervous trembling and other distressing symptoms, acting as a narcotic, and in inferior animals even

*The introduction of tea cultivation into Java had also been delayed by a lack of interest on the part of the relevant (Dutch) East India Company.

producing paralysis. Its exciting effect upon the nerves makes it useful in counteracting the effects of opium and of fermented liquors, and the stupor sometimes induced by fever.'

In fact, green tea was not generally taken strong in Britain; but, for many people, the expectation that green tea would affect their nerves was sufficient for it to do so. In *Cranford*, Mrs Gaskell described how if Miss Matty 'was made aware that she had been drinking green tea at any time, she had always thought it her duty to lie awake half through the night afterward (I have known her to take it in ignorance many a time without such effects), and consequently green tea was prohibited in the house.'

Green tea was also more likely than black to be adulterated. To make it bright instead of its natural grey-green, it had to be treated with various substances, of which Prussian Blue and verdigris (crystals formed by the action of acetic acid on copper) were the most lethal. It was therefore in the commercial interest of the British government that it should have introduced effective control of the adulteration of tea in the Sale of Food and Drugs Act of 1875. This encouraged the consumption of Indian black tea at the expense of China green. By the 1880s grocers were finding it difficult to sell their China teas unless they could guarantee them 'pure' or 'free from colouring matters', and, even then, much was only sold at a loss, and not restocked. The adulteration of China tea was no longer a problem by the end of the century, but by then it was too late.

The process whereby British consumers were persuaded to convert from China to Indian tea was a gradual one. As was explained in the 1880s by Colonel Edward Money, a tea-planter in India, in his book *The Tea Controversy*, 'Before tea came from India in such quantities as to make its use general, China teas . . . were sold alone and on their own merits. The vendors of tea soon discovered that, owing to the greater strength of the Indian article, most China teas were improved if a dash of Indian were added. As time went on, and Indian teas increased in quantity and became cheaper, the retail dealers mixed larger proportions of Indian teas with Chinese until, little by little, they arrived at what, speaking generally, is the rule today, when the teas sold consist of two-thirds Chinese and one-third Indian tea. The public have thus been, little by little, educated to appreciate the Indian tea flavour, and to despise teas which lack the strength to which they are now accustomed . . . The Chinese teas which were sold pure a dozen years ago would find no purchasers now.'

The conversion from China to Indian tea was ensured by the development of proprietary blends of brand-name tea from the 1880s on; these relied on Indian in preference to China tea, because Indian tea was more consistent in quality and price. Whereas, up to 1870, more than 90 per cent of Britain's tea came from China, by 1900 50 per cent came from India, 35 per cent from Ceylon and only 10 per cent from China. Exports of tea from India had grown from one million pounds (in weight) in 1860 to a hundred million pounds by the end of the century.

Thanks to the economic dependence of the East India Company on the tea trade with China up to 1833, and the desire of both the Company and the Government to encourage the development of the Indian tea trade after that date, the incipient taste for coffee, which had been so popular among the bourgeoisie who frequented the coffee houses of the late seventeenth and early eighteenth centuries and among the working men who patronized the coffee houses of the first half of the nineteenth century, was aborted. Britain became a nation of tea- rather than coffee-drinkers.

This process was not reversed until the 1950s, when coffee bars became fashionable; indeed, one of the reasons for their popularity amongst young people was precisely the fact that coffee was an exotic, foreign drink. To consume coffee was an act of rebellion against generations of tea-drinkers, against tea as the traditional, established British drink. In the coffee bars young people acquired a taste for coffee without knowing how to make it; so, when they bought coffee for drinking at home, they chose the instant in preference to the real version. Instant coffee, made by brewing coffee and then spray-drying it in a heated tower (or, increasingly nowadays, freeze-drying it in a vacuum), was invented just before the Second World War. In the last thirty years it has been marketed with great success as a smart, up-market modern drink, a cup of which is sufficient to seduce one's young, attractive and successful next-door neighbour. In the same period, coffee consumption has increased markedly: having been only one-sixth as much as tea in the 1960s, it is now half as large, and growing. It would not be an exaggeration to say that the popularity of coffee in Britain today should be attributed primarily to the marketing skills of instant-coffee companies. After all, 90 per cent of the coffee that is drunk in Britain today is instant, compared with between 30 and 40 per cent in most of the rest of Western Europe. It is a legacy of the political and economic interests that ensured that tea rather than coffee became the British national hot drink that the coffee that is drunk today in Britain is generally inferior in quality to what is consumed elsewhere in Europe.

Trading interests not only explain why Britain became a tea-rather than a coffee-drinking nation but they also explain why it did not, until very recently, become a significant wine-drinking one. Although there had been a number of vineyards in England in the Middle Ages,* most of them had disappeared by the end of the sixteenth century, possibly as a result of the cooling of the climate – although whether such a cooling ('The Little Ice Age') ever took place remains a matter of dispute among meteorologists. Certainly it had been evident, even in the Middle Ages, that the climate for growing vines in England was a marginal one; producing white wines might have been possible in most vintages, but there was rarely enough sun to ripen black grapes sufficiently to produce red wines. When, therefore, colonists began to settle the eastern seaboard of North America, where the summers were substantially warmer than in England, the hopes for the future of a wine industry travelled with them. Indeed, one of the reasons why people emigrated to North America during the seventeenth century was that they hoped to provide their homeland with the wine, oil and silk that it was currently compelled to import from its rivals on the Continent of Europe. The prospect of producing wine appeared to be a bright one, since a profusion of wild grapes grew naturally. But these wild grapes came from a variety of vine that was different from the one that produced wine in Europe, and they did not produce wine of the same quality. Wines were made from native grapes almost from the first settlement of Virginia in 1607. In 1622 some Virginian wine that had been made from native grapes was sent to London; it is not known how it tasted initially, but it was spoilt by a musty cask and a long voyage, and by the time it arrived in London it did not taste pleasant at all. From London, the Virginia Company wrote to the

*These will be discussed in the Conclusion.

colonists to say that the wine 'hath been rather of scandal than of credit to us'.

Rather than persevering with the native vines, the colonists attempted to introduce European vines into America. Already, in 1619, the Virginia Company had sent out a consignment of European vines, together with eight French vine-growers from the Languedoc. But these vines did not grow successfully. Nor did the vines that were sent out to New England in the 1640s, nor those sent out to Maryland in the 1670s, nor those brought out by the first organized company of Huguenot refugees from France that landed in Carolina in 1680, nor those brought from Bordeaux to Pennsylvania by William Penn on his first voyage in 1682, nor those that were brought to Georgia in the 1740s and 1750s. The colonists' efforts to grow European vines in America failed for the simple reason that vines already grew there, and therefore there were already pests that preyed upon them – pests to which the native vines had developed a certain amount of resistance but against which the European vines were powerless.* The most famous of these pests was the phylloxera louse, to which the native American vines were largely resistant; later, in the nineteenth century, when phylloxera swept across the vineyards of Europe and California, a solution was found in the grafting of European vines on to the roots of phylloxera-resistant American ones.

Largely because hopes rested at the time on the American colonies, therefore, the seventeenth and eighteenth centuries were not periods that saw a great deal of vine-planting in England. The suggestion that England should produce its own wine was made by the quasi-anonymous author of *The Vineyard . . . Observations made by a Gentleman on his Travels*, who argued that neglecting the possibilities of vine-growing in England had led to 'the reproach of the natives of our island and the impoverishment of the nation in general, who have annually remitted large sums of specie to purchase this exhilarating liquor from foreigners, which we might as well raise at home with a little industry and by a right application.' But few people took up his challenge. Only two important English vineyards were established in the eighteenth century, both of them in Surrey: Westbrook near

---

* Apple, pear and peach trees, on the other hand, were a new introduction to the continent; there were no pests to prey on them so they succeeded almost at once.

Godalming, which was created in the early 1720s by James Oglethorpe, later the founder of Georgia, and Painshill near Cobham, created by Charles Hamilton in the early 1740s. The more famous, and more successful, of the two was Hamilton's. He succeeded, by trial and error, in producing a wine that (by his own account) 'sparkled and creamed in the glass like champagne. It would be endless to mention how many good judges of wine were deceived by my wine, and thought it superior to any champagne they ever drank; even the Duc de Mirepoix preferred it to any other wine; but such is the prejudice of most people against anything of English growth, I generally found it most prudent not to declare where it grew, till after they had passed their verdict upon it.' The visiting French wine connoisseur Pierre Grosley passed a less favourable verdict. 'To the eye,' he wrote, 'it was a liquor of darkish grey colour; to the palate, it was like verjuice* and vinegar blended together by a bad taste of the soil.' But he knew what he was tasting, and maybe his prejudice got the better of him.

English farmers in the seventeenth and eighteenth centuries were generally uninterested in trying to produce a pale imitation of French wine because they had discovered that the English equivalent of fine French wine already existed: it was cider. John Evelyn told in his *Pomona* of how, in the 1630s, a gentleman called Taylor, who was apparently well known in Herefordshire, challenged a visiting London wine merchant that he could produce a cider that would excel the merchant's best French or Spanish wines. Three separate competitions were held, with a varied selection of judges; on all three occasions the judges preferred 'a good Redstreak' to all the wines that the merchant could offer.

Supposedly, the Redstreak cider apple had been developed at his country seat at Holme Lacy in Herefordshire by Lord Scudamore, who later served Charles I as ambassador in Paris; but, if Evelyn's chronology is correct, the development of the Redstreak must predate Scudamore's devotion to the improvement of his orchards in the late 1620s and early 1630s – not least because cider apple trees take many years to reach maturity. What is evident is that it was to the excellence of the Redstreak, and to

---

*Verjuice was the juice of unripe grapes, which was used in cooking and for making mustard.

the assiduity of the gentleman farmers such as Scudamore who cultivated it, that the rise in the quality and reputation of cider was due. Indeed, some years before anyone thought of putting wine into bottles, Scudamore and his fellow countrymen were bottling cider in order to preserve it. They soon discovered – as did those people who imported champagne in bottles for a similar reason after the Restoration – that it continued gently to ferment in bottle, producing a sparkling drink of the highest quality.

Whereas, in the 1630s, cider had been drunk almost exclusively in the West Country, in the middle of the century its reputation was spread across England by soldiers who had acquired a taste for it while they had camped in Herefordshire, Worcestershire and Gloucestershire during the Civil War, and after the Restoration a number of cider houses opened in London and Oxford. In the later part of the century, the agricultural writer John Worlidge, in a treatise in which he advocated the application of improved methods of pomiculture in what he called 'Britain's vineyard', claimed that cider was 'valued above the wines of France', pointing out that, if it had been made from Herefordshire Redstreak apples and matured for two or three years, it sold for £20 the hogshead* – much the same as the most prestigious of all French wines, Château Haut-Brion. 'If at any time,' wrote Evelyn, 'we are in danger of being hindered from trade in foreign countries, our English indignation may scorn to feed at their tables, to drink of their liquors, or otherwise to borrow or buy of them, so long as our native soil does supply us with such excellent necessaries.'

If cider has long since fallen into decline, and its manufacturers have long since abandoned their aspirations to produce the 'wine of England', it is largely because cider was given to agricultural labourers as part of their wages and came in time to be identified with them. In order to encourage the consumption of this domestically-produced agricultural product, cider was generally exempt from excise duty of any kind; instead of increasing its popularity, this only served to lower its image still further as the favourite drink of those segments of society that were too poor to afford any other form of alcohol.† This image survives today.

*About fifty gallons.
†Ironically, growth in the sales of English wine has been impeded by a governmental policy that has continued to regard wines as a foreign product, and has taxed them accordingly.

Indeed, the Somerset cider-maker Julian Temperley says that many of the people who come to his door to buy his traditionally-made Burrow Hill cider pretend that they are not buying the cider for themselves but for their friends.

Because of the failure of vine-growing in North America, and the greater attention that was paid by English farmers to cider than to wine manufacture, the wine that the English had forced upon them in the eighteenth century for reasons of politics and trade was neither American nor English but Portuguese. If people drank a great deal of port in this period, it was because it was cheap and strong; it was not because they especially liked the taste. The extent to which port was disdained by sophisticated palates is evident from the lengths to which some of them went in order to smuggle French wines into England. And the lack of sophistication of the majority of wine-drinkers is evident from the fact that much of the port that they consumed in this period came from much closer to home than Portugal. Pierre Grosley was told by a wine merchant that 'The country people gather in the hedges round London the sloes and blackberries, which they publicly sell to the wine merchants; that many of these merchants have in the country brambles and wild shrubs, which bear fruits of this sort; and when they are ripe, the vintage commences in London: that is to say, the wines then begin to be brewed, the chief ingredient of which is the juice of turnips boiled to a total dissolution. This juice, mixed with that of wild fruit, with beer and litharge, after a slight fermentation, produces the port wine drunk at taverns and places of public diversion in and about London.' Litharge, otherwise known as 'sugar of lead', was added to the wine in order to sweeten it. Unfortunately, the combination of litharge and wine produced lead acetate which was poisonous. In a notorious incident at Nancy in France in 1696, wine sweetened with litharge had caused the death by convulsion of more than fifty people.

As well as being made from domestic turnips and hedgerow fruits, wine was also produced on a commercial scale from imported raisins. This had begun, under patent, in 1635; the trade had then fallen into decline, only to be revived, on a substantial scale, in the middle of the eighteenth century by a Quaker called Mark Beaufoy. Having abandoned his original trade of distilling because it offended his conscience, Beaufoy went to Holland to learn how to make malt vinegar, and on his return set up a vinegar factory on the site of the old tea garden at Cuper's Gardens. He fined and flavoured the vinegar with 'rape': that is, the solid matter in raisins. At first he threw away the water in which the raisins had been steeped. But then he was shown by Dr Fothergill, another Quaker, how he could make wine from the raisin juice.* Indeed, the wines that he made from this raw material won the admiration of contemporaries for their apparently close resemblance to genuine imported wines. Towards the end of the eighteenth century it was estimated that half of the port and five-sixths of the white wines consumed in London had also been produced there.

In the early nineteenth century, however, these domestically-produced wines fell into decline, following the capture by the British navy of the Cape of Good Hope from the Dutch. Here, the Boers had been producing wine from grapes since the second half of the seventeenth century; indeed, they were responsible for the manufacture of one of the most celebrated wines of the world, the sweet red – or rather, topaz-coloured – wine of Constantia. When Britain annexed the Cape in 1806, therefore, it appeared that, at long last, the Government would be able to fulfil its ambition of owning a colony that was capable of providing the mother country with inexpensive, wholesome table wine. Accordingly, it abandoned its preferential duty on Portuguese wines and applied it instead to wines coming from the Cape. This did not, however, produce the flood of wholesome wines that had been expected. Instead, wine merchants imported only the cheapest Cape wines, regardless of quality. They were not interested in selling them on their own merits but wanted them to fulfil the role that had previously been played by wine made from hedgerow fruit and imported raisins: they wanted them for mixing with port and sherry in order to reduce the amount of duty that they had to pay overall.

Nor is it likely that any Cape wine, other than the very expensive and exclusive Constantia, would have been capable of selling on its own merits. The Boers, it seems, were simply uninterested in producing good wines. 'The mother country

---

*This would now be called 'British' wine and is made, no longer from raisins, but from imported grape-juice concentrate. It should not be confused with 'English' wine, which is made from domestically-produced fresh grape juice.

possesses no colony where a more congenial soil exists, or where better wines might be grown,' observed the wine writer Cyrus Redding. Yet, he added, 'In no wine country is there room for greater improvement . . . The obstinacy of the Dutch character is proverbial. The Boers are an ignorant, dogged race of people . . . content to do, in the same mode, what their fathers did before them, and no more; contented with "the wisdom of their ancestors".' The wines, he pointed out, suffered from an 'earthy taste' as a result of the carelessness of the vine-growing and wine-making methods of the Dutch farmers, who failed even to shake off the earth that clung to the bunches of grapes before throwing them into the fermentation vat. In the middle of the century, a second attempt was made to sell Cape wines to the British market, by relabelling them as 'South African'. Some consumers were conned into imagining that they were being offered wine from a hitherto undiscovered country, but not for long. The wine merchant Thomas George Shaw observed that 'I have not yet met with anyone courageous enough to place a bottle on his table.'

The requirement for a colony capable of supplying inexpensive, wholesome wine was not, therefore, solved by the annexation of the Cape of Good Hope, complete with its pre-existing Dutch-owned vineyards. Instead, it was provided by the discovery of a new continent in which the cultivation of the vine had hitherto been unknown. Vines had been introduced into Australia at the same time as the first convicts, when Captain Arthur Phillip, the governor of the new penal colony, planted vine cuttings that he had brought with him from Europe at Port Jackson (now Sydney) in 1788. In theory, therefore, it would have been possible for Australia to have had a thriving wine industry by the time that Britain annexed the Cape. But viticulture was not a subject that was on the minds of the first, or indeed the next, generation of colonists. As was pointed out, nearly half a century after Phillip's first landfall, by the man who is now generally considered to be the founder of the Australian wine industry, James Busby, 'Had New South Wales been settled by a colony from France, or by any other country whose climate is favourable to the growth of the vine, we should at this day have seen few corn fields without their neighbouring vineyards . . . but the settlers of New South Wales, reared in a country where the vine does not flourish and where the place of wine is supplied by malt liquors and ardent spirits, have brought with them to the colony their prejudice in favour of these liquors, which they continue to use at home, forgetting that even in old countries they form but a poor substitute for wine, and that their pernicious effects are increased tenfold by the heat of a climate such as this.'

Busby had emigrated to Australia from Scotland in 1823–1824 with his parents, his father having been contracted to assist in the engineering of a water supply for the city of Sydney. Before leaving for the New World, Busby had visited the vineyards of France, and he had spent the long voyage east writing *A Treatise on the Culture of the Vine and the Art of Making Wine*, in which he argued that New South Wales should develop a wine industry in order that it should become less dependent on the mother country and better able to establish the natural relationship between a colony and a parent state: the exchange of the raw produce of the former for the manufactures of the latter. The opportunity existed, he pointed out, because the wines of the Cape had failed to fulfil their potential.

While this book was 'intended to rouse the attention of the higher classes, and those who might naturally be expected to take a lead in a new pursuit', Busby's second production, *A Manual of Plain Directions for Planting and Cultivating Vineyards in New South Wales*, written after he had settled in Australia and established his own vineyard, was 'addressed to that more numerous portion of the community, constituting the class of smaller settlers. Its object is to convince them that they and each member of their families may, with little trouble and scarcely any expense, enjoy their daily bottle of wine, the produce of their own farms.' Busby's motive, therefore, was the improvement of the economy of the colony and of the manners of its inhabitants, who had hitherto been inclined to the consumption of excessive quantities of rum. He was not concerned with the wealth of the mother country or the health of its inhabitants.

In support of his exhortation that the natives of New South Wales should establish their own wine industry, Busby took advantage of a business trip back to England in 1831–1832 to visit the vineyard regions of France and Spain and collect cuttings of a range of vines that might prove suitable for cultivation in the Australian climate. These were then transported on the convict ship *Lady Harewood* and were planted both in the Botanic Gardens in Sydney and at Busby's own vineyard at Kirkton in the Hunter Valley, a hundred miles to the north. Among them were cuttings of Chardonnay and Pinot Noir that he had obtained from the Clos de Vougeot in Burgundy; it is quite possible, although it is far from certain, that the vines from which many of Australia's best present-day Chardonnays and Pinot Noirs are produced have descended directly from the plants that Busby brought back with him from France. In 1833, having laid the foundations of an Australian wine industry, Busby left for New Zealand, where he had been appointed British Resident and where he was to spend the rest of his life.

Busby may have laid the foundations, but, for all his efforts, there was not, in 1833, any Australian wine industry of which to speak. The same year saw the publication in London of what has been described as the first modern wine book, Cyrus Redding's *History and Description of Modern Wines*. This surveyed the vineyards of the world, from Chile to China, but the existence of viticulture in Australia was not mentioned. It was the generation following Busby's departure from the scene that saw the establishment of the Australian wine industry; it was not until 1854, thirty years after Busby had arrived in Australia, and sixty-six years after Captain Phillip had planted the first vines at Sydney, that Australian wines were first exported on a commercial basis to the mother country.

By this time, the attitude of the British government towards trade with its colonies and with its neighbours had changed completely. It had abandoned the belief in protectionism and self-sufficiency that had characterized the colonial development of the seventeenth and eighteenth centuries, and now adhered to the principle of free trade. It put this principle into practice in 1860, when the preferential rates of duty on colonial wines, from which the Cape had failed to benefit and from which Australia was beginning only belatedly to benefit, were abandoned, and duties on all imported wines were equalized. Then, in 1861–1862, a new type of preferential duty was introduced, on wines below twenty-six degrees proof spirit, the equivalent of just under 15 per cent alcohol by volume. These changes damaged the nascent imports of Australian wines because their effect was not simply to make French wines more affordable than they had been previously but actually to impose a lower duty on wines produced in the vineyards of Britain's old enemy than on those made in its new colony. The reason for this was that Australian wines were generally stronger than French ones. Hardly any French wines were made from grapes so ripe that their natural alcohol content surpassed the limit of twenty-six degrees proof spirit above which a higher rate of duty applied. But the opposite was true of Australian wines – most of them full-bodied red wines bearing the designation of 'burgundy', many of which had been made from very ripe grapes that naturally exceeded the limit for the lower rate of duty.

This obstacle to the importation of Australian wines into Britain was not overturned until 1886, when the limit for the lower rate of duty was raised from twenty-six to thirty degrees proof, that is, to just over 17 per cent alcohol by volume. It was at this point that Britain's first Australian wine boom occurred: at their peak in 1902 imports reached nearly one million gallons – much the same quantity as was imported in the first year of the current Australian wine boom, eighty-five years later. From that point, however, imports of wines, not only from Australia but also, more markedly, from Spain and Portugal and, most notably of all, from France, fell into decline. The duty changes of 1860–1862, and the adjustment of 1886, had failed to turn Britain into a wine-drinking nation. Indeed, by the time that the First World War broke out, *per capita* consumption had fallen to a level lower than it had been in 1859.

There were a number of reasons why Britain did not become a wine-drinking country during the half-century after 1860. One of them was that, however cheaply wine might be made available to them, the majority of the working classes were simply not prepared to abandon their traditional preference for beer and spirits. This was hardly surprising. If they had been reluctant to abandon their old tastes after settling in Australia, ten thousand miles away, where wine could be produced cheaply and where the consumption of spirits, at least, was hardly suited to the hot climate, then it was evident that they would be many times more reluctant to do so in the cold and damp climate of Britain.

This reluctance was demonstrated by the experience of William Winch Hughes, the founder of Victoria Wine, which he related to the House of Commons Select Committee on Wine Duties that met in 1879. Hughes had taken advantage of the reduction in wine duties – and of the introduction of a 'single bottle' Act that enabled shopkeepers to obtain a licence to sell wines by the bottle for consumption off the premises – to open his first branches in the East End of London in the second half of the 1860s; as well as selling wine by the bottle, he tried to encourage working-class people who had not yet acquired a taste for wine to try it, by offering a glass for the very low price of one penny. By the time that he gave his evidence to the Committee, however, he had all but abandoned the experiment. He had given up the glass trade, he told the Committee, 'because we found that people do not drink wine, they prefer beer and spirits. We were asked to open places to sell wine in poorer neighbourhoods by several clergymen, and we did so . . . It was a fabulous business that we got at first, but it dropped off gradually, and people went back to their beer and spirits.'

Most people had gone back to their beer and spirits – but not all of them. To say that the mass of the English population were not interested in drinking wine, or at least could not be persuaded to do so if the price were right, is something of a simplification of the truth. Hughes, after all, founded a great business upon the sale of wine to the masses. 'There is no doubt,' he told the Committee, 'that we have popularized wine to a great extent. Many a man will have a decanter of wine on his table on Sunday who would never have had it before, because he can now have it cheap and good. Instead of drinking beer, he would drink a glass of wine, and he could afford to give a glass of wine to his friends. They look upon it as a more genteel thing than drinking a glass of beer.' The wines that Hughes succeeded in popularizing among the working classes, however, were not the light wines that the Government had favoured by the changes in duty in the early 1860s, but sweet, fortified wines such as port and sherry. Certainly, the duty on these wines had been lowered, but not by nearly as much as the duty on the light wines. They were much cheaper than they had been – but they were not yet cheap enough. Hughes sold his cheapest ports and sherries for 11d a pint, the equivalent of about 1s 2½d a bottle. At this time beer cost 2d a pint. Wine, therefore, was much more of an expensive luxury than it is today, when everyday wine of acceptable quality can readily be purchased for £2.50 a bottle, and a pint of beer in a pub costs anything between £1 and £1.50 a pint.*

The existence of a potential for wine consumption among the working classes, if the kind of wine that they wanted to drink could be obtained cheaply, was clear enough. But it was not demonstrated again until half a century later, between the two world wars. This was a period in which the consumption of alcoholic drinks in general fell dramatically, not so much because of the Depression as because people preferred to spend their money on other vices and other forms of entertainment. This was also a period that saw a great decline in dining out, or at least in the consumption of wine with meals in restaurants. Despite the consumption of French wines by vast numbers of soldiers while on service on the Continent during the First World War, imports of French wines fell dramatically in the period that followed, from 3.7 million gallons in 1920 to 1.9 million gallons in 1938 – the lowest level since the duty had been reduced more than three-quarters of a century earlier. Yet, during the same period, overall wine imports increased, from 13.5 to 15.2 million gallons. Imports of French wines may have declined, but those of Australian and South African wines increased markedly, thanks to the reintroduction of preferential rates of duty for wines produced in the former colonies, in fulfilment of a promise that had been made by the Imperial War Cabinet in 1917.

'We made that undertaking,' Winston Churchill later explained, 'out of the sincere gratitude and affection which we felt towards the Dominions who at that moment had sent armies thousands of miles across the sea to fight in the line in France.' In the early 1930s, the international depression and the general introduction of protectionist tariffs added another reason to buy Australian and South African wines: the patriotic necessity of supporting the economy of the British Empire. In the 1930s Australia alone regularly exported three million gallons of wine a year to the United Kingdom. These were not, however, the dry red wines that had been popular among the middle classes in the later nineteenth

*The reduction in the differential is attributable principally to the measures introduced during the First World War, when duties on all alcoholic drinks were increased but those on beer and spirits much more than those on wine, partly because fewer people drank wine and therefore it was a less fruitful source of revenue, and partly because one of the intentions behind the increases in duty was to stop the working classes from drinking excessive quantities of beer and spirits.

century but were sweet wines of a kind that appealed to the palates of less sophisticated consumers. Whereas, in 1920, France had accounted for 27 per cent of wine imports, and Australia and South Africa only 4 per cent, by 1938 France's share had fallen to 13 per cent, whilst that of Australia and South Africa had risen to 30 per cent. The system of preferential rates of duty for colonial wines that had been in force from 1813 until 1860 might have failed to create a substantial trade between the colonies and the mother country in reliable, inexpensive wines, and to popularize the consumption of wine in Britain, but the same could hardly be said of the 1920s and 1930s, when a boom in Australian and South African wines presaged the wine boom that has occurred since the Second World War.*

The wines that have become popular in the second half of the twentieth century, however, are very different from the ones that were favoured by the working classes in the later part of the nineteenth century, or that grew in popularity between the wars. Although there was a substantial growth in the popularity of generally sweet, relatively high-strength wines such as sherry and vermouth in the 1960s and 1970s, when people speak of the wine boom and of the fact that Britain has, at long last, become a wine-drinking nation, what is meant is the growth in the popularity of light dry wines of a kind suited to consumption with meals.

Given that the wine boom has coincided with Britain's membership of the European Union, it might be imagined that the growth in the consumption of the wines that are produced in such profusion by several of its European partners is associated in some way with efforts by the Government to promote trade within Europe. The evidence does not, however, support this supposition. Certainly the excise duty on wine was virtually halved – reduced from 25p to 13½p a bottle – in 1973, the year in which the United Kingdom joined what was then called the Common Market, and certainly imports of light table wines increased by 30 per cent in the year that followed. The reason for the reduction in duty, however, lay neither in a desire to stimulate trade nor in a concern to harmonize duties with other member

---

*The period between the wars also saw a quadrupling in the sales of 'British' wines, on which no duty at all was payable before 1927, and only a nominal amount afterwards.

countries, but simply in the need to compensate for the introduction of VAT – the effect of which was significantly to increase the prices of all wines, especially of the more expensive ones.

The Government, far from stimulating the wine boom for reasons of trade or Europhilia, has sought to milk it for reasons of income. Indeed, the enormous increase in sales of wine in the first half of the 1970s tempted the Chancellor, Denis Healey, virtually to double the excise duty in 1975, from 21p to 41p a bottle; this certainly increased governmental revenues during a recession, but it also served to slow down the wine boom for a while. Since then, with the exception of 1984 – when the then Chancellor, Nigel Lawson, was ordered by the European Court of Justice to reduce excise duties on wine relative to those on beer – the Government has increased excise duties on wine every year. It has also gone out of its way to stall proposals by the European Commission to harmonize excise duties within the Union at a lower level than those currently obtaining in Britain.

If Britain has today become a wine-drinking nation, it is no thanks to the Government. Wine-drinking has been popularized by the development of branded wines, which have taken away the fear of buying wine: people who were deterred by the foreign names on wine labels, and who did not wish to betray their ignorance by asking shop assistants for advice, now found the task of wine-buying less daunting. It has been made popular by the supermarkets, which have removed any stigma that might have attached to wine-buying by treating it as just another grocery product, and have therefore attracted respectable women who would no more have thought of entering an off-licence than they would a bookmaker's or a pornographic bookshop.* It has been popularized by wine bars, which have attracted women who have felt alienated by pubs; it has been popularized because an increasing number of people have taken to travelling abroad and to eating out at European-style restaurants; and it has been popularized by the marketing of Australian wines made in a modern style, having an exaggeratedly fruity taste that appeals to people who have previously been put off white wines by their

---

*A similar explanation had been advanced in the 1730s to help account for the popularity of gin among 'female servants': the fact that it was sold at chandlers' shops, the supermarkets of their day.

thinness and acidity or their tendency to oxidize and who have rejected red wines because of their harsh tannins. Finally, at the third attempt, it seems that Australian wines have established a permanent place on the tables of the British public, and this time, the increase in sales – from half a million gallons in 1986 to ten million gallons in 1993 – owes absolutely nothing to any kind of help from the Government. It must be accounted one of the ironies of vinous history that the greatest period of popularity in Britain for the wines of a colony or former colony should have occurred at a time when, far from benefiting from a preferential rate of duty, they are in fact discriminated against in favour of wines coming from Britain's former trading rivals on the Continent of Europe.

6

'DRINK WATER AND DIE'

FOR THOUSANDS OF YEARS, WINE HAS BEEN USED AS A MEDICINE. In the Old Testament it is described as being mixed with oil and balsam in order to serve as an antiseptic and wound dressing, and prescribed as a treatment for disease. The Talmud describes wine as 'the foremost of all medicines; wherever wine is lacking, medicines become necessary.' In the New Testament Jesus told the story of the Good Samaritan, who treated the wounds of the man he found lying injured on the road with oil and wine. And the Apostle Paul expressed the comtemporary medical view of wine when he advised Timothy to 'Drink no longer water, but use a little wine for thy stomach's sake and thine often infirmities.'

Early Islamic doctors may have ranted against the evils of intoxication, but at the same time they wrote numerous lengthy tracts on the medicinal values of wine. In a famous passage in the *Arabian Nights* wine was eulogized on the grounds that 'It disperseth stone and gravel from the kidneys and strengtheneth the viscera and banisheth care, and moveth to generosity and preserveth health and digestion; it conserveth the body, expelleth disease from the joints, purifieth the frame of corrupt humours,

239

engendereth cheerfulness, gladdeneth the heart of man and keepeth up the natural heat; it contracteth the bladder, enforceth the liver and removeth obstructions, reddeneth the cheeks, cleareth away maggots from the brain and deferreth grey hairs. In short, had not Allah (to whom be honour and glory!) forbidden it, there were not on the face of the earth aught fit to stand in its stead.' In fact, the Koranic prohibition of wine has seldom interfered with its medicinal use in Muslim countries, because Islamic law has long been interpreted to permit the use of wine as medicine, on the grounds that necessity makes it lawful.

Not only was wine used as a medicine as well as a beverage, but spirits were regarded as medicines long before anyone thought of drinking them for pleasure. Given the limitations of medieval medical knowledge, it is easy enough to understand why doctors in this period should have regarded spirits as being of medicinal value. It was demonstrated by practical observation that they gave the people who drank them a feeling of warmth; as far as doctors were concerned, this made them the ideal medicine for people who were suffering from fevers and other cold diseases. Spirits were also prescribed as prophylactics against, and treatments for, the plague. Indeed, it is quite possible that the spread of the use of spirits across the Continent of Europe in the fourteenth century occurred largely as a consequence of the Black Death. Spirits were also applied externally to old people, in an attempt to warm them up. According to one, perhaps legendary, account, such a treatment was applied to the ailing King Charles II of Navarre in 1386–1387. On the advice of his doctors, he was wrapped in pieces of cloth that had been soaked in spirits; these were then sewn together in order to provide him with complete protection. One night, the servant whose job it was to stitch the cloth together, instead of breaking off the end of the thread when he had finished, tried to burn it off with a candle. The thread caught on fire; this spread to the cloth which burst into flame. Nothing could be done to put out the fire; the King cried out continually and suffered from the most terrible agonies as he was burnt to death. It appears that his death was little mourned by those who survived him: Charles II is known to posterity as Charles the Bad.

There was also a philosophical basis to the medieval belief in the medical efficacy of spirits. Distilling was thought to release the finer essence of the substance distilled – its spirit – and the alchemists, who were trying to relate chemistry to a philosophic world system, believed that distilling would help them to attain the Elixir of Life, which would render men immortal. This appeared to be confirmed by the fact that spirits kept substances such as meat from rotting; it seemed reasonable to deduce from this that they were able to keep human flesh from corruption and thus to ensure long life on earth. As Michael (Puff von) Schrick claimed in the 1450s, 'Anyone who drinks half a spoon of brandy every morning will never be ill; . . . when someone is dying and a little brandy is poured into his mouth, he will speak before he dies.'

The prevailing belief in the medical efficacy of spirits led monks, who had a long tradition of preparing herbal remedies, to seek to preserve these remedies for longer – and supposedly to add to their powers – by distilling them. In order to counteract the bitterness of the resulting distillation, they added sugar or honey to produce cordials and liqueurs – some of which survive more or less unchanged today. For example, Bénédictine was first devised by Don Bernardo Vincelli at the Benedictine Abbey of Fécamp in Normandy about 1510, using a combination of the wild plants and herbs that grew in profusion on the seaside cliffs and spices from the East* in order to produce an elixir that was supposed to combat the diseases that were prevalent in the countryside around the monastery. Today, in Western Europe, Bénédictine is taken as a digestive, which may perhaps be regarded as a degradation of its original medicinal status; in the Far East, however, it continues to be taken by workers in tin mines, who spend long periods knee-deep in water and believe that Bénédictine helps prevent them from contracting rheumatism and other muscular problems.

It is not known precisely when these spirits and liqueurs, along with their supposed medicinal virtues, arrived in the British Isles. According to legend, the art of distillation was introduced into Ireland from the Continent of Europe by Saint Patrick in the fifth century AD, and the word 'poteen' is derived from his. Unfortunately, the only evidence that exists relevant to this assertion

---

*Spices were considered to have medicinal powers because it was believed that diseases were caused by miasmas (bad odours), which the spices would counteract.

contradicts it: 'poteen' actually means 'little pot', referring to whisky that has been distilled on a small scale. It is also alleged that when the English first invaded Ireland in 1170–1172 whisky was in common use among the people of the country, but, again, evidence is lacking. It is possible only to surmise that Irish monks returning from pilgrimages to Spain may have brought the knowledge of distillation back with them and begun to distil whisky in their monasteries. Not until the fifteenth century was distillation commonly practised; and it may well not have been until that period that the art was brought to the west coast of Scotland by Irish settlers. By this time, brandy was being imported into England from the Continent.

There is little evidence to show the manner in which spirits were used in the British Isles in this period. They appear to have been used to inspire courage in soldiers,* to judge from an account given by Edmund Campion in his *History of Ireland*. He tells of an occasion in 1350 when the English soldier Sir Robert Savage, 'having prepared an army against the Irish, allowed to every soldier before he buckled with the enemy a mighty draught of *aqua vitae*†.' Campion, who wrote his history in 1569, himself attributed the Irish propensity for spirits to the marshy and watery state of the country, which caused the Irish to fall ill from colds and flu, 'for remedy thereof they use an ordinary drink of *aqua vitae*, so qualified in the making that it drieth more and inflameth less than other hot confections'.

In England, spirits were widely drunk in the plague year of 1593, but with little success; as a result, they fell out of favour for some years, although attempts to devise a cordial that would prove efficacious in the treatment of all diseases continued. When Sir Walter Raleigh returned from his voyage of exploration to Guyana in 1595 with many new plants, it was hoped that he would be able to add the ingredients that had been lacking in previous attempts to produce the Elixir of Life. When he was imprisoned in the Tower of London by King James I, Raleigh was allowed to set up a small laboratory in which he concocted

*It is not known when the term 'Dutch courage' was first employed: certainly not before the late sixteenth century; probably not until considerably later than that.
†*Aqua vitae*, the Latin for 'water of life', was translated into Gaelic as *uisge beatha*; this was usually rendered in English in the sixteenth and seventeenth centuries as 'usquebaugh'; it was then contracted into 'whisky'.

a Great Cordial by macerating forty roots, seeds and herbs in spirit, distilling the result and then adding powdered bezoar stones*, pearls, coral, deer's horn, amber, musk, antimony and sugar. The Queen, Anne of Denmark, and the heir to the throne, Prince Henry, were supporters of Raleigh, and did their best to secure his release. The Queen was convinced that the Great Cordial had saved her life in a serious illness, and the Prince took a particular interest in Raleigh's experiments. When, in 1612, the Prince was taken severely ill, Raleigh sent him some of the cordial, reportedly with a message that it would certainly cure him providing he had not been poisoned. Such a comment was hardly likely to endear Raleigh to the King, since it was rumoured that the King himself had poisoned his son because he was jealous of his popularity. Henry died, in any case, and Raleigh was eventually executed in 1618.

One plant that was regarded as possessing medicinal virtues, and could be obtained considerably closer to home than Guyana, was juniper: a diuretic that was recommended in the treatment of diseases of the kidneys, liver and heart. Juniper berries also offered the advantage that they improved the flavour of spirits that had been produced from poor-quality raw materials. In the sixteenth century they began to be used by Dutch apothecaries in order to enliven the dull taste of spirits that had been distilled from rye. In the seventeenth century the use of this new medicine – 'juniper water' – spread to England; in 1663 Samuel Pepys recorded in his diary having been advised by his doctor to take it for his health. Admittedly, it was not long before this medicine was being abused by much of the population, especially in London, who took it, not for medical purposes, but in order to get drunk. Nevertheless, doctors in the eighteenth century persevered in their belief that this product – now called geneva after the Dutch word for juniper (*jenever*), later corrupted to 'gin' – was a medicine and not a beverage. In his *Essay Upon Health and Long Life*, published in 1724, the physician George Cheyne insisted that 'Strong liquors were never designed for common use'; he pointed out that they had always been sold in the past alongside other medicines in apothecaries' shops, and had been prescribed by doctors in the same way as other medicines, 'to refresh the weary,

*Stones formed in the stomachs of animals.

to strengthen the weak, to give courage to the faint-hearted, and to raise the low-spirited.' It was no less reasonable, he said, for a man to drink off a draught of spirits for his amusement than it was to see him sit down to a dish of Sir Walter Raleigh's Cordial.

The fact that spirits were now consumed for their intoxicating qualities did not mean that they ceased to be used as medicines. A new medical theory founded upon the use of spirits was developed in the late eighteenth century by John Brown, a teacher at Edinburgh and founder of what has been called the Brunonian school of medicine. Brown argued that strong drinks were antiseptics, and that they prevented decay; the link with alchemical theory is evident. One of Brown's biographers, Thomas Beddoes, told how on one occasion a student of medicine had died despite the application of Brown's methods. When the body was opened and examined, Brown remarked that the body was unusually fresh, and that its lack of putrefaction was proof of the efficacy of his treatment. The Brunonian system caused much controversy in his lifetime and continued to do so after his death in 1788. According to the *Dictionary of National Biography*, in 1802 'the university of Göttingen was so convulsed by controversy on the merits of the Brunonian system that contending factions of students in enormous numbers, not unaided by professors, met in combat in the streets on two successive days, and had to be dispersed by a troop of Hanoverian horse.'

The medical administration of alcohol then fell into decline during a twenty-year vogue for Broussaisism in the early nineteenth century. Dr Broussais based his system on his understanding of the process of inflammation and on the advanced practice of blood-letting with leeches. Broussaisism represented the apogee of the 'heroic' style of medicine: that is to say, a dependence on drastic remedies and drugs that produced violent reactions in the body. The reason why blood-letting was frequently indicated in the cases of fever or inflammation was that doctors generally viewed a treatment that produced a significant change in the condition of the patient as being beneficial, and blood-letting clearly relaxed and apparently cooled restless patients. Emetics and cathartics, which cleaned out the system, were also popular – at least among doctors.

By the 1840s, however, heroic medicine was in decline. Doctors underwent a crisis of confidence about the excessive use of such extreme practices as blood-letting and purging, and replaced the lancet with the brandy bottle. Alcohol had long been considered to be a stimulant, and therefore useful in any disease of weakness or debility where greater activity or excitement in the body was indicated. Spirits had commonly been administered to persons in accidents in which breathing was impaired or shock had occurred – the origin of the practice of administering brandy in cases of shock – while wine, being weaker than spirits, was administered to patients who were slowly wasting away from long debilitating fevers. Now, however, alcohol was regarded by many physicians as a panacea for all acute diseases. Physicians 'brandied' patients suffering from conditions as diverse as pneumonia, typhus and rheumatic fever. Prescriptions of as much as three pints of brandy a day, administered for between several days and a month or more, were not uncommon. In order to explain away the change in their practice physicians formulated the explanation that they had been forced to change their methods because disease had changed: previously it had been an overstimulating type which demanded depletive therapy like blood-letting, but now it was an enfeebling kind which demanded supportive and stimulative treatment with nutriments and alcohol.

The most influential proselytizer of 'alcoholic therapeutics' in mid-nineteenth-century Britain was Robert Bentley Todd, a practising London physician who held the chair in physiology and morbid anatomy at King's College. Todd believed that diseases could only be cured by natural processes and not by the direct influence of any known drug or remedial practice. However, therapeutic support with alcohol and other nourishment could promote and assist these natural curative processes, sustaining the debilitated system and keeping the patient alive until nature provided a cure. In constructing his theories Todd drew heavily on the principles of nutritional physiology that Justus Liebig had put forward in the early 1840s: the claim that alcohol prevented the wastage of nervous tissue by offering itself up for combustion.* Behind Liebig's and Todd's theories lay the premise that the alcohol taken into the body was not excreted unchanged but was retained and transformed in the

---

*This was associated with the then popular theory of spontaneous combustion: that a person who drank heavily converted his body into combustible tissue that could catch fire spontaneously and burn without fuel until it was reduced to ashes.

system: it acted as nourishment, and was transformed into nervous tissue.

Unfortunately, Dr Todd's method of treating fevers with alcoholic stimulants did not do much good for Charles Hindley, the Member of Parliament for Ashton, in 1857. Mr Hindley was being treated by his family physician, Dr Granville, and apparently some progress was being made, until the assistance of Dr Todd was sought. Todd made Hindley swallow six pints of brandy in about seventy-two hours. As Hindley's condition deteriorated, Granville begged Todd to stop giving him brandy but Todd refused, so Granville walked out in disgust. Hindley died that night. Granville refused to sign the death certificate and afterwards wrote and circulated a pamphlet in which he stated that he had died because of the brandy he had been given. In 1860, Todd himself died as the result of an overdose of his own medicine. The next year saw the death of the most eminent of the patients to be given the benefit of this treatment, Prince Albert. It was subsequently suggested in some quarters that he might have recovered from his illness but for the alcohol he had been given.*

It might have seemed that the theory of 'alcoholic therapeutics' would be overturned by new experimental evidence that was presented by researchers after Todd's death, showing that alcohol was not transformed in the body but rather was eliminated unchanged. But, instead of abandoning alcohol now that the theory on which its administration had been based had been discredited, doctors simply constructed new theoretical models to explain the beneficial actions of alcohol in treating disease. While Todd had argued that alcohol stimulated the system because it nourished it, the adherents of the new school believed that alcohol, while not food, stimulated the nervous system and supported the vital power. Just how alcohol stimulated the nervous system was not made clear. But no-one seemed to mind. Instead, the focus of medical debate now changed from how alcohol nourished or stimulated the body to how alcohol changed the body's temperature. Hitherto, medical, scientific and popular opinion had held that alcohol raised the body's temperature. Physiological research conducted in the late 1860s, however, purported to show that alcohol lowered the body's temperature. This new research gave

*The cause of Albert's illness will be discussed later in this chapter.

rise to the belief that alcohol could reduce the temperature of febrile patients. This made the therapeutic use of alcohol even more widespread and it did not diminish until the end of the century.

By this time, however, the prescription of alcohol was beginning to be seriously questioned. Doctors who prescribed alcohol for their patients encountered the same problem as those who prescribed morphine: many of the people who were instructed to take alcohol while they were sick continued to take it, in substantial quantities, after they had recovered. One anti-drink campaigner cited the case of a man advised to take brandy as a prophylactic against cholera who had then followed this advice so enthusiastically that in six months he had delirium tremens. And in his *History of Drink* James Samuelson accused the medical profession of promoting drunkenness by 'too freely prescribing alcohol as a remedy for bodily ailments', claiming that 'The downfall of many a man or woman has dated from the first dose prescribed by a heedless or mercenary physician'.

The principal reason for the disappearance of alcohol from medical practice at the end of the nineteenth century, however, was that new methods took its place. For example, for hundreds of years the only antiseptic successful in preventing infection without injury to tissue had been alcohol, applied directly to wounds. The alternative method was to subscribe to the doctrine that wounds healed best by 'second intention', which involved inserting needles, setons and irritant substances under the skin to provoke the generation of 'laudable pus'; or, in the case of amputations, to apply boiling oil to the stump to check haemorrhage. Alcohol, 'second intention' and boiling oil were all rendered obsolete when modern antiseptic surgery was introduced by Lord Lister in the second half of the nineteenth century. By 1900, new medicines were appearing, such as aspirin, vitamins, hormones, antibiotics and tranquillizers. Each new product was accompanied by clinical data attesting to its efficacy. For alcoholic drinks, such proofs were lacking. According to Salvatore P. Lucia, who wrote a history of the medical uses of wine in the early 1960s, 'The only conclusive evidence of its value was the test of centuries – as a harmless stomachic, diuretic and sedative, gently beneficial in virtually all ailments, in all segments of the population, uniformly effective despite the biologic variations which so frequently nullify, and often violently repulse, treatment by modern drugs. While things new captured medical interest, the old fell into disuse. Ancient healing in general came under professional and popular scorn, and volumes purporting to expose medieval and folk medicine became national best sellers.'

Today, far from prescribing alcohol, doctors are warning their patients not to drink it. In the United States in 1990 warning labels were introduced on all bottles of alcoholic drinks, saying that women should not drink them during pregnancy because of the risk of birth defects, and that the consumption of alcoholic beverages impairs the ability to drive a car or operate machinery, and may cause health problems. The government-funded Health Education Authority has considered the possibility of introducing similar health warnings in Britain, pointing to research that says that two-thirds of people believe bottles of alcoholic drink should carry a government health warning. And the government-funded campaign group Alcohol Concern has specifically recommended that drinks should carry a statutory health warning, similar to those on cigarette packets, outlining the dangers of drinking too much and advising on 'safe limits'*.

It is as much for nutritional as for clinical reasons that the medical profession has generally turned against alcoholic drink. Historically, beer was regarded more as a food than as a means of dulling the pain of existence. This was how, in the early eighteenth century, Benjamin Franklin's companion at the printing press justified his daily consumption of six pints of strong beer: he insisted that it was necessary if he was to be strong at his work. A hundred years later, the passage of the Beer Act that opened up the beer trade was underpinned by the belief that it would lead working men to convert from gin to beer. 'They [will] have good beer instead of bad spirits,' said Henry Brougham, a future Chancellor, in the debate on the Bill in the House of Commons. 'To the poor the beer [is] next to a necessity of life.'

The fact that beer was considered to play a fundamental part in people's diets placed a major obstacle in the way of teetotal campaigners in the second quarter of the nineteenth century.† Early teetotallers, like pioneer vegetarians, were thought to be

*'Safe limits' will be discussed in the next chapter.
†These campaigns will be discussed in the next chapter.

throwing away their lives as surely as motor-cycle despatch riders or promiscuous male homosexuals today. In Warrington the Temperance Society regarded beer so highly that when, in 1830, an ex-drunkard asked for a teetotal pledge to sign, one had to be drawn up specially for him, and a friend tried physically to prevent him, calling out, 'Thee mustn't, Richard, thee'll die.' And when, in 1840, Robert Warner, a young Quaker, applied to a London life insurance company to take out a policy on his life, he was told that, as a total abstainer, he would have to pay an additional premium.

These beliefs outlasted the nineteenth century. Before the First World War, agricultural workers continued in their conviction that it was impossible to bring in the harvest without the assistance of harvest beer. And, during the war, commissioners who were sent out to north-east England to find out the causes of recent industrial unrest determined that one of the main ones had been an insufficiency of beer. 'Rightly or wrongly,' they commented in their report, 'the workers are convinced that beer is an indispensable beverage for men engaged in "hot" or "heavy" trades.' After the end of the war the perceived healthfulness of beer was used in beer advertisements, not only but most famously for Guinness. The campaign that claimed that 'Guinness is good for you', which ran from 1929 to 1937, was devised by Guinness's advertising agents Oswald Greene and Bobby Bevan, who had conducted their research by visiting pubs and asking people why they drank Guinness. Many of the people they met said that they drank Guinness because it was good for them; in other words, it was the continuing popular belief in the healthfulness of beer that inspired the campaign, not the campaign that led people to believe that beer might do them good. As part of the Mass-Observation survey of Bolton in 1937–1938 a competition was organized in the local press to find out why people drank beer. This brought a number of replies, most of which gave the same reasons of health that had recently been stressed in brewers' advertisements. Ten per cent said that they drank beer partly or principally because of its laxative effect, and 6 per cent because it contained vitamins.

These attitudes have been abandoned altogether today. When, at the end of the 1980s, market researchers asked a sample of people why they drank beer, the answers were that it was enjoyable, had a good flavour, was refreshing and offered good value for money. Health was not mentioned. Yet the old belief that beer was good for the drinker was not unreasonable. It was calculated just after the Second World War that the energy value of a pint of fairly weak beer (3 per cent alcohol) was about two hundred calories, and that a single pint of beer provided between 10 and 20 per cent of a man's daily requirement of riboflavin, nicotinic acid, calcium and phosphorous. Using this calculation, it is possible to obtain a rough idea of the amount of their daily calorific requirements that people obtained from beer in the past.* During the period of beer's greatest popularity, from the sixteenth to the early eighteenth century, it has been estimated that people of all ages and sexes drank on average a quart of beer a day. Obviously, labouring men drank much more. In the 1730s it was said that an ordinary labourer consumed about two quarts of strong beer per day but those in heavy, well-paid jobs like coal-heaving reportedly quaffed as much as a gallon. And of course Franklin's companion at the printing press drank six pints. Thus from beer alone, an ordinary labourer who drank porter in the first half of the eighteenth century was obtaining about 1,000 calories a day, Franklin's companion was getting 1,500 and a worker in a heavy, well-paid job would have got 2,000 calories. Not only did beer provide manual labourers with energy and vitamins, as well as alleviate the monotony of their diets, but it freed them from having to obtain their calories by eating a quantity of bread that would have been so large as to be indigestible.

Even though beer consumption declined significantly in the second half of the eighteenth and first half of the nineteenth century, it remained an important element of working men's diets. Average consumption among men was roughly a pint per head per day, and among working-class beer-drinkers probably a quart, thus providing about 500 calories a day. This said, as working men came to rely less on beer for nutrition, it changed in style: once people began to drink beer simply for refreshment, it became lighter, paler and lower in alcohol.

The reason why beer consumption had fallen was that many labouring families had turned to tea. As was explained in 1812

---

*It is not possible to obtain a precise computation because the strength of beer varied considerably, from 'small beer' at between 2 and 3 per cent alcohol to strong beer such as porter at as much as 7 per cent.

by the historian David Macpherson in his *History of the European Commerce with India*, since the reduction of the duty in 1784 tea had become an 'economical substitute' for beer among the middle and lower classes. They still drank some beer, but it had become too expensive for them to be able to buy enough of it to rely on it alone for their supply of liquid. Macpherson pointed to the absurdity of the fact that 'We are so situated in our commercial and financial system that tea brought from the eastern extremity of the world, and sugar brought from the West Indies, and both loaded with the expense of freight and insurance . . . compose a drink cheaper than beer.'

The replacement of beer by tea in the diets of working people in the eighteenth and early nineteenth centuries was undoubtedly detrimental to their health. Although they were able to derive a certain amount of nutritional value from drinking tea, since it was normally taken with sugar and often with milk, it was a very poor substitute for beer. It is the inadequacy of tea as a dietary replacement for beer that explains the apparently extraordinary denunciation of tea by the social reformer William Cobbett in his book *Cottage Economy*. Tea-drinking, he said, was a 'troublesome and pernicious habit . . . Is it in the power of any man, any good labourer who has attained the age of fifty,' he wondered, 'to look back on the past thirty years of his life without cursing the day in which tea was first introduced into England? . . . I view the tea-drinking as a destroyer of health, an enfeebler of the frame, and engenderer of effeminacy and laziness, a debaucher of youth, and a maker of misery for old age . . . It is notorious that tea has no useful strength in it; that it contains nothing nutritious; that it, besides being good for nothing, has badness in it, because it is well known to produce want of sleep in many cases, and in all cases to shake and weaken the nerves. It is, in fact, a weaker kind of laudanum, which enlivens for the moment and deadens afterwards.'

A much better drink than tea, from a nutritional point of view, was saloop. Between the second quarter of the eighteenth and the second quarter of the nineteenth century, it was saloop, rather than tea or coffee, that was sold at stalls in the streets of London in the night and early morning. Saloop was prepared from a powder made from orchid roots, to which milk and sugar were then added. This produced a thicker drink than tea or coffee, a greasy-looking beverage that was a favourite of porters, coal-heavers and other heavy labourers. The root from which it was made was said to contain more nutritious matter in proportion to its bulk than any other; it was thought that a man could live on an ounce of saloop a day. In the 1820s Charles Lamb took the trouble to investigate the popularity of saloop among artisans at breakfast time, but he did not go so far as to taste it. He said that he could tell from the smell that it would make him sick. Saloop fell out of favour after the reduction in the duty on coffee in 1825, and the saloop-sellers were replaced by stalls selling coffee.

Although neither tea nor coffee was as nutritious as saloop, they all shared the advantage that the drinker did not need to fear that the water they contained might be contaminated, because it had been sterilized by boiling. In the manufacture of beer, too, the wort – water in which the malted barley had been steeped and to which hops had been added – was boiled before fermentation; and, after the yeast had done its work, the finished beer was sufficiently high in acidity to prevent the growth of any harmful bacteria. If, before the late nineteenth century, people who were simply in search of liquid refreshment were forced to choose between hot drinks such as tea and coffee and alcoholic drinks such as beer, it was because they did not generally consider plain, unboiled water to be a healthy option. 'Water is not wholesome sole by itself for an Englishman,' observed the sixteenth-century dietitian Andrew Boorde. 'If any man do use to drink water with wine, let it be purely strained, and then seethe* it; and after it be cold, let him put it to his wine.'

It was not in fact necessary to boil the water before adding it to the wine. The fact that water could be made safe to drink by adding wine to it was known to the Persian armies that conquered much of Asia in the sixth century BC and to the Roman armies that conquered much of Europe in the first century AD; indeed, this knowledge was central to the organization of their campaigns. It was not for nearly another two millennia, however, that it was discovered why this should have been the case. Only in the 1950s did medical researchers trace the bactericidal power of wine to compounds contained in the skins of the grapes; these were

*Boil.

inactive if extracted from the grapes and only became potent as a result of the process of fermentation. Thus, red wine was much more effective than white because the grape skins were included during the fermentation of red wines but were removed before the fermentation of white ones. Moreover, although the bactericidal power of red wine depended upon the process that made it alcoholic, it remained largely independent of its alcohol content.*

Alcohol did kill bacteria, but only in much higher concentrations; despite their much greater alcoholic strength, spirits were not necessarily as effective as red wine. It is therefore unclear whether the spirits that were used by British sailors for more than three centuries served as effectively to sterilize their water as did the wine that was used by the soldiers of ancient Persia and classical Rome. Certainly the water that was carried by ships in the British navy needed to be treated in some way: kept on board in wooden casks, it developed an unpleasant, fetid taste and aroma after only a few weeks. As a result, it was used for washing the men and the ship, and for cooking – but not for drinking. Instead, the men were supposed to drink beer, of which they were allowed a ration of a gallon a day each. But the beer did not keep good indefinitely, either, and it could rarely be restocked at foreign posts. Wine could be found in some places – but not in the Caribbean. So, beginning after the capture of Jamaica from the Spanish in 1655, rum was substituted. Officially, it was no more than a replacement for beer or wine, to be given when the latter were unavailable, but it was not long before the rum was being given as a matter of right, in a ration of half a pint a day, served out a little before noon. If sailors wanted their beer, they could have that as well. But they preferred rum – since its taste did not spoil.

Unfortunately, the consumption by sailors of a daily half-pint of rum – at the strength that it came off the still, twice as alcoholic as the watered-down rum that is sold today – was conducive neither to their good health nor their good discipline. It gave rise, stated Admiral Vernon in an Order to Captains in 1740, to 'a brutal disregard to their duty as Christians and their being

---

*Red wine did not work immediately – it was necessary to add it to water half an hour in advance of drinking in order for it to be fully effective.

thoughtlessly hurried into all sorts of crimes as well as being visibly debilitated and destroyed in their constitutions, which it may be justly apprehended is owing to their drinking their allowance of spirituous liquor at once, and without any mixture to allay the heat of it, which of itself is sufficient to intoxicate and gradually to destroy them.' Vernon ordered that the rum ration be mixed throughout the fleet in a ratio of four parts water to one part rum, and that it no longer be served all in one go but half of it at about eleven in the morning and the other half at about five in the afternoon. Vernon, a war hero as a result of his capture from the Spanish of Porto Bello on the isthmus of Panama the previous year, had acquired the nickname 'Old Grogram', in reference to the material out of which his waterproof boat-cloak was made; the drink that his Orders created therefore came popularly to be called 'grog'.

Before long, the use of grog spread throughout the Navy. Not only did the mixture mitigate the more noxious effects of the rum – as Vernon had intended – but it served to make the water more pleasant and safer to drink.* Admittedly, when it was diluted according to Vernon's directions, the alcoholic strength of the mixture may well not have been sufficient fully to sterilize the water, but the rum was not always diluted to the extent that Vernon might have wished. Sometimes it was served as strong as an equal mixture of spirits and water ('half and half grog'), in which case it would almost certainly have been strong enough to kill any bacteria. At this strength, however, it was considerably less likely to prevent the sailors from becoming drunk. The obvious solution to the problem of grogginess on board ship would have been to reduce the ration, rather than merely to dilute it, but sailors were so attached to their rum that the Admiralty feared that they might mutiny if the supply were reduced, and therefore shrank back from doing so. It was only after the end of the Napoleonic wars, when the country was no longer in peril, that the Admiralty took steps to reduce the rum ration. By now, it was possible to keep the water fresh for longer by storing it in iron tanks rather than wooden casks. In 1825 the rum ration was halved; it was

*Grog also served as a medium to which lemon or lime juice could be added, for the better prevention of scurvy. It was believed by many sailors that the anti-scorbutic powers of this cocktail should not be attributed to the citrus juice but to the rum.

halved again in 1850. At the same time, the introduction of steam ships made it possible to introduce effective on-board distillation apparatus; indeed, the consumption of large quantities of plain water now became not only possible but necessary for the stokers who worked in unbearably hot conditions. This said, the rum ration did not disappear altogether until 1970.

On dry land, the problem was not one of keeping water fresh but of preventing contamination. The effectiveness of filtration as a means of purifying water contaminated by pathogenic bacteria had in fact been known for a long time. The Chinese had for thousands of years used alum as a coagulant in muddy water in order to accelerate clarification; the filtration of water through charcoal was recommended in Sanskrit medical literature four thousand years ago. It was one thing, however, for individual householders to fill their cisterns with sand or charcoal and filter water through it for their personal use, and quite another for water companies to establish slow sand filters to treat all the water that they piped to homes. Until piped supplies became common, there was simply no incentive to introduce water filtration on a commercial scale. In London, the first slow sand filter was introduced by the Chelsea Waterworks Company in 1829. It was some time before other companies followed suit.

The importance of filtration was only fully realized as a result of the arrival of cholera in Britain from India in 1831. Doctors were perplexed as to its causes; some believed that it was caused by an air-borne poison produced by the putrefaction of bodies or rotting vegetables. Temperance campaigners had no such doubts: cholera, they said, was caused by drunkenness. As a result of his researches in the epidemic of 1848–1849, Dr John Snow proved that cholera was in fact water-borne. Having shown that the highest casualty rates were among those who drew water from a pump in Broad Street, he persuaded the authorities to remove the handle from this pump, and the incidence of cholera in the area quickly dropped. The Metropolitan Water Act of 1852, which required the filtration of domestic water, marked a turning-point in the supply of drinkable water.

The improvement in the quality of domestic water did not mean, however, that the problem of water-borne disease had been solved. Indeed, it has generally been held that the most eminent of its victims was Prince Albert, who was not saved from death at the end of 1861 by the administration of large quantities of brandy. In November Albert had learned that, during a course of training at a military camp in Ireland in the summer, his son Edward, the Prince of Wales, had formed a liaison with an actress, whom he had subsequently brought home to Windsor Castle. This not only caused Albert a great deal of mental agony, but prevented him from sleeping. He then went to Sandhurst to inspect the buildings for the new Staff College and Royal Military Academy; it was a pouring wet day and he contracted a chill. This was compounded by his insomnia. A few days later, Albert went to visit the Prince of Wales in Cambridge, where the latter was supposedly studying, and they went for a long walk during which Albert painfully discussed the liaison with his son. The next day, his illness took a turn for the worse; two and a half weeks later, he died.

According to Dr William Jenner, one of the physicians who attended him during his final illness, Albert had died from typhoid, a disease that is contracted from contaminated water. If this was indeed the cause of Albert's death, he either contracted it at Sandhurst or – more probably – at Windsor Castle, where, according to the Lord Chamberlain, 'The noxious effluvia which escapes [sic] from the old drains and numerous cesspools . . . is [sic] frequently so exceedingly offensive as to render many parts of the castle almost uninhabitable.' On the other hand, it is perfectly possible that the original diagnosis of Albert's death was incorrect and that he actually died from cancer or renal failure. Whatever the medical cause of Albert's death, Queen Victoria had no doubts where the responsibility lay: for the rest of her life she blamed the death of her husband on her son.

Certainly, despite the improvement in water supplies, the danger of contracting water-borne disease remained a very real one. It was not sufficient that a supply of clean domestic water should be available; it was also necessary to establish an adequate means of removing sewage. In London, in the first half of the nineteenth century, the problem of sewage disposal, far from ameliorating, had worsened – originally as a consequence of the enormous increase in population, which grew from 1 million to 2.5 million in the course of these fifty years. Sanitation generally took the form of a cesspit under the house; in poor districts this would often overflow through the floor boards into the rooms above. In order to rectify this situation the Metropolitan Commission of Sewers was formed in 1847, and this decreed that all cesspits must be abolished – which meant that all sewage was now discharged in the Thames. The absurdity of this measure was revealed by the Great Stink of 1858, during an unusually hot, dry summer: the stench given off by the river was so bad that the windows of the Houses of Parliament had to be draped with sheets soaked in chloride of lime. Tons of chalk lime, chloride of lime and carbolic acid were poured into the river, but to little effect; Disraeli described the Thames as 'a Stygian pool reeking with ineffable and unbearable horror'. The following year Joseph Bazalgette began the construction of London's underground sewage network, which was opened between 1865 and 1875, with 1,300 miles of sewers. From this point on, water ceased to be regarded as a source of disease and came to be looked upon as a source of refreshment: in the 1870s many Londoners abandoned their belief that water should only be drunk if it had first been purified with spirits; in the same decade, the pupils of public schools such as Eton and Winchester converted from drinking beer to drinking water with their meals.

Before the nineteenth century, water had been unpopular not only because it often carried pathogenic bacteria but also because it was free. The peasantry may have drunk water in the early Middle Ages but once their incomes began to rise in the fifteenth century and they could afford to drink ale, they turned away from water – which was thereafter tainted with the stigma of poverty, in the same way as rye bread later became. Comparing French and English habits in the 1460s, the judge and writer on legal affairs Sir John Fortescue pointed out that the English 'drink no water, unless at certain times upon a religious score and by way of doing penance'. 'Would you believe it,' wrote César de Saussure in the 1720s, 'though water is to be had in abundance in London, and of fairly good quality, absolutely none is drunk? In this country . . . beer . . . is what everyone drinks when thirsty.' It was thus as much for reasons of status as of health that, when beer became expensive in the late eighteenth century, the labouring classes turned not to water but to tea.

At the same period, however, water became fashionable among the upper classes – admittedly in a rarefied form. At the beginning of the seventeenth century Dudley, Lord North had travelled to the Low Countries and visited the town of Spa, which had long been famous for its medicinal waters.* On his return to England, he fell in with Prince Henry, the son of King James I, and together they indulged their desires and abused their bodies to excess. North fell ill, and the doctors ordered him to go to the country for the sake of his health. So he went down to stay at a friend's estate in Kent. The countryside bored him, however, and his health failed to improve – until, at the beginning of his journey back to London, he noticed a clear spring that left a ruddy-coloured track, reminding him of the effect of the iron in the waters of Spa. He had some of this water bottled, and sent to his physician. The latter analysed it and found that it contained not only iron, which he believed to be effective in treating hypochondria and diseases of the bladder and kidneys, but also 'vitriol', which was considered to be capable of curing the colic, the melancholy and the vapours, as well as of warding off the plague. Lord North drank the water, and felt better; he recommended it to his friends; soon the invalids of the court were travelling down to the spring at what is now called Tunbridge Wells.

The greatest proponent of the waters of Tunbridge Wells was a local doctor called Lodowick Rowzee, who wrote a book on the subject in 1632. In order to ensure that people actually visited the spa – and took the treatments that he prescribed – he developed the theory that there was little point in bottling Tunbridge water and exporting it to London because mineral waters deteriorated away from their source. Mineral waters contained a 'volatile spirit', a substance that could not be detected by analysis but without which they were valueless. Indeed, Tunbridge water was so delicate that not only was it ruined by carriage but its virtues evaporated in the heat of the sun. Dr Rowzee's patients were therefore required to drink from the spring every morning before breakfast.

The spa waters of Bath had been known long before those of Tunbridge; indeed, the Romans had held them in such high esteem that they had built a city around them. After the departure of the Romans, however, the waters fell largely out of use, and their popularity was not revived until after the experience of Lord

---

*The term spa, meaning a watering-place, is derived from the name of the town.

North and the enterprise of Dr Rowzee had made Tunbridge a favoured watering-place. Bath was made fashionable once again by Charles II and his wife Catherine of Braganza, who visited the town in the autumn of 1663 in the hope that the Queen would 'find the waters remedial in sterility', and as a result of the organization of the social life of the town by Beau Nash, who served as 'master of ceremonies' throughout the first half of the eighteenth century.

Bath enjoyed an advantage over Tunbridge Wells in that its waters were warm, and so could be bathed in as well as drunk – but then, it was not only warm waters that became popular for bathing in the eighteenth century. In the second half of the century, sea-bathing came into fashion, notably at Brighton; the activity was not at first regarded as a pleasurable one but simply as a treatment for diseases of the glands. Indeed, it would have been difficult to have derived much enjoyment from the experience, given that doctors recommended their patients to bathe in the water in chilly weather, when they considered that the pores of their skin were safely closed. Another less than pleasurable aspect of the Brighton treatment was that the patients were supposed not only to bathe in the sea-water but also to drink it, as it was said that this helped in the cleaning of the glands. Obviously, the consumption of large quantities of neat sea-water would have been impossible, so patients were instructed to drink the water in quantities of no more than a quarter of a pint at a time, mixed with an equal quantity of milk.

In the early nineteenth century, a solution was finally found to the coldness of the sea and the unpleasantness of the water at Brighton. The lack of a natural spring was rendered irrelevant by the establishment of a spa that produced a variety of artificial mineral waters both for bathing and for drinking. The means of manufacturing carbonated waters had originally been discovered by Joseph Priestley in 1767, a few years before he discovered oxygen. Priestley supplied the technology for carbonating distilled water for experimental use by Captain Cook on his voyage of discovery to the Antarctic in the *Resolution* in 1772–1775 but otherwise did nothing to exploit his invention. Instead, it was exploited in Geneva by Nicholas Paul and his partner, one Jacob Schweppe, who manufactured soda water – carbonated water to which soda had been added for medical purposes.

The next stage was to produce imitations of natural mineral waters; they were first manufactured on a commercial basis in the second decade of the nineteenth century by a German doctor called Friedrich Adolph Augustus Struve, who prepared precise copies not only of several German mineral waters but also those of Spa. He opened pump rooms in Germany, in Russia and then, in 1825, at Brighton. Initially he called this the German Spa, but he soon obtained the patronage of King George IV, and changed the name to the Royal German Spa. Invalids came to his pump room in preference to natural springs, and some medical men recommended his waters as being quite equal to the natural waters they imitated. Struve also sold his waters through agents in London for 1s 4d per dozen bottles – roughly the same price as a case of the cheapest champagne. The Royal German Spa and Struve's Brighton Seltzer Water remained popular until the 1880s.

By the late nineteenth century, most Britons were perfectly happy to drink tap water. This was not the case in France, where the struggle to eliminate contaminated water supplies continued for many years; as late as 1943 only 38 per cent of French communes had safe drinking water. This serves to explain why the French have acquired a reputation for being drinkers of mineral water – a habit that returned to Britain in the 1980s. The revival in the popularity of mineral water in Britain today is therefore to be explained by very different reasons from those that led to its popularity in the eighteenth and early nineteenth century. Mineral water is drunk, not because it is considered positively to improve the health of the drinker, but – at least in part – because it is considered that tap water is unsafe to drink.

It is not in fact generally the case that consumption of tap water in Britain today poses any dangers, but the issue is one of perception, not of reality. It is believed that the quality of tap water has deteriorated, partly as a result of the publicity that has been given to certain cases in which there has undoubtedly been contamination. The most famous of these concerns an incident at Camelford in Cornwall in July 1988, when twenty tons of aluminium sulphate were mistakenly emptied into the wrong tank at the treatment works that supplied water to the town and the surrounding villages, thus entering the mains water supply. People who drank the affected water suffered from diarrhoea, headaches and nausea and rashes. Two years after the incident some of them were complaining that their memory was impaired and expressed the fear that they might suffer in the long term from brain damage. It is possible that their fear is justified, as there exists a body of research that points to a link between Alzheimer's disease, premature senile dementia, and high concentrations of aluminium in drinking water – but only time will tell. This means that the incident will continue to receive publicity for years to come, thus maintaining popular concern about the possible dangers of tap water.

In 1989 an independent panel that had been appointed to look into the medium- and long-term effects of the incident at Camelford concluded that, where people suffered from lasting illness, this had nothing to do with the toxicity of the chemicals they had ingested but probably resulted from sustained anxiety, which the panel attributed partly to the failure of the South-West Water Authority to give out adequate information, and partly to alarmist reports in the media. The panel may not have been correct in its conclusions, but it was right to point to the role played by the media in creating popular conceptions about the risks of drinking water. It is not as if newspapers have shrunk back from producing scare stories about the poor quality of Britain's water. For example, one *Sunday Times* 'Insight' feature in 1989 was illuminated by a headline that declared that 'One in five sewage works illegally discharges human filth into Britain's rivers', and that 'untreated human waste pours daily into streams and rivers, diluted sewage floods city streets, and thousands of miles of overloaded sewers are near collapse'.

Nor has the Government served to improve its profile as the guardian of the health of its citizens by fighting a running battle with the European Commission over the date at which it is prepared to conform to European Union standards for drinking water. In 1980 a European Union (then Community) directive required all member states to pass legislation by 1982 requiring certain standards of water purity to be met by 1985. The British government has indulged in such prolonged delaying tactics on this issue that the European Commission brought legal proceedings which resulted in 1992 in the British government being found guilty by the European Court of Justice of breaching the water directive. The Government promised that it would ensure compliance by the end of 1995 – although there was no guarantee that this promise would be fulfilled.

The British government has thus been seen for many years to have been supporting agricultural and commercial interests to the detriment of consumers. Again, it is more a matter of perception than of reality. The issue is that the nitrate levels in water in parts of Britain, notably East Anglia, exceed the European Union limit of fifty milligrams per litre. These high nitrate levels have been caused by intensive agricultural practices, in which pastures have been ploughed up for crops and large quantities of nitrate fertilizer applied. There is no evidence, however, that they pose a substantial danger to health. The European Union standard for nitrates in drinking water is based on ensuring avoidance of a disease called methaemaglobinaemia or 'blue baby syndrome', which affects bottle-fed infants. There have only been fifteen cases of methaemaglobinaemia in Britain in the last thirty years, and the last death was in 1948.

In these circumstances it is not surprising that John Bellak, then Chairman of the Water Services Association, should have told the 'Water 2000' conference in London in 1991 that the defects of the water industry had been 'exaggerated beyond measure and beyond reason'. Certainly, consumers had good reason to be concerned about the possibility of the contamination of their domestic water supplies with lead – the ingestion of which supposedly contributed to the fall of the Roman Empire – but, as Bellak pointed out, where this occurred, it was not the fault of the water companies: it was caused by the old lead pipes that some people had in their houses. There had in fact been substantial improvements in the treatment of drinking water, bathing water and sewage – yet public satisfaction with water supplies had fallen. 'The disparity between reality and perception is alarming,' Bellak said. The perception was demonstrated by a survey, conducted in advance of the privatization of the water supply industry, in which more than 40 per cent of those interviewed expressed fears about health risks and 28 per cent said that they never drank from their taps at all. Instead, they drank mineral water.

In 1984, 85 per cent of all the mineral water consumed in Britain was sparkling. Ten years later, however, 60 per cent of mineral water, and nearly all of that drunk in homes, was still.

Only in restaurants, pubs and wine bars had sparkling water retained its popularity. Evidently, mineral water started to become popular in the late 1970s and early 1980s as a type of soft drink and was therefore preferred in a sparkling form, whereas in the late 1980s and early 1990s it was largely being drunk as an alternative to tap water – except in restaurants, pubs and wine bars where it was still being consumed as an alternative to alcohol.* This change has been reflected in a change in the style of advertisements. In the early 1980s bottled water was promoted as a fashionable accessory to food, but by the 1990s the emphasis was on purity and health. Although companies that market mineral waters in Britain are prohibited by the regulations from making the sort of health claims that were made for mineral waters in the past – and are still made on the Continent – they have not shrunk back from playing on public fears about the healthfulness of tap water. In 1992 an advertisement for Spa showing a pregnant woman with the strapline, 'Before you drink, think Spa . . . source of purity,' had to be withdrawn after the Advertising Standards Authority ruled it made 'an unwarranted appeal to the scare factor' when there was no evidence that Spa water was any healthier than any other.

It might have been imagined that the belief that mineral water was healthier than tap water would have taken a knock as a result of the discovery in February 1990 of traces of benzene – a chemical that is used to manufacture plastics, insecticides and polyurethane foam and is capable of causing cancer in humans – in bottles of Perrier during routine testing of its mineral content in North Carolina in the United States. Although levels of benzene were found to be up to four times as high as the American environmental standard for drinking water allowed, a spokesman for the United States Food and Drug Administration said that, even at the highest level detected, a person drinking a pint of Perrier a day for many years would raise his risk of cancer by no more than one in a million. Nevertheless, Perrier withdrew its water from sale in the United States. At this point the company stated that the water on sale in Britain was free from

*Another explanation for the change is that people had needed initially to convince themselves about spending money on water by buying it in a different form to that in which it came out of the tap, but once they had become used to the idea of buying water they converted to the still version.

contamination. But tests on British supplies that were carried out by the Ministry of Agriculture found levels of benzene contamination similar to those found in America. Perrier then withdrew its water from sale everywhere in the world. Its chairman, Gustave Leven, confessed that the pollution had been caused by a failure to clean the filters that had been supposed to remove the benzene from the natural gases that emerged from the source of the water at Vergèze in the south of France. Dr Derek Miller, assistant director of the independent Water Research Centre, commented that it was 'astonishing' that carbon filters were being used to clean a 'natural mineral water' in the first place.

Thus, not only was the world's most popular brand of mineral water shown to contain a carcinogen, but it was revealed that the water had to be filtered in order that this substance should be removed. It might have seemed that this would damage the popular belief in the naturalness of natural mineral water – but it did not. Perrier may not have regained the dominance of the mineral water market that it held before the benzene scare, but sales of other waters continued to increase enormously. The consumption of bottled waters in Britain, which stood at 55 million litres in 1983, had reached 570 million litres ten years later. In 1990 the owners of one of the leading brands of sparkling mineral water, Badoit, withdrew their product from supermarkets in Britain and in 1992 withdrew it from restaurants because the increase in sales in Britain was threatening its ability to supply the demand in its home market of France.

The average cost of the mineral water that is purchased in shops in Britain is now 43p a pint. Just as it seemed absurd two hundred years ago that the working classes drank tea from China, sweetened with sugar from the West Indies, because it was cheaper than British beer, so it seems absurd today that so many people are prepared to pay more for a bottle of water – much of it imported from the Continent of Europe – than for a bottle or carton of domestically-produced milk.

The popularity of milk is in itself a relatively recent phenomenon. In the sixteenth and seventeenth centuries cow's milk was drunk in some parts of the countryside but hardly at all in towns. It was considered by doctors that cow's milk was suitable only for young children and very old people; some even had their doubts about the wisdom of giving male children milk from any source but their mothers, frowning upon not only cow's milk but also the practice of wet-nursing, on the grounds that it would influence the child's character adversely. 'For as lambs sucking she-goats bear coarse wool, and kids sucking ewes bear soft hair,' explained the physician Thomas Muffet,* 'so fine children degenerate by gross woman's milk, losing or lessening that excellency of nature, wit and complexion, which from their parents they first obtained.' At the end of the seventeenth century it was calculated that average per capita consumption of milk was less than two pints a week.

In the eighteenth century, the quality of the milk available in towns was generally appalling. Most of it was produced by herds of cows living in insanitary underground dens, and then watered down by milk-women who hawked it around the streets in open-top pails contaminated by dirt and saliva. And it was quite expensive, up to 2d a pint in the later part of the century. It was only likely to be drinkable if it were purchased straight from the udder, from cows that had been driven round the streets. The best milk in London was that obtained direct from the cows grazing in St James's Park, which was usually drunk on the spot.

The quality of the milk available in towns did not improve significantly until the source of supply changed in the latter part of the nineteenth century. Until then, most of the milk available was produced in town dairies. The cattle that lent themselves best to this artificial town life were imported Dutch cows. They proved, however, to be more susceptible to disease than country animals, and in 1866 more than half of the ten thousand cows in London were killed by cattle plague. This led to the imposition of such strict sanitary regulations on town dairies that most of them closed down, and from this time onwards the industrial towns were supplied almost entirely by country milk. This soon improved in quality, largely as a result of the concentration of the wholesale milk trade into the hands of a few large firms which established contacts with farms that enabled them minutely to control the quality and condition of the milk as well as the general

*Reputedly the father of the Little Miss Muffet who 'Sat on a tuffet/Eating her curds and whey/[When] came a big spider/Who sat down beside her/And frightened Miss Muffet away.'

sanitary condition of the farm. By 1902 the consumption of milk among middle-class families had risen to six pints per person per week, although the fact that it was still relatively expensive meant that much less milk was consumed by the labouring classes, less than a pint a head.

The next major step forward in the popularity of milk resulted from the introduction of pasteurization, thus ensuring that children were no longer risking disease and death by drinking commercially-produced cow's milk. In the summer of 1911, when infantile diarrhoea killed off 203 out of every 1,000 babies, the epidemic was blamed on the contamination of raw (un-pasteurized) cow's milk; by 1921, when half the milk in London was pasteurized, the infantile death rate in the capital had fallen to 90 per 1,000. The pasteurization of milk had begun in 1906, but the methods that were used in early plants were unreliable. The milk was flash-pasteurized by being splashed onto a steam-heated surface at about 80°C; because of the short time involved, the temperature was critical, and the milk was often either not heated sufficiently (in which case it might be contaminated) or heated to excess (which ruined the flavour). It was only from 1923 onwards that a more sophisticated holding technique was developed, in which the milk was held at 65°C for thirty minutes.*

The new holding technique may have ensured that the milk was pasteurized efficiently, but it required a change in methods of distribution. Milk that was pasteurized by the holding technique had first to be put into bottles. But bottles were much more subject to variations in external temperature than churns, and thus the new system of pasteurization required the introduction of a new system of refrigerated distribution and storage. In the 1920s small refrigerators, hitherto unknown in Britain, were introduced by the American Frigidaire company, and installed in dairies nationwide.

Now that milk was safe, it became fashionable. Dairy shops that sold milk for consumption on and off the premises were replaced by American-style milk bars that young men patronized without shame. Now that milk was safe, moreover, a scheme was established for supplying milk in schools. By 1939 more than half

---

*This later gave way to the compromise 'high-temperature, short-time' treatment of 15 seconds at 70°C that continues to be used today.

of the children in state schools were receiving a third of a pint daily, for which some paid half the retail price and others nothing at all; during and after the Second World War this scheme was extended to independent schools. There was also a scheme to promote the consumption of milk by workers in industry.

At the outbreak of the Second World War milk consumption in Britain had reached three pints per person per week. By 1953 this had further increased to five pints. This had nothing to do with the milk companies, but was the result of the shortage of other foods during and after the war, and the subsidization of the price by the Government, which actively encouraged its citizens to drink more milk. As Sir John Boyd Orr, one of the principal architects of the Government's food policy, explained in a lecture in 1940, 'Every child should have at least one and a half pints of milk a day . . . Except for young children milk is, of course, not an essential food. All that is contained in milk could be obtained from other sources. But it is so rich in first-class protein, minerals and most of the vitamins that it is the most valuable and the cheapest food available for making good the major deficiencies in the diet of the poor.' During the war the Ministry of Food proclaimed that milk was vital to the national health. Milk, and the tea to which it was added in liberal quantities, became symbols of the British nation, and when the war ended, milk was regarded as one of the instruments of victory.

The belief in the virtues of milk long outlasted the war. Milk bars were replaced by coffee bars, most of whose customers drank *cappuccino*, essentially frothy milk with a small amount of coffee in the bottom. The Milk Marketing Board spent large sums of money on advertising. The continuing public belief in the importance of milk was demonstrated by the reaction to the decision in 1971 of Margaret Thatcher, then Secretary of State for Education and Science, to withdraw free milk from schoolchildren above the age of seven, a decision that earned herself the epithet of 'Thatcher the Milk Snatcher'.

In the 1970s, however, public attitudes to milk began to change as people stopped worrying about good nutrition and started worrying about obesity and whether the cholesterol in their bloodstreams might give them a heart attack. At the same time, soft drinks became more popular. Those people who had gone to coffee bars in their youth and drank hot milk with a little coffee in it continued to do the same thing at home. But as they grew older and became parents, their children rebelled against their tastes and took up soft drinks. Milk consumption fell from five to four pints per person per week.

Those people who had been brought up on milk might have been more inclined to continue drinking it if an acceptable low-fat version had been available. In the early 1980s, however, the only low-fat milk that could be found was UHT 'skimmed' milk. UHT stood for 'Ultra-Heat Treated', meaning that the milk had been heated to a very high temperature in order to sterilize it and ensure a long shelf-life – a process that affected the flavour adversely. UHT might have been the form in which milk was sold in many Continental European countries but it was not the form to which British consumers had become accustomed. Nevertheless, sales of UHT skimmed milk soon increased to a point at which it became viable for the Milk Marketing Board to introduce a fresh version. Even this fresh skimmed milk, however, did not taste the same as the milk with which consumers were familiar. Because virtually all the fat had been skimmed off, it did not taste as creamy as whole milk. The next stage was the development of an inter-mediate form of 'semi-skimmed' or 'half-fat' milk, which offered the appeal of skimmed milk for health considerations while retaining more of the taste of whole milk. By 1993 low-fat milks accounted for more than half of all milk consumption; most of that was semi-skimmed. The fall in milk consumption had been halted.

One feature that emerges from the changes in the popularity of milk is that attitudes towards the healthfulness and utility of particular drinks tend to be cyclical in their nature. This is demonstrated, not only by the rise, fall and rise of milk, but by changes in attitudes to tea and coffee.

Tea was originally popularized in China in the third century BC, when the megalomaniac 'First Emperor' Qin Shi Huanghi regularly drank an elixir of powdered jade and tea, in the hope that his life would be prolonged indefinitely, since it was believed that tea was an Elixir of Life. This idea was promoted by adherents of the Taoist religion, many of whom were tea merchants and therefore derived economic advantage from the belief. To ensure long life people swallowed special Elixir of Life pills washed down with cups of Elixir of Life tea. As 'proof' to substantiate claims that tea was the Elixir of Life, it was generally believed that one could subsist on tea alone. Many scholars and holy men were said to take no nourishment except for bowls of tea. For centuries the holiest monks demonstrated their faith by living only on tea – at least until the fourteenth century, when it was discovered that they had fraudulently used tea-like shreds of meat instead of tea leaves.

Similar claims were made when tea was introduced into Europe, in Holland in the mid-sixteenth century. One of the first European physicians to sound the praises of tea, and one of the most influential, was Dr Nikolas Dirx in his *Observationes Medicae* in 1641. 'Nothing is comparable to this plant,' he wrote. 'Those who use it are for that reason alone exempt from all maladies and reach an extreme old age. Not only does it procure great vigour for their bodies, but it preserves them from gravel and gallstones, headaches, colds, ophthalmia, catarrh, asthma, sluggishness of the stomach and intestinal troubles.'

In England, too, tea was promoted on medical grounds. In an advertisement for his coffee house behind the new Royal Exchange in the City of London which he published at the beginning of the 1670s, Thomas Garway claimed that, among other attributes, tea 'maketh the body active and lusty . . . removeth the obstructions of the spleen . . . taketh away the difficulty of breathing . . . prevents and cures agues, surfeits and fevers . . . prevents consumptions and powerfully assuageth the pain of the bowels.' Indeed, 'the said leaf is of such known virtues that those very nations famous for antiquity, knowledge and wisdom do frequently sell it among themselves for twice its weight in silver.' At Garway's Coffee House it could be obtained for between 16s and £2 10s a pound.

Despite such enthusiastic expressions of support, many people treated tea with caution. Having no experience of the effects of this exotic new drink, they took precautions to insure themselves against any possible ill consequences. In London in the late seventeenth century some ladies took brandy after their tea as a corrective. Similarly, in some parts of Scotland in the eighteenth century it was the custom to add a gill of whisky to the last cup from the pot 'to correct all the bad effects of the tea'. It is also probable that the practice of adding milk to tea originated in the middle of the eighteenth century as an attempt to counteract what were perceived as its more harmful qualities.* The effect of the addition of milk to tea is to mitigate the taste of its mouth-puckering tannins, with which the casein in the milk combines; this chemical process may not have been understood at the time but the effects on its taste certainly were.

It was felt by many that tea was simply not suited to Western constitutions. As the Danish physician Simon Paulli explained, 'Being Europeans, we ought to use the drinks peculiar to Europe; for it is no less generally than justly observed that the natural produce of any country is best suited to the constitution of its inhabitants. Thus tea seems by nature adapted to the inhabitants of China, coffee to those of Persia, chocolate to those of America, and ale and wine to those of different parts of Europe. Thus the ancient inhabitants of Saxony and Mecklenburg, before they became fond of foreign delicacies, used to say proverbially, "Drink wine, and reap benefit from it; drink ale, and become fat; drink water, and die." . . . Europeans then must have their constitutions impaired and their strength exhausted, by living like the inhabitants of Asia, Africa and America.'

The most famous of all attacks on tea was made in the middle of the eighteenth century by the traveller and philanthropist Jonas Hanway.† Having described it as an 'intoxicating liquor', a 'fashionable drug' and an 'epidemical disease', he went on to ask rhetorically, 'To what height of folly must a nation be arrived, when the common people are not satisfied with wholesome food at home, but must go to the remotest regions to please a vicious palate . . . Were they the sons of tea-sippers who won the fields of Crécy and Agincourt, or dyed the Danube's streams with Gallic blood?'

By the nineteenth century, however, tea was regarded not only as a nutritional necessity but also as having contributed in no small effect to the great change that had taken place in the manners and morals of the nation. As was pointed out in a history of the tea trade, published in 1832, 'The introduction of this beverage into England has materially contributed to the health and morals

---

*The origin of the practice of adding milk to tea is usually attributed to a French gentlewoman, Madame de la Sablière, in 1680, but this arises from a misreading of the letter of Madame de Sévigné from which the information is derived: Madame de la Sablière added milk to tea, not to improve the taste of the tea, but to disguise that of the milk.
†Hanway is best remembered by posterity for being the first man to carry an umbrella in wet weather in London.

of the nation at large, by superseding in a great measure the immoderate drinking of spirituous, vinous and all other fermented potations.'

Nor was it any coincidence that medical support for tea, that vital ally of the temperance and teetotal movements,* reached its zenith at the same time as the aims of the teetotal movement were most fully realized – during the First World War, which saw the introduction of prohibitively high taxes on alcoholic drinks and of drastic restrictions on the opening hours of public houses. The famous Ty-phoo brand of tea was created by a Birmingham grocer named John Sumner in 1905. His sister bought a packet of small-leaf tea, found that it was good for her digestion, and suggested that he make up a similar blend. He followed her advice, with considerable commercial success. At this time most grocers sold a wide variety of teas, which they blended themselves for their customers; Sumner, however, went direct to the source: he purchased small-leaf (fannings) teas in Ceylon and had them blended in Colombo; all that he had to do on their arrival in England was to put them in packets. Ty-phoo, which was sold at one price only, was the first successfully branded tea. Sumner advertised Ty-phoo as 'leaf-edge tea, free from injurious gallo-tannic acid'. This was a double lie: all tea contains gallo-tannic acid, and it is completely harmless, being simply the water-soluble form of tannin. But the advertisements worked; indeed, many people bought their Ty-phoo from chemists rather than grocers. During the First World War most of the tea imported into Britain was 'pooled' and sold, not under brand names, but simply as 'tea'; but, having canvassed the support of nearly four thousand doctors, John Sumner succeeded in having Ty-phoo exempted from this requirement.

Like the changes in attitudes to milk, the secular changes in medical attitudes to tea have been cyclical in nature. As has been suggested by Denys Forrest, a specialist writer and authority on the history of tea, they have in fact followed a standard cycle for new foodstuffs: first they are promoted, when still little known, as a panacea; then they are denounced, when showing signs of popularity, as a health menace; only then can they be promoted, when universally accepted, on various hygienic and dietary

---

*These will be discussed in the next chapter.

grounds. He points out that the inhabitants of the former Yugoslavia are still in the first phase and drink tea as a prophylactic against influenza, while Mexicans are at the second stage and consider it ruinous to the nerves.

Coffee has gone through a comparable cycle. It first became popular in the Yemen in the fifteenth century, among adherents of Sufism, who took coffee during their religious services. Sufism was a movement whose members sought mystically to reach out for God, to merge spiritually with the divine. They did so by holding communal services at night, in which they devoted their energies to achieving a trance-like concentration on God. They were assisted in obtaining the requisite state of mental excitement by the consumption of coffee.

Thus, coffee was first consumed as a stimulant. Within a few decades the consumption of coffee had spread throughout the Muslim Near East. It had become popular partly for social reasons: coffee houses fulfilled a need for places to go out and socialize in a part of the world where alcohol was scorned and where a restaurant culture was lacking. But coffee also became popular because of its pharmacological effect on the people who drank it. The way in which coffee affected the drinker was described as '*marqaha*' by its earliest devotees: the term refers to 'coffee euphoria', to the fact that coffee makes the heart beat faster and contributes to a feeling of renewed vigour. This pharmacological effect was the reason – or at least the excuse – that was given by Kha'ir Beg, the *muhtasib* in Mecca, when he banned the consumption of coffee in 1511. The ban was introduced after two doctors had stood up at a meeting of the *ulema* (the leading religious scholars) of the city and declared that coffee was unhealthy. The *ulema* then pronounced that coffee-drinking was contrary to Islamic law, on the grounds that it caused harm to the drinker.

Thus, in the Muslim world, in which coffee was first popularized, doubts about its healthfulness were expressed by doctors and scholars almost from the beginning. There was no consensus: some scholars condemned it while others supported it; the status of coffee remained vague. In the light of this confusion, it may seem surprising that coffee was promoted with such vigour by its supporters in seventeenth-century Western Europe. No Muslim scholar, not even the staunchest supporter of coffee, had claimed that it was a panacea. Yet it was precisely this claim that was made by its European admirers. Sir Henry Blount, who travelled extensively in the Levant in the seventeenth century, went so far as to claim that the Turks, Persians and 'most of the eastern world . . . acknowledge how it freeth them from crudities caused by ill diet or moist lodging, insomuch as they, using coffee morning and evening, have no consumptions, which ever come of moisture, no lethargies in aged people, or rickets in children, and but few qualms in women with child . . . When a Turk is sick, he fasts and takes coffee, and if that will not do, he makes his will, and thinks of no other physic.'

It seems that European admirers of coffee, such as Blount, were inclined to pass on whatever anybody said to them about coffee's medicinal value, because they were otherwise unable to understand why anyone should want to drink it. 'Although the taste of this drink is not agreeable in any respect,' wrote Jacques de Bourges, a priest who accompanied the Bishop of Beryte on his journey to Turkey in 1661, 'it is nevertheless highly esteemed by these people, on account of the good effects that they find in it.'

There was also another reason why coffee (and tea) were promoted so vigorously by their admirers. They became popular at the end of a period that saw a significant change in the bodily type of many Englishmen. As a very broad generalization, men were thin in the Middle Ages but became fatter in the sixteenth century. This distinction is exemplified by the popular conception of the appearances of Henry VII and Henry VIII. The change in bodily type was attributed by contemporaries, not to increased consumption of food, nor to the consumption of different types of food, but to increased consumption of beer. The heavy drinking of the sixteenth century produced an increase in the number of people suffering from disorders such as gout, digestive troubles and acute headaches.

In their search for an antidote to these disorders doctors experimented with a number of new drugs, among which were tea and coffee. 'Were the custom of drinking [tea] as universal here as it is in the eastern countries,' argued John Ovington in his *Essay upon the Nature and Qualities of Tea*, then men 'might even double the days of their natural life, by converting it all into enjoyment, exempt from several painful and acute diseases, occasioned very often by a pernicious excess of inflaming liquors, which render it rather a burden than a blessing to us.' It was as a drug, and an antidote to the ill-effects of too much alcohol, that Sir William Harvey, the physician credited with discovering the circulation of the blood, experimented with coffee. According to legend, when on his deathbed in 1657, Harvey summoned his lawyer and held up a coffee bean. 'This little fruit,' he whispered, 'is the source of happiness and wit.' Harvey then bequeathed his entire supply of coffee, fifty-six pounds, to the London College of Physicians, directing them to commemorate the day of his death every month by drinking his coffee in the morning, so long as the supply lasted.

Doctors in the seventeenth century believed in humoral medicine, according to which it was supposed that a person's body fluids dictated his mood. There were four fluids (blood, yellow bile, black bile and phlegm), four temperaments (sanguine, choleric, melancholic and phlegmatic) and four properties (warm and moist, warm and dry, cold and dry, and cold and moist). Blood, being warm and moist, produced a sanguine temperament; yellow bile, which was warm and dry, produced a choleric temperament; black bile, which was cold and dry, produced a melancholic temperament; phlegm, being cold and moist, produced a phlegmatic temperament. Now, coffee was regarded as a dry and dessicating substance, probably because the beans had been roasted, thus removing their natural moisture. It was therefore believed that coffee dried out the body's phlegm, thus robbing the phlegmatic temperament of its very foundation. Previously, the phlegmatic temperament, in which the body was made portly by a diet of beer, had been regarded as the natural one. But now it was argued that the opposite was true: that the dryness produced by coffee was beneficial, that sobriety was a desirable state in which to find oneself.

Not only was coffee considered to be a sober drink, but it was regarded as a means of curbing sexual urges, and even of inducing impotence. It was therefore especially recommended to Catholic priests, to support their commitment to live in celibacy. For the rest of the population, however, the supposedly anaphrodisiac properties of coffee were not necessarily regarded as beneficial. The story was told of a King of Persia who has been 'so accustomed to the drinking of coffee that he had an inconceivable aversion for women . . . The Queen standing one day at her chamber window, and perceiving that they had got down a horse on the ground, in order to the gelding of him, asked some that stood by, why they treated so handsome a creature in that manner. Whereupon answer being made her that he was too fiery and mettlesome, and that the business of those who were about him was, with the taking away of the excess of mettle, which stone-horses* are guilty of, to deprive him of all generative virtue, the Queen replied that the trouble might have been spared, since the coffee would have wrought the same effect; and that, if they would keep the stone-horse with that drink, he would, in a short time, be as cold as the King her husband.'

Even after it was realized that the consumption of coffee alone was insufficient to ensure that priests lived in celibacy, the fact that coffee was a sober drink that stimulated the intellect rather than the libidos of the people who drank it was not necessarily considered by doctors to be beneficial. The celebrated eighteenth-century Swedish botanist Linnaeus suggested that the popularity of coffee might be regarded as one of the disadvantages of progress, that coffee 'might be considered useful by those who set a higher worth upon saving their time than on maintaining their lives and health'. Linnaeus's meaning was clarified by the warning that was given by the homoeopath Samuel Hahnemann in 1803: coffee, he said, created 'an artificially heightened sense of being'; it threw life off its natural rhythm.

In Britain, however, as the nineteenth century progressed, coffee first contributed to the growth in size of the temperance and teetotal movements, and then benefited from their growth in influence and their gradual winning over of doctors to their cause. At a time when the range of soft drinks on offer was limited to soda water, lemonade and ginger beer, coffee – even more than tea – was the quintessential temperance drink. The support of teetotal campaigners led them to sponsor the establishment of coffee public houses, which were designed to have the social qualities of the pub but with the alcohol left out. During a period when the social and medical consequences of alcohol were under concerted attack, coffee was free from medical criticism.†

---

*Stallions.
†Coffee was attacked by the opponents of the teetotal movement, who alleged that one teetotaller from Minehead in Somerset had died as a result of drinking several quarts of coffee a day, a post-mortem supposedly revealing nine pounds and fourteen ounces of it in his body.

This is far from the case today. The principal physiologically active component in coffee is an alkaloid, caffeine, which may well have evolved as a natural herbicide to help growing shrubs overcome competing plants. It stimulates the brain by fitting itself into brain receptors designed for adenosine, a natural sedative that tells the body's cells to slow down. By overriding it, caffeine fools the body into staying in top gear. There is plenty of evidence, both anecdotal and scientific, to suggest that people who consume coffee on a regular basis – meaning two or more cups a day – experience lowered mood states and headaches and drowsiness when they are deprived of dietary caffeine. The Institute of Food Research has also found that there exists a relationship between these withdrawal symptoms and drink preference. That is to say, one factor contributing to the widespread consumption of coffee is its ability to alleviate the symptoms of caffeine withdrawal. In other words, it is addictive.

Concern about the possible ill effects of the caffeine in coffee has encouraged many inveterate coffee-drinkers to abandon conventional coffee for the decaffeinated version – even though the process of decaffeination, which most commonly involves soaking the beans in a solvent to dissolve the caffeine and then steaming the beans and washing several times with water in order to remove residues of the solvent, affects the flavour of the coffee adversely. Indeed, at the beginning of the 1990s there were some people in the coffee industry who believed that decaffeinated coffee would become more popular than the regular version – just as low-fat milk is now more popular than the original in which all the fat is retained.

This has not turned out to be the case. The proportion of the coffee drunk in Britain that is decaffeinated has stabilized at about 13 per cent. It is likely – although there is no firm evidence – that some people have been dissuaded from converting from pure coffee to the decaffeinated version, or persuaded to reconvert to coffee that contains caffeine, because of the publication of information that appears to throw doubts over the safety of the decaffeination process. The solvent that is most commonly used for decaffeination is methylene chloride, which is also used in some paint-strippers, aerosols and dry-cleaning solutions, and when inhaled at high concentrations can cause faintness, headaches and skin irritation. It has also been found to cause liver cancer in mice.

In fact, for human beings to ingest the quantity of methylene chloride that has been proved to cause damage to mice they would need to drink twenty million cups of coffee a day. If they tried to do this, the water would kill them before the coffee would. But that is not the point. Someone who has converted from ordinary to decaffeinated coffee for fear that he might be becoming addicted to caffeine or because he hopes that it will enable him to sleep better at night is quite likely to convert back again if he has been told that the decaffeinated coffee has been treated with a solvent that definitely causes cancer in laboratory animals.

It might also be wondered why the popular concern about the effects of the caffeine in coffee has not transferred to other drinks that contain caffeine, notably tea and colas. Certainly, these drinks contain less caffeine than coffee, but they do not contain as much less as is popularly imagined. It is impossible to state precisely how much caffeine is contained in a cup of coffee or tea, because it depends on the type of coffee or tea used, and the means by which it has been brewed. For example, a cup of *espresso* may contain as much as 300 milligrams of caffeine, whereas a cup of instant coffee contains only one quarter as much. Since the vast majority of the coffee that is drunk in Britain is instant, this is the relevant figure. The caffeine content of a cup of tea depends principally on the length of time for which it has been brewed, but is likely to be a little less than that of a cup of instant coffee, maybe 40 to 50 milligrams. This would appear to confirm the popular belief that tea is healthier than coffee because it contains less caffeine – were it not for the fact that the average Briton drinks twice as much tea, in terms of liquid volume, as he does coffee, and therefore ingests considerably more caffeine from tea than he does from coffee.

Equally, cola drinks may seem relatively harmless compared to tea and coffee, since they contain only about half as much caffeine for the same amount of volume as tea and a third as much as instant coffee.* But children are smaller than adults: if one allows

*There was a time when Coca-Cola contained just as much caffeine as coffee, and considerably more than tea. In 1911, however, the Coca-Cola Company was accused by the United States government of adulterating its product by the addition of a harmful ingredient, that is to say, caffeine. This case, memorably entitled *The United States v Forty Barrels and Twenty Kegs of Coca-Cola*, lasted until 1917, when it was settled out of court, the Coca-Cola Company having reformulated the drink in order to halve the amount of caffeine it contained.

for size, a child receives a similar dose of caffeine from the same quantity of cola as does an adult from coffee. Very few research studies have been carried out to determine the effect of caffeine on children compared with those that have been conducted on adults, but a behavioural study that was carried out by psychiatrists from the United States National Institute of Mental Health in the early 1980s found that children who drank six cans of cola a day (or the equivalent) were initially more alert, but then became fidgety, irritable and nervous, although not clinically hyperactive. In the opinion of Dr Michael Jacobson, Director of the Center for Science in the Public Interest in Washington DC 'It is crazy even to put this kind of substance in drinks consumed by so many children.'

If people do not feel the same concerns about tea and colas as they do about coffee, it is largely because they are ignorant of the relative amounts of caffeine that they are ingesting from these various drinks, but maybe also partly because of the publicity that has been given to recent scientific studies that have connected the regular consumption of large quantities of coffee with an increased risk of heart disease. In 1986 the results were published of a study of 1,130 middle-aged men who had once been students at the Johns Hopkins Medical School in Baltimore. It was found that the risk of heart disease increased in proportion to the number of cups of coffee drunk per day, and that people who drank more than five cups a day were three times more likely to suffer from heart disease than those who did not. There had been previous studies that found links between heart disease and coffee-drinking but these had been explained away on the grounds that heavy coffee-drinkers also tend to be heavy smokers. This was the first coffee study to separate the risks of smoking from those of coffee-drinking. The fact that the risk of heart disease increased in proportion to the number of cups of coffee drunk strengthened the conclusion that coffee was the cause. The researchers were not clear why this should have been so, but suggested that it might have had something to do with caffeine causing irregular rhythms in the heart. This research was supported in 1990 by the publication of the results of an even larger survey of 38,564 middle-aged men and women that had been carried out by researchers from the National Health Screening Service in Norway. The researchers found that the number of cups of coffee that the men and women drank each day was directly related to the number of them who had died from heart disease, even when other risk factors, such as smoking and high blood pressure, were taken into account.

If British coffee-drinkers have been encouraged to convert to decaffeinated coffee by research linking coffee with heart disease, they have been wrong to do so. The survey of the former students of the John Hopkins Medical School in Baltimore did not investigate the methods by which the coffee had been brewed, nor were the people who took part in the Norwegian study asked how they made the coffee they drank. However, it is common practice in Norway and the other Scandinavian countries to prepare coffee by boiling it. Boiling coffee extracts fatty substances from the ground beans; this raises blood cholesterol, which leads to a greater incidence of coronary heart disease. Caffeine has nothing to do with it. There is no evidence of any link between coffee consumption and an increased risk of heart disease in Britain, where the vast majority of the coffee that is drunk is made by adding boiling water to instant coffee powder or granules.

This said, it is perfectly understandable that the publication of research linking the consumption of coffee with an increased risk of heart disease should have caused concern among coffee-drinkers. After all, heart disease is the largest single cause of death in Britain; indeed, Scotland and Northern Ireland have (along with Finland) the highest rate of death from heart disease in the world. Not only is heart disease the largest single cause of death, but it is a major cause of premature death. Approximately one third of all deaths from heart disease in England and Wales are of men under sixty-five. Moreover, during the 1980s doctors and public health officials concentrated their efforts on reducing the risk of heart disease by improving people's diets. It might therefore be expected not only that research linking coffee with heart disease would have led some consumers to turn to decaffeinated coffee, or indeed to other hot drinks such as herbal teas, but also that growing evidence that a particular drink contributes to the reduction of the risk of heart disease would have led to a very substantial increase in that drink's popularity. Certainly this is what has happened in the United States. On 17 November 1991 the CBS news magazine programme 'Sixty Minutes' included an item on the 'French Paradox' – the fact that French people suffer much less from heart disease than British or Americans, despite their consumption of saturated fats, tendency to smoke heavily and general aversion to exercise. The presenter Morley Safer interviewed American and French doctors and medical researchers about the relationship between diet, wine consumption and heart disease. He travelled to Lyons, the capital of French gastronomy, to interview Serge Renaud, director of the Institut National de la Santé et de la Recherche Médicale and one of the two authors of the report. Renaud explained that the reason why the rate of heart attacks in Lyons was much lower than in American cities was that the French regularly drank moderate amounts of alcohol with their meals, in the form of red wine.

This programme, which was watched by 21.8 million households, unleashed a red wine mania. Wine retailers and restaurateurs reported that people were buying red wine who had never tried it before in their lives. In Pennsylvania, the state liquor control board recorded a 97 per cent increase in sales of red wine in the week following the broadcast. And this was not a nine days' wonder. In 1992 sales of red wine – which had been in decline in the 1980s – increased by 39 per cent.

It is understandable why Americans, having been told for so many years by their doctors that alcohol was bad for them, should have taken with such enthusiasm to red wine after being shown a glimpse on television of the apparently beneficial effects of a lifestyle that was so much more attractive than their own. What is more difficult to comprehend is why it was not until 1991 that publicity of this kind was given to evidence of which the medical community had known for years.

One of the American researchers who was interviewed by Safer for the 'Sixty Minutes' programme was Curtis Ellison, chief of preventive medicine and epidemiology at the Boston University School of Medicine. As he later admitted to the American wine magazine *The Wine Spectator*, doctors had been reticent about publicizing material that showed alcohol in a positive light. 'We've known for quite some time that alcohol tends to decrease the rate of heart disease,' he said. 'We hadn't been suppressing it, but we hadn't been making it widely known, either.'

At the beginning of the twentieth century, it had generally been believed by medical practitioners that the regular consumption of alcohol necessarily shortened the life of the person who drank it.

This belief was overturned in 1926 by Raymond Pearl, a statistics professor at the Johns Hopkins University, who showed in his book *Alcohol and Longevity* that, if people who drank appeared to die younger than those who did not, this was to be explained by the enormous damage caused by alcohol to the health of people who drank very heavily. If they were removed from the equation, then it appeared that moderate drinkers lived at least as long as abstainers – if not longer. 'Reading Pearl's monograph,' commented the cardiologist Arthur Klatsky at a symposium in Amsterdam in 1982, 'one has the impression that, for basically political reasons, Pearl tried to avoid placing too much emphasis upon the findings of the lower mortality of moderate drinkers. He realized the public health implications of his results. He seemed a little afraid of the attack upon his study which would follow publication.' In fact, Pearl's findings were not so much attacked as almost totally ignored. This is hardly surprising, given that they appeared at a time when the sale of alcoholic beverages within the United States was prohibited.

American (and British) doctors might not have wished to contemplate the health benefits of alcohol in the early twentieth century, but the opposite was true of their counterparts in the wine-drinking countries of the Mediterranean. In France, between the wars, medical journals that undertook surveys of medical opinions of general practitioners about the problem of alcoholism received replies that noted a marked increase in the consumption of wine, which was generally regarded as a healthy sign; indeed, doctors in the south-west extolled the health of peasants who drank five or more litres of wine a day. An association called the Medical Friends of the Wines of France was established, under the leadership of Adolphe Portmann, a senator from the Gironde and an ear-nose-and-throat specialist. Not only did the Friends extol the medicinal virtues of wine at their congresses, but these were on occasions followed by applied research: after one congress in Bordeaux, members adjourned for a two-day visit to the major vineyards of the region, including Château Margaux and Château d'Yquem.

Although it was believed by many French health professionals that people who drank wine lived longer than those who did not, proof for this belief was lacking. In *The Black Horse of the Apocalypse*, an attack on American Prohibition, Célestin

Cambiare could contest the claim by anti-alcohol campaigners that abstinence prolonged life only by pointing to the longevity of many wine-drinking Frenchmen. Citing examples such as Marshal Foch, who won the First World War at the age of sixty-six, he pointed out that 'Many Frenchmen reach a very old age, and keep their mental faculties and vigour up to the end. At an age when men of other nations are generally incapacitated for any kind of work, many Frenchmen . . . are still very active.'

The proof to support Cambiare's argument only began to emerge after the Second World War, and not in France but in its neighbour, Italy. Here, too, it had been widely believed by doctors that the regular use of wine in the diet helped to prevent heart disease – a belief that was given support by the discovery that certain plant compounds, which lowered the formation of blood cholesterol in animals, were present in wine. Then, at the beginning of the 1960s, a study was made of the eating and drinking habits of eighty people convalescing from heart attacks in Rome. It was found that thirteen of them were abstainers – an unusually high proportion in a country where wine-drinking was a part of everyday life – and that twenty-five of the others had significantly decreased their consumption of wine in the period preceding their heart attack. The researcher, Claudia Balboni, made the point that 'An intensive study of the drinking habits in coronary cases is urgently required'.

At the same time, a comparison was being conducted in the United States between the death rate in the town of Roseto, Pennsylvania, where the vast majority of the population was of Italian origin and retained their Italian dietary habits, and mortality in five other communities, of German, Welsh and mixed ethnic groups. It was found that a far smaller proportion of the population of Roseto than of the other towns had died from heart disease, even though they consumed many more calories and much more fat than the majority of Americans. They also drank vastly more wine. Despite this clear evidence of a French – or rather Italian-American – paradox, more than a generation before its existence became a matter of public knowledge, the researchers shrank back from concluding that the low death rate from heart disease was directly related to the high consumption of wine. 'The reason for the relatively salubrious condition of the Rosetans is not clear at the present moment,' they observed.

'Whether or not their . . . way of life contributes to their good health is still to be determined.'

It was not until the 1970s that American medical researchers felt confident enough even to suggest that there might be a causal correlation between alcohol consumption and a reduced risk of heart disease. Arthur Klatsky, having trawled through the computerized medical records of 120,000 patients at the Kaiser-Permanente Medical Center in Oakland, California, in an attempt to find factors that significantly affected the risk of heart disease, discovered that those who consumed alcohol in moderation were significantly less likely to suffer heart attacks than non-drinkers. After examining the possible causes of this relationship, Klatsky suggested, a little guardedly, that, 'Although the finding of a statistically significant negative association between use of alcohol and a first [heart attack] cannot at this time be interpreted as proof of the protective effect of alcohol on the coronary vessels, this happy possibility does exist.'

It was not long before other studies began to appear in support of Klatsky's findings. In 1981, for example, the results were published in *The Lancet* of a ten-year study of 1,422 male civil servants in London, which found that proportionately fewer of the moderate drinkers among the sample had died from heart disease than of either the non-drinkers or the heavy drinkers. The researchers offered a plausible explanation for their findings: they suggested that the protective effect of alcohol could be explained by the fact that it increased the level in the blood of 'good' cholesterol (HDL, high-density lipoprotein), a substance that moves around the arteries retrieving and eliminating 'bad' cholesterol (LDL, low-density lipoprotein), which would otherwise clog them up.

These studies were not alone. But nothing was done to spread the news among the general public. There were several reasons for this. In the first case, the fact that several studies showed the existence of an inverse relationship between moderate alcohol consumption and heart disease, even if they also offered reasons to account for it, did not prove that there was anything more than a statistical, as opposed to causal, connection: these studies did not necessarily lead to the conclusion that it was the moderate drinking itself that did people good. It was suggested in some quarters that any apparent beneficial effect of moderate alcohol consumption on the state of the heart might be explained by the phenomenon of 'competing risk': that is, people who drank alcohol regularly would be more inclined to die from heart attacks as a result if the alcohol did not cause them to die prematurely from other causes. Furthermore, it was argued by Gerald Shaper, Professor of Clinical Epidemiology at the Royal Free Hospital in London, that many of the people who were classified in studies as non-drinkers included a large number who had given up alcohol because of ill-health. Having given up alcohol they were included among the non-drinkers; because many of them were predisposed to heart disease, they caused the death rate among non-drinkers to be inflated.

On the surface, Shaper's argument appeared to be persuasive. But it suffered from a crucial flaw. If the higher mortality rate for teetotallers were to be explained, as Shaper suggested, by the fact that this group contained a large number of unhealthy ex-drinkers with heart disease, then it should also have included a disproportionate number of people at risk from other diseases that were known to be caused by excessive alcohol consumption, such as cirrhosis. But it did not. An increase in death from those diseases was to be found only in those consuming large amounts of alcohol daily, and not among non-drinkers.

If doctors chose generally to follow the arguments of detractors such as Shaper rather than to accept the ever-increasing body of research that indicated a connection between moderate alcohol consumption and a reduced risk of heart disease, it was because – like Pearl half a century earlier – they considered it impolitic to show alcohol in a good light. Doctors had just been persuaded to abandon their traditional belief that alcohol-related disease should be treated on an individual basis and to subscribe to a theory according to which the amount of alcohol-related harm in society was directly related to the *average* alcohol consumption of its members.* They were therefore concerned to encourage even moderate drinkers to reduce their alcohol consumption. So they were hardly going to be interested in promoting research that showed that moderate alcohol consumption was positively beneficial.

They were not going to promote research, but, as Ellison

*This 'Ledermann theory' will be discussed in the next chapter.

pointed out, they were not going to suppress it, either. By the beginning of the 1990s the evidence in favour of the benefits of moderate alcohol consumption had become irresistible. It was now much stronger and better attested than, for example, the evidence that linked the consumption of increased amounts of cholesterol with an increased risk of contracting heart disease. For researchers to deny the existence of a link between moderate alcohol consumption and a reduced risk of heart disease on the grounds that the correlation was merely statistical rather than causal was beginning to appear as perverse as the continued insistence of the tobacco industry that the link between smoking and lung cancer was also simply a statistical coincidence. Indeed, researchers were now competing with one another to provide explanations for why alcohol should be beneficial. It was suggested, for example, that alcohol exerts an effect on platelets, the smallest of the blood cells, which are thought to contribute to heart disease because they cling to fatty deposits on the artery wall, clogging the artery. It may well be that alcohol, when consumed in moderation, helps to flush away the platelets from the artery wall.

Further evidence was also provided to support the belief that viewers had taken away with them from the 'Sixty Minutes' programme: that wine, and especially red wine, may be more effective in preventing heart attacks than other forms of alcohol. Researchers have returned to the same area of investigation as was explored in Italy after the Second World War and have suggested that compounds such as tannins that are contained in red wine inhibit the process of oxidation that causes the 'bad' cholesterol (low-density lipoproteins) in the bloodstream to thicken and sometimes to clog arteries, causing heart attacks. These non-alcoholic compounds are not present in white wine because they come principally from the skins of the grapes, which (as has already been mentioned) are included during the fermentation of red wines but are removed before the fermentation of white ones.*

On the other hand, it may well be that all forms of wine are equally beneficial because the benefits of wine should principally

---

*They may or may not be the same compounds that are responsible for the bactericidal power of red wine.

be explained by social factors. It may be that wine is more salutary than other forms of alcohol principally because it is usually consumed regularly and slowly during meals, rather than irregularly and at uncertain speed on its own. It therefore gives the body a gradual protective dose of alcohol at precisely the same time as its drinker is ingesting potentially dangerous saturated fats. It also helps to reduce stress and to make people feel happier. If doctors have generally rejected the medical benefits of wine and other forms of alcohol during the twentieth century, it is because they have been obsessed with what can be analysed scientifically: they have wanted to retain, and enhance, the mystique and inaccessibility of their profession. They have been hostile to alcohol because the harm that it causes has been so much easier to analyse than its benefits. But now the tables have been turned: the benefits of moderate alcohol consumption have been proven scientifically. Maybe this will make it easier for doctors to accept the obvious fact that the ingestion of moderate quantities of alcohol improves the health of their patients for the simple reason that it gives them pleasure.

7

'THE BANE OF THE NATION'

THE FACT THAT MODERATE ALCOHOL CONSUMPTION IS (AND was) positively beneficial does not mean that excessive alcohol consumption has not been positively harmful. The disease, degradation and death that were caused by the excessive consumption of gin in London in the first half of the eighteenth century have already been described in some detail. Among the various solutions that were tried in order to deal with the problem was the imposition in 1736 of an Act that sought to prohibit the retailing of spirits both by imposing an unaffordably high level of duty and by requiring retailers to take out an unaffordably expensive annual licence. In effect, the sale of spirits was prohibited. This Act had been introduced in response to the petition to Parliament from the justices of peace of the Middlesex Bench that had described how the children of gin-sodden mothers were born feeble, and were soon taught to acquire a taste for 'this great and certain destroyer'; the justices added that gin also destroyed the strength of the men who drank it, rendering them incapable of heavy labour, and raised their spirits, carrying them into 'a degree of outrageous passion' in which they committed robberies and other crimes.

The Middlesex Bench had not been alone in stirring up anti-gin propaganda. There was, for example, the claim that a dram shop in Southwark advertised itself with a sign saying 'Drunk for a penny, dead drunk for two pence, straw for nothing' – a tale that was never substantiated and that indeed was discredited as apocryphal soon after it appeared. There was also *Distilled Spirituous Liquors the Bane of the Nation*, a book written by Thomas Wilson, the son of the Bishop of Sodor and Man and an earnest young man then in shameless pursuit of clerical preferment, which not only repeated some of the tales of the most noxious effects of gin-drinking on the underclass in London but provided detailed arguments in an attempt to demolish the belief of the Government that the imposition of a prohibition on the distillation and sale of spirits would damage its revenues. Wilson argued that the damage to the national economy as a result of the sickness and laziness and criminality caused by gin far exceeded the revenue that was derived by its taxation.

Wilson and a number of the Middlesex justices formed part of a loose association of upper-class moral reformers; since it was they who were the principal movers of the 1736 Act, this should therefore be regarded as the first manifestation of temperance reform. Another of the group was James Oglethorpe, a Member of Parliament who had in 1729 presided over a committee that brought about prison reforms; this had given him the idea of founding a new colony where the poor and destitute could start afresh. In November 1732 Oglethorpe had sailed across the Atlantic with 120 settlers* and founded Savannah in what became Georgia. It was not long, however, before the settlers were dying as a result of the ill-effects of drinking too much rum. In 1734 Oglethorpe had returned to England and guided a Bill through Parliament that prohibited the sale of distilled spirits in the new colony, the intention being that the colonists should restrict themselves to healthier drinks such as wine – a substance that Oglethorpe himself produced at his vineyard near Godalming in Surrey.

*Wilson had been asked to join the colonists but had refused on the grounds that his father needed him in England to help fight opposition to his efforts to improve the morals of the clergy within his diocese.

The temperance movement, therefore, began as a campaign that was directed against spirits – and was in favour of beer and wine. In America before the Revolution the Philadelphian naturalist and traveller John Bartram dreamed of establishing viticulture in America for the sake of leading men away from strong drink, and travelled the country seeking out suitable grapes with which to fulfil his aim. The federal government granted lands to the Swiss in Indiana and to the French in Alabama in the hope of creating a plentiful source of native wines, and, in 1819, lowered taxes on imported wines in order to encourage temperance. This measure received the approbation of Thomas Jefferson, who had not only drafted the Declaration of Independence and served as the third President of the United States but was reputed as a wine connoisseur and vine-grower in his own right. 'It is an error,' he wrote, 'to view a tax on [wine] as merely a tax on the rich. It is a prohibition of its use to the middling class of our citizens, and a condemnation of them to the poison of whisky, which is desolating their houses. No nation is drunken where wine is cheap; and none sober, where the dearness of wine substitutes ardent spirits as the common beverage. It is, in truth, the only antidote to the bane of whisky.'

It is not, however, as a moderationist movement that sought to turn people from spirits to wine that the temperance movement is remembered today. Indeed, the word itself has lost its original sense of moderation and has come to refer to a campaign that sought first to persuade people to abandon the consumption of all forms of alcoholic drink and later to compel them to do so, by illegitimating the trade in liquor. Whereas the energies of the first generation of temperance campaigners in the first half of the eighteenth century came to be directed elsewhere – towards the resettlement in America of that class of people who had been the principal victims of the gin age, and towards the righting of other iniquities that manifested themselves most clearly in the American and West Indian colonies, such as the slave trade – this was not true of the temperance movement that re-emerged in the early nineteenth century.

Like its predecessor of the best part of a century earlier, this movement was initially inspired by a concern with the manner in which legislation had led to an excessive consumption of spirits. As has already been described, the Government responded to the enormous loss of revenue that had been caused by the smuggling of spirits in Scotland in the late eighteenth and early nineteenth centuries by reducing the excise duty in 1823. The reduction succeeded in diverting illegal production and sales to legal channels. But it occurred at the same time as the development of a more efficient method of distillation, and between them these led to widespread fears of an increase in alcoholism and alcohol-related crimes in towns. It was these fears that led to the establishment of the first of the nineteenth-century temperance societies, in Greenock in Renfrewshire, in 1828 or 1829. The nascent movement then spread from Scotland to England in 1830, when the first temperance society was established in Bradford by a Scottish worsted manufacturer, Henry Forbes. This was soon followed by societies in Leeds and London.

In England, as in Scotland, the foundation of temperance societies was inspired by fears of what the working classes would do after drinking too much spirits. In 1825, the duty on spirits had been reduced from 11s 8¼d to 7s a gallon, and official statistics for consumption had at once risen markedly. Many contemporaries assumed that this indicated a real increase in consumption; since malt consumption was falling, it was assumed that this meant that popular taste had switched from beer to spirits. What the statistics really showed was a diversion of spirits consumption from illegal to legal channels, but this was not appreciated at the time. Public alarm at the consequences of this apparent increase in spirits consumption was stimulated by a quadrupling of criminal convictions in the London area between 1811 and 1827, which it was believed reflected a rapid increase in crime; in fact it was the result of increased police efficiency.

Fears of an uncontrolled, gin-soaked populace were reinforced by the spread of lavishly decorated gin palaces. In fact, the gin palace revolution was not a response to increased consumption of spirits but part of a general retail revolution – but again, this was not appreciated at the time. Regardless of whether the gin shops served to increase working-class drinking, they certainly illuminated it and made it more flagrant. In 1829 the justices of the peace of the Middlesex Bench issued another of their celebrated broadsides, in which they declared that their attention had 'been called to the demoralizing consequences likely to ensue in the middling and lower classes from the alarming increase of gin shops in every direction, in and around the metropolis, by the conversion of what used to be quiet respectable public houses, where the labouring population could find the accommodation of a tap room or parlour in which to take the meals or refreshment they might require, into flaming dram shops, having no accommodation for persons to sit down, and where the only allurement held out was the promise of "Cheap Gin".'

So far the temperance movement resembled its eighteenth-century predecessor. The campaign changed from advocating temperance to preaching teetotalism* largely as a result of the response of the Government to the gin scare of the 1820s. This was to pass in 1830 the Beer Act, which (as has already been described) removed all taxes on beer and permitted anyone to open a beer shop who wished to do so. This Act was successful in so far as that by the end of the year, 24,000 of the new beer shops had opened across the country. They did not put an end to drunkenness, however. It turned out that the working classes were no less capable of getting drunk on beer than they had been on gin. Writing only a fortnight after the Act came into operation, the celebrated clergyman-journalist, the Revd Sydney Smith, previously a supporter of free trade in ale, stated, 'The new Beer Bill has begun its operations. Everybody is drunk. Those who are not singing are sprawling. The sovereign people are in a beasty state.'

Nor did the Beer Act succeed in its intention of weaning the urban masses off gin: it did not put a stop to the growth in the number of gin palaces and in the conspicuous consumption of spirits. Contemporaries noticed that the number of gin palaces continued to grow, and concluded that the Beer Act had been counter-productive: that the new competition from the beer shops encouraged licensed publicans to open up gin palaces. In fact, the converse had been true: it was not the Beer Act that had created the gin palace but the gin palace that had led the Government to create the Beer Act. But, once again, this was not understood by contemporaries.

Instead, the conclusion was drawn that the only solution to the problems that appeared to be posed by the gin palaces, and to

---

*The word derives from the exclamation of one Dicky Turner at a temperance meeting in Preston in 1833. 'I'll have nowt to do wi' this moderation, botheration pledge,' he said. 'I'll be reet down and out tee-tee-total for ever.'

have been worsened by the Beer Act, was to seek to persuade the working classes to renounce alcoholic drink altogether. Great campaigns were undertaken by teetotal missionaries who travelled round the British Isles in an effort to convert the mass of the people to their cause.

The first of them was James Teare, a bootmaker from the Isle of Man, who in the course of twelve months in 1836 and 1837 travelled eight thousand miles and held four hundred meetings. He made many thousands of converts – not least a businessman at Street in Somerset who used the contents of his wine cellar to moisten the cement for a new home – but his achievements were as nothing compared with those of 'Father' (Toby) Mathew in Ireland in the late 1830s and early 1840s. According to contemporary accounts, Mathew persuaded between five and six million people – virtually three-quarters of the population – to forswear alcoholic drink. There was, however, no means of ensuring that those people who signed a pledge to turn teetotal kept their promise. After the failure of the Irish potato harvest, much of the population fled to America; those who remained and were in a position to do so turned once again to the consoling powers of drink.

'It has been computed that three-fourths of those who sign the pledge fall again,' later stated the campaigner Frederick Powell in his book *Bacchus Dethroned*. 'There are thousands of our fellow-countrymen so sunk and saturated in moral and physical dilapidation that they are beyond the powers of reclamation; *without a change in the social conditions by which they are surrounded*, no power can arrest them in their perdition-ward career.' It was insufficient, he believed, to further the teetotal cause simply by a process of moral suasion – of seeking to persuade people voluntarily to abandon alcoholic drink. 'Even if we take for granted that moral suasion will finally prove successful,' he explained, 'its staunchest advocates must confess that a "consummation so devoutly to be wished" can only be accomplished *after a very long period*. In fact, if we are to judge its final success by the operation of other great movements, as for instance the preaching of the gospel, it cannot succeed till the lapse of some thousand years; and, in the meantime, myriads of victims must be sacrificed upon the altar of Mammon and Indifference . . . We cannot suffer this to go on. We cannot stand by the turgid swollen waters, and gaze upon the wailing victims borne helplessly past us, and wait till the waters shall subside, so that we may go over dry-shod.'

The only solution, Powell and others insisted, was to change the social conditions – to introduce prohibition. Not only, they claimed, would it prevent those who took the pledge from backsliding, and ensure that the moral reformation of the people would be far more rapidly achieved, but it would bring economic benefits upon the nation as a whole: no longer would money be wasted on alcoholic drink; no longer would the strength of labouring men be weakened; no longer would they descend to the pursuit of crime.

Powell's comments about the economic benefits of prohibition may have echoed those of the Middlesex magistrates and Thomas Wilson more than a century before, but the new philosophy owed its origins, not to the history of Britain, but to contemporary America. For nineteenth-century British moral reformers, America represented both a laboratory for political experiment and a model society, on which a new vision of Britain should be based. And, in America, prohibition was already being introduced. The conclusion that banning all forms of alcoholic drink was the only possible solution to the harm that it caused had first been reached by campaigners in the state of Maine, who had secured in 1851 the passage of a law forbidding the sale or manufacture of alcoholic drink within the state boundaries. Similar laws were then adopted in twelve other states between 1852 and 1855; because they were based on the legislation that had first been introduced in the state of Maine, they were known collectively as the Maine Law. At the same time, American prohibitionists crossed the Atlantic and encouraged teetotallers to establish a campaign dedicated to the introduction of prohibition in Britain. They succeeded: the United Kingdom Alliance for the Suppression of the Traffic in all Intoxicating Liquors was founded in 1853.

In the first years of its existence, the aim of the Alliance was simply to have the Maine Law introduced in Britain. It was not long, however, before it realized that the implementation of its dream of national prohibition would be long delayed, and that it would be a more practical policy to seek its introduction piece-meal. Accordingly, the Alliance began to campaign for what was called 'local veto' or 'local option' – essentially a system of local prohibition, whereby, if a two-thirds majority of the ratepayers in a particular locality voted 'No licence', all licences in the area would, after a notice period, be withdrawn.*

The Alliance found great difficulty, however, in persuading any government to give even such a gradualist measure its whole-hearted support. Proposals to introduce a limited form of local option were introduced in the Liberal Party's Licensing Bill of 1871, but this was to apply only to the granting of new licences, not old ones, and it was only to come into force after a period of ten years. This Bill was criticized by the Alliance for not going far enough; but it was not for this reason that the Government was forced to drop its proposals after a few weeks. It was widely considered in the country that the Bill went much too far: that it should be regarded as an unwarranted attempt to interfere with public liberties and private property. 1,160 petitions organized against the Bill collected 822,965 signatures between them; the *Sunday Times* declared that 'A more imbecile, inconsistent, impracticable and intolerable measure never challenged our con-demnation'. The Liberal Party replaced the 1871 Bill with a much milder one in 1872, but this still led to popular protests; the Liberals were then roundly defeated in the 1874 General Election. It was the result of this election that encouraged the polarization of the drink issue on party political lines. The licensing proposals of 1871–1872 had been non-partisan in their nature, but now increasingly the brewers, distillers and licensees supported the Conservative Party, and the Conservative Party favoured their interests. If the Alliance was still to entertain any prospect of the introduction of local option legislation, that prospect lay with the Liberal Party alone.

Following its defeat in the 1874 General Election, however, the Liberal Party was reluctant to introduce local option proposals, in any form. When the party was returned to government in 1880, Sir Wilfrid Lawson, the President of the Alliance and the Liberal Member of Parliament for Carlisle, proposed that the House of Commons introduce a Resolution that called upon the Government to sponsor local option legislation. The House supported his proposal, and the Prime Minister, William Ewart Gladstone, promised to introduce a Bill – but failed to do so. Lawson

*Exceptions were to be made for hotels, restaurants and railway refreshment rooms.

introduced two further Resolutions in 1881 and 1883, which were again carried; indeed, Gladstone himself supported the proposal on the second of these occasions – but no Bill was forthcoming. It was not until 1890 that the Liberals, when in opposition, adopted local option as official party policy, and not until 1893 that a Bill to this effect was introduced. This, however, was abandoned because of Parliament's absorption in Irish Home Rule; the same happened to a milder Bill in 1895. The Liberals were routed in the ensuing election, and attributed their defeat to their advocacy of local option.

To blame a single issue in this way was patently absurd. It was not as if its dedication to the poll tax or to privatization prevented voters from returning the Conservative Party in the 1987 and 1992 General Elections. It is not ideological issues that cause governments to lose elections, but economic ones. The Liberal Party lost the 1895 election because of disappointment with its record on more fundamental issues, such as wages, prices and employment. Nevertheless, many influential members of the Liberal Party now abandoned the policy of local option.

Although it is unlikely that voters rejected the Liberal Party in 1895 simply or principally because they objected to the policy of local option, it is quite possible that some of them were persuaded to vote Conservative by pressure from the drinks trade. Certainly, supporters of prohibition claimed that the trade spent large sums on elections, and insinuated that the trade bribed electors with drink or money. But they failed to produce any evidence to substantiate their claims. As an historian who has recently examined the issue has pointed out, 'The legendary sums which the trade spent on elections seem to have been just that'.

The real source of the trade's political power lay in the influence exerted by publicans over voters. Few industries could match the drinks trade in its access to the newly enfranchised working class for whom the pub served as a major recreational centre. There were more than 100,000 pubs and thousands more off-licences. Now, in the 1895 election the Conservatives and Unionists won 270 seats. A few years later it was calculated that, even if each pub had caused the transfer of only one vote from the Liberals to the Conservative and Unionist cause, it was the influence of the publicans that had won the Conservatives and Unionists the election. If the influence of these on-licences had been eliminated, only 187 of these 270 seats would have been won by the Conservatives and Unionists, 83 of them would have been won by the Liberals instead, and the Liberals would have won the election. Unfortunately, there is no evidence for how retailers sought to win the votes of their customers (other than by giving out leaflets and putting up posters). And, if publicans were instrumental in persuading working-class voters to vote for Conservative candidates in the 1895 election, their influence was short-lived, because from the beginning of the twentieth century it was undermined by the rise of the Labour Party and the development of a working-class political consciousness.

It was only after the publicans had lost their political influence that local option once again became a political issue – this time as the result of a law case, *Sharp v Wakefield*. It had generally been assumed that a licence, once granted, would be renewed each year subject to good conduct. But Mrs Sharp, the owner of a pub in a remote part of Westmorland, was refused renewal of her licence by the Kendal magistrates on the grounds that the pub was both unnecessary and remote from police supervision. This became a test case, and was appealed up to the House of Lords, which ruled that the justices had absolute discretion to refuse licences as they thought fit.

This had been in 1892. But the justices did not make any substantial exercise of their power of refusal until the beginning of the new century, the reason being that they did not have the power or the funds to give compensation to licensees whose applications for renewal they rejected, and most of them thought it was unfair to do so without compensation. Once the justices had begun to act on the powers given them by the *Sharp v Wakefield* judgment and to refuse to renew licences on the grounds that they were excess to requirements, without any form of compensation being available to the former licensee, the licensed trade began to put pressure on the Prime Minister, Arthur Balfour, through Members of Parliament who owned a financial interest in brewing and distilling companies. The pressure was sufficient to persuade Balfour to pass the 1904 Licensing Act, which dramatically curtailed the powers of the justices.

This Act was popularly known as the Balfour Act and described by the trade's opponents as the 'Brewers' Endowment Bill'. It removed from the justices the right to withdraw licences except in the case of misconduct or the unsuitability of licensed premises. The renewal of existing well-conducted licences could only be refused at the Quarter Sessions – and then compensation would have to be paid out of a fund levied on all the licensed houses in the districts. The number of licences the renewal of which could be refused in any one area was limited to the funds available from the compensation fund, together with any money borrowed on the security of that fund.

In 1906 the Liberal Party was returned to government with a massive majority; and there were 53 Labour members, most of whom (including Keir Hardie) were non-drinkers. The 1908 Licensing Bill proposed that compensation was to be paid only for the next fourteen years to licensees, the renewal of whose licences had been refused – after that time every application for renewal would be treated as an application for a wholly new licence.

Rather different accounts of the public reaction to this Bill are given by the brewer Sydney Nevile and the temperance historian George Wilson. According to Nevile, the opposition to the Bill came not only from the licensed trade but from the financial world, who feared that it was a first instalment of confiscation on a large scale, likely to threaten the security of many industries in which public money was invested. 'But the most startling opposition came from the general public . . . It became abundantly apparent that the people of this country were not willing to submit to the threat of prohibition, and the Government must have been astonished at the turmoil that resulted . . . I doubt if any Bill has been met with such a fury of opposition. During the Bill's progress through the House there were several by-elections, all of which the Government lost by crushing majorities.'

Wilson, on the other hand, describes how the Bill 'brought the whole Trade out in the most violent political campaign of its history. Meetings in support of the Bill were disturbed and sometimes broken up by organized Trade opposition of somewhat rowdy character, and when a by-election took place in Peckham during the progress of the Bill before Parliament, it was marked by scenes which recalled the old bad days of electioneering.' The brewers' and licensed victuallers' organizations organized an open-air demonstration against the Licensing Bill in Hyde Park on 27 September 1908, booking special trains to bring supporters to London. According to two recent historians of the temperance movement, who have based their account on contemporary temperance sources, 'In many instances ridiculously low prices were paid for tickets on the understanding that passengers would attend the demonstration and vote for a resolution condemning the Bill. In many cases sums of money were given for expenses, and it was even hinted that unemployed men had been paid two shillings to join the demonstration.'

Nevile later claimed that 'The public disapproval of this Bill was so marked that the Government abandoned it'. This was a somewhat partial interpretation of the facts. The 1908 Licensing Bill was passed by the Commons but rejected by the Lords; it was in fact a trial of strength between the two. It is true that the Lords believed that their action would meet with popular approbation, but that was not why they voted against the Bill. Lord Lansdowne, the leader of the Conservative Party in the House of Lords, offered a number of very sensible reasons for rejecting the Bill, not least the fact that it did nothing to promote true temperance principles; but the fundamental reason for the Lords' rebuttal of the Bill was that it represented the intention of an elected first chamber with a Liberal majority to impose its wishes on an unelected second chamber with a Conservative majority.

The rejection of the Licensing Bill was followed a few months later by Lloyd George's 'people's budget', in which the Liberal government proposed a substantial increase in taxation. For the Lords to reject a Budget would fly in the face of established political convention; it would also make it impossible for the Government to run the country. The Lords did reject the Budget; a general election was called; it was won by the Liberal Party. The Prime Minister, Herbert Asquith, introduced a Parliament Bill by which the power of the Lords to prevent the implementation of legislation initiated in the Commons would be reduced to a power to delay. It was evident that such a Bill would not be passed by the Lords as it was currently constituted, but Asquith persuaded the King, Edward VII, to agree to create, if need be, a sufficient number of Liberal peers for the Government to be able to muster a majority in the Lords. The Conservative majority in the Lords backed down, and passed the Parliament Bill. The most significant consequence, therefore, of the 1908 Licensing Bill was that the powers of the House of Lords were reduced.

*   *   *

The next time that the issue of the control of the drinks trade came to a head was during the First World War. It might seem, with hindsight, that the introduction of Prohibition in the United States of America in 1919–1920 was a naïve, impractical and extreme measure of a kind that would never have been contemplated by the British government. In fact, the only unusual feature of the introduction of Prohibition in America in this period was that it had relatively little to do with the consequences of going to war. There had been a very real possibility that the national requirement for good order and maximum efficiency in wartime would have led to the introduction of prohibition in Britain in 1914–1918; it was, after all, a measure that had been or was in the process of being introduced in several countries.

Certainly, in Russia, the Tsarist government had sought to improve the war effort through sobriety. In August 1914 it outlawed the sale of spirits for the duration of the conflict. The sale of wine and beer was permitted, but local governments were given the right to forbid the sale of all alcoholic beverages – an opportunity of which the majority were quick to avail themselves. The Tsarist government also declared that the sale of vodka would be forbidden even after the war. Although the Tsar was not able personally to oversee the maintenance of prohibition, this was indeed what happened. Before the war, the Bolsheviks had shown little interest in the drink issue. But the anarchy that developed during the course of 1917 led to an increase in drunkenness, with workers, peasants and soldiers ingesting alcohol in any form in which they could obtain it. Some resorted to moonshine, industrial alcohol, eau-de-Cologne, varnish or furniture polish. Others tried to get their hands on the remaining stocks of vodka. In November and December Petrograd was convulsed by a series of liquor riots, chiefly by soldiers. At times the struggle over liquor supplies escalated into pitched battles involving armoured cars and machine-guns; one such clash at the Petrov Vodka factory left three guardsmen and eight soldiers dead. These riots caused the Bolshevik government to reaffirm the principle of prohibition, which it maintained until it was forced by financial pressure to reintroduce the state vodka monopoly in 1924.

In Canada, prohibition ought really to have been introduced back in 1898. A Liberal government was elected; it had promised that, if it were elected, it would put the issue of introducing prohibition to a referendum; the referendum was duly held, and the country voted in favour of prohibition, by a slim majority. But the Prime Minister, Wilfrid (later Sir Wilfrid) Laurier, refused to fulfil his promise by bringing in legislation. In the referendum poll, every province had voted to go 'dry' – with the exception of Quebec, where French speakers and Roman Catholics had voted overwhelmingly in favour of allowing the trade in alcohol to continue. Laurier did not want to split the country. So he used the pretext that only about 44 per cent of the electorate had bothered to vote in the referendum in order to stall on the issue of introducing prohibition. As a result, it was not until the First World War that prohibition was introduced into Canada. Now, prohibitionist campaigners succeeded in presenting the issue of the abolition of the trade in alcoholic drinks as a matter of pure patriotism: that the production of liquor consumed products that were better used for food, and that the consumption of liquor reduced industrial and military efficiency. In 1915 and 1916 province after province voted to go 'dry' – and in 1917 Quebec was forced to follow them, when the government introduced the total prohibition of all beverages containing more than 2.5 per cent proof spirit (1.4 per cent alcohol by volume).* This national prohibition lasted until the war had ended, till 1919.

For a long time, it looked as if prohibition would be introduced in New Zealand, too. Here, the strength of the prohibitionist movement before the war meant that it had been the practice of parliamentary candidates to claim that they would support its introduction – in order to ensure that they would be elected. In the 1908 Parliament there was a majority of members who were pledged to support a Bill granting a National Prohibition poll, which would be carried on a 55:45 majority. This Bill was introduced in 1910. When the division came, there was surprisingly a majority of five against it – the reason being that some members had been bribed to oppose the Bill or at least to miss their trains and so fail to make the vote. So the prohibition poll was carried out in 1911 on a 60:40 majority basis and, sure enough, the majority in favour of prohibition was more than the

*An exception was made for the purchase of alcohol for 'medicinal' purposes. In Vancouver in the period before Christmas queues a mile long could be seen waiting to enter liquor stores in order to have their prescriptions filled.

55 per cent that would have been required had the 1910 Bill been passed, but less than the 60 per cent that was in fact required. During the war, the liquor lobby accepted the introduction of the 6 p.m. closing time because it was better than the alternative of prohibition. After the war another prohibition poll was held in 1919. This time only a straight majority was required. The liquor lobby aimed so much propaganda at the overseas service vote that servicemen overseas voted four to one in favour of Continuance, which helped give Continuance a narrow 51:49 victory.

In Britain, it had seemed quite possible in the early months of the war that prohibition would be introduced. It was believed that drink was hampering war production; indeed, Lloyd George (then Chancellor of the Exchequer) delivered a speech at Bangor in February 1915 in which he declared that 'Drink is doing us more damage in the war than all the German submarines put together'. Then, early in March, came the Battle of La Neuve Chapelle in which the failure of the British bombardment was attributed by its commander, Sir John French, to a lack of shells. In order to deal with this problem the new Coalition Cabinet hurriedly created a Ministry of Munitions, to which Lloyd George was transferred. At the end of the month he received a deputation of shipbuilding employers, who urged him to introduce prohibition because (they said) heavy drinking by their employees was affecting production. He replied that 'Nothing but root and branch methods will be of the slightest avail in dealing with this evil . . . We are fighting Germany, Austria and drink; and, as far as I can see, the greatest of these three deadly foes is drink.'

In making these comments, and giving them immediately to the Press, Lloyd George appeared to be giving the employers his support. Trade unionists were angry that Lloyd George should have accepted the employers' statements at face value. The chairman and the general secretary of the Boilermakers' Society wrote to several newspapers to say that 'The tales told by the Shipbuilding Employers' Federation are the same old misrepresentations, exaggerations and contradictions that we have heard from them many times. They are the tales they usually give us instead of money . . . The wholly unjustifiable attack of the Shipbuilding Employers' Federation will do more than all the drink in the country to diminish output.'

This riposte led Lloyd George to enquire more closely into the facts, having previously gone on hearsay. He asked for reports from factory inspectors and local police officers. The detailed evidence showed that each side had overstated and oversimplified its case. For example, the factory inspector reporting from Barrow-in-Furness said that, while much loss of time was due to drinking, another cause was that many workers were earning good enough wages to be able to maintain their ordinary standard of living with four or five days' work a week. The police reports pointed out that 'The question of drinking and the remedies is freely discussed by the workmen themselves. Many of them believe in further restriction . . . and their minds are prepared for some drastic measures. There was, however, a general consensus of opinion that complete prohibition would be resented by a large number of the workmen, and that if it were adopted as a policy it would lead to retaliatory measures on their part.'

So prohibition was not introduced in England in the early stages of the First World War. Lloyd George did consider the possibility of introducing a limited form of prohibition, of spirits only, but was persuaded to abandon this idea by a deputation from the distillery companies who pointed out that if he closed them down he would be deprived of the many and varied contributions of industrial alcohol to the munitions industry. Then Lloyd George thought about nationalizing the liquor trade. This had to be ruled out, however, because the cost (at £225 million) would have been excessive. What Lloyd George ended up doing was introducing the Liquor Control Board, in May 1915. It was the Control Board that introduced the closing of pubs in the mornings, in the afternoons and early at night. A year and a half later the possibility of nationalizing the drinks trade was raised again, when the Control Board told the Government that the successful prosecution of the war was still being hampered by the excessive consumption of alcohol, and suggested that the State assume direct control of the manufacture and sale of alcoholic drinks. This proposal had to be abandoned, however, after industrial discontent broke out in the spring and summer of 1917, as a result of a shortage of beer. The Government responded by increasing the supply of beer, and decided that further interference with the drink trade was undesirable.

The Government may no longer have been considering the introduction of prohibition or even nationalization after this point, but the drinks trade continued to be frightened by prohibitionist campaigns. In 1916 a new prohibitionist group, called The Strength of Britain Movement, had been formed. The movement's chief propagandist, Arthur Mee, focused his attack on the use of scarce raw materials, especially grain, by the drinks trade. The threat of prohibition had led the major Scottish distillery companies to set up the Whisky Association in the spring of 1917. Within two years a fighting fund of £100,000 had been raised, and a new pressure group, The Freedom of Britain Movement, had been formed. The whisky distillers devoted greater resources to fighting this campaign for prohibition than it had to any of the other threats to the spirits trade in the preceding generation.

The whisky distillers had good reason for their concern, because the introduction of a limited form of prohibition in some parts of Scotland had already been envisaged before the war had begun. Under the Temperance (Scotland) Act 1913, local option had been introduced, with the first possibility of voting on it in 1920. The reason why it was feasible to introduce the possibility of voting for local option in Scotland was that under Scottish law all licences were granted for one year only, and there was no right to compensation if a licence was refused. Under the 1913 Act a poll could be taken every three years, if a requisition had been signed by one-tenth of the voters in the area. For the first local option polls in 1920 the entire staffs of whisky companies were sent out to campaign, and the shareholders were mobilized. Since only 40 of the 584 areas in which polls were held voted to go dry, the outcome was generally regarded as a defeat for the prohibitionists.

Throughout the 1920s, the whisky companies kept up their campaign. In 1922 the Distillers Company appointed Field Marshal Earl Haig to the Board. Haig was then still regarded as a war hero, and brought instantaneous respectability to the trade's cause; he had connections with the whisky industry through his family firm John Haig & Co. In the second set of polls in 1923, no further areas went dry, and five of the areas that had gone dry in 1920 voted to go wet again. In the third series of polls in 1926, no new area went dry and two of the dry areas reintroduced licences.

In 1927 the General Assembly of the Church of Scotland

unanimously adopted a report that stated that 'People in No-licence areas are at a loss to understand how their fellow countrymen in other places are so slow to believe and so unwilling to act . . . The benefits of No-licence are so great and the communal sacrifice that is its price so small, that how the movement moves so slowly is a mystery.' In the same year the temperance writer George Wilson visited six towns that had gone dry in 1920 – Lerwick, Stromness, Wick, Kirkintilloch, Kilsyth and Stewarton – and found that in each of these places drinks expenditure had been transferred to better channels; children were better fed and clothed and savings had increased despite the industrial depression.

In his history of British pubs and licensing laws, published the next year, Lord Askwith, an eminent barrister and member of many government committees, expressed a different opinion. 'Far from local veto [local option] having done good,' he wrote, 'it has certainly in many localities done harm. The polls have been responsible for infinite turmoil and ill-feeling, and a lavish expenditure which has been wholly wasteful. In the few "No-licence" areas shebeening is common and the drinking of methylated spirit and Sunday drinking are on the increase.' Whereas, in remote country areas, the introduction of local option led to illicit distillation, in Lowland towns such as Kirkintilloch and Kilsyth, just outside Glasgow, it simply meant that people had to make the effort of travelling to a pub beyond the boundary of the area. Nevertheless, local option did survive in a few places for many years. Kirkintilloch and Kilsyth did not vote to go wet until the late 1960s, and there were still a handful of dry areas when local option was abolished in the Licensing Act of 1976.

The ineffectiveness of prohibitory measures, whether on a national or local scale, whether of all alcoholic drinks or of spirits alone, has been abundantly demonstrated by history. It was exposed in the 1730s and 1740s, when the attempts effectively to prohibit the consumption of spirits both in England and in Georgia proved to be failures.

The English Parliament, when passing the Gin Act in 1736, failed to consult the Excise Board about possible difficulties in enforcing the new legislation, yet it was the Excise Board that was principally responsible for enforcing the law in the metropolis.

The difficulty that the Excise Board encountered in discovering the petty dram shops and street vendors against whom the legislation was principally directed led Parliament to pass the Sweets Act in 1737, which empowered the Excise Board to offer rewards to informers. Informing became a highly organized operation; informers invented a variety of dirty tricks to entrap retailers; many informers were attacked, and some were killed.

'Since the populace saw that they could not evade the law,' said Lord Carteret in the House of Lords, 'they openly and avowedly transgressed it; and the transgressors were so numerous that they even set the Government itself at defiance. No private man, no under-officer durst inform, no magistrate durst punish, without being in danger of being de-witted* by the mob as he passed along the streets.' The Act was effectively abandoned in 1739, when the outbreak of war with Spain and growing ministerial instability combined with a risk of major public disorder because of a calamitous harvest failure. The Act was repealed and replaced with another in 1743, which took a wholly different approach, seeking to make the sale of gin public and respectable.

Nor was the attempt to prohibit spirits in the Georgian colony a success. All that happened was that rum was smuggled over the border from South Carolina. Savannah was soon full of illegal tippling shops. In 1749, the prohibition was repealed. Oglethorpe's successor, President Stephens, later expressed the opinion that less rum was consumed in the colony after its use was permitted than when it had been obtained and drunk clandestinely.

It would therefore have been possible for the English and American prohibitionists of the nineteenth century to have learned the lesson that prohibition does not work, from the experience of a hundred years earlier. But, as Hegel famously stated, the only thing that we learn from history is that we do not learn from history. The Maine Law was introduced in response to the immigration in the 1840s of large numbers of Irish, who drank a great deal of whisky, and Germans, who drank a substantial amount of beer. This law served to validate 'American family values' in the same way as the laws against adultery, duelling and

---

*From the Dutch statesmen John and Cornelius De Witt, who were murdered by a mob in 1672.

lotteries that were then passing through most state legislatures. Its function was largely symbolic, because it was almost entirely ineffective. The fact that liquor had been prohibited in state after state did not mean that people stopped making it, selling it or drinking it. Indeed, between 1850 and 1860, the per capita consumption of beer, wine and whisky in the country as a whole actually increased. The major fall in consumption had occurred in the 1830s and 1840s; that is to say, the Maine Law served to validate a change that had already occurred, not to effect something that had not yet happened.

Prohibition was effective in ending the manufacture and sale of beverage alcohol only within those jurisdictions where public officials committed themselves to enforcing it, such as Portland in Maine, the city where the movement had begun. Elsewhere, it spurred drinkers to resistance. Restrictive legislation short of prohibition led to the Lager Beer Riots in Chicago in 1855 and the New York City Riots of 1857. Far from providing stability in an age of social change, the Maine Law created disorder of its own. The law did not last for long. In most of the states in which it had been introduced it had collapsed by the end of the 1850s – maybe because the nation had become absorbed in the slavery issue. Even in those few states where prohibition remained on the statute book, all attempts at effective enforcement were abandoned; even in Maine – even in Portland – by the end of the nineteenth century, prohibition had become a by-word for hypocrisy.

To a substantial extent, the national Prohibition that was introduced in the 1920s was a repeat of the Maine Law, only on a larger scale: it was impelled by a similar motivation, it offered a similar symbolic value, it manifested a similar lack of enforcement. Once again, its purpose was to assert the primacy of the principles of the White Anglo-Saxon Protestant nuclear family over those of recent immigrants, to draw a line between what was acceptable and what was deviant behaviour. To a certain extent, it can be compared to the abolition of slavery in the 1860s, which did not end the oppression of blacks but did validate the personal dignity that was enshrined in the Bill of Rights. It can also be compared to the current argument as to whether or not laws establishing greater federal control over the possession of guns should be passed in the United States. Banning guns would not stop people from having them, or from using them in the furtherance of crime; it would simply serve to validate the values of those members of society who regard the free use of guns in the modern world as morally reprehensible.

This said, it was believed by those who promoted it that national Prohibition would be more effective than the Maine Law had been, that it would remove one of the principal obstacles that had stood in the way of enforcement in the 1850s – and indeed during the Georgian prohibition of a hundred years earlier – namely the traffic in alcoholic beverages across state borders. It was hoped that, by turning the whole country dry, trans-border traffic would be prevented. This hope was not fulfilled. The Prohibition Bureau was very poorly equipped to deal with smugglers: there were, for example, only twenty agents in the Twentieth District, which included the Pacific North-West. Nor is it likely that even a substantial increase in the number of agents would have enabled the Prohibition Bureau effectively to police the Canadian border: as one wag pointed out at the time, it was impossible to keep liquor from dripping through a dotted red line. It was certainly not in the interests of the Canadian government to discourage smuggling across the border into the United States, since it made a great deal of money by taxing the liquor first. There are no statistics to indicate the quantity of alcoholic drinks that were imported into the United States from Canada during Prohibition, but the revenues derived by the Canadian government from liquor taxes increased fourfold during the period, while the consumption of spirits by the Canadian population virtually halved. It may safely be assumed that the discrepancy in the figures is to be explained by the transfer of most of the drink across the border.

Liquor also reached the United States from islands in the West Indies, although the smuggling activities of the rum-runners has probably attracted more subsequent publicity than the size of their trade deserved. The most celebrated of them was Bill McCoy, who had a reputation for bringing in only high-quality merchandise – the Real McCoy. In all, it has been calculated that between five and ten million gallons of spirits a year were smuggled into the United States during Prohibition.

Most of the alcoholic drink that was consumed during Prohibition, however, was in the form of spirits that had been illegally produced within the borders of the United States itself. The production of moonshine made from corn sugar alone is estimated to have been at least 70 million gallons a year. This was then mixed with glycerine and oil of juniper in an attempt to replicate the flavour of gin. This concoction came to be called 'bathtub gin' not – as is popularly supposed – because it was mixed in bathtubs but because it was diluted with water before being sold on; the bottles were too tall to fill with water from a sink tap but they fitted under the taps of a bathtub. Some of this illicit liquor was purchased directly by consumers, or sold to retailers, but the majority went to speakeasies, of which a Prohibition agent estimated in 1926 there were 100,000 in New York alone.

The scale of smuggling, illegal distillation and illicit consumption in America in the 1920s was so great that it has sometimes been supposed that the consumption of alcohol actually increased during the period that its sale was prohibited. This would certainly be a pleasant irony if it were true, but it is wrong. In fact, consumption of alcohol fell significantly during national Prohibition, to between half and two-thirds of its pre-Prohibition level. It is quite clear why this should have been the case. It was evident that most of those people who had supported the introduction of Prohibition would have wanted to obey the new law and abstain from alcoholic refreshment. Other people who had opposed Prohibition or believed that it should apply only to others often balked at the price of bootleg liquor, which was four or five times as expensive as legal liquor had been. A cocktail that had cost 15 cents before Prohibition cost 75 cents in the 1920s.

Prohibition did not prevent people from drinking if they wanted to and could afford it. What it did was to cause them to do their drinking illegally. The customers of speakeasies were not interested in beer or wine; what interested them was hard liquor. Before Prohibition, most of the alcohol drunk in America was drunk in the form of beer. During it, three-quarters was spirits. Not only were bathtub spirits easier to manufacture and smuggle than beer, but beer was essentially a working-class drink, and the working classes could not, for the most part, afford the new, higher prices.

Prohibition also served to turn people from table wines to spirits. The culture of wine-drinking, which had been growing in America at the turn of the century, was killed off by Prohibition and has barely revived today. During Prohibition, European immigrant families simply made wine for themselves rather than trying to sell it commercially. One of the legacies of Prohibition is thus a tradition of home wine-making, and it is the tradition of home wine-making that explains why the United States is not yet a wine-drinking country. This consequence of Prohibition is especially ironical given that the prohibitionist movement had originated in the early nineteenth century as an anti-spirits temperance movement, whose purpose had been to turn people from spirits to wine.

It was not because it failed to stop people from drinking, however, that Prohibition was repealed. Proponents of Prohibition, like British campaigners of the eighteenth and nineteenth centuries, had claimed that the abolition of alcoholic drink would benefit the country economically: that expenditure would be diverted from alcoholic drink to dry goods, leading to increased production, more jobs and higher wages. This claim appeared to have been borne out by the prosperity of the 1920s – but it was exploded by the Great Depression, which began at the end of the decade.* The Depression forced the government to look for new sources of income; since liquor had provided between 30 and 40 per cent of its revenues at the beginning of the century, the solution was obvious. Prohibition was repealed in 1933.

Despite the failure of the Maine Law in the 1850s and of national Prohibition in the 1920s, there is substantial evidence of the growth of what is generally described as 'neo-prohibitionist' sentiment in the United States today. It has been encouraged by the health movement, which combines an emphasis on exercise and nutritious food with the avoidance of tobacco and alcohol, and by the national obsession with the problems caused by narcotic drugs, among which alcohol is generally classified. Nor have the White Anglo-Saxon Protestants in American society abandoned the attitudes that led to prohibition in the past. It has been estimated that 35 per cent of Americans are teetotal and that, of these, 51 per cent abstain for religious reasons.

Anti-alcohol campaigners have already succeeded in persuading the United States Congress to introduce legislation that requires

---

*In fact, the claim was never correct. Although less liquor was drunk during Prohibition, it cost more; the amount of money that was spent on it was much the same.

all bottles of alcoholic drink to carry a health warning. The warning labels are supplemented in several states by signs which must be posted in every establishment where drinks are sold and which declare that the consumption of alcoholic drinks during pregnancy can cause birth defects. This is true – but what the warnings do not say is that Foetal Alcohol Syndrome has been evidenced only among mothers who drink very heavily during pregnancy. There is no evidence that moderate alcohol consumption poses a significant risk. But the warnings have generally been taken at face value; it has become accepted that pregnant women should not drink at all – and certainly not in public. This was demonstrated by the experience of Jane McMurray, who ordered a pink daiquiri in a restaurant just outside Seattle in 1991. McMurray was pregnant, and very obviously so. Instead of taking her order, two waiters lectured her about her unborn foetus and how it would be born with defects if she drank a daiquiri. In this instance, the manager of the restaurant took McMurray's side and fired the waiters; but the story became a topic of much discussion throughout the United States.

As the story about the pregnant woman and the pink daiquiri demonstrates, the significant change in the United States has been manifested not so much in the form of legislation as in public attitudes. Wine consumption in restaurants has fallen dramatically, despite a growing popular interest in wine and food. People who drink more than a glass of wine in a restaurant fear that they will encounter opprobrium and therefore prefer to do their drinking at home. On one recent occasion a French wine merchant, dining alone in a Boston steakhouse, tried to sample a rival's brand, which was available only by the bottle. His order was refused by a waitress who told him that a bottle was too much for one person and that she risked being held legally responsible for his actions if he consumed it.

Some people do not even feel that they are permitted to buy wine to drink at home – such as the superintendent of schools in McAlester, Oklahoma, who has explained to the editor of the American trade magazine *Wines and Vines* that she would not dare to enter an off-licence. McAlester is not a rural backwater, but rather a small city with its own university. But if the superintendent were ever seen entering an off-licence, a number of influential people in the city would consider her to be unfit to be in charge of their children's education – and she would expect to lose her job. The most famous demonstration of the new public disapproval of alcohol consumption occurred at the beginning of 1989, when John Tower, who had been a United States Senator from Texas from 1961 until 1984, was nominated by George Bush to be Secretary of Defense. He was rejected by the Senate, at least in part, on the grounds that his drinking made him 'morally unfit'. Tower had admitted that he used to drink too much in the 1970s but had promised that he would swear off drink if his appointment were confirmed. He was killed in an air crash in 1991.

As has been pointed out by Dr David F. Musto, Professor of Psychiatry and of the History of Medicine at the Yale University School of Medicine and possibly the country's leading expert on temperance trends, the change in popular attitudes towards drinking during the 1980s was so profound that many people simply did not notice that they had changed their views. At the beginning of the 1990s he predicted that, by the end of the century, the consumption of alcoholic beverages would be ostracized in the same way as smoking had been in the 1980s. He also explained that the concerns and tactics of modern campaigners have very closely paralleled those of the mid-nineteenth and early twentieth centuries: they have emphasized public concern with the safety and healthfulness of food, they have converted from discussing beer, wines and spirits separately to discussing one form, alcohol, they have moved from attacking alcohol abuse to attacking alcohol itself, and they have graduated from urging moderation to urging abstinence. He believes that if the current anti-alcohol movement follows the pattern of its two predecessors, it will last another ten or twenty years, becoming increasingly severe and moralistic, before ending with a wild backlash in an era of excess.

Not only does history suggest that the anti-alcohol movement in the United States is likely to become more virulent, but it also indicates that what happens today in America happens tomorrow in Britain. American campaigners had helped to sow and encourage the spread of temperance sentiment in Britain and Ireland at the end of the 1820s and beginning of the 1830s; the American origins of the local option campaign that began in the 1850s have already been mentioned. There were also attempts to transfer the prohibitionist movement to Britain in the 1920s. Once American campaigners were confident that the battle to introduce prohibition had been won in the United States, they turned to the prospect of securing worldwide prohibition – which was essential if smuggling were to be prevented. Accordingly, the American prohibitionist William Eugene 'Pussyfoot'* Johnson came to Britain in 1918 and first helped in the campaign for local option in Scotland before setting up an office in London and establishing a Campaign for Prohibition in Britain. This came to an early end, however, following a debate at Essex Hall off the Strand, in which he was 'ragged' by medical students who broke up the debate by throwing flour bags and stink-bombs and then carried him in procession through the West End. In Great Portland Street the rag turned sour when someone in the crowd threw a stone that hit him in the eye, which had as a result to be removed.

The reason why the prohibitionist movement that had succeeded in implementing its aims in the United States failed to do so in Britain is clear enough. The extent by which Prohibition reduced alcohol consumption in America was much the same as the reduction achieved by the much less drastic control measures that had been introduced during the First World War in Britain. In this respect, Britain was a far more fortunate country than America, because the sort of licensing system that worked so well in reducing alcohol consumption and drunkenness in Britain could never have been introduced successfully in the United States. Britain had a tradition of public order and regard for law; in many areas of the United States – which saw a boom in organized crime during Prohibition – this simply did not exist.

It might have seemed that the rise to power of the Labour Party, which had supported the campaign for local option before the First World War, would have made the introduction of prohibition into England more probable. And certainly, in 1920, the Labour Party declared in favour of local option at its annual conference. After that, however, the attitudes of its members began to change. There were two principal reasons for this: the marked decline in the consumption of alcoholic drink in Britain, and the

*The nickname derived from his stealthy work in hunting down drink.

failure of the American experiment with prohibition. Not only had the American example played a crucial role in the origins and development of the British temperance, teetotal and prohibitionist movements in the nineteenth centuy, but it had played a vital part in their downfall between the two world wars.

As for today, the fear that the current anti-alcohol campaign will spread from the United States to Britain has certainly impressed the major British drinks companies, a consortium of whom – Allied, Bass, Courage, Guinness, IDV (International Distillers and Vintners), Scottish & Newcastle, Seagram and Whitbread – has founded the Portman Group in order 'to promote sensible drinking and reduce alcohol-related harm'. According to John Rae, the Group's Director, it was set up because companies such as Seagram and Guinness, which played a major role in the American market, felt threatened by events in the United States and wanted to win over the British government to their arguments before the anti-alcohol lobby spread to Britain.

It is not certain, however, that Rae's comments should be taken at face value. A temperance* campaign had been growing in Britain for several years before the establishment of the Portman Group in 1989; it is quite possible that the Group was established in an attempt to hijack this campaign and pervert it for its own ends. The origins of this campaign owed absolutely nothing to events in the United States; indeed, it arose out of the development of an attitude towards the treatment of alcohol-related harm that differed fundamentally from the view that prevailed, and still prevails, in America.

In the beginning – in colonial times – American doctors had regarded the excessive consumption of drink as no more than a personal failing, and indeed as a matter of choice. Then, in the late eighteenth century, they had developed the idea that habitual drunkenness was a disease: that, once a person had become addicted to drink, he was helpless to resist. Drunkenness was no longer a personal failing, because the drinker no longer controlled the alcohol; instead, the alcohol controlled the drinker. In the

---

*There is still a problem of terminology. 'Temperance' is generally used only of a marginal group of campaigners who wish to see the use of alcohol abandoned altogether, while the majority of modern campaigners, who simply profess a desire that people should drink less, tend to be described as the 'anti-alcohol lobby'. Evidently, these terms are used the wrong way round. In this book, 'temperance' has been used in its original sense of 'moderation'.

middle of the nineteenth century this view was institutionalized in the foundation of asylums specifically designed for the medical treatment of habitual drunkenness – which was then described as 'inebriety' rather than 'alcoholism'. The American Association for the Study of Inebriety was formed, and this funded research into the causes of the problem. Research then lapsed during national Prohibition and was not resumed until the end of the 1930s. A review of the literature that had previously been published on the subject was then undertaken by a distinguished biometrician* called Elvin Morton Jellinek. It was Jellinek who popularized the word 'alcoholism', and it was Jellinek who formulated the modern concept of alcoholism as a disease. This theory rapidly found favour in America because it appeared to provide a scientific explanation of heavy drinking that differed significantly from the view of drunkenness as a social problem that had led to the disastrous experiment of Prohibition. Jellinek's theory of alcoholism as a disease that can be treated by doctors remains the prevailing philosophy in the United States today because it suits the psychological need of many Americans to blame their own failings on an outside agency that is beyond their control, and because it supports the philosophy and methods of Alcoholics Anonymous, an immensely influential organization.

Despite its continuing dominance in American medical circles, however, the 'disease concept of alcoholism' remains no more than a theory of the most tendentious kind. It is scientific only in so far as it was originally articulated by a scientist; neither of its fundamental terms – alcoholism and disease – has ever been adequately defined; none of its propositions has ever been proven by a substantive body of controlled empirical research. If it survives today, it is not because it is correct but because it is useful. In Britain, where the 'disease concept' was never as strongly established as in the United States, its dominance was challenged in the 1970s by sociologists, a profession whose star was then in the ascendant. It was sociologists who pointed out – quite correctly – that alcohol causes a lot of problems, not only among alcoholics but also among people who consume large amounts of drink in a social context, and indeed among people who drink much less than alcoholics do. In effect, sociologists

*Someone who applies statistical methods to biology.

challenged the medical ownership of the problem of alcoholism: they argued that it was *their* problem, that is, a social and not a medical one. It would not have been possible successfully to propound such an argument in America because it would have smacked of the policies that had led to Prohibition, but in Britain, where prohibition had never been introduced, it rapidly found favour.

The change to a socially-based approach to alcohol-related problems found support in a theory that had been developed by a French statistician called Sully Ledermann, and published in Paris in 1956, but not discovered by English-speaking researchers until about ten years later. Following an examination of French mortality statistics in the 1930s, when the supply of alcohol appeared to be limitless, and during the German occupation, when it was rigorously controlled, Ledermann had developed a hypothesis that levels of alcohol consumption and alcohol-related harm are inextricably linked: that is to say, the higher the level of alcohol consumption in a given society, the greater the amount of alcohol-related harm. Once sociologists had accepted, and doctors had been persuaded to accept, the 'Ledermann theory', it was but a short step to the 'control theory': that the amount of alcohol-related harm in a given society can be diminished simply by taking measures that reduce the overall level of alcohol consumption.

The conversion from the disease concept of alcoholism to the Ledermann and control theories came at a time when the existing indicators of alcoholism – admissions to hospital, mortality from cirrhosis, and arrests for public drunkenness – were on the increase. So, too, was alcohol consumption. Indeed, between 1950 and 1980 the average consumption of alcohol per head of the adult population of the United Kingdom approximately doubled. If evidence was needed to support the application of the new theories to the United Kingdom experience, it was available. The theories were taken up by Robert Kendell, Professor of Psychiatry at the Royal Edinburgh Hospital, in a lecture that he gave at the Royal College of Physicians in 1978 and published in the *British Medical Journal* a year later. 'There are sound reasons,' he argued, 'for believing that all the consequences of alcohol abuse would be reduced if total population consumption could be reduced; and that, within fairly broad limits, total population consumption could be reduced by legislative changes to increase the price or restrict the availability of alcoholic beverages . . . Until we stop regarding alcoholism as a disease, and therefore as a problem to be dealt with by the medical profession, and accept it as an essentially political problem, for everyone and for our legislators in particular, we shall never tackle the problem effectively. The medical profession and the caring professions in general are just as incapable of dealing with the harm and suffering caused by alcoholism as the medical services of the Armed Forces are incapable of dealing effectively with the harm and suffering caused by war.'

The change in medical attitudes to the treatment of alcohol-related problems, and the perception that these problems were growing, coincided with a change in attitude within the relevant governmental department, which was then called the Department of Health and Social Security (DHSS). This was increasingly concerned to give priority to preventive medicine, partly because insufficient attention had been given to it in the past, and partly because it was cheaper than curing people. It was therefore attracted to a new theory that suggested that it was more effective to prevent the occurrence of alcohol-related problems by discouraging people from drinking too much in the first place than by treating them after they had become addicted. At this time there were four government-aided voluntary bodies working to counter alcoholism, but they were criticized in some quarters for duplicating each other's work, and there were rumours that they were fighting amongst themselves. Following an inquiry by the DHSS and the National Council for Voluntary Organizations (NCVO) they were wound up and their grant was passed in a slightly reduced form to a new organization called Alcohol Concern. The inquiry also recommended that the Health Education Council, a quango financed by the DHSS, should assume the responsibility for educating the public about the consequences of alcohol misuse, and that an independent campaigning body should be established, on the initiative of the Royal Colleges of Medicine.

Accordingly, in 1983 the Royal Colleges established Action on Alcohol Abuse (AAA, or 'Triple A') under the direction of a sociologist called Don Steele. Twelve years earlier, the Royal Colleges had set up Action on Smoking and Health (ASH) in the hope that it would be given government money; and it was. They entertained the hope that the same would happen in the case of AAA. It did not. Steele had to raise most of the funds for AAA out of voluntary donations; throughout the 1980s his organization remained chronically underfunded; nevertheless, it was the most vociferous, and most effective, of the temperance groups of the period.* 'We were very weak,' says Steele; 'we had no money. But we appeared everywhere. We did it simply by being outrageous. What we said was true – but much of it was unverified fact.'

This is a moot point. The measures for which modern temperance groups have campaigned have been tendentious in the extreme. They have called for the imposition of higher taxes and for the tightening of the licensing laws on the grounds that, by making alcoholic drink more expensive and harder to obtain, these measures would serve to reduce consumption. The logic may appear impeccable, but it is unsupported by historical evidence. Attempts in the past to control consumption by increasing taxation have tended to divert consumption from legal to illegal channels. This has not invariably been the case, but it has been more likely to happen in those places or periods of history in which there has been little respect for the laws in question or in which smuggling has been especially easy to carry out. Since the opening of the border with the Continent at the beginning of 1993, allowing people to import as much alcoholic drink as they want provided that it is destined for their personal consumption, smuggling has increased enormously. One means of making this problem worse would be to increase taxes. Fortunately, this is unlikely to happen: the Government cannot realistically be expected to take measures substantially to increase taxes on alcohol relative to inflation when it is busy fighting off attempts by the European Commission to force it to reduce taxes to the level of its partners in the European Union. The demands of temperance campaigners for increased taxes are not only unjustifiable but also unrealizable.

Similar criticisms can be made of the demands by temperance campaigners that the licensing laws be made stricter. Where this has been done in the past, it has generally led to a growth in

*AAA closed down in 1989, having run out of money.

317

home-brewing and distillation and the provision of illegal drinking dens; moreover, the stricter the laws, the more unhealthy the drinking culture, and the greater the speed at which people drink. Certainly this was the case before 1976, when the closing time of pubs in Scotland was 10 p.m. The consequence of closing the pubs at so early an hour was recalled by Allan Stewart, Conservative Member of Parliament for Eastwood, when introducing a Private Member's Bill for all-day opening in England and Wales at the end of 1986. 'When I was a student at St Andrew's University,' he said, 'I remember going into pubs at 9.45 p.m., after an evening studying, and witnessing the "late-night swill", where people used to line up large whiskies and half-pints of beer and gulp them down in rapid succession before closing time at 10 p.m. It was absurd and crazy.' Stewart's Bill was talked out by Members of Parliament who supported the temperance cause, but it was succeeded a few months later by a government-sponsored Bill, which became law in 1988. This has not led to any increase in drunkenness – as Alcohol Concern now admits.

Temperance campaigners have also called for tighter restrictions on drinks advertising, on the grounds that this leads people to drink who would not otherwise do so. Again, this is disputable. For forty years after the introduction of commercial television in Britain in 1955, advertisements for spirits were absent from the screen. In the 1950s Scotch whisky producers, who could not afford to advertise, persuaded other spirits companies to enter into a gentlemen's agreement not to do so, either. In the 1970s this understanding was converted into a formal, but voluntary, agreement with the television companies. Their absence from television screens did not harm the spirits producers. In forty years spirits consumption trebled whereas beer consumption increased by only one quarter as much – even though, by the 1990s, more than £100 million was being spent each year on advertising beer, mostly on television. Admittedly, in 1995, some spirits companies declared their intention to start advertising on television – but they did so, at least in part, because they feared that some people imagined that their absence was involuntary and that they had been banned because the alcohol in spirits was somehow more noxious than that in wine or beer.

If the principal purpose behind the advertising of alcoholic drinks were to persuade people to drink alcohol who would not otherwise do so, then the alcoholic drinks companies would club together in order to advertise their products generically. But they do not. They advertise individual products, because their aim is to persuade people to drink one brand in preference to another. This is especially true of advertisements for lager, which have succeeded in giving the impression that different brands have different tastes – the fallacy of which is evident to anyone who takes the trouble to compare them. For example, Stella Artois is considered in the United Kingdom to be a 'premium' lager, for a pint of which Van Gogh would willingly have given away a painting at his local bar. This high-class image is evidently the creation of advertisers, since in Belgium, where it was originally produced, it is regarded as a lager of ordinary quality. Advertisements have also created an up-market image for Carlsberg, 'probably the best lager in the world'. This designation would come as a surprise to Danish consumers of Carlsberg, who regard the low-strength, British-brewed version as a pale substitute for the original.

Temperance groups have also compaigned for the introduction of stricter laws on drink-driving. Indeed, Steele regards it as the most significant achievement of AAA to have been the party that originally suggested that causing death by careless driving while under the influence of alcohol should be made into a separate offence, as it was in the 1991 Road Traffic Act. Drink-driving, however, is not a temperance issue; it is a road-safety one. There is no direct relationship between the number of deaths and serious injuries caused by people who drive when drunk and the incidence of alcohol-related disease and deaths from cirrhosis of the liver among people who consume excessive quantities of alcohol. It is true that people are much less inclined to drive a car after drinking than they used to be, but it would be wrong to attribute this change in attitudes to the temperance movement. After all, the most important measure that has been taken to prevent people from driving while under the influence of drink – the introduction of the breathalyzer and with it a maximum permitted level of alcohol in the blood – was taken in the Road Traffic Act of 1967, long before the revival of the temperance campaign. It is not the temperance movement that has politicized the issue of drink-driving, but the politicization of the issue of drink-driving that has enabled the temperance movement to achieve a greater degree of attention for its cause than it would otherwise have been able to do.*

When pressed to specify the other achievements of the temperance campaigns, Steele generalizes. 'We have succeeded in changing the whole public consciousness about alcohol,' he says. 'A lot of the changes since the 1970s cannot be quantified; some of the things that happened in the 1980s are still being felt.' This position is supported by Eric Appleby, Director of Alcohol Concern, who says that alcohol misuse can only be reduced by changing public attitudes towards alcoholic drink, and towards the amount of it that the majority of people consume.

This philosophy is enshrined in the concept of the 'safe limit' – a further development of the Ledermann theory. If, as the Ledermann theory suggests, the amount of alcohol-related problems in a given population is related to the average consumption of that population, it follows that, if a sufficient proportion of the population can be persuaded voluntarily to reduce its alcohol consumption to below a notional safe limit, the amount of alcohol-related problems should be reduced. Accordingly, the medical Royal Colleges and the two interested government-funded bodies, the Health Education Authority (the successor of the Health Education Council) and Alcohol Concern, came to an agreement in 1987 to recommend that men should drink no more than twenty-one units (glasses of wine, shots of spirits or half-pints of beer) per week, and women no more than fourteen; above that level, they said, the risk of alcohol-related harm was increased.

The role of teaching the public about 'units' and 'safe limits' was given to the Health Education Authority. Five years later, roughly 30 per cent of the population between the ages of sixteen and fifty-four knew the size of a 'unit' of alcohol, and a little less than 25 per cent knew what the 'safe limits' were for their sex. Wittingly or unwittingly, in many cases these safe limits were being exceeded. According to the Government's General Household Survey, 28 per cent of men and 11 per cent of women drank more than the 'safe limits'. In its White Paper *The Health of the Nation* the Government declared that its aim was to reduce the proportion of the population drinking more than the 'safe

---

*The same is true of 'lager loutism'.

limit' to 18 per cent of men and 7 per cent of women by 2005.

Teaching people about 'units' and 'safe limits' seems to be a much more sensible way of trying to reduce their consumption of alcoholic drink than increasing taxes, tightening the licensing laws, or introducing other legislative controls. This approach suffers from certain defects, however. In the first case, no reliance can be placed on the figures in the General Household Survey and it will be impossible ever to tell for sure whether the targets set out in *The Health of the Nation* have been attained. Statistics for alcohol consumption that have been obtained by market research simply cannot be relied upon. People rarely tell market researchers the truth about their alcohol consumption; indeed, the interview technique of gathering information on drinking habits never accounts for more than 60 per cent of the alcohol that is shown by Customs and Excise statistics to have been sold.*

Secondly, the concept of the 'safe limits' cannot medically be justified. Back in 1982 both the Royal College of Psychiatrists and the British Medical Journal's *ABC of Alcohol* were giving fifty-six units a week as the safe upper limit for male alcohol consumption. Yet, five years later, this limit was reduced to twenty-one units a week, without any reasons for the change being given, and without there being any substantive new research to back it up. Richard Smith, now the Editor (then the Deputy Editor) of the *British Medical Journal*, was a member of the working party that established the new 'safe limits' in 1987. 'We just pulled them out of the air,' he says.

Not only was no new evidence forthcoming to support the reduction in the 'safe limits' but subsequent research has suggested that they are lower than the level of alcohol consumption that offers the best protection against heart disease. In 1994 the eminent epidemiologist Sir Richard Doll of the Cancer Studies Unit in Oxford published the results of a survey of twelve thousand male doctors, which found that the group that suffered least from heart disease was non-smokers who drank between twenty-five and thirty-five units a week, and that mortality rose above the level found in non-drinkers only among those who

---

*It may be that a more accurate method of obtaining statistics of drinking habits is by examining the contents of dustbins ('garbology'). In one survey in 1986 in Tucson, Arizona, 85 per cent of people questioned said they did not drink beer, yet 75 per cent of all dustbins inspected had beer cans in them.

drank more than forty-two units a week – the equivalent of three pints of beer a day. It is possible to place greater confidence in these statistics than in other surveys of alcohol consumption because Doll used health professionals, thus obviating the problems of inaccurate reporting by people who cannot remember their drinking habits, and of underestimation by people who are too embarrassed to recall how much they have drunk.

Admittedly, it can be argued that it does not matter that the 'safe limits' are lower than can be justified on medical grounds, provided that they are presented as guidelines rather than limits. But the Department of Health believes in presenting them as limits on the grounds that some people will always assume that they have been set too low and therefore exceed them. And the Department of Health has actually softened its position: it used to claim that the risk to health increased *exponentially* after the limits of twenty-one units for men and fourteen for women had been passed.

The very idea of 'safe limits', moreover, shows up a fundamental weakness in the modern temperance movement that was not shared by the teetotal and prohibitionist movements of the nineteenth century. With temperance, there is no clear goal, no simple course to follow, no possibility of making a pledge and sticking to it. Presumably those people who wish to pay attention to the recommended 'safe limits' are supposed to keep a written record of all the occasions on which they drink and the quantities that they consume; presumably each time that two people share a bottle of wine they should take the trouble to calculate how much of it each of them drinks. With teetotalism, there is no such problem. It is just a matter of stopping. Indeed, the greater moral certainties that are offered by teetotalism help to explain why it was not until nineteenth-century campaigners converted from advocating temperance to preaching teetotalism that their movement took off. Teetotalism inspired a religious fervour in its adherents, who were driven by a conviction that their work had been given to them by God; they regarded the refusal of many temperance campaigners to embrace the new doctrine as the equivalent of the rejection by the Jews of the teachings of Jesus Christ. There was a logic to the progression of the nineteenth-century campaign from temperance to teetotalism and prohibition, but no such progression is possible today. A campaign that advocates moderation may be damaged by its internal con-tradictions, but a movement that insisted that people gave up drinking alcohol altogether would be laughed out of court.

The principal defect of the concept of 'safe limits', however, derives from the theory that inspired it. It is hardly surprising that the belief of temperance campaigners in the 'safe limits' is misplaced, because the Ledermann theory on which they are founded has never been proved, and must be looked upon with considerable scepticism. It is simply not possible to substantiate an argument that says that, in all societies, there is a direct relationship between average alcohol consumption and the level of alcohol-related disease. *A priori*, it is improbable that such a relationship should exist, since societies differ so greatly in the manner and frequency of their alcohol consumption. There is no reason, for example, why the incidence of alcohol-related disease in Scandinavia, where people tend to drink spirits in binges at weekends, should be related to its occurrence in Mediterranean Europe, where most of the consumption of alcohol is of wine with meals.

The subscription of present-day temperance campaigners to the Ledermann theory may be compared to the belief of their nineteenth-century predecessors that there was a direct relation-ship between the number of pubs in a given area and the amount of drunkenness – a belief that contributed substantially to their efforts to press for the introduction of parliamentary legislation that would make it possible for the number of pubs to be reduced. Certainly, an association existed – not least because it was in the commercial interest of pub and brewery groups to open more outlets in an area where there were more customers who were likely to drink large amounts of beer. Certainly, there often exists an association today between the average consumption of alcohol in a particular society and the incidence of alcohol-related disease – not least because the presence of a large number of people who drink to such an excessive extent as to do harm to their bodies inevitably increases the average. But the fact that these associ-ations should exist is quite different from saying that an increase in the average consumption of alcohol *leads* to an increase in alcohol-related disease or that a reduction in the number of pubs *leads* to a reduction in drunkenness. The links are tenuous ones; they are neither direct nor causal.

It may reasonably be wondered, then, why the Ledermann theory has been so widely accepted; why, for example, the Director General of the World Health Organization stated it as an apparently established fact in 1978 that 'Any reduction in per capita consumption will be attended by a significant decrease in alcohol-related problems.' If the Ledermann theory has found favour, it is because it serves conveniently to support a sociologically-based approach to alcohol problems; it provides an apparent grounding for the purely hypothetical argument that alcohol-related problems can be lessened by publicity campaigns and regulatory measures taken by the Government, that alcohol is a political, rather than a purely medical, problem. Propounding the Ledermann and control theories as though they have been proven to be true, and to be effective, may therefore be compared with other instances in which scientific findings have been exaggerated, misrepresented or ignored in order to foster a particular public policy, such as the idea that reducing cholesterol in the diet will reduce the incidence of heart disease, the notion that the Star Wars project could have protected the United States from missile attack, the supposition that there will be a heterosexual AIDS epidemic in Britain, the theory that lead-free petrol in cars and catalytic converters benefit the environment, and the conjecture that the world's climate is under threat from a man-made 'greenhouse effect'.

Admittedly, at first sight there appears to be some evidence that points to the success of the application of the Ledermann theory to the United Kingdom experience. After all, the modern temperance movement grew up in response to evidence of a substantial increase in alcohol consumption since the Second World War, and, since it began its campaigns, the consumption of alcohol has stopped growing. It would be foolhardy, however, to assume that an historical coincidence necessarily implies a causal correlation. The increase in alcohol consumption between 1950 and 1980 was simply one phase of a cycle. In the period between the wars alcohol had fallen out of fashion. It was commented in the *New Survey of London Life and Labour* in 1935 that 'The social status of drunkenness has steadily fallen in the eyes of the working-class population. Where once frequent drunkenness was half-admired as a sign of virility, it is now regarded as, on the whole, rather squalid and ridiculous.' The new unfashionableness of alcohol was as much a generational change as anything else. In the second of his social surveys of working-class habits in York, carried out in 1935, Benjamin Seebohm Rowntree was told by publicans that habitual middle-aged and older drinkers continued to spend all the money they had to spare on drink, but that no fresh class of heavy drinkers was taking their place.

The fashion having turned against alcohol between the wars, it swung back again afterwards. Young people had more money – which they were more inclined to spend on alcohol, principally because of the development and marketing of drinks that were specifically designed to appeal to their unsophisticated palates. They benefited in the 1960s and 1970s from the marketing of clear-coloured, neutral-flavoured spirits such as vodka and white rum; they could mask the flavour of the alcohol by adding orange or other fruit juices to the vodka, and cola or other carbonated drinks to the rum. They benefited in the 1970s and 1980s from the development of new spirit-based drinks such as Bailey's Irish Cream and other blends of whisky, cream and chocolate, Captain Morgan Spiced Rum, Archers Peach Country Schnapps, the coconut-flavoured liqueur Malibu, and Mirage and Taboo, mixtures of white wine, vodka and fruit essences. These, and other similar drinks, were intended to satisfy people who, in the words of one American advertising man, 'want to chug stuff. They don't want to acquire the taste. They want it to taste like candy the first time going down.'

By the mid-1980s, however, the fashion among young people, having turned away from alcohol after the First World War and then turned back again after the Second, began to swing away from alcohol again. In the period when alcohol was unfashionable between the wars, young people had preferred to spend their money on going to cinemas and dance halls. In the late 1980s and the 1990s they have increasingly chosen to spend it on 'raves' and narcotic drugs. Indeed, it is possible that, by seeking to show alcohol in a disapproving light, temperance campaigners have encouraged this development, that the most significant effect of the temperance movement has simply been to shift what it had identified as a social problem into another sphere. It is uncertain whether those young people who now amuse themselves with narcotic drugs will turn to alcohol as they grow older and more conservative: whether they will eventually conform to the values of a society that regards recreational drug-taking as a dangerous and deviant activity. If they do, then the next generation of young people may well in their turn prefer narcotic drugs to alcohol, in a simple act of rebellion against their parents' taste. It is possible that alcohol will never again be as universally popular as it was in the late 1970s and early 1980s.

Certainly, it would be wrong to regard the fact that alcohol consumption has stopped increasing at the same time as the modern temperance movement has been conducting its campaigns as an achievement for that movement. At best, like the Maine Law of the 1850s, it has simply served to validate a change in social attitudes: it has symbolized the fall in the fashionableness of alcohol. At worst, it has proved a dangerous irrelevance: an echo of a time when the excessive consumption of alcoholic drink was indeed a major cause of social and medical problems; a by-product of an attempt by sociologists to assert increasing dominance over medical theory and practice; a focus for knee-jerk reactions to social problems to which nobody was inclined to seek out the underlying causes or to propose a practical solution.

CONCLUSION: WASSAIL!

ONE OF THE BIGGEST OBSTACLES FACED BY NINETEENTH-CENTURY anti-alcohol campaigners was the part that was played by alcoholic drink, and especially wine, in the stories of the Bible and the rituals of the Christian Church. The fact that the Bible contained several hundred references to alcohol might have seemed an insuperable obstacle in an age when men took Scripture literally. In fact, various sophistical arguments were developed in an attempt to justify the theory that, where wine was mentioned in the Bible, what was intended was grape juice. The most influential of these was the 'two wines' theory that was developed by the celebrated prohibitionist orator Frederic Lees: that the Hebrew words for wine and strong drink meant unfermented grape juice in places where drink was referred to approvingly, and alcoholic wine only where it was mentioned critically.

In co-operation with the Revd Dawson Burns, Lees produced in 1868 *The Temperance Bible Commentary*, in which 493 references to drink in the Old Testament and 144 in the New Testament had been rewritten in order to conform to the theory; it was suggested, for example, that the correct translation of the phrase in the Song of Solomon that had previously been rendered into English as 'Stay me with flagons' was in fact 'Sustain me with cakes of grapes'. Even Lees and Burns proved unable, however, to resolve the knotty problem of St Paul's advice to Timothy that he should drink a little wine for his stomach's sake. One possible solution was offered seventeen years later by John Kirton in a book entitled *The Waterdrinkers of the Bible*. Timothy, he argued, was evidently a teetotaller because St Paul's advice to him implied that he normally drank only water.

In the long term, at least, these arguments proved unsuccessful. In 1912, in the Eleventh Lees and Raper Memorial Lecture – an institution that had been intended to perpetuate the memory and continue the work of Lees and his fellow campaigner James Raper – Edward Hicks, the Bishop of Lincoln and Vice-President of the prohibitionist United Kingdom Alliance, declared that the 'two wines' theory 'is steadily repudiated by the best Biblical scholars and has, in my opinion, seriously hindered the acceptance of our principles by the thoughtful Christian public . . . I have decided to postpone [the question of unfermented wine] altogether until the time comes when the temperance movement has a far greater hold on the popular mind.'

In insisting that the wine that was mentioned so often in the Bible was in fact unfermented grape juice, anti-alcohol campaigners had struck at the central ceremony of the Christian faith: the Eucharist, the ceremony of thanksgiving that formed part of Holy Communion. Non-conformist clergy who were themselves teetotallers, or who supported the prohibitionist cause, took to celebrating the Eucharist with grape juice, or, in some cases, with tea. Very few Anglican clergy followed them. Even Bishop Hicks declared himself 'content with a mixed chalice of weak wine and water'. The defect in the teetotallers' argument was not simply that they were wrong: that the wine that had been drunk in the Holy Land in Biblical times had indeed been the alcoholic and not the non-alcoholic version. The symbolic value of the ceremony of the Eucharist depended substantially on the fact that what was used was fermented wine.

The origins of the Christian ceremony of the Eucharist are to be found – at least in part – in the pagan cult of Dionysos, the god of wine. It is not possible precisely to describe the Dionysiac legend, because there were a number of different legends about him and the beliefs of his followers changed with time. It was generally believed, however, that during the winter, when the vines were dormant, Dionysos travelled on a long voyage. According to some accounts, he travelled to the underworld: he died along with the crushed grapes and was resurrected in the spring, when the vines sprouted again. Certainly, it was to celebrate his return in the spring that the main Dionysiac feasts were held. Thus, the Dionysos cult offered an example of death and rebirth to the early Christians.

The Dionysiac legend that exerted most influence on Christianity, however, was the one described in Euripides's last play, *The Bacchae*,* which told the story of Dionysos's arrival in Greece at the city of Thebes. According to Euripides's account, Dionysos was the son of a divine father – Zeus – and a mortal mother – Semele, daughter of Cadmus the king of Thebes. Not only was he, like Jesus, the son of a god and a mortal woman, but he had also worked miracles and had been persecuted.

The similarity between Bacchic and early Christian rituals led the Romans to confuse them. Both were performed in secret, or at least in private. The followers of Bacchus had claimed to be eating their god's flesh and drinking his blood. So did the early Christians. Given that Christians have been arguing about the matter for hundreds of years, it is not surprising that the symbolic nature of the sacrament was lost on the Romans. By the late second century there were widespread charges that Christians were involved in clandestine rites involving promiscuous intercourse and ritual meals at which human flesh was eaten.†

Early Christian theologians reasoned that, in writing *The Bacchae*, Euripides had been divinely inspired to prepare the way for Christianity. Once Christianity was established, however, the continuing existence of a Dionysiac or (as it was now called) Bacchic cult posed a threat. It was a rival ideology, which Christianity was only eventually able to defeat by adopting some of its essential elements. It is the competition offered by the cult

---

*The name Bacchus was that by which Dionysos was known across the Aegean in Lydia.
†From the twelfth century onwards similar accusations were levelled by Christians against Jews: the 'blood libel' that they murdered Christian children at Passover and used their blood in the manufacture of unleavened bread. The last time that a Jew was put on trial for the alleged ritual murder of a Christian child was in the Ukraine in 1911; the blood libel also featured in Nazi propaganda.

of Dionysos that explains why St John in his Gospel cites Jesus as saying, 'I am the true vine.' He was dissociating himself from the false vine: the vine that led people astray because it concealed within it a false god and a false religion.

It is possible also that the continuing existence of the cult of Dionysos serves to explain why Mohammed banned the consumption of wine, in an attempt to distance his religion as far as possible from the Dionysiac one. In his history of vine-growing the polymath and philosopher Edward Hyams suggested that 'The Christians were cleverer than the Muslims; for whereas the latter tried to prohibit wine and stop the drunkenness which was also a Dionysian rite, the former took over, and civilized, in the Eucharist, part of the wine ritual and made it their own.'

In the Christian ceremony of the Eucharist, the wine that is offered to celebrants serves as a symbol of Christ's blood, which he had offered to his disciples at the Last Supper. Here, in the words of the Gospel according to St Matthew, Jesus 'took the cup, and gave thanks, and gave it to them, saying "Drink ye of it; for this is my blood of the new testament, which is shed for many for the remission of sins." ' The connection between wine and the blood of Christ was explained by a sermon on the theme of Christ in the wine press that was preached in the early seventeenth century by Lancelot Andrewes, Bishop of Winchester (and one of the principal translators of the Authorized Version of the Bible). 'He was himself trodden and pressed: He was the grapes and clusters Himself . . . The press He was trodden in was His cross and passion . . . The wine or blood (all is one) came forth at all parts of Him . . . before He came to be wine in the cup.'

In the Christian ceremony of the Eucharist, wine symbolizes blood partly because – through the connection with the cult of Dionysos (or Bacchus) – the vine symbolizes death and rebirth but principally because of the idea of the 'blood taboo'. Among ancient civilizations, it was believed that plants such as vines were animate because they bled when they were cut. It was also believed that the souls of animate beings such as humans and plants lived in their blood because they died when blood was spilled. Therefore, by drinking their blood, it was possible to take in their souls. The idea that souls lived in the blood explains the Biblical insistence that flesh be drained of its blood before eating, a practice still observed by orthodox Jews today.

Moreover, ancient priests and kings offered wine in libation to the gods, because they thought that it was the blood of beings who had once fought against them, the vines having grown out of their rotting bodies. They thus explained drunkenness by saying that the spirit of the grape had entered the body of the drinker, that the blood enemies of the gods had agitated the drunkard.

It was on account of notions such as these, rather than any association between the colour of red wine and that of blood,* that wine played a vital part in sacrifices in the early days of classical Rome. Indeed, wine was considered so important, and the supply was so limited, that men under the age of thirty and women and servants of any age were forbidden to drink it except at religious ceremonies. According to Dionysius of Halicarnassus, Romulus was the author of a law that permitted a husband to kill his wife for drinking wine or committing adultery. In his *Natural History* Pliny cited the story of a man by the name of Mercenius who murdered his wife for taking a drink of wine and was acquitted by Romulus. Cato added that it was the custom for men to give their female relatives a kiss on the lips in order to discover whether or not they had been drinking wine.

Not only has the symbolic value of wine made it essential to the religious ceremonies of many cultures but so too – in those societies in which wine has not been available – have those of other forms of alcohol. The Aztecs of medieval Mexico drank *pulque*, the fermented juice of the agave cactus. As in the case of wine in ancient Rome, this played such an important part in their religious ceremonies that young people who were found to have consumed so much of it socially as to be intoxicated were put to death. At religious celebrations, on the other hand, drunkenness was not merely permitted, it was compulsory. Worshippers were expected to drink to the point of insensibility, in order to avoid displeasing the gods. It was believed that the gods took pleasure in witnessing the consumption of excessive quantities of alcohol at the ceremonies that were held in their honour because alcohol was regarded as a miracle that they had sent down to earth. And it is easy to understand why such a belief

---

*The fact that red wine is the same colour as blood is irrelevant. There is no reason why the Eucharist should not be celebrated with white wine; indeed, this is preferred by many Anglican clerics today as it reduces cleaning expenses.

should have been entertained. Before the introduction of distilled spirits, the only means whereby alcoholic drinks were produced was a natural process of fermentation, in which barley and water were transformed into beer, grapes turned into wine, apples into cider and cactus juice into *pulque*. It was not understood by the Romans nor by the early Christians nor by the Aztecs that this transformation was achieved by the action of yeasts. Instead, the process of fermentation was regarded as miraculous – as a no less inexplicable form of transubstantiation than turning bread into flesh, and blood into wine. It was not until as recently as the second half of the nineteenth century that the miracle of fermentation came scientifically to be explained, when Pasteur discovered that it was the product of yeast metabolism.

Spirits, too, were regarded as miraculous in the Middle Ages. That is why they were considered to be such potent medicines; that is why they were thought to be stages in the quest for the Elixir of Life. It is not known whether spirits existed before this period, but, if they did, it is most likely that they were used for religious purposes. There being no conclusive proof of any spirits having been distilled before the twelfth century, most historians have tended to follow the line that they were not. On the other hand, the art of distillation had been known for hundreds of years before that: it had been applied to chemicals and to herbal juices. It has recently been suggested by the food-and-drink historian Constance Anne Wilson that – contrary to received opinion – distillation was also used to produce alcoholic spirits in the Near East in the early centuries AD. These spirits were, however, used for purposes that were very different, not only from the ones for which they are used today, but also from their medicinal applications in the Middle Ages.

The first spirits, Wilson argues, were not intended for drinking at all. They were described in Latin as *aqua ardens*, or 'burning water', because what mattered was their ability to burn. According to Wilson's theory, it was a ritual among gnostic Christian sects of the period to distil wine upon the altar to produce spirits, to which they set fire. They then poured the burning 'water' upon the head of the person whom they were initiating into their sect – they provided a literal baptism of fire. Providing that the spirit had not been distilled to more than 35 per cent alcohol, it would burn without causing any harm to the person to whose head it was applied.

Certainly the baptism of fire accorded with the belief of the gnostic Christians that they were able mystically to achieve revelation of the divine. They believed that, by baptizing their initiates with lighted 'water', the heavenly soul that was represented by the light given off by the flame would unite with the human soul of the person baptized, guaranteeing that the latter would spend his afterlife in a heaven full of light, beyond the stars. Moreover, if Wilson's theory is correct, it would explain some of the less readily explicable claims that were later made for spirits: that they cured blindness and deafness, and restored memory. Baptism with 'burning water' took away the blindness of the person who was ignorant of the heavenly life; it took away the deafness of the person who had not heard the gnostic message about life; it restored the memory of the heavenly life to the convert who was baptized. It was not just *aqua ardens* – 'burning water' – but *aqua vitae* – 'water of life'.

It is simple enough to understand why the religious connotations of baptism with spirits – if they ever existed – should have been forgotten, and spirits have come to be used instead as medicines in the Middle Ages. Because gnostic theories of baptism were spread to Western Europe in the twelfth century by heretical movements, such as the Cathars, at first the distillation of spirits was forbidden by the Church. It was not long, however, before their earthly medicinal virtues were being recognized; indeed, it may well have been realized by the ecclesiastical authorities that the heretical undertones of these 'waters' could be silenced by positively encouraging their use as medicines. So, with the suppression of gnostic heresies by the Inquisition in the Middle Ages, spirits were freed of their ritual connotations; from then on, the only form of alcohol that continued to be used by Christians for religious purposes was wine.

One advantage that spirits offered over wine was that they could be made anywhere, from whatever fermented fruit or cereal was locally available. Wine was more of a problem. Since it was needed to celebrate Holy Communion often in places and at times when wine was not commercially available, it was necessary for the founder of a church or abbey or monastery or mission to plant vines at the same time as the foundation. The importance of having wine for the performance of religious ceremonies therefore goes a long way to explain where and why vineyards have been planted. Indeed, it is possible that the need to have wine to celebrate Holy Communion explains why the knowledge of wine survived the destructive barbarian invasions of the Dark Ages, rather than following other elements of Graeco-Roman culture into desuetude and being revived only in the Renaissance.

It is possible, but it is not known for sure. The theory that the monks saved the arts of vine-growing and wine-making during the Dark Ages because they needed wine for Mass was first advanced by the Catholic apologist the Comte de Montalembert in the 1860s. Although the Count offered little evidence, his claim was widely accepted. It was not until a century after Montalembert had advanced his claim that it was criticized by William Younger in his book *Gods, Men and Wine*. Younger argued that the vineyards that were attached to churches, abbeys and monasteries were intended, not to provide wine for the Mass, but simply to contribute to the upkeep of the foundation. Although Younger, unlike Montalembert, did not have an axe to grind, it is impossible to say which claim is correct. Too little evidence survives to prove the argument either way. What is clear is that enormous quantities of wine were needed for the monasteries in the early Middle Ages. Their population, including brethren, servants and pupils, and serfs and artisans and their families, might amount to several thousand. At this time every adult man and woman communicated in both kinds three times a year and received additional unconsecrated wine after Mass every Sunday, while priests communicated every day.

Much of Younger's argument concerns the establishment of vineyards in England, most of them after the Norman Conquest. He identified 139 vineyards in all, of which he was able to attribute 78 to lay and 52 to ecclesiastical ownership. Maybe so, but the fact that the growth of a thriving wine industry in England in the late eleventh and twelfth and thirteenth centuries had a great deal to do with the thirst of royalty and nobility does not prevent it from having also had a great deal to do with the Church and its need to have wine to celebrate Holy Communion. It is no coincidence that the heyday of English viticulture in the twelfth and thirteenth centuries occurred at the same time as a growth in the number of monasteries and abbeys during this period. In the 1120s William of Malmesbury, the librarian of Malmesbury Abbey and therefore perhaps to be regarded as a biased source, not only claimed that the wines of the Vale of Gloucester were the best in the country (which may well have been true) but also suggested that they were 'little inferior to the French'.

In the late Middle Ages vine-growing in England fell into decline, not to be revived on a serious scale until the second half of the twentieth century. Several reasons have been suggested to explain this decline: the disappearance of much of the monastic workforce as a result of the Black Death, the cooling of the climate, and increased competition from imported wines. But the event that turned the decline into a collapse was the Dissolution of the Monasteries in 1536. Regardless of the part that the need for wine to celebrate Holy Communion might have played in the birth of the medieval English wine industry, the diminution of this need was the principal cause of its death.

While the English wine industry was collapsing, that of the New World was being created. In their belief in the importance of having wine for Mass, there was little difference between the Spanish *conquistadores* of the sixteenth century and the missionaries who accompanied them. Hernando Cortès, the conqueror of Mexico, was a man of such fanatical piety that he had to be restrained by his own chaplains from destroying idols on the most inappropriate occasions, and from encouraging mass-conversions of the Aztecs, which his religious advisers knew to be worthless.

It was possible for Spanish settlers in America to have wine sent out from Europe, but it was an expensive and lengthy process, and highly impracticable in the case of the more remote countries such as Peru and Chile. Moreover, vines grew in the wild in America, so it was clear to the Spaniards that, if they brought their own vines from home and grafted them onto the American vines, they would grow too. So this is what they did. Cortès first sent out to Spain for cuttings in 1522, not long after his conquest of Mexico had begun. In Peru and Chile, vines were planted somewhat later, mostly in the 1550s and 1560s. In Chile, the vineyard area grew to such a size that militant natives appear to have regarded the vines as a symbol of the religion that the white men had brought with them. It is quite possible that, having noted the religious importance of wine, the native Chileans thought that by striking at the sacred plant they would be making war on that Christian God in whose name they were being enslaved and massacred. Certainly, when the people of Concepción rose under their *cacique* Antecul, they destroyed every vineyard they could reach.

Further north the expansion, of the vineyards at least, was obtained more peacefully. Vines were taken north from Mexico by Jesuit missionaries to Baja California, where the first Jesuit mission was established among the Indians in the 1680s. Padre Eusebius Kino planted vine cuttings as soon as he arrived, declaring that 'We have planted [vines] in the hope that this land of California will produce wine for the Mass.'

Today, Baja (Lower) California is the only part of California to remain under Mexican control; what used to be called Upper (Alta) California is now one of the United States of America. Until 1846, however, all of California was Mexican-owned. And it was during this period that the Californian wine industry was established, thanks primarily to missions set up by Franciscan friars. The Franciscans had taken over from the Jesuits, whose activities, both in the New World and back in Europe, had aroused a great deal of hostility, and whose order had in consequence been suppressed. The Jesuit missions in Lower California were handed over to the Franciscans, and it was they who took the faith into Upper California. According to tradition, the first vines in Upper California were planted by Padre Serra when he founded the first mission station at San Diego in 1769. In fact, there is no evidence that wine was produced in California before 1782, at the mission of San Juan Capistrano.

Whenever the first mission vineyards were established, they preceded by some years the first plantation of a vineyard by a non-missionary. Again, it is not known exactly when this first occurred, but it was probably not until nearly the end of the eighteenth century. The process appears to have been that the missionaries began their vineyards for religious purposes but, with the arrival of more settlers, started to sell the surplus produce; by 1833 the Franciscans dominated a thriving wine industry. At this point, however, the dominance of the missions was brought forcibly to an end when they were secularized by the Mexican government, causing most of them to be abandoned.

The most famous of the former Franciscan vineyards today is Buena Vista, which was planted by missionaries in 1832. It was made famous, not by the Franciscans, but by 'Count' Agoston Haraszthy, a political exile from Hungary, who bought the estate twenty-five years later and planted it with vines that he had brought with him from Europe. The good condition of the sixteen acres of vines that survived from the earlier period played a major part in persuading Haraszthy, a brilliant publicist, to devote from this point all his time and attention to viticulture. He wrote pamphlets extolling California's vine-growing climate and sold cuttings of his vines to farmers throughout the state. Haraszthy may not have deserved the title of 'Father of California Viticulture' that he was subsequently awarded, but he played a significant part in its growth. His efforts came to an end in 1869 when, in Nicaragua in order to set up a rum factory, he fell into a stream and was eaten by an alligator.* By this time the Californian wine industry was so well established that it was exporting wine to Europe.

This said, the symbolic significance of wine extends far wider than the celebration of religious rites and the needs of religious communities. The link between blood and wine means not only that, by drinking wine, it is possible for a religious celebrant to take in the soul of a god, but also that two people who share a glass of wine are entering symbolically into a blood covenant – an affirmation of friendship and fidelity. Certainly, this would serve to explain why, even today, orthodox Jews will not accept wine from Gentiles: there is but a small step from establishing such a social bond to the dilution of the race by intermarriage. Orthodox Jews are permitted only to drink Kosher wine, the production of which is controlled in such a way as to ensure that no Gentile (or even unobservant Jew) has tampered with it in any way. Every stage in the vinification process, from the pressing of the grapes to the bottling of the wine, must be undertaken by a Sabbath-observant Jew, under rabbinical supervision. After bottling, the wines may not be transported by unobservant Jews or Gentiles unless they are protected by two seals – a cork and a capsule – and, if they are drunk in a restaurant, they remain

---

*Buena Vista is now owned by a German company, which produces wine of high quality from imported French grape varieties.

Kosher only if they have been opened and poured by an orthodox Jew.*

And it is not just wine, but drinks of all kind, that serve as symbols of human association; indeed, they serve much more effectively as a symbol of sharing than food does. With food, and especially with roast meats, which have been central to ceremonial meals, some people are given better pieces than others. This can as easily lead to disputes as to fellowship. Certainly, this was what happened among the Celtic tribes of central Gaul – modern France – in the first century BC. Here, the feast was the central ceremony by which the social order was displayed and reaffirmed. It was the occasion when the assembled nobility observed the ceremonial cutting of the joint and the response of each of their number to the portion he was offered. The portion that was due to the bravest warrior was the thigh. If the carver offered this piece to someone, but someone else thought that he was the bravest warrior, then he would claim the piece instead. If the warrior to whom the piece had originally been awarded opposed this claim, the two warriors would fight there and then, and, if necessary, to the death.

With drink, on the other hand, everyone shares the same liquid.† Indeed, in the past everyone drank out of the same vessel. Until the middle of the sixteenth century there was often only one glass or goblet for the whole table – which was why a man of good breeding would wipe his mouth with a napkin before drinking, and would empty the entire content of the glass in one draught. When people stopped drinking out of the same vessel they started clinking their glasses together, to show that they were still sharing the same substance. Glasses grew in popularity from the sixteenth century onwards partly because of their 'ring': the sound they made when tapped. The 'ring' improved where the raw material contained plenty of lead oxide; indeed, British and Irish glass of the seventeenth, eighteenth and early nineteenth centuries is still famous for its 'rich bell-notes' of F or G sharp. Even today, moreover, there remain some symbolic occasions on

---

*A slight exception is allowed in the case of *mevushal* wines, which have been pasteurized; these can be transported and poured by anyone. Unfortunately, the process of pasteurization affects the flavour. The best Israeli wines, notably the Yarden range from the Golan Heights Winery, are therefore not treated in this way.

†Except, it seems, Voltaire, who wrote to the owner of Château Corton-Grancey in Burgundy to ask him to send him more of his Corton, which Voltaire said he secretly drank himself while serving a simple Beaujolais to his friends.

which everyone drinks out of the same container, such as when a loving cup is passed round at the end of a formal dinner in the hall of an Oxford or Cambridge college or a City of London livery company or in the Mansion House, home of the Lord Mayor of London, in order to indicate the fellowship that the diners feel for each other.

It is the fact that drink serves so effectively as a symbol of sharing that explains the development of the customs of drinking to someone's health, and of pledging the drinker while he did so.

In his *History of the Kings of Britain* the twelfth-century chronicler Geoffrey of Monmouth attributed the introduction of the practice of drinking to the health of another person to the first settlement of Britain by the Angles and Saxons in the middle of the fifth century AD. Geoffrey told how the first of the 'English' to settle in Britain were the Saxon leaders Hengist and Horsa, who, having been asked by Vortigern, King of South Britain, to come over to help him fight the Picts, landed on the Isle of Thanet in 449. In return for their assistance, Vortigern made Thanet over to them. But their ambitions were greater than this. Hengist invited Vortigern to a feast, at which he plied him with large quantities of drink. At the end of the feast, Hengist's daughter Rowena, 'one of the most accomplished beauties of that age,' appeared, bearing a golden goblet filled with wine. She approached Vortigern, curtseyed, and said, 'Laverd King, was hail!'

The King, who was struck by her beauty, and filled with desire, asked his interpreter what she had said. 'She called you, "Lord King",' he was told, 'and did you honour by offering to drink your health. You must answer her, "drinc hail!" ' Vortigern immediately said the words, 'drinc hail!' and bade her to drink. After Rowena had drunk from the goblet, Vortigern took it from her hand, kissed her, and drank in his turn. He then asked her father for her hand in marriage; the price that Hengist demanded for this union was the whole of Kent. 'From that day to this,' added Geoffrey of Monmouth, 'the tradition has endured that one who drinks first at a banquet says "was hail" to his partner and he who takes the drink next replies "drinc hail".'

Now, it is true that the term 'wassail!' meant 'be in good health!', and by the time that Geoffrey was writing had become the contemporary equivalent of 'cheers!'* But the account that Geoffrey gives of its origins cannot be relied upon. After all, later in the same book Geoffrey describes the prophecies of Merlin and tells the tale of King Arthur. *Pace* Geoffrey of Monmouth, it is simply not known when the custom of drinking to someone's health originated, nor, indeed, when and where the term 'wassail!' was first used.

According to another legend, the practice of pledging originated during roughly the same period as that of drinking to someone's health, in this case in connection with a genuine historical event. Supposedly, pledging originated as a result of the murder of the fifteen-year-old King Edward by the henchmen of his step-mother Elfryth, at Corfe Castle in Dorset in AD 978, so that her son Ethelred† could ascend the throne in his stead. Certainly, the treachery of this deed shocked even the hardened people of the time; 'No worse deed was ever done among the English . . . since they first sought the land of Britain,' commented the *Anglo-Saxon Chronicle*. Before long, miracles were being wrought at Edward's tomb, and he was declared a saint and a martyr by the Church.‡

As a result of the canonization of the King, who was now called Edward the Martyr, the story of his death came to be elaborated. Several medieval chroniclers told the tale of how, when out hunting one day, Edward had ridden to visit his step-mother at Corfe Castle, where she was living with Ethelred. The Queen came out, received him with apparent kindness, and begged him to alight from his horse, but he refused to do so. 'Then drink to me while you are on horseback,' said the Queen. 'Willingly,' replied the King, 'but first you will drink to me.' The butlers filled a horn with wine and handed it to her. She drank half of it, and then handed it on to the King. While he was drinking, one of her henchmen (or, according to some accounts, Elfryth herself) stabbed him. Dropping the horn, he spurred his horse and fled to join his companions, but while on his way fainted from loss of blood and fell from the saddle. His feet hanging from the

---

*Since the seventeenth century, 'wassail!' has only been used in this sense as a deliberate archaism. 'Cheers!' is a modern introduction.
†Known in his own time as 'Ethelred *unraed*,' the Anglo-Saxon for 'ill-advised'; this was later corrupted to 'Ethelred the Unready'.
‡His saint's day is still celebrated on 18 March.

stirrups, he was dragged through the woods by his horse, leaving a trail of blood behind him.

If these elaborations are to be believed, then it was in order to avoid the risk of repeating Edward's unfortunate experience that it became customary in the Middle Ages for a man who intended to take a drink to ask the man sitting next to him at table if he would 'pledge' him – that is to say, guarantee his safety. The person addressed would then pledge the drinker by holding up his knife or sword to guard him, the drinker being unable to draw his sword to defend himself while in the process of drinking.

Thus, pledging began as a practical and necessary activity. In time, however, it came to mean something quite different, much closer to 'wassail!' – drinking to someone's health. 'Pledging' came to refer to a person who gave an assurance of fidelity by drinking to a second person, often in response to the second person having drunk to the first person's health. Doubtless, the meaning changed as a result of the development of more civilized behaviour and the abandonment of the practice of carrying arms. Instead, in the sixteenth and seventeenth centuries, the practices of pledging and drinking to the health of another person became bound up in an arcane English ritual, which led to much derision on the part of foreign visitors, and contributed to the development of the international reputation of the English as a nation of drunkards.

As has already been described, it was claimed by contemporaries that heavy drinking was introduced into England from the Low Countries as a result of the wars there in the sixteenth century. In his history of the reign of Queen Elizabeth, written a few years after her death, William Camden recalled that 'The English, which of all northern nations had been least drinkers, and most commended for their sobriety, learned by these Netherland wars to drown themselves in immoderate drinking, and by drinking to others' healths to impair their own.' Barnaby Rich, who had served in the campaigns in the Low Countries in his youth in the mid-sixteenth century, later settled in Ireland and became a writer. At the age of seventy-seven in 1617 he published a book entitled *The Irish Hubbub, or the English Hue and Cry*, in which he denounced the manners of contemporary society, among them the practices of pledging and drinking healths. 'The institution in drinking of a health is full of ceremony and observed by tradition, as the Papists do their praying to the saints,' he wrote. He went on to describe how, at a dinner, each person in turn removed his hat, took a full cup in his hand, called for silence, and named another member of the company to whose health he proposed to drink. The person whose health was being drunk – the pledger – responded by taking off his own hat, kissing his fingers and bowing 'in sign of reverent acceptance'. The person who was drinking the health then swallowed the contents of his cup, turned it upside-down, 'and in ostentation of his dexterity gives the cup a phillip, to make it cry *twango*.'

At this time, the term 'toasting' had not yet been invented. It was, however, common practice in the seventeenth century to put a piece of toasted bread in a cup of sack or ale; it was supposed to improve the flavour. According to an account given in *The Tatler* in 1709, the means whereby the word came to be transformed from an object that was put into a drink into the object of the act of drinking occurred as the result of an incident that occurred in Bath during the reign of Charles II. A celebrated beauty was bathing under the gaze of a large number of admirers, one of whom took a cup of water from her bath and drank her health to the assembled company. Another admirer responded that he would prefer to jump into the water and carry off the lady: that he did not like the liquor, but he would have the toast.*

The most ostentatious manner of drinking to the health of a beauty was witnessed at the Castle Tavern in Covent Garden half a century later. As was described in the magazine *The Connoisseur*, 'Some bloods being in company with a celebrated *fille de joie*, one of them pulled off her shoe, and in excess of gallantry filled it with champagne, and drank it off to her health. In this delicious draught he was immediately pledged by the rest, and then, to carry the compliment still further, he ordered it to be dressed and served up for supper. The cook set himself seriously to work upon it: he pulled the upper part (which was of damask) into fine shreds, and tossed it up in a ragout; minced the sole; cut

---

*Another term that was coined in the eighteenth century was 'hob-nob', to refer to the practice of two people drinking to the health of each other; it derived from 'hab or nab' or 'hab-nab', meaning 'to have or not to have', that is to say, one person asked another, 'Will you or will you not have [a drink]?'

the wooden heel into very thin slices, fried them in butter, and placed them round the dish for a garnish. The company, you may be sure, testified their affection for the lady by eating very heartily of this exquisite *impromptu*.'

From a modern viewpoint, the conventional toasting rituals of the period do not seem significantly less ridiculous than drinking a toast from a shoe; as has been stated, they seemed ludicrous to foreign visitors at the time. Henri Misson de Valbourg, a Frenchman who spent some time in England at the end of the seventeenth century, and generally commented favourably upon English society, considered the custom of drinking healths to be 'impertinent and ridiculous . . . There are two principal grimaces which are universally observed, upon this occasion, among persons of all degrees and conditions: the first is that the person whose health is drank, if an inferior or even an equal, must remain still as a statue while the drinker is drinking. If, for instance, you are about to help yourself to something out of the dish, you must stop suddenly, lay aside your fork or spoon, and wait without stirring any more than a stone till the other has drunk. After which, the second grimace is to make a low bow, to the great hazard of dipping your peruke in the sauce upon your plate.'

More than a century later, the German Prince Hermann Ludwig Heinrich von Pückler-Muskau, who wrote up an account of his visit to England in the 1820s, having described precisely the same practices, commented that 'Many of the customs of the South Sea islanders, which strike us the most, are less ludicrous'. Pückler-Muskau also pointed out that it was unusual to take wine without drinking to the health of someone else,* which posed a problem if there were few people at dinner and a man had drunk with all of them; he had then to wait for his next drink until the dessert. From a present-day point of view, however, it would seem that the ubiquity of the practice of toasting posed an ever greater problem if there were a large number of people at the dinner. If one person drank to the health of another then the latter was obliged to return the favour and 'pledge' the first person by downing a glass of wine in his turn. It was therefore virtually

---

*It was regarded as rude. In his reminiscences of Scottish life at the turn of the eighteenth and nineteenth centuries, the judge Lord Cockburn recalled that when the Duke of Buccleuch took a glass of sherry by himself at dinner at the home of the Lord Advocate, this act was 'noticed afterwards as a piece of Ducal contempt'.

impossible for any diner to complete a meal in the company of several others without taking part in so many toasts as to become quite inebriated.*

The only practical justification for the survival of the practices of toasting and pledging had lain in the questionable loyalties of the Civil War and the Jacobite resistance of the late seventeenth and early eighteenth centuries. It would not have been surprising if people had pledged each other for real in the Jacobite period in England, but there is no evidence of this; instead, they demonstrated their loyalty by toasting either the King in port or the King Over The Water in claret, passing their glasses over a bowl of water as they did so. This was no longer a relevant issue by the second half of the eighteenth century. There had never been any purpose behind the gestures and grimaces that were required as part of the toasting ceremony; now there was no purpose behind the ceremony itself, besides a symbolic demonstration of fellowship; yet it survived, and survives, to the present day. Certainly, toasting is no longer imposed as an obligation upon diners, but people do still toast each other in order to express congratulation or wish someone good luck. And people still cement bonds of friendship and establish ties of obligation by buying rounds of drinks for each other in pubs.

Even the practice of pledging still survives in the form of the loyal toast to the Queen that is taken at official banquets and military messes. And when a loving cup is passed round at the end of a formal dinner, it is common practice for three people to stand up at any one time: the first has just drunk from the cup and hands it on to the second person, who will be the next to drink from it, while the third person stands guard over the drinker. In some places the third person goes so far as to turn his back on the second and face the assembled company, in order to be alert to the possibility of an attack – in a relic of pledging in the original sense of the word.

The respect in which the symbolic importance of drink survives most strongly, however, and imposes itself most forcibly upon the

---

*This also explains why it would have been difficult to match wine with food at this period. The rules forbidding someone from drinking except to the health of another, and requiring him to drink if another person asked him, often meant that a diner, having had no wine for half an hour, was compelled to swallow five glasses in five minutes.

imagination of drinkers, lies in the drinks themselves rather than in the ceremonies that surround them. Not only did the mystery of the natural process of fermentation serve in the past to enhance the religious value of alcoholic drinks, not only did the natural cycle of death and rebirth of the vine in the Dionysiac legend provide a model for the beliefs of Christianity, but the fact that wine continues today to reflect the rhythm of the seasons in the countryside makes its appeal especially potent to the increasingly urbanized or suburbanized communities of the Western world.

Certainly, it would be hard to explain in any other terms the popularity each November of Beaujolais Nouveau, which, if it were simply to be judged on quality and value for money, would have generally to be regarded as a feeble and disappointing wine. It is true that there have been extensive commercial interests behind the marketing of Beaujolais Nouveau since the 1950s: originally its promotion was taken up in 1950 by merchants in Burgundy, who were attracted by the notion of a wine that they could sell within a few weeks of the harvest in order to generate the cash they needed to finance the purchase and storage of the fine wines of the region. But Beaujolais Nouveau would not have taken off if it had not been that its seasonality appealed to consumers, especially in cities.

In Britain, the seasonal aspect of Beaujolais Nouveau was emphasized by the race to be the first person to bring it into the country each year. This began in the mid-1960s and was formalized by the *Sunday Times* in 1974, when the wine was released in Beaujolais at midnight on Thursday 14 November. The race was won by John Patterson, the director of Dateline, who, flying in his own aeroplane, reached the newspaper's offices at 2.30 a.m. on Friday. After three years of operation, this race was effectively abolished by the police in 1977 because it led to speeding on the roads. After that, lorries carrying the wine started to race each other across France, which was considerably more dangerous. The producers themselves put an end to this race by allowing the wine to be released, not in Beaujolais, but from the port of Calais at midnight.

The success of Beaujolais Nouveau has led to many copies, not least in the Southern Hemisphere, where it is possible to beat the Beaujolais Nouveau to shop shelves by six months or more. But none of these wines has achieved the same appeal. It is their own autumn that drinkers of Beaujolais Nouveau wish to commemorate, not the autumn on the other side of the world. Even those wine connoisseurs who regard Beaujolais Nouveau as a frivolous wine that sells for an excessively high price are happy to drink it on the day it is released, as an act of commemoration of that year's grape harvest.

The efforts of wine-makers in the most celebrated regions of France in arguing with their counterparts in the New World that French wines are the inimitable product of the soil has already been mentioned. So has their resistance to the introduction of refrigeration, on the grounds that it seems to be too much like cheating. So, too, has their desire to create an aura around their wines: to establish them as natural phenomena, beyond the control of man.

It is not only in the interests of French wine-makers, however, that fine wines should be regarded as natural phenomena; it is also in the interests of wine-makers in the New World – and of consumers worldwide. This was demonstrated in 1986, when there emerged the possibility of using modern technology to turn ordinary wine into something of much higher quality. Leo McCloskey, a researcher at Ridge Vineyards in the Santa Cruz Mountains in California, announced that he had identified a substance called oenin which he said represented up to half the flavour of a fine red wine. He also announced that he had developed a means of accelerating the natural development of oenin, which is formed by the grouping together of tannins as a red wine matures. He declared that 'We should soon be able to deliver wines that possess this very desirable flavour more often and better, so that fine wines will be more available and cheaper.'

When McCloskey revealed his discovery to the newspapers, he had not realized that what would interest them most was the question of whether or not it was, or would become, possible to synthesize oenin, in order artificially to produce fine wines. In the opinion of Paul Draper, the wine-maker at Ridge Vineyards, synthesis is impossible because wine is much too complex a substance, a mess of polymers (long chains of tannins) that simply cannot be analysed.

Draper and McCloskey did, however, discuss what would happen if it ever did become possible to synthesize fine wines. Would there still be a place for Ridge? They concluded that there would. As Draper pointed out, 'People drink wine as a corrective to the high technology of today, as a link with the seasons and the soil. Wine naturally made is the foremost symbol of transformation: that is why it has been part of so many religions . . . It is an essential truth which human beings need to keep themselves in touch with nature, in touch with art, in touch with magic, in touch with God.'

A philosopher by training, Draper has developed an understanding of the appeal and importance of wine that transcends the limited view of most of his colleagues. Wine – and indeed other fermented drinks – have played a fundamental role in the history of the western world. Without them, the civilization of Europe and the New World could not have evolved in the way that it has, nor could it continue to flourish in the way that it should.

BIBLIOGRAPHY AND REFERENCES

THIS IS NOT A LIST OF ALL THE BOOKS AND ARTICLES THAT HAVE been consulted for this book, but of the major works on each subject, and of the sources of particular stories and quotations.

INTRODUCTION

Mohammed: cited in Hugh Johnson, *The Story of Wine* (London, 1989), p.100. History of coffee: William H. Ukers, *All About Coffee* (2nd ed., New York, 1935). Kha'ir Beg: Ralph S. Hattox, *Coffee and Coffeehouses: the origins of a social beverage in the medieval Near East* (Seattle, 1988), pp. 29–45. Katib Çelebi, *The Balance of Truth* (tr. G. R. Lewis, London, 1957), p. 60. Mehmed Köprülü: Antoine Galland, *De l'Origine et du Progrès du Café* (Caen, 1699), pp. 59–61. Early English coffee houses: Edward Forbes Robinson, *The Early History of Coffee Houses in England* (London, 1893); Aytoun Ellis, *The Penny Universities* (London, 1956). James Howell, testimonial prefaced to Walter Rumsey, *Organon Salutis* (London, 1657). *The Character of a Coffee House*, by an Eye- and Ear-Witness (1665), p. 6. James Douglas,

A Description and History of the Coffee Tree (London, 1727), Supplement, p. 14. Arthur Young, *Travels in France* (ed. M. Betham-Edwards, 2nd ed., London, 1889), pp. 153–4.

Early history of tobacco: Sarah Augusta Dickson, *Panacea or Precious Bane: tobacco in sixteenth-century literature* (New York, 1954); Jerome E. Brooks, *The Mighty Leaf* (London, 1953); Jordan Goodman, *Tobacco in History* (London, 1993). James I: *Two Broadsides Against Tobacco* (London, 1672), pp. 1–12; Thomas Rymer, *Foedera*, vol. 16 (1715) pp. 601–2. Failure of other attempts to ban tobacco: Joel Best, 'Economic interests and the vindication of deviance: tobacco in seventeenth-century Europe', *Sociological Quarterly*, vol. 20 (1979) pp. 171–182.

Henry Fielding, *Enquiry into the Causes of the Late Increase of Robbers* (London, 1751), p. 18. Petition from the Parish of St Martin's in the Fields: cited in M. Dorothy George, *London Life in the Eighteenth Century* (London, 1925), pp. 27–37. Viscount Goschen: *Hansard*, 3rd Series, vol. 285 col. 1969 (23 April 1866). Leo Tolstoy, 'The ethics of wine-drinking and tobacco-smoking', *The Contemporary Review*, vol. 59 (1891) pp. 170–187. Arthur Mee, *The Fiddlers: drink in the witness box* (London, 1917), p. 20. Judge Parry, *Drink and Industrial Unrest*, True Temperance Monographs No. 8 (London, 1919).

History of drugs: Brian Inglis, *The Forbidden Game: a social history of drugs* (London, 1975); Virginia Berridge and Griffith Edwards, *Opium and the People: opiate use in nineteenth-century England* (London, 1981); Terry M. Parssinen, *Secret Passions, Secret Remedies: narcotic drugs in British society 1820–1930* (Manchester, 1983); Virginia Berridge, 'Drugs and social policy: the establishment of drug control in Britain 1900–1930', *British Journal of Addiction*, vol. 79 (1984) pp. 17–29; Marek Kohn, *Dope Girls: the birth of the British drug underground* (London, 1992); Terence McKenna, *Food of the Gods* (London, 1992). Coca-Cola: Mark Pendergrast, *For God, Country and Coca-Cola* (London, 1993), pp. 24–30, 89–91. W. G. Mortimer, *History of Coca: the 'divine plant' of the Incas* (New York, 1901), p. 17.

Restrictions on spirits in the First World War: Arthur Shadwell, *Drink in 1914–1922: a lesson in control* (London, 1923), pp. 36–43. Prohibition and drugs: David T. Courtwright, *Dark Paradise: opiate use in America before 1940* (Cambridge, Massachusetts, 1982), p. 179 n. 60; David F. Musto, *The American Disease: origins of narcotics control* (New Haven, Connecticut, 1973), pp. 138, 140, 302. Senator Reed: cited in Andrew Sinclair, *Prohibition: the era of excess* (London, 1962), pp. 374–5. *Daru* and *bhang*: G. M. Carstairs, 'Daru and bhang: cultural factors in the choice of intoxicant' in *Beliefs, Behaviours and Alcoholic Beverages: a cross-cultural survey* (ed. Mac Marshall, Ann Arbor,

Michigan, 1979), pp. 297–312. Aldous Huxley, *The Doors of Perception* (London, 1954), p. 16. Placebos: Gordon Claridge, *Drugs and Human Behaviour* (London, 1970), pp. 35–6; Oliver Gillie, 'No booze may be good news', *The Independent*, 30 December 1986; G. Alan Marlatt and Damaris J. Rohsenow, 'The think-drink effect', *Psychology Today*, vol. 15 no. 12 (December 1981) pp. 60–9, 93. Peter Marsh: Roger Tredre, 'The unhappiest hours of the week', *The Independent on Sunday*, 2 February 1992. American students: L. H. Bowker, 'The relationship between alcohol, drugs and sexual behaviour on a college campus', *Drug Forum*, vol. 7 (1978) pp. 69–70. Two Fingers: cited in Eric Clark, *The Want Makers* (London, 1988), p. 265.

CHAPTER 1

History of drunkenness: Richard Valpy French, *Nineteen Centuries of Drink* (London, 1884). Saint Boniface, cited in French, *op. cit.*, pp. 27–8. William of Malmesbury, *Chronicle of the Kings of England* (tr. John Sharpe, ed. John A. Giles, London, 1847), p. 279. John of Salisbury, cited in French, *op. cit.*, pp. 68–9. Alehouses: Peter Clark, *The English Alehouse: a social history* (London, 1983), pp. 108–115. Philip Stubbes, *The Anatomie of Abuses* (London, 1583), folio 62. Thomas Nash, *Pierce Penniless's Supplication to the Devil* (ed. J. P. Collier, London, 1842), p. 52. The Dutch Wars: David W. Davies, *Dutch Influence on English Culture 1558–1625* (Ithaca, New York, 1964); John J. Murray, 'The cultural impact of the Flemish Low Countries on sixteenth- and seventeenth-century England', *American Historical Review*, vol. 62 (1957) pp. 837–54. Daniel Defoe, *A Brief Case of the Distillers and of the Distilling Trade in England* (London, 1726), pp. 17–31. Thomas Tryon, *Health's Grand Preservative* (London, 1682), pp. 9–10. César de Saussure, *A Foreign View of England in the Reigns of George I and George II* (tr. and ed. Madame van Muyden, London, 1902), pp. 157–65. Baron d'Archenholz, *A Picture of England* (London, 1789), vol. 2 pp. 107–114.

History of port: Sarah Bradford, *The Story of Port* (2nd ed., London, 1983). John Croft, *Treatise on the Wines of Portugal* (London, 1787), p. 23. Claret in Scotland: Billy Kay and Caileen MacLean, *Knee Deep in Claret: a celebration of wine and Scotland* (London, 1983), pp. 108–9. *Travail à l'anglaise*: André Jullien, *Topographie de tous les Vignobles connus* (Paris, 1816), pp. 204–5; Alexander Henderson, *The History of Ancient and Modern Wines*, (London, 1824), p. 183; Paguierre, *Classification and Description of the Wines of Bordeaux* (Edinburgh,

1828), pp. 64–7. *Moniteur Viticole*: cited in Thomas George Shaw, *Wine, the Vine and the Cellar* (London, 1863), p. 466.

Rees Howell Gronow: *The Reminiscences and Recollections of Captain Gronow* (London, 1892), vol. 1 pp. 33–4. John Mytton: 'Nimrod' (Charles James Appleby), *Memoirs of the Life of the Late John Mytton* (London, 1915), pp. 63, 126–7; Richard Darwall, *Madcap's Progress* (London, 1938), pp. 148–9. Bolingbroke: *The Autobiography and Correspondence of Mary Granville, Mrs Delaney* (ed. Lady Llanover, 2nd Series, London, 1861–1862), vol. 3 p. 168. Dr Johnson: *Boswell's Life of Johnson* (ed. George B. Hill, Oxford, 1934), vol. 3 p. 245, vol. 5 pp. 59–60. Boswell: *Lord Eldon's Anecdote Book* (ed. Anthony L. J. Lincoln and Robert L. McEwen, London, 1960), pp. 19–20. Benjamin Franklin, *Autobiography* (ed. William N. Otto, Boston, 1928), pp. 55–6.

Charles Tovey, *Wine and Wine Countries* (2nd ed., London, 1877), p. 87. Middle classes and claret: James L. Denman, *The Vine and its Fruit* (2nd ed., London, 1875), pp. 481–4. The Gilbeys: Nicholas Faith, *Victorian Vineyard: Château Loudenne and the Gilbeys* (London, 1983); Alec Waugh, *Merchants of Wine* (London, 1957). Working classes and port: J. L. W. Thudichum, *Cantor Lectures on Wines* (London, 1873), p. 31.

History of beer: Peter Mathias, *The Brewing Industry in England 1700–1830* (Cambridge, 1959); H. S. Corran, *A History of Brewing* (Newton Abbot, 1975); Terry R. Gourvish and Richard G. Wilson, *The British Brewing Industry 1830–1980* (Cambridge, 1994). Martineau, cited in Mathias, *op. cit.*, pp. 76–7. Bass: 'Messrs Bass and the Burton Breweries' in *Fortunes Made in Business* (London, 1884), vol. 2 p. 422. Banning of alcohol from the Great Exhibition: *The National Temperance Chronicle*, New Series, vol. 1 no. 1 (July 1851) p. 102. Disraeli: *Hansard*, 3rd Series, vol. 120 cols 395–406 (30 March 1852). The London market: Kevin H. Hawkins, *History of Bass Charrington* (Oxford, 1978), pp. 7, 12–13.

Lager in England in the late nineteenth century: Eric M. Sigsworth, 'Science and the brewing industry 1850–1900', *Economic History Review*, 2nd Series, vol. 17 (1964–1965) pp. 536–50. The first light bottled beers: Alfred C. Chapman, 'The production of light bottled beer', *Journal of the Institute of Brewing*, vol. 2 (1896) pp. 274–86; Alfred C. Chapman, *Brewing* (London, 1912), p. 119. *Brewing Trade Review*, cited in Hawkins, *op. cit.*, pp. 111–12.

Early English coffee houses: Edward Forbes Robinson, *The Early History of Coffee Houses in England* (London, 1893); Aytoun Ellis, *The Penny Universities* (London, 1956). Anthony à Wood: *The Life and Times of Anthony Wood . . . described by himself* (ed. Andrew Clark,

Oxford, 1891–5), vol. 1 p.168. Daniel Edwards and Pasqua Rosee: John Houghton, *A Collection for the Improvement of Husbandry and Trade* no. 458 (2 May 1701); Bryant Lillywhite, *London Coffee Houses* (London, 1963), 'Pasqua Rosee's Coffee House'. History of tea: William H. Ukers, *All About Tea* (New York, 1935). Jonas Hanway, *A Journal of Eight Days' Journey . . . to which is added an essay on tea* (London, 1757), vol. 2 pp. 20–22, 270–8. Edward Chamberlayne, *Angliae Notitia, or the Present State of England* (15th ed., London, 1684), pp. 40–41. French influence: Louis Charlanne, *L'influence française en Angleterre au dix-septième siècle* (Paris, 1906). History of champagne: André Simon, *The History of Champagne* (London, 1962); Nicholas Faith, *The Story of Champagne* (London, 1988). History of claret: Edmund Penning-Rowsell, *The Wines of Bordeaux* (5th ed., London, 1985). Samuel Pepys, *Diary* (ed. Robert Latham and William Matthews, London, 1971), vol. 4 p. 100 (10 April 1663). John Locke, *Journal*, in *Locke's Travels in France 1675–1679* (ed. John Lough, Cambridge, 1953), pp. 142–143.

Joseph Farrington, *Memoirs of the Life of Sir Joshua Reynolds* (London, 1819), p. 65. Christopher Driver, *The British at Table 1940–1980* (London, 1983), p. 5. Shaw: *Report from the Select Committee on Import Duties on Wines* (London, 1852), Q. 1248, p. 198. Drunkenness of the English: Brian Harrison, *Drink and the Victorians* (London, 1971), pp. 102–3. *Journal of the Institute of Brewing*: Chapman, *art. cit.* Wine in the First World War: H. E. Laffer, *The Wine Industry of Australia* (Adelaide, 1949), p. 120. Stuart Pigott, *Life Beyond Liebfraumilch* (London, 1988), p. 9.

The British in India: David Burton, *The Raj at Table: a culinary history of the British in India* (London, 1992), pp. 203–13. César de Saussure, *loc. cit.* Mrs Isabella Beeton, *The Book of Household Management* (London, 1861), p. 892. Calcutta merchant: W. L. Tizard, *The Theory and Practice of Brewing* (2nd ed., London, 1846), pp. 521–5. History of Burton: Colin C. Owen, *The Development of Industry in Burton-upon-Trent* (Chichester, 1978). Thomas Allsopp and Samuel Allsopp: John S. Bushnan, *Burton and its Bitter Beer* (London, 1853), pp. 88–111. Shipwreck story: William Molyneux, *Burton-on-Trent: its history, its waters and its breweries* (London, 1869), pp. 229–31; *Fortunes Made in Business, loc. cit.* Tonic water: Douglas A. Simmons, *Schweppes: the first two hundred years* (London, 1983), p. 45.

Invention of *espresso*: Edward and Joan Bramah, *Coffee Makers: three hundred years of art and design* (London, 1989), pp. 142–4. History of coffee bars: Edward Bramah, *Tea and Coffee* (London, 1972), pp. 67–74. *Times Educational Supplement*, 'Coffee Comes to Town', (8 July 1955). Cocaine: Virginia Berridge, 'The origins of the English drug "scene" 1890–1930', *Medical History*, vol. 32 (1988) pp. 51–64. Milk bars: Robert Graves and Alan Hodge, *The Long Weekend: a social history of Great Britain 1918–1939* (London, 1940), pp. 295–6. Coca-Cola on the Continent: Mark Pendergrast, *For God, Country and Coca-Cola* (London, 1993), pp. 241–6; Ely J. Kahn Jr, *The Big Drink* (London, 1960), pp. 22–3.

Simon Hoggart, *America: a user's guide* (London, 1990), pp. 68–70, 127. Hot weather in Philadelphia: *Moreau de Saint-Méry's American Journey* (ed. Kenneth and Anna M. Roberts, New York, 1947), p. 323. Early refrigeration in America: Oscar Edward Anderson, *Refrigeration in America: the history of a new technology and its impact* (Princeton, New Jersey, 1953), pp. 1–13; Richard O. Cummings, *The American and his Food: a history of food habits in the United States* (2nd ed., Chicago, 1941), pp. 36–40. *The New York Mirror*, vol. 16 (14 July 1838) p. 23. Americans drink only water: George M. Towle, *American Society* (London, 1870), vol. 1 p. 270; Peter L. Simmonds, *The Popular Beverages of Various Countries* (London, 1888), p. 102; Richard J. Hooker, *Food and Drink in America: a history* (Indianapolis, 1981), pp. 272–3. Wenham Lake Ice: Sylvia P. Beamon and Susan Roaf, *The Ice Houses of Britain* (London, 1990), pp. 41–6. *De Bow's Review*, vol. 19 (1855) p. 709. Early refrigeration: Johann Beckmann, *A History of Inventions and Discoveries* (tr. William Johnston, 2nd ed., London, 1814), vol. 3 pp. 322–54. British ice houses: Beamon and Roaf, *op. cit.*, pp. 18–19. George Saintsbury, *Notes on a Cellar Book* (London, 1920), pp. 67–8, 75–6.

Peter Mathias, *op. cit.*, pp. 12–21, 413–14. Louis Pasteur: Sigsworth, *loc. cit.* Charles Tovey, *op. cit.*, pp. 51, 64–5. Alexander C. Kelly, *The Vine in Australia* (Melbourne, 1861), pp. 116–20. Tchelistcheff: Hugh Johnson, *The Story of Wine* (London, 1989), pp. 450–1.

CHAPTER 2

Rees Howell Gronow: *The Reminiscences and Recollections of Captain Gronow* (London, 1892), pp. 33–4. Edward Ramsay, *Reminiscences of a Scottish Life and Character* (22nd ed., Edinburgh, 1874), pp. 111–12. Changes in the dinner hour: Arnold Palmer, *Movable Feasts* (Oxford, 1984). *Real Life in London* (London, 1822), vol. 1 pp. 273–6. Macaulay: Sir George Otto Trevelyan, *The Life and Letters of Lord Macaulay* (London, 1893), p. 575. De Quincey: *The Collected Writings of Thomas De Quincey* (ed. David Masson, Edinburgh, 1890), vol. 7 pp. 24, 36–7. Tea: Dorothy Constance Peel, 'Homes and habits' in *Early Victorian England 1830–1865* (ed. George M. Young, London, 1934), vol. 1 pp. 90–103. Queen Victoria: Peel, *op. cit.*, pp. 111–22. Smoking: Sir Algernon West, *Recollections 1832 to 1886* (London, 1899), vol. 1 pp. 83–4; Lord Frederic Hamilton, *The Day Before Yesterday* (London, 1920), p. 322; *Leaves from the Note Books of Lady Dorothy Nevill* (ed. Ralph Nevill, London, 1907), pp. 136–8. Conversion from *service à la française* to *service à la russe*: J. Rey, *The Whole Art of Dining* (London, 1921), pp. 66–9. John Burnett, *Plenty and Want* (2nd ed., London, 1983), p. 225.

Mrs Isabella Beeton, *The Book of Household Management* (London, 1861), p. 12. Grimod de la Reynière, cited in Giles MacDonogh, *A Palate in Revolution: Grimod de la Reynière and the 'Almanach des Gourmands'* (London, 1987), p. 156. *Apéritifs* in France: Andrew V. Kirwan, *Host and Guest* (London, 1864), p. 302; Margaret Visser, *The Rituals of Dinner* (London, 1992), pp. 119–21. H. Lorenz Feuerheerd, *The Gentleman's Cellar and Butler's Guide* (London, 1899), p. 59. *Apéritifs* before the First World War: George W. E. Russell, *Collections and Recollections* (2nd Series, London, 1909), pp. 26–7. Dennis Wheatley, *The Seven Ages of Justerini's* (London, 1949), p. 75. Cocktail parties: Alec Waugh, *In Praise of Wine* (London, 1959), pp. 216–17, 245; Kenneth P. Kirkwood, *The Diplomat at Table* (Metuchen, New Jersey, 1974), pp. 251–3. Sherry parties: Wheatley, *op. cit.*, pp. 80–1. Ernest Cockburn, *Port Wine and Oporto* (London, 1949), pp. 88–9. Alan Jackson, *The Middle Classes 1900–1950* (Nairn, 1991) pp. 82–101. Robin McDouall, 'Convivial in clubs' in *The Compleat Imbiber*, no. 3 (ed. Cyril Ray, London, 1960), pp. 33–4. *The Times*, 22 January 1949. Drinking 'injurious to the digestion': Thomas Carling, *Wine Etiquette* (Whitstable, 1949), p. 16. Market research: Mintel, *Market Intelligence*, November 1988.

History of dining: Ann Willan, *Great Cooks and their Recipes from Taillevent to Escoffier* (London, 1977); Stephen Mennell, *All Manners of Food: eating and taste in England and France from the Middle Ages to the present* (Oxford, 1985); Reay Tannahill, *Food in History* (2nd ed., London, 1988). History of wine: William Younger, *Gods, Men and Wine* (London, 1966); Hugh Johnson, *The Story of Wine* (London, 1989). 'The forefathers of our vermouths': Johnson, *op. cit.*, p. 71. Lead poisoning: Tannahill, *op. cit.*, pp. 90–1. Duke of Clarence: Shakespeare, *Richard III*, Act I, Scene 4. Falstaff: Shakespeare, *2 Henry IV*, Act IV, Scene 3. Sack: Julian Jeffs, *Sherry* (3rd ed., London, 1982), pp. 51–2, 247–8. Andrew Boorde, *A Dietary of Health* (ed. F. J. Furnivall, London, 1870), pp. 252–8. William Harrison, *Harrison's Description of England in Shakespeare's Youth* (ed. Frederick J. Furnivall, London, 1877), vol. 1 pp. 149, 166. Elizabethan fish days: Harrison, *op. cit.*, p. 144; John C. Jeaffreson, *A Book About the Table* (London, 1875), vol. 2 pp.

223–40. French v English food: Henri Misson de Valbourg, *Memoirs and Observations in his Travels over England* (tr. John Ozell, London, 1719), pp. 313–17. Pehr Kalm, *Kalm's Account of his Visit to England on his Way to America in 1748* (tr. Joseph Lucas, London, 1892), pp. 14–15. Richard Ames, *The Search after Claret* (London, 1691), Canto 1, Verse 1. Alexander Henderson, *The History of Ancient and Modern Wines* (London, 1824), pp. 318–19. The 1820 port vintage: Thomas George Shaw, *Wine, the Vine and the Cellar* (London, 1863), pp. 82–91; Joseph James Forrester, *A Word or Two on Port Wine!* (London, 1844). Richard Shannon, *Practical Treatise on Brewing . . . with an appendix on the culture and preparation of foreign wines* (London, 1805), Appendix, p. 178. Sherry: Cyrus Redding, *A History and Description of Modern Wines* (3rd ed., London, 1851), p. 206; Henry Vizetelly, *Facts About Sherry* (London, 1876), pp. 48–9; Feuerheerd, *op. cit.*, pp. 79, 81–7. Dry Sack: Jeffs, *loc. cit.* Henri Misson de Valbourg, *op. cit.*, pp. 144–7. Walter Besant, *Fifty Years Ago* (London, 1888), pp. 160–74. Shaw, *loc. cit.* Gronow, *op. cit.*, vol. 1 pp. 36–8. *The Times*, 29 October 1861. *Dublin University Magazine*: H. S. Spencer, 'Cheap wines', vol. 80 (September 1872) pp. 357–9.

Ruffs and reeves: Abraham Hayward, 'Dinners, clubs etc.', *Quarterly Review*, vol. 55 no. 110 (February 1836) p. 465. Grimod de la Reynière, cited in MacDonogh, *op. cit.*, pp. 135, 152–6. Brillat-Savarin, *Physiologie du Goût/Physiology of Taste*, Aphorisms and Meditation no. 14, 'On the pleasure of the table'. Abraham Hayward, *The Art of Dining* (London, 1852), pp. 120–2. History of champagne: André Simon, *The History of Champagne* (London, 1962). Thomas Walker, *Aristology, or the Art of Dining* (London, 1881), p. 73. '*Vous buvez ce poison-là*': Nathaniel Newnham-Davis and Algernon Bastard, *The Gourmet's Guide to Europe* (London, 1903), pp. 116–17. Feuerheerd, *op. cit.*, pp. 61–71. Serena Sutcliffe, *A Celebration of Champagne* (London, 1988), pp. 25–6. George Saintsbury, *Notes on a Cellar Book* (London, 1920). Wine not drunk with cheese: 'Oenismus' (Thomas Cosnett), *The Footman's Directory and Butler's Remembrancer* (4th ed., London, 1825), p. 111; *The Butler*, by an Experienced Servant (London, 1855), p. 97. André Simon, *In The Twilight* (London, 1969), pp. 90–1.

Matching wine and food: David Rosengarten and Joshua Wesson, *Red Wine with Fish: the new art of matching wine with food* (New York, 1989). Comparison between medieval European and modern Indian cookery: Willan, *op. cit.*, pp. 10–11. Charles Francatelli, *The Modern Cook* (29th ed., London, 1896), pp. 477–80. Dr Johnson: *Boswell's Life of Johnson* (ed. George B. Hill, Oxford, 1934), vol. 1 p. 468. Philippa Pullar, *Consuming Passions* (London, 1970), pp. 125–31. Edward P. Thompson, *The Making of the English Working Class*

(London, 1980), p. 411. American commentator: Timothy Edward Howard, *Excelsior, or Essays on Politeness, Education and the Means of Attaining Success in Life* (Baltimore, 1868), p. 87, cited in John F. Kasson, 'Rituals of dining: table manners in Victorian America' in *Dining in America 1850–1900* (ed. Kathryn Grover, Amhurst, Massachusetts, 1987), pp. 134–5. Development of London restaurants: Robert Thorne, 'Places of refreshment in the nineteenth-century city' in *Buildings and Society: essays in the social development of the built environment* (ed. Anthony D. King, London, 1980), pp. 228–53. 'Fast, if not disreputable': Clement Scott, *How they dined us in 1860 and how they dine us now* (London, c. 1900), p. 8. *The Epicure's Almanack* (London, 1815), pp. 133, 150–1. Marie Louise Ritz, *César Ritz* (London, 1938), pp. 100–1, 150–3. 'The exhibiting of magnificent dresses': Auguste Escoffier, *A Guide to Modern Cookery* (London, 1907), Preface, pp. v–vi. Nathaniel Newnham-Davis, *Dinners and Diners: where and how to dine in London* (2nd ed., London, 1901), p. 4. Ceremony distracted diners from the food: Derek Taylor, *Fortune, Fame and Folly: British hotels and catering from 1878 to 1978* (London, 1977), p. 83. Havelock Ellis, cited in Pullar, *op. cit.*, p. 156n. Sucking: Hans D. Renner, *The Origin of Food Habits* (London, 1944), pp. 64–5, 70–1.

CHAPTER 3

Theodore Zeldin, *France 1848–1945* (Oxford, 1977), vol. 2 ('Intellect, Taste, Anxiety') pp. 754–5. California wines in the nineteenth century: Vincent P. Carosso, *The California Wine Industry: a study of the formative years 1830–1895* (Berkeley, California, 1951), pp. 100–1, 183–5; Charles L. Sullivan, *Like Modern Edens: wine-growing in Santa Clara Valley and Santa Cruz Mountains 1798–1981* (Cupertino, California, 1982), pp. 54–5; Leon D. Adams, *The Wines of America* (3rd ed., New York, 1985), pp. 18–21, 223–9; Thomas Pinney, *A History of Wine in America from the Beginnings to Prohibition* (Berkeley, California, 1989), p. 360. Jack Davies, cited in *The Wine Spectator*, 15 June 1991, p. 25. Philippe Guermonprez: *The New York Times*, 13 February 1991; *The Wine Spectator*, 31 January 1992, p. 12. Oregon Pinot Noir: Andrew Barr, *Pinot Noir* (London, 1992), pp. 234–55. Medieval Burgundy: Roger Dion, *Histoire de la Vigne et du Vin en France* (Paris, 1959), pp. 291–300. Petrarch, cited in Claude Courtépée and Edmé Béguillet, *Déscription générale et particulière du Duché de Bourgogne précédée de l'abrégé histoire de cette province* (Dijon, 1775), vol. 1 p. 190. Spurrier 'rigs' his tasting: Simon Loftus,

Anatomy of the Wine Trade: Abe's Sardines and other stories (London, 1985), p. 120; *The Wine Spectator*, 1–15 April 1986, pp. 41–2. 'California Cabernets do age': *The Field*, 11 October 1986. *Terroir* and *terroiristes*: Barr, *op. cit.*, pp. 6–10. Anthony Hanson, *Burgundy* (London, 1982), pp. 147–8. Monastic *pigeage*: Edward Ott, *A Tread of Grapes* (Bidford-on-Avon, 1982), pp. 38–9. Bacteria in burgundies: Barr, *op. cit.*, pp. 29–33.

Brand in Alsace: Tom Stevenson, *The Wines of Alsace* (London, 1993), pp. 161–2. Gold in Tokay: Zoltán Halász, *Hungarian Wine Through the Ages* (Budapest, 1962), pp. 88–9. Robert Townson, *Travels in Hungary in 1793* (London, 1797), p. 269. Cyrus Redding, *A History and Description of Modern Wines* (3rd ed., London, 1851), pp. 286–7. 'Rotten wines' in Sauternes: cited in Henri Enjalbert, 'Comment naissent les grands crus: Bordeaux, Porto, Cognac', *Annales* 1953, p. 324. Dom Pérignon legend: Nicholas Faith, *The Story of Champagne* (London, 1988), pp. 20–39. Patrick Forbes, *Champagne: the wine, the land and the people* (London, 1967), pp. 105–29. 'Costa Brava champagne' case: Robert Keeling, 'The "Spanish champagne" case' in André Simon, *The History of Champagne* (London, 1962), pp. 160–74. 'The spirit of Agincourt lives on': cited in *The Daily Telegraph*, 9 February 1993. Traditional 'elderflower champagne': Dorothy Hartley, *Food in England* (London, 1954), pp. 445–6.

Sweet German wines: Andrew Barr, *Wine Snobbery: an insider's guide to the booze business* (London, 1988), pp. 104–5. Kermit Lynch, *Adventures on the Wine Route: a wine buyer's tour of France* (New York, 1988), p. 203. New oak in Burgundy: Barr, *Pinot Noir*, pp. 26–9. Guy Accad: Barr, *Pinot Noir*, pp. 20–2. Steve Philpott, cited in *Off Licence News*, 30 January 1992. CAMRA attacks 'canned draught' beers: *What's Brewing*, November 1992, January and March 1993; *Off Licence News*, 2 July 1992, 11 February and 29 April 1993. Thornton Mustard: Victoria McKee, 'A bitter man, or ale and hearty?' *The Times*, 30 December 1989. Pub Design of the Year Awards: *What's Brewing*, April 1994.

CHAPTER 4

Cáceres: *The Guardian*, 14 October 1991. History of the licensing laws: Sidney and Beatrice Webb, *The History of Liquor Licensing in England principally from 1700 to 1830* (London, 1903); Lord Askwith, *British Taverns: their history and laws* (London, 1928); George B. Wilson, *Alcohol and the Nation* (London, 1940); Rob Baggott, *Alcohol, Politics and Social Policy* (Aldershot, 1990). Turmoil on Sunday mornings:

Arthur Shadwell, *Drink, Temperance and Legislation* (London, 1902), pp. 36–8. 1872 Licensing Act: Brian Harrison, *Drink and the Victorians* (London, 1971), pp. 262–85. The First World War: Henry Carter, *The Control of the Drink Trade: a contribution to national efficiency 1915–1917* (London, 1918); Arthur Shadwell, *Drink in 1914–1922: a lesson in control* (London, 1923). Sanders, cited in Central Board of the Licensed Victuallers' Central Protection Society of London, *An Examination of the Evidence before the Royal Commission on Licensing (England and Wales) 1929–1930* (London, 1931), p. 40. Reade, cited in *ibid.*, p. 36. Australia: John M. Freeland, *The Australian Pub* (Carlton, Victoria, 1966), pp. 170–6; Walter Phillips, ' "Six o'clock swill": the introduction of early closing of hotel bars in Australia', *Historical Studies: Australia and New Zealand* vol. 19/no. 75 (October 1980) pp. 250–66; Jan Morris, *Sydney* (London, 1992), pp. 143–7. New Zealand: Conrad Bollinger, *Grog's Own Country* (Wellington, 1959). James C. Parker, *Mission Work Among Licensed Victuallers* (2nd ed., London, 1892), p. 7.

Maudling: *Hansard*, 5th Series, vol. 819 col. 1568 (24 June 1971). Effect of implementation of Clayson's recommendations in Scotland: John C. Duffy and Martin A. Plant, 'Scottish liquor licensing changes: an assessment', *British Medical Journal*, vol. 292 (1986) pp. 36–9; Philip Tether, 'Liquor licensing: theory, practice and potential' in *Drinking to your Health: the allegations and the evidence* (ed. Digby Anderson, London, 1989), pp. 137–56. Kenneth Clarke's Licensing (Amendment) Bill: *Hansard*, 5th Series, vol. 906 cols 820–869 (27 February 1976). Douglas Hurd: *Hansard*, 6th Series, vol. 122 cols 37–44 (9 November 1987). Chief Superintendent Stevens, cited in *The Independent*, 23 August 1989. OPCS survey: Eileen Goddard, *Drinking in England and Wales in the late 1980s* (London, 1991).

1987 Sunday survey: Public Attitudes Surveys Research Ltd, 'Attitudes to Longer Pub Hours', cited in *Hansard*, 6th Series, vol. 122 col. 93 (9 November 1987). History of Sunday closing laws: R. P. Durnford, *The Englishman's Brief for Sunday Closing* (London, 1898). 1854 Manchester survey: *Report from the Select Committee on Public Houses* (London, 1854), p. xvi. 'Well corked down': *ibid.* pp. xix, 39. Hyde Park Riots: Brian Harrison, 'The Sunday trading riots of 1855', *The Historical Journal*, vol. 8 (1965) pp. 219–45; Norman Longmate, *The Waterdrinkers* (London, 1968), pp. 158–71. Sunday closing in Wales: W. R. Lambert, 'The Welsh Sunday Closing Act, 1881', *The Welsh History Review*, vol. 6 (1972–1973) pp. 161–89. *The Times*, cited in Askwith, *op. cit.*, pp. 107–12. George and Weedon Grossmith, *Diary of a Nobody* (Bristol, 1892), pp. 29–32. John Major, cited in *Off Licence News*, 2 February 1995. Mrs Thatcher's defeat: *Guardian*, 30 November

1991. Lord Ferrers: *The Times*, 23 April 1988; Baggott, *op. cit.*, pp. 116–32. Michael Schluter: 'Today', Radio 4, 25 January 1995; *The Independent*, 26 January 1995. George Howarth: *Hansard*, 6th Series, vol. 254 cols 1019–20.

Impossibility of enforcing laws: Guy Thorne, *The Great Acceptance: the life story of F. N. Charrington* (London, 1912), p. 69; Harrison, *Drink and the Victorians*, pp. 376–7. Illegal drinking in Scotland: Edwin A. Pratt, *The Licensed Trade: an independent survey* (London, 1907), pp. 143–9. Nightclubs in First World War: James Bishop, *The Illustrated London News Social History of the First World War* (London, 1982), pp. 112–13; Marek Kohn, *Dope Girls: the birth of the British drug underground* (London, 1992), pp. 28–30. Nightclubs in the 1920s: Robert Graves and Alan Hodge, *The Long Weekend: a social history of Great Britain 1918–1939* (London, 1940), pp. 119–20; Ronald Blythe, *The Age of Illusion: glimpses of Britain between the wars 1919–1940* (2nd ed., Oxford, 1983), pp. 34–6. Bottle parties: Graves and Hodge, *op. cit.*, pp. 225–7. Henley Centre for Forecasting, *Leisure Futures* (1993). Richard Carr, cited in Elizabeth Heathcote, 'Nightclubs agonize over Ecstasy', *The Independent*, 17 August 1992.

Douglas Hurd, cited in *What's Brewing*, December 1988. Peter Marsh: cited in *The Independent*, 10 August and 5 December 1990 and in *The Independent on Sunday*, 2 February 1992; Peter Marsh and Kate Fox Kirby, *Drinking and Public Disorder* (London, 1992), pp. 135–40, 161. 'Out of Hours': Ken Worple, *Towns for People: transforming urban life* (Buckingham, 1992). Bootlegging during Prohibition: Norman H. Clark, *Deliver Us From Evil* (New York, 1976), pp. 146–53. Leeds: *The Independent*, 2 July 1993. Scottish brasseries: David Goymour, 'Open all hours', *Caterer and Hotelkeeper*, 9 March 1989, pp. 43–4. Michael Howard, cited in *The Independent*, 12 March 1992. *Marketing Week*: Iain Murray, 'Not in front of the children', 20 March 1992. Steve Cox: *What's Brewing*, April 1992. Neville Marshall and Richard Ridler: *What's Brewing*, June 1993.

Early English coffee houses: Edward Forbes Robinson, *The Early History of Coffee Houses in England* (London, 1893); Aytoun Ellis, *The Penny Universities* (London, 1956); Bryant Lillywhite, *London Coffee Houses* (London, 1963). Henri Misson de Valbourg, *Memoirs and Observations in his Travels over England* (tr. John Ozell, 1719), pp. 39–40. Three thousand coffee houses: Edward Hatton, *A New View of London* (London, 1708), p. 30. Rosee and Edwards: John Houghton, *A Collection for the Improvement of Husbandry and Trade* no. 458 (2 May 1701). Tea Gardens: Warwick W. Wroth, *The London Pleasure Gardens of the Eighteenth Century* (London, 1896); Edwin Beresford Chancellor, *The Pleasure Haunts of London during four centuries*

(London, 1925). Coffee-house keeper, cited in George R. Porter, *The Progress of the Nation* (3rd ed., London, 1851), pp. 673–81. 'Friends of the beer-house interests': Harrison, *Drink and the Victorians*, p. 323.

Heavy drinking in the 1870s: A. E. Dingle, 'Drink and working-class living standards in Britain 1870–1914', *Economic History Review*, vol. 25 (1972) pp. 608–22. John Ruskin, 'Fors Clavigera' in *Works* (ed. E. T. Cook and Alexander Wedderburn, London), vol. 19 (1907) p. 23. Benjamin Seebohm Rowntree, *Poverty and Progress: a second social survey of York* (London, 1941), pp. 363–4, 370–3. Cinemas: Jeffrey Richards, *The Age of the Dream Palace: cinema and society in Britain 1930–1939* (London, 1984). Mass-Observation, *The Pub and the People: a worktown study* (London, 1943), pp. 136–7. 'Dancing mad': *The Social and Economic Aspects of the Drink Problem*, (ed. Walter Meakin, London, 1931), pp. 60–1. No more 'soaking': Wilson, *op. cit.*, p. 247. Competitive expenditure: *ibid.*, pp. 223–8, 253–4. Gambling a similar vice to drink: J. Martin, 'Gambling' in *New Survey of London Life and Labour* (London, 1935), vol. 9 p. 271.

Charles Forte: *Forte: the autobiography of Charles Forte* (London, 1986), pp. 24, 49. *The Times*, 29 July and 2 August 1935, 4 September 1936 and 30 August 1937. Mass-Observation, *op. cit.*, pp. 319–20. *The Times Educational Supplement*, 'Coffee comes to town', 8 July 1955. Consumers' Association survey: *Which?*, June 1989, pp. 282–4. Andrew Knowles, cited in *Marketing Week*, 11 May 1990. Artisan groups: Marianna Adler, 'From symbolic exchange to commodity consumption: anthropological notes on drinking as a symbolic practice' in *Drinking: behaviour and belief in modern history* (ed. Susanna Barrows and Robin Room, Berkeley, California, 1991), pp. 376–98. John Dunlop, *The Philosophy of Artificial and Compulsory Drinking Usages in Great Britain and Ireland* (London, 1839). Treating in First World War: Arthur Mee, *The Fiddlers: drink in the witness box* (London, 1917), p. 33; Longmate, *op. cit.*, pp. 260, 269. Prohibition of treating: Shadwell, *Drink in 1914–1922*, pp. 119–20.

History of pubs: Askwith, *op. cit.*; Herbert A. Monckton, *A History of the English Public House* (London, 1969); Mark Girouard, *Victorian Pubs* (London, 1975); Peter Clark, *The English Alehouse: a social history 1200–1830* (London, 1983); Wolfgang Schivelbusch, *Tastes of Paradise: a social history of spices, stimulants and intoxicants* (tr. David Jacobson, New York, 1992), pp. 188–203; Peter Haydon, *The English Pub: a history* (London, 1994). Karl Kautsky, 'Der Alkoholismus und seine Bekämpfung', *Die Neue Zeit*, 1891, cited in Schivelbusch, *loc. cit.* 'Traffic innovation': *ibid.* Class segregation: *Report from the Select Committee on Import Duties on Wines* (London, 1852), Q. 3817, pp. 523–4; Harrison, *Drink and the Victorians*, pp. 45–6. Sydney Nevile,

Seventy Rolling Years (London, 1958), pp. 64–7, 71, 167, 172. Ernest Oldmeadow, cited in Central Board of the Licensed Victuallers' Central Protection Society of London, *op. cit.*, p. 85. Strauss, cited in Hermann Levy, *Drink: an economic and social study* (London, 1951), pp. 238–42. Roadhouses: Alan A. Jackson, *The Middle Classes 1900–1950* (Nairn, 1991), pp. 283–6. George Orwell, *The Road to Wigan Pier* (London, 1937), p. 72.

Patrick Colquhoun, *Observations and Facts Relative to Licensed Alehouses in the City of London and its Environs* (London, 1794), p. 17. Gustave d'Eichthal, *A French Sociologist Looks at Britain* (ed. B. M. Ratcliffe and W. H. Chaloner, Manchester, 1977), p. 312. Barmaids banned in New Zealand: A. R. Grigg, 'Prohibition and Women: the preservation of a myth', *New Zealand Journal of History*, vol. 17 (1983), pp. 144–65. 1977 survey: cited in *The Sunday Times*, 19 April 1992. Julia Carpenter: Richard Milner, 'The wine bar boom', *The Sunday Times*, 12 May 1974. Wine-bar design: Worple, *op. cit.* Children in the nineteenth century: Wilson, *op. cit.*, pp. 160–2. Food in pubs in First World War: Shadwell, *Drink in 1914–1922*, pp. 46–51, 75–6; Central Board of the Licensed Victuallers' Central Protection Society of London, *op. cit.*, p. 71. Food in wine bars in the 1970s: Acumen Marketing Group, *A Report on the British Market for Food in Pubs and Wine Bars* (London, c.1978–1979). 66 per cent of people attracted by pub food: MORI survey, cited in *The Times*, 2 September 1992. Wine bars in decline: Mintel survey, cited in *The Independent*, 12 August 1993. Fay Maschler, *The Evening Standard*, 8 September 1992. G. K. Chesterton, 'The Rolling English Road' in *Collected Poems* (London, 1927), pp. 183–4.

CHAPTER 5

The Gin Age: M. Dorothy George, *London Life in the Eighteenth Century* (3rd ed., London, 1951); Lord Kinross, 'Prohibition in Britain', *History Today*, July 1959, pp. 493–9; John Watney, *Mother's Ruin: a history of gin* (London, 1976). Middlesex justices, cited in Thomas Wilson, *Distilled Spirituous Liquors the Bane of the Nation* (2nd ed., London, 1736), Appendix, pp. xi–xii. Judith Dufour: *Old Bailey Session Papers*, 1734, cited in George, *op. cit.*, p. 42. Peter Clark, 'The "Mother Gin" controversy in early eighteenth-century England', *Transactions of the Royal Historical Society*, 5th Series, vol. 38 (1988) pp. 63–84. Corbyn Morris, *Observations on the Past Growth and Present State of the City of London* (London, 1751), p. 23. Charles Davenant, *An Essay Upon Ways and Means of Supplying the War* (London, 1695), pp.

137–8. Lord Hervey: William Cobbett, *The Parliamentary History of England*, vol. 12 (London, 1812) cols 1193, 1315, 1430.

History of taxation: Basil E. V. Sabine, *A Short History of Taxation* (London, 1980). Alcohol price inelastic: H. M. Treasury, *Macroeconomic Model Equation and Variable Listing* (London, 1986), cited in Faculty of Public Health Medicine of the Royal College of Physicians, *Alcohol and the Public Health* (Basingstoke, 1991), pp. 101–2. Institute of Fiscal Studies: Paul Baker and Stephen McKay, *The Structure of Alcohol Taxes: a hangover from the past* (London, 1990), p. 33; Peter Temple, 'Games without frontiers', *Wine and Spirit*, August 1988, pp. 44–6. Presumption of innocence: *The Daily Telegraph*, 11 February 1992. Gillian Shepherd, cited in *Off Licence News*, 19 March 1992. Bill Keen, cited in *The Sunday Telegraph*, 19 December 1993. Vic Bassi, cited in *The Mail on Sunday*, 13 June 1993. John Marek, cited in *The Observer*, 12 July 1992. Bracewell-Miles: The Adam Smith Institute, *A Disorderly House* (London, 1993).

The wine trade in the eighteenth century: André Simon, *Bottlescrew Days* (London, 1926); A. D. Francis, *The Wine Trade* (London, 1972). Robert Walpole: John H. Plumb, *Sir Robert Walpole* (London, 1956), pp. 120–2. History of Scotch whisky: Michael S. Moss and John R. Hume, *The Making of Scotch Whisky* (Edinburgh, 1981). Stein and Stewart, cited in T. M. Devine, 'The rise and fall of illicit whisky-making in northern Scotland, c. 1780–1840', *Scottish Historical Review*, vol. 54 (1975) pp. 155–77. Superiority of poteen: Caesar Otway, *Sketches in Ireland* (2nd ed., Dublin, 1839), p. 60. Smuggling of spirits in England: George Bishop, *Observations, Remarks and Means to Prevent Smuggling* (Maidstone, 1783), pp. 10–11. The Beer Act: Brian Harrison, *Drink and the Victorians* (London, 1971), pp. 64–86; Terry R. Gourvish and Richard G. Wilson, *The British Brewing Industry 1830–1980* (Cambridge, 1994), pp. 3–22.

Tea taxation: Stephen Dowell, *A History of Taxation and Taxes in England* (2nd ed., London, 1888), vol. 4 pp. 213–30. Tea-smuggling: Hoh-Cheung and Lorna H. Mui, 'Smuggling and the British tea trade before 1784', *American Historical Review*, vol. 74 no. 1 (October 1968) pp. 44–73. Duncan Forbes, *Some Considerations on the Present State of Scotland* (3rd ed., Edinburgh, 1744); George Menary, *The Life and Letters of Duncan Forbes of Culloden* (London, 1936), pp. 143–6. Boston Tea Party: Benjamin Woods Labaree, *The Boston Tea Party* (New York, 1964). Franklin and *Boston Broadside*: cited in John F. Greden, 'The tea controversy in colonial America', *Journal of the American Medical Association*, vol. 236 no. 1 (5 July 1976) pp. 63–6. 'British tea': Richard Twining, *Observations on the Tea and Window Act and on the Tea Trade* (London, 1784), pp. 41–4. Tea adulteration in the nineteenth century: John Burnett, *Plenty and Want* (2nd ed., London, 1983), pp. 106–7, 265–6.

Coffee shops in London: Robert Montgomery Martin, *The Past and Present State of the Tea Trade* (London, 1832), pp. 56–63. Beneficial effect of cheap price of coffee: George R. Porter, *The Progress of the Nation* (3rd ed., London, 1851), pp. 548–51. Coffee stalls and chicory: Henry Mayhew, *London Labour and the London Poor* (London, 1861), vol. 1 pp. 183–4. George Dodd, *The Food of London* (London, 1856), pp. 414–20. Peter L. Simmonds, *The Popular Beverages of Various Countries* (London, 1888), pp. 178–219. Heinrich Jacob, *The Saga of Coffee* (tr. Eden and Cedar Paul, London, 1935), p. 142. Andrew V. Kirwan, *Host and Guest* (London, 1864), pp. 235–44. British preference for tea: Ian Bersten, *Coffee Floats, Tea Sinks* (Sydney, 1993), pp. 49–54.

History of coffee: William H. Ukers, *All About Coffee* (2nd ed., New York, 1935); Jacob, *op. cit.* Ressons: *L'Encyclopédie* vol. 2 (Paris, 1751), pp. 527–9. De Clieu: *L'Année Littéraire*, vol. 6 (1774) pp. 217–19. History of tea: William H. Ukers, *All About Tea* (New York, 1935); James M. Scott, *The Tea Story* (London, 1964); Denys Forrest, *Tea for the British* (London, 1973); Henry Hobhouse, *Seeds of Change: five plants that transformed mankind* (London, 1985), pp. 93–137. History of tea in China: John C. Evans, *Tea in China* (Westport, Connecticut, 1992). History of tea in India: Sir Percival Griffiths, *The History of the Indian Tea Industry* (London, 1967); John Weatherstone, *The Pioneers, 1825–1900, the early British tea- and coffee-planters and their way of life* (London, 1986). Dutch and sage: Philippe Sylvestre Dufour, *Traités nouveaux et curieux du Café, du Thé et du Chocolat* (Lyon, 1685), pp. 240–3. The East India Company: Sir Cyril H. Philips, *The East India Company 1784–1834* (2nd ed., Manchester, 1961). Banks and Macartney: J. L. Cranmer-Byng, *An Embassy to China* (London, 1962), pp. 374–5 n. 57. James Johnston, *The Chemistry of Common Life* (Edinburgh, 1855), vol. 1 p. 169. Elizabeth Gaskell, *Cranford* (Classics Book Club, 3rd ed., London, 1941), p. 157. Edward Money, *The Tea Controversy: Indian versus Chinese teas* (2nd ed., London, 1884).

History of wine: William Younger, *Gods, Men and Wine* (London, 1966); Hugh Johnson, *The Story of Wine* (London, 1989). History of vine-growing: Edward Hyams, *Dionysus: a social history of the wine vine* (London, 1965). History of vine-growing in England: Hugh Barty-King, *A Tradition of English Wine* (Oxford, 1977). History of vine-growing in America: Thomas Pinney, *A History of Wine in America from the beginnings to Prohibition* (Berkeley, California, 1989). England should produce its own wine: S. J., *The Vineyard* (London, 1727), Dedication. Hamilton, cited in Sir Edward Barry, *Observations,*

Historical, Critical on the Wines of the Ancients and the Analogy between them and Modern Wines (London, 1775), pp. 471–5. Pierre Grosley, *A Tour to London* (tr. Thomas Nugent, London, 1772), vol. 1 p. 83. History of cider: Roger K. French, *The History and Virtues of Cyder* (London, 1982); Stuart Davies, ' "Vinetum Britannicum": cider and perry in the seventeenth century' in *'Liquid Nourishment': potable foods and stimulating drinks* (ed. Constance Anne Wilson, Edinburgh, 1993), pp. 79–105. John Evelyn, *Pomona* (Appendix to *Sylvia*) (London, 1664), Preface, p. 3. John Worlidge, *Vinetum Britannicum* (1st ed., London, 1676 and 3rd ed., London, 1691), Preface. Grosley, *op. cit.*, pp. 81–2. Mark Beaufoy: Thomas Pennant, *Some Account of London* (3rd ed., London, 1793), pp. 32–3; 'A day at a vinegar and British wine factory', *Penny Magazine*, New Series, vol. 11 (October 1842).

Adulteration of Cape wines: Thomas George Shaw, *Wine, the Vine and the Cellar* (London, 1863), pp. 336–40. Cyrus Redding, *A History and Description of Modern Wines* (London, 1833), pp. 284–8; (3rd ed., London, 1851), pp. 312–18. Shaw, *loc. cit.* History of Australian wine: H. E. Laffer, *The Wine Industry of Australia* (Adelaide, 1949); John Beeston, *A Concise History of Australian Wine* (Sydney, 1994). Prejudice of settlers: James Busby, *A Manual of Plain Directions for Planting and Cultivating Vineyards in New South Wales* (Sydney, 1830), Introduction, pp. 7–9. Natural relationship between colony and mother country: James Busby, *A Treatise on the Culture of the Vine and the Art of Making Wine* (Sydney, 1825), Introduction, pp. ix–xxxiv. 'Enjoy their daily bottle': Busby, *Manual, loc. cit.* Biography of Busby: *Journal and Proceedings of the Royal Australian Historical Society*, vol. 26 (1940) pp. 361–86. William Winch Hughes: *Report of the Select Committee on Wine Duties* (London, 1879), Qs 3732–3854, pp. 180–3; Asa Briggs, *Wine for Sale: Victoria Wine and the liquor trade 1860–1984* (London, 1985). Winston Churchill: *Hansard*, 5th Series, vol. 208 cols 311–323 (28 June 1927). Wine sales between the wars: *The Measurement of Consumers' Expenditure and Behaviour in the United Kingdom 1920–1938* (ed. Richard Stone, Cambridge, 1954), vol. 1 pp. 175–87. Gin at chandlers' shops: Wilson, *op. cit.*, Introduction, p. vii.

CHAPTER 6

History of the medicinal use of wine: Salvatore P. Lucia, *A History of Wine as Therapy* (Philadelphia, 1963). Arabian Nights: Sir Richard Burton, *The Book of the Thousand Nights and a Night* (London, 1894–1897), vol. 4 pp. 176–7 (452nd night). Early history of spirits:

Robert J. Forbes, *Short History of the Art of Distillation* (Leiden, 1948); Constance Anne Wilson, 'Burnt wine and cordial waters: the early days of distilling', *Folk Life*, vol. 13 (1975) pp. 54–65; Constance Anne Wilson, 'Water of Life: its beginnings and early history' in *'Liquid Nourishment': potable foods and stimulating drinks* (ed. Constance Anne Wilson, Edinburgh, 1993), pp. 142–64. Charles of Navarre: cited in Henri Martin, *Histoire de France* (4th ed., Paris, 1878), vol. 5 p. 408. Bénédictine in the Far East: Peter A. Hallgarten, *Spirits and Liqueurs* (2nd ed., London, 1983), pp. 17–27. History of spirits in Ireland: Edward B. MacGuire, *Irish Whiskey* (Dublin, 1973). Edmund Campion, 'History of Ireland' in *Ancient Irish Histories* (ed. James Ware, Dublin, 1809), p. 13, 123. Sir Walter Raleigh: A. C. Wootton, *Chronicles of Pharmacy* (London, 1910), vol. 2 pp. 310–15. Samuel Pepys, *Diary* (ed. Robert Latham and William Matthews, London, 1971), vol. 4 p. 329 (10 October 1663). George Cheyne, *An Essay of Health and Long Life* (London, 1724), p. 43. John Brown: Thomas Beddoes, preface to John Brown, *The Elements of Medicine* (London, 1795), vol. 1 p. lxxv. Alcoholic therapeutics in the nineteenth century: Sarah E. Williams, 'The use of beverage alcohol as medicine, 1790–1860', *Journal of Studies on Alcohol*, vol. 41 (1980), pp. 543–66. John Harley Warner, 'Physiological theory and therapeutic explanation in the 1860s: the British debate on the medical use of alcohol', *Bulletin of the History of Medicine*, vol. 54 (1980) pp. 235–57. Todd, Hindley and Prince Albert: Augustus B. Granville, *Dr Todd and the Late Member for Ashton* (London, 1860); Frederic R. Lees, *An Inquiry into the Reasons and Results of the Prescription of Intoxicating Liquors in the Practice of Medicine* (London, 1866), pp. 36, 96, 100. Taking brandy to keep away cholera: Revd William R. Baker, *The Curse of Britain* (London, 1838), p. 144. James Samuelson, *History of Drink* (London, 1878), p. 231.

Health Education Authority, cited in *Marketing Week*, 20 October 1989. Alcohol Concern, *Warning: Alcohol Can Damage Your Health*. Benjamin Franklin, *Autobiography* (ed. William N. Otto, Boston, 1928), pp. 55–6. Brougham: *Hansard*, 2nd Series, vol. 24 cols 419–422 (4 May 1830). 'Thee musn't, Richard, thee'll die': cited in Norman Longmate, *The Waterdrinkers* (London, 1968), p. 55. Robert Warner: George B. Wilson, *Alcohol and the Nation* (London, 1940), p. 262. Harvest beer: George Bourne, *Change in the Village* (London, 1912), p. 77. ' "Hot" or "heavy" trades': His Honour Judge Parry, *Drink and Industrial Unrest* (London, 1919). Guinness: Brian Sibley, *The Book of Guinness Advertising* (Enfield, 1985), pp. 37–43. Mass-Observation, *The Pub and the People* (London, 1943), pp. 42–4. Market research in 1980s: Mintel, *Market Intelligence*, March 1989. Calculation of energy value of beer: H. J. Bunker, 'The nutritive value of yeast, beer, wines and spirits', *Chemistry and Industry* 1947, pp. 203–4. Average consumption of beer in the past: Peter Clark, *The English Alehouse: a social history 1200–1830* (London, 1983), pp. 109, 209. David Macpherson, *The History of the European Commerce with India* (London, 1812), p. 132 n.1. William Cobbett, *Cottage Economy* (London, 1828), no. 2, 'Brewing beer', paras 23–33. Nutritiousness of saloop: Richard Valpy French, *Nineteen Centuries of Drink in England* (2nd ed., London, 1891), p. 273. Nastiness of saloop: Charles Lamb, *The Essays of Elia* (London, 1868), pp. 140–7.

Andrew Boorde, *A Dietary of Health* (ed. Frederick J. Furnivall, London, 1870), pp. 252–8. History of rum in the Navy: A. James Pack, *Nelson's Blood* (Havant, 1982). Prince Albert: Daphne Bennett, *King Without a Crown* (London, 1977). Lord Chamberlain, cited in Cecil Woodham-Smith, *Queen Victoria* (London, 1972), p. 279. Disraeli, cited in *The London Encyclopaedia* (ed. Ben Weinreb and Christopher Hibbert, London, 1983), pp. 237–8. Sir John Fortescue, *De Laudibus Legum Angliae* (tr., London, 1737), p. 83 (chapter 36). César de Saussure, *A Foreign View of England in the Reigns of George I and George II* (tr. and ed. Madame van Muyden, London, 1902), pp. 157–65. Tunbridge Wells: Lewis Melville, *Society at Royal Tunbridge Wells* (London, 1912); Margaret Barton, *Tunbridge Wells* (London, 1937). Lodowick Rowzee, *The Queen's Wells* (London, 1632). Bath: A. Barbeau, *Life and Letters at Bath in the Eighteenth Century* (London, 1904); Lewis Melville, *Bath under Beau Nash – and after* (London, 1926). Brighton: Lewis Melville, *Brighton* (1909); Osbert Sitwell and Margaret Barton, *Brighton* (London, 1935). Drinking sea-water: John Awsiter, *Thoughts on Brightelmston* (London, 1768), pp. 18–20. Artificial mineral waters: William Kirkby, *The Evolution of Artificial Mineral Waters* (Manchester, 1902); Charles Ainsworth Mitchell, *Mineral and Aerated Waters* (London, 1913); Douglas A. Simmons, *Schweppes: the first two hundred years* (London, 1983). *The Sunday Times*, 12 March 1989. John Bellak, cited in *The Independent*, 24 October 1991. Survey of attitudes to tap water: Robens Institute at Surrey University, cited in *The Sunday Correspondent*, 27 May 1990. Spa advertisement 'unwarranted': *The Times*, 6 September 1993. Derek Miller, cited in *The Sunday Correspondent*, 18 February 1990.

History of milk: Alan Jenkins, *Drinka Pinta* (London, 1970). Thomas Muffet, *Health's Improvement* (ed. C. Bennett, London, 1655), pp. 119–28. Sir John Boyd Orr, 'National food requirements' in *The Nation's Larder and the housewife's part therein* (London, 1940), p. 51.

Tea the 'Elixir of Life': John C. Evans, *Tea in China* (Westport, Connecticut, 1992), pp. 20–1. Nikolas Dirx, cited in William H. Ukers,

All About Tea (New York, 1935), vol. 1 pp. 31–2. Thomas Garway, *An Exact Description of the Growth, Quality and Virtues of the Leaf Tea* (London, c. 1670); Bryant Lillywhite, *London Coffee Houses* (London, 1963), 'Garraway's Coffee House'. Brandy a corrective to tea: Walter Besant, *London in the Time of the Stuarts* (London, 1903), pp. 292–6. Whisky a corrective to tea: Billy Kay and Caileen MacLean, *Knee Deep in Claret: a celebration of wine and Scotland* (London, 1983), pp. 108–9. Madame de la Sablière, *Lettres de Marie de Rabutin-Chantal, Marquise de Sévigné* (ed. U. Silvestre de Sacy, Paris, 1861), vol. 6 pp. 361–6 (16 February 1680). Simon Paulli, *A Treatise on Tobacco, Tea, Coffee and Chocolate* (tr. Robert James, London, 1746), pp. 132–4. Jonas Hanway, *A Journal of Eight Days' Journey . . . to which is added an essay on tea* (London, 1757), vol. 2 pp. 20–4, 270–8. Beneficial effect of tea on manners: Robert Montgomery Martin, *The Past and Present State of the Tea Trade* (London, 1832), p. 196. Ty-phoo: Denys Forrest, *Tea for the British* (London, 1973), pp. 198–9. Cyclical changes: Denys Forrest, *The World Tea Trade* (Cambridge, 1985), p. 188.

Early coffee-drinking: Ralph S. Hattox, *Coffee and Coffee Houses: the origin of a social beverage in the medieval Near East* (Seattle, 1988). Sir Henry Blount, testimonial prefaced to Walter Rumsey, *Organon Salutis* (London, 1657). Jacques de Bourges, *Relation du Voyage de Monseigneur l'Evêque de Beryte Vicaire Apostolique du Royaume de la Cochinchine* (Paris, 1666), pp. 40–1. Change in bodily type: Aytoun Ellis, *The Penny Universities* (London, 1956), pp. 10–17. Sir William Harvey, cited in Heinrich E. Jacob, *The Saga of Coffee* (tr. Eden and Cedar Paul, London, 1935), p. 128. Coffee and humoral medicine: Wolfgang Schivelbusch, *Tastes of Paradise* (tr. David Jacobson, New York, 1992), pp. 39–49. Coffee recommended to Catholic priests: Liselotte of the Palatinate, cited in Lewis Lewin, *Phantastica: narcotic and stimulating drugs* (New York, 1931), pp. 257–8. King and Queen of Persia: Adam Olearius, *The Voyages and Travels of the Ambassadors from the Duke of Holstein to the Great Duke of Muscovy and the King of Persia* (tr. John Davies, London, 1662), pp. 322–3. Linnaeus and Hahnemann, cited in Schivelbusch, *loc. cit.* Coffee public houses: Mark Girouard, *Victorian Pubs* (London, 1975), pp. 171–6.

The Institute of Food Research, cited in *The Independent*, 24 July 1993. Decaffeinated coffee: *Which?*, June 1990, pp. 314–17. Caffeine and children: *The Daily Telegraph*, 5 October 1993. Caffeine in Coca-Cola: Mark Pendergrast, *For God, Country and Coca-Cola* (London, 1993), pp. 114, 124, 469. Johns Hopkins Medical School study: Andrea La Croix et al., 'Coffee consumption and the incidence of coronary heart disease', *New England Journal of Medicine*, vol. 315

(1986) pp. 977–82. Norwegian study: Aage Tverdal et al., 'Coffee consumption and death from coronary heart disease in middle-aged Norwegian men and women', *The British Medical Journal*, vol. 300 (1990) pp. 566–9.

Effects of 'Sixty Minutes' programme: *The Hertford Courant*, 28 November 1991; *The Chicago Tribune*, 30 December 1991; *The Wine Spectator*, 30 June 1992 and 15 March 1994. Curtis Ellison: *The Wine Spectator*, 15 March 1994. Raymond Pearl, *Alcohol and Longevity* (New York, 1926). Arthur Klatsky, 'Alcohol, cardiovascular disease and mortality: is moderate drinking healthier than abstinence?' in *Alcohol, Health and Society* (ed. R. J. J. Hermus, Wagenigen, Holland, 1983), pp. 71–90. France between the wars: Patricia E. Prestwich, *Drink and the Politics of Social Reform: anti-alcoholism in France since 1870* (Palo Alto, California, 1988), pp. 224–5. Célestin Cambiare, *The Black Horse of the Apocalypse* (Paris, 1932), pp. 265–76. Claudia Balboni, 'Alcohol in relation to dietary patterns' in *Alcohol and Civilization* (ed. Salvatore P. Lucia, New York, 1963), pp. 61–74. Roseto study: Clarke Stout et al., 'Unusually low incidence of death from myocardial infarction: study of an Italian-American community in Pennsylvania', *Journal of the American Medical Association*, vol. 188 (1964) pp. 845–9. Arthur Klatsky, 'Alcohol consumption before myocardial infarction: results from the Kaiser-Permanente epidemiologic study of myocardial infarction', *Annals of Internal Medicine*, vol. 81 (1974) pp. 294–301. Study of civil servants: Michael Marmot et al., 'Alcohol and mortality: a U-shaped curve', *The Lancet*, 14 March 1981, pp. 580–3. 'Competing risk' explanation: The Royal College of Psychiatrists, *Alcohol: our favourite drug* (London, 1986), pp. 96–7. Gerald Shaper, 'Alcohol and mortality in British men: explaining the U-shaped curve', *The Lancet* 1988, vol. 2 pp. 1267–1273; 'Alcohol and mortality; a review of prospective studies', *British Journal of Addiction*, vol. 85 (1990) pp. 837–47, 859–61. Shaper's argument flawed: Michael Marmot, 'Alcohol and cardiovascular disease: the status of the U-shaped curve', *The British Medical Journal*, vol. 303 (1991) pp. 565–8. Effect of alcohol on platelets: S. Renaud and M. de Lorgeril, 'Wine, alcohol, platelets and the French paradox for coronary heart disease', *The Lancet*, vol. 339 (1992) pp. 1523–6. Beneficial effect of tannins: E. N. Frankel et al., 'Inhibition of oxidation of human low-density lipoprotein by phenolic substances in red wine', *The Lancet*, vol. 341 (1993) pp. 454–7. Health and pleasure: James Le Fanu, 'Drink, smoke and beware Dr Killjoy', *The Sunday Telegraph*, 17 April 1994.

CHAPTER 7

Middlesex justices, cited in Thomas Wilson, *Distilled Spirituous Liquors the Bane of the Nation* (London, 1736), Appendix, pp. 14–24. 'Dead drunk for a penny': *A Supplement to the Impartial Enquiry into the Present State of the British Distillery* (London, 1736), p. 13. Thomas Wilson, *Diaries* (ed. C. L. S. Linnell, London, 1964). Moral reformers: Peter Clark, 'The "Mother Gin" controversy in early eighteenth-century England', *Transactions of the Royal Historical Society*, 5th Series, vol. 38 (1988) pp. 63–84. Georgia: Charles C. Jones, *The History of Georgia* (Boston, 1883), vol. 1 pp. 189, 427 and n. Promotion of vine-growing in America: Thomas Pinney, *A History of Wine in America from the beginnings to Prohibition* (Berkeley, 1989), pp. 88, 121–6, 136–9, 435. Thomas Jefferson, letter to Monsieur de Neuville, 13 December 1818, cited in *Jefferson and Wine* (ed. R. de Treville Lawrence, The Plains, Virginia, 1976), p.185. Nineteenth-century temperance, teetotal and prohibitionist movements: Norman Longmate, *The Water-drinkers* (London, 1968); Brian Harrison, *Drink and the Victorians* (London, 1971). Gin palaces: Mark Girouard, *Victorian Pubs* (London, 1975), pp. 23–34. Sydney Smith: Lady Holland, *A Memoir of the Reverend Sydney Smith* (London, 1855), vol. 2 pp. 309–10 (24 October 1830). Father Mathew: Elizabeth Malcolm, *Ireland Sober, Ireland Free* (Dublin, 1986), pp. 101–50. Frederick Powell, *Bacchus Dethroned* (London, 1871), pp. 209–12.

History of local option legislation: Lord Askwith, *British Taverns: their history and laws* (London, 1928); George B. Wilson, *Alcohol and the Nation* (London, 1940), pp. 106–13, 184–6; Sir Sydney O. Nevile, *Seventy Rolling Years* (London, 1958), pp. 53–63; David W. Gutzke, *Protecting the Pub: brewers and publicans against temperance* (Wood-bridge, 1989). *The Sunday Times*, cited in Lord Kinross, *The Kindred Spirit* (London, 1959), pp. 57–8. 1895 election and local option: Philip Snowden, *Socialism and the Drink Question* (London, 1908), pp. 111–12. 'Legendary sums': David M. Fahey, 'Brewers, publicans and working-class drinkers: pressure-group politics in late Victorian and Edwardian England', *Histoire Sociale/Social History*, 13 May 1980, pp. 85–103. Drink and votes in the 1895 election: Joseph Rowntree and Arthur Sherwell, *The Temperance Problem and Social Reform* (7th ed., London, 1900), pp. 102–3. Two recent historians of the temperance movement: Gwylmor P. Williams and George T. Brake, *Drink in Great Britain 1900–1979* (London, 1980), p. 35.

Russia: Neil Weissman, 'Prohibition and alcohol control in the U.S.S.R.: the 1920s campaign against illegal spirits', *Soviet Studies*, vol. 38 (1986) pp. 349–68; Boris M. Segal, *Russian Drinking: use and abuse of alcohol in pre-revolutionary Russia* (New Brunswick, New Jersey, 1987). Canada: Robert C. Brown and Ramsay Cook, *Canada 1896–1921: a nation transformed* (Toronto, 1974). New Zealand: Conrad Bollinger, *Grog's Own Country* (Wellington, 1959). Lloyd George: John Grigg, *Lloyd George: from peace to war 1912–1916* (London, 1985), pp. 215, 229–37. Drink in the First World War: Arthur Shadwell, *Drink in 1914–1922* (London, 1923); Henry Carter, *The Control of the Drink Trade* (London, 1918). Whisky distillers: R. B. Weir, 'Obsessed with moderation: the drink trades and the drink question 1870–1930', *British Journal of Addiction*, vol. 79 no. 1 (March 1984) pp. 93–107. Local option in Scotland: Wilson, *op. cit.*, pp. 120–1, 173–4; Askwith, *op. cit.*, pp. 243–6; *Report of the Royal Commission on Licensing (Scotland)* (London, 1931). Lord Carteret: William Cobbett, *The Parliamentary History of England*, vol. 12 (London, 1812) col. 1224.

Georg Hegel, *Lectures on the Philosophy of History* (tr. J. Sibree, London, 1857), Introduction, p. 6. Maine Law and Prohibition: Andrew Sinclair, *Prohibition* (London, 1962); Norman H. Clark, *Deliver Us From Evil* (New York, 1976); Mark E. Lender and James K. Martin, *Drinking in America: a history* (2nd ed., New York, 1987); Joseph Gusfield, *Symbolic Crusade* (2nd ed., Urbana, Illinois, 1988); Jack S. Blocker, *American Temperance Movements* (Boston, 1989). Economic effects of Prohibition: Clark Warburton, *The Economic Results of Prohibition* (New York, 1932).

French wine merchant: *The Financial Times*, 4 July 1992. Superintendent of schools: *Wine and Spirit*, September 1990, p. 29. Musto, cited in *The New York Times*, 23 May 1990 and 1 January 1991. 'Pussyfoot' Johnson: Williams and Brake, *op. cit.*, pp. 70–1. Difference between British and American systems: Raymond B. Fosdick and Albert L. Scott, *Toward Liquor Control* (New York, 1933), pp. 39–41.

The modern British temperance movement: *Drinking to Your Health: the allegations and the evidence* (ed. Digby Anderson, London, 1989); Rob Baggott, *Alcohol, Politics and Social Policy* (Aldershot, 1990); Derek Rutherford, 'The drinks cabinet: U.K. alcohol policy', *Contemporary Record*, vol. 5 no. 3 (Winter 1991) pp. 450–67. Sully Ledermann, *Alcool, Alcoolisme, Alcoolisation* (Paris, 1956). Robert Kendell, 'Alcoholism: a medical or a political problem?' *The British Medical Journal*, 10 February 1979, pp. 367–71. Enquiry into voluntary bodies: *National Voluntary Organizations and Alcohol Misuse* (London, 1982). Allan Stewart: *The Observer*, 25 January 1987; *Hansard*, 6th Series, vol. 115 col. 498 (1 May 1987). Knowledge of 'safe limits': Health Education Authority, *Health Update No. 3: Alcohol* (London, 1993). Percentage exceeding 'safe limits': *General Household Survey 1990* (London, 1992), pp. 138–53. Target reduction: Department of

Health, *The Health of the Nation* (London, 1992), p. 20. Inadequacy of interviewing technique: Jancis Robinson, *On the Demon Drink* (London, 1988), p. 277. Tucson dustbin survey: *The Times*, 28 April 1986. Sir Richard Doll et al., 'Mortality in relation to consumption of alcohol: thirteen years' observations on male British doctors', *British Medical Journal*, vol. 309 (1994) pp. 911–18. Director General of World Health Organization, cited in Dwight D. Heath, 'Policies, politics and pseudo-science: a cautionary tale about alcohol controls' in *Drinking to Your Health*, pp. 38–52. Misrepresentation of scientific findings: *ibid.* Drunkenness regarded as 'ridiculous': B. D. Nicholson, 'Drink' in *New Survey of London Life and Labour* (London, 1935), vol. 9 pp. 243–69. Benjamin Seebohm Rowntree, *Poverty and Progress: a second social survey of York* (London, 1941), pp. 363–4. 'Taste like candy': cited in Eric Clark, *The Want Makers* (London, 1988), pp. 269–70.

CONCLUSION

Wine in the Bible: Norman Longmate, *The Waterdrinkers* (London, 1968), pp. 182–91. 'Stay me with flagons': Song of Solomon II: 4–5. 'Sustain me with cakes of grapes': Frederic Lees and Dawson Burns, *The Temperance Bible Commentary* (London, 1868), p. 151. Timothy: John W. Kirton, *The Water-Drinkers of the Bible* (London, 1885), pp. 152–7. Edward Hicks, *The Church and the Liquor Traffic* (c. 1912–1913), pp. 10, 15. History of wine: William Younger, *Gods, Men and Wine* (London, 1966); Hugh Johnson, *The Story of Wine* (London, 1989). Christians eating human flesh: Robert L. Wilken, *The Christians as Romans Saw Them* (New Haven, 1984), pp. 17–19. 'I am the true vine': St John's Gospel XV:1; C. Kerényi, *Dionysos* (tr. Ralph Manheim, London, 1977), pp. 257–8. Edward Hyams, *Dionysus: a social history of the wine vine* (London, 1965), p. 215. St Matthew's Gospel XXVI: 26–29. Lancelot Andrewes, cited in Desmond Seward, *Monks and Wine* (London, 1979), p. 32. Blood and symbolism: Salvatore P. Lucia, *A History of Wine as Therapy* (Philadelphia, 1963); Reay Tannahill, *Flesh and Blood: a history of the cannibal complex* (London, 1975). Colour of wine: Thomas E. Bridgett, *History of the Holy Eucharist in Great Britain* (London, 1881), pp. 171–2; *The Guardian*, 24 February 1990. Wine in ancient Rome: Jacques André, *L'Alimentation et la Cuisine à Rome* (2nd ed., Paris, 1981), pp. 162–74. Aztecs: John Eric Thompson, *Mexico Before Cortez* (New York, 1933), p. 68. History of spirits: Robert J. Forbes: *Short History of the Art of Distillation* (Leyden, 1948); Constance Anne Wilson, 'Burnt Wine and Cordial Waters: the early days of distilling', *Folk Life*, vol. 13 (1975) pp. 54–65. Gnostic ritual: Constance Anne Wilson, 'Philosophers, Iosis and Water of Life', *Proceedings of the Leeds Philosophical and Literary Society*, vol. 19 (1984) pp. 101–19; Constance Anne Wilson, 'Water of Life: its beginnings and early history' in *'Liquid Nourishment': potable foods and stimulating drinks* (ed. Constance Anne Wilson, Edinburgh, 1993), pp. 142–64.

Monks and wine: Seward, *op. cit.*; Comte de Montalembert, *Les Moines de l'Occident* (Paris, 1860–1877); William Younger, *op. cit.*, pp. 232–44. History of vine-growing in England: Hugh Barty-King, *A Tradition of English Wine* (Oxford, 1977); Tim Unwin, 'Saxon and Early Norman viticulture in England', *Journal of Wine Research*, vol. 1 no. 1 (1990) pp. 61–75. William of Malmesbury, *De Gestis Pontificum Anglorum*, cited in Hyams, *op. cit.*, p. 188. Introduction of vines to America: *ibid.*, pp. 255–302. Cortès: William H. Prescott, *History of the Conquest of Mexico* (London, 1901), vol. 1 pp. 467–71. History of vine-growing in California: Vincent P. Carosso, *The California Wine Industry 1830–1895* (Berkeley, California, 1951); Thomas Pinney, *A History of Wine in America from the beginnings to Prohibition* (Berkeley, California, 1989); Leon D. Adams, *The Wines of America* (4th ed., New York, 1990). Padre Eusebius Kino, cited in Seward, *op. cit.*, p. 144.

The symbolism of drinking: Elvin M. Jellinek, 'The symbolism of drinking: a culture-historical approach', *Journal of Studies on Alcohol*, vol. 38 (1977) pp. 852–66. Celtic tribes: Barry Cunliffe, 'Wine for the barbarians' in *Origins: the roots of European civilization* (ed. Barry Cunliffe, London, 1987), pp. 161–6. 'Rich bell-like notes': G. J. Monson Fitzjohn, *Drinking Vessels of Bygone Days* (London, 1927), p. 128. Voltaire, cited in Hubrecht Duijker, *The Great Wines of Burgundy* (London, 1983), p. 93. History of toasting and pledging: Richard Valpy French, *The History of Toasting* (London, 1882) and *Nineteen Centuries of Drink in England* (London, 1884); Frederick W. Hackwood, *Inns, Ales and Drinking Customs of Old England* (London, 1909), pp. 141–152. Pamela Vandyke Price, *Wine Lore, Legends and Traditions* (London, 1985). Geoffrey of Monmouth; *Old English Chronicles* (ed. John A. Giles, London, 1908), pp. 186–7. Origin of 'wassail': Michael Drayton, *Poly-Olbion* (ed. John Selden, London, 1612), pp. 153–4. Murder of King Edward: Henry of Huntingdon, *Chronicle* (ed. Thomas Forester, London, 1853), p. 177; William of Malmesbury, *Chronicle of the Kings of England* (ed. John A. Giles, London, 1847), pp. 163–5; 'Vita Oswaldi Archiepiscopi Eboracensis' in *The Historians of the Church of York and its Archbishops* (ed. James Raine, London, 1879), vol. 1 pp. 448–51; *The Anglo-Saxon Chronicle* (tr. G. N. Garmonsway,

London, 1953), p. 123. William Camden, *The History of the Most Renowned and Victorious Elizabeth, Late Queen of England* (London, 1630), p. 3. Barnaby Rich, *The Irish Hubbub, or the English Hue and Cry* (London, 1622), p. 24. *The Tatler*, no. 24 (2 June 1709). *The Connoisseur*, vol. 1 (1754) p. 112. Henri Misson de Valbourg, *Memoirs and Observations in his Travels over England* (tr. John Ozell, London, 1719), pp. 69–70. Prince von Pückler-Muskau, *Tour in Germany, Holland and England in the years 1826, 1827 and 1828* (London, 1832), vol. 3 pp. 84–5. Henry Cockburn, *Memorials of His Time* (Edinburgh, 1856), pp. 36–7. Five glasses in five minutes: *Real Life in London* (London, 1822), vol. 1 pp. 273–6.

Beaujolais race: *The Sunday Times*, 10 and 17 November 1974. Paul Draper, cited in *The Vine*, no. 87 (April 1992) p. 46.

INDEX